pub @ £25

£10

£25.00 N
7840

INTERIOR LIGHTING

INTERIOR LIGHTING

Prof. J. B. de Boer
Prof. Dr. D. Fischer

M   **PHILIPS TECHNICAL LIBRARY
KLUWER TECHNISCHE BOEKEN B.V. -
DEVENTER - ANTWERPEN**

First published in the United Kingdom 1978 by
THE MACMILLAN PRESS LTD
London and Basingstoke

ISBN 0 333 25670 0 (English edition)

This book is sold subject to the standard conditions of the Net Book Agreement

ISBN 90 201 1032 2 (Dutch edition)

© 1978 Kluwer Technische Boeken B.V. - Deventer - Antwerpen

1e druk 1978

Niets uit deze uitgave mag worden verveelvoudigd en/of openbaar gemaakt door middel van druk, fotokopie, microfilm of op welke andere wijze ook, zonder voorafgaande schriftelijke toestemming van de uitgever.

No part of this book may be reproduced in any form, by print, photoprint, microfilm or any other means without written permission from the publisher.

Preface

The purpose of this book is to outline the principles of indoor lighting practice and lighting design and to leave the lighting engineer, architect, interior designer, or student of these or related disciplines with a better understanding of both the background to and the application of these principles.
Much of what we practise in lighting today stems from the results of extensive laboratory and field research into the quantity and quality aspects of lighting, from experience continually being gained from the study of existing installations and from information gathered in the allied fields of acoustics and air conditioning.
Lighting engineering is not an exact science. On the contrary, it deals with people as well as things, and the lighting in a given interior is not good unless the occupants like it. An awareness of the fact that lighting is as much an art as a science is, indeed, central to a full appreciation of what interior lighting is all about.
This book is divided into four parts. Part One is devoted to the fundamentals of indoor lighting. Each of the first four chapters makes extensive reference to the relevant research work carried out in this field, both in the lighting laboratories of Philips and elsewhere. The findings most significant to practical lighting design to emerge from this research are analysed and summarised. The section concludes with two chapters in which indoor lighting is seen in the greater context of building design. The first of these chapters considers the interrelation between lighting, ventilating, air conditioning and acoustics and the role played by each of these disciplines in determining the quality of the interior environment, while the second tackles the important question of energy conservation.
Part Two of the book begins by taking a look at the lighting equipment – principally lamps and luminaires – suitable for use in interior lighting. The emphasis here is placed more on the practical features of this equipment than on the technical background to its development, the intention being to help those who select this equipment rather than those who design it. Because new lighting equipment is constantly being introduced, no attempt has been made to furnish technical data; it has been anticipated that those

seeking detailed information will be better served by making recourse to manufacturers' literature. A chapter on the electrical aspects of the lighting installation supplies the reader with a framework of good engineering practice on which to build. Finally in this section, the benefits to be gained from pursuing a well-conceived maintenance programme are outlined.

The three chapters comprising Part Three of the book bridge the gap between theory and practice and supply the reader with the basic 'tools' needed for effective lighting design. A review of the main lighting criteria, which in fact forms a summary of the results arrived at in Part One, is followed by an examination of how these criteria have been incorporated into the various national and international lighting codes. The concluding chapter in this section provides a step-by-step approach to the various calculations employed during the design of a lighting project, as well as an insight into the the techniques currently used to measure the basic lighting quantities.

The final section of the book takes the reader out of the classroom, so to speak, and into each of the main fields of application in turn. Practical advice, based on a consideration of the various lighting criteria discussed earlier in the book, is offered on the best approach to adopt for the solution of a given type of lighting project. In several instances, examples of lighting installations have been chosen from projects completed in the Philips Lighting Design Centres throughout the world.

The emphasis throughout is on artificial lighting and not lighting by natural means. The provision of the latter is rarely, if ever, the concern of the lighting engineer, and his interest in how daylight has been employed for a given interior is limited to the way it will influence his lighting design.

Finally, it should be added that the lighting of domestic interiors has not been dealt with here. This is a sector in which personal taste and preference invariably override many of the established principles of lighting.

We wish to express our warm thanks to G. F. Söllner of the Philips Research Laboratories, Aachen (Germany) for preparing the first drafts of the chapters comprising Part One of this book. Thanks are also due to N. J. Quaedflieg of the Lighting Division of Philips Netherlands for his suggestions regarding the chapter Lighting Maintenance and to A. B. de Graaff of the Philips Lighting Design and Engineering Centre for his help in compiling the chapter Calculations and Measurements. Finally, we wish to record our indebtedness to D. L. Parker, at present attached to the same Lighting Design and Engineering Centre, for his invaluable advice and assistance in preparing the manuscript.

Eindhoven, mei 1978   J. B. de Boer
                                                                                      D. Fischer

Contents

Part 1 – FUNDAMENTALS
1. Lighting Levels 11
2. Preferred Luminances 42
3. Glare 73
4. Colour 89
5. Ventilation, Air Conditioning and Acoustics 113
6. Energy Considerations 133

Part 2 – LIGHTING EQUIPMENT
7. Lamps 143
8. Luminaires and Other Equipment 165
9. The Electrical Installation 181
10. Lighting Maintenance 192

Part 3 – LIGHTING DESIGN
11. Lighting Criteria 201
12. Lighting Codes 216
13. Calculations and Measurements 226

Part 4 – APPLICATION FIELDS
14. Industrial Lighting 252
15. Offices and Schools 261
16. Shops and Stores 272
17. Museums and Art Galleries 278
18. Hotels 284
19. Hospitals 291
20. Sports Buildings 299

BIBLIOGRAPHY 310
GLOSSARY 315
APPENDIX 327, 330
LIST OF COLOUR PLATES 331
INDEX 332

Part 1

FUNDAMENTALS

Chapter 1

Lighting Levels

The obvious first question to be asked when planning an interior lighting installation is 'What lighting levels are needed?'. But before this question can be answered it is necessary to clarify exactly what is meant by the term 'lighting level'.

The output of a light source is the so-called luminous flux measured in lumens. The luminous flux incident per unit area of a surface is called the illuminance, which is measured in lumens per square metre, or lux. The brightness of the surface illuminated by the source, or more precisely its luminance measured in candelas per square metre, is directly proportional to the product of the illuminance and the surface reflectance, the latter being the ratio of the reflected luminous flux to the incident luminous flux. These two quantities, illuminance and luminance, are therefore closely interrelated, the connecting link being the reflectance of the surface illuminated. In the case of diffusely reflecting surfaces, for example, the equation connecting these two quantities is

$$L = \frac{E\rho}{\pi}$$

where L is the luminance in cd/m^2, E the illuminance in lx and ρ the reflectance. It is because of this close interrelationship that the two quantities illuminance and luminance are referred to collectively as lighting levels.

To return to the question posed above, the answer will depend on the type of interior being considered. In rooms or areas in which visual tasks have to be carried out, the so-called 'working interiors', the required lighting levels will usually depend on the difficulty of the task and the level of performance desired; although a worker's satisfaction with his visual environment must also be considered. In circulation areas and places intended for social contact and relaxation, other than sports areas, the visual performance criterion is not so valid and the emphasis is then placed almost entirely upon the criterion of visual satisfaction.

The way in which these two criteria, visual performance and visual satisfaction, have been used to find lighting levels suitable for recommendation in different types of interior is considered here in some detail. The chapter concludes with a brief outline of the research done to investigate the possible effect that age might have on each of these criteria.

1.1 Lighting for Visual Performance

There are two approaches that can be adopted when seeking to arrive at a lighting level suitable for the performance of a given visual task. One can investigate the effect of lighting level on visibility threshold for artificial tasks under laboratory conditions. Adequate visual performance can then be guaranteed by ensuring that the lighting level is, in practice, well above the threshold value appropriate for the task in question. Alternatively, one can investigate directly the effect on visual performance of lighting levels in the supra-threshold range. The lighting level is then found from the value corresponding to that giving the required visual performance.
The first approach offers the advantage that one obtains an insight into the limitations of the seeing process. The benefit of the second approach is that one is able to draw conclusions concerning the effect that a particular lighting level will have in a practical situation. The CIE has tried to integrate both approaches in one unified framework for evaluating visual performance aspects of lighting (CIE, 1972).

1.1.1 Investigations into Threshold Visibility

The degree of visibility of an object of given size and contrast (as measured relative to a homogeneous background) exposed to view for a given period of time is determined by the visual acuity, contrast sensitivity and speed of vision of the observer.
These terms are defined as follows

Size
For the purposes of visibility investigations the size of an object, or the size of its critical detail, is commonly defined as the angle subtended by the object or detail at the eye of the observer, this angle usually being expressed in minutes of arc.

Contrast
The (luminance) contrast C of a small object of uniform luminance seen against a background of uniform luminance is the difference between object luminance L_o and background luminance L_b, expressed as a proportion of the background luminance. Thus
$$C = \frac{L_o - L_b}{L_b} = \frac{\Delta L}{L}$$

Visual acuity (1/D)
1. Qualitatively: Capacity for distinguishing fine detail.
2. Quantitatively: Reciprocal of the angular separation D (generally in minutes of arc) of two neighbouring objects (e.g. points or lines) that the eye can just perceive as being separate.

Contrast sensitivity (symbol S_c)
1. Qualitatively: Capacity for distinguishing luminance difference.
2. Quantitatively: Reciprocal of the minimum perceptible relative luminance difference. Thus
$$S_c = \frac{L}{\Delta L} = \frac{1}{C}$$

Speed of perception (or speed of vision) (1/t)
Reciprocal of the time interval, usually in seconds, between the instant at which an object is presented and the perception of its form.

These faculties of visual acuity, contrast sensitivity and speed of perception are closely interrelated, and the luminance of the visual field has a considerable positive influence on all three. An improvement in one's visual faculties is, indeed, immediately apparent when the light is switched on in a poorly-lit room.

Investigations into threshold visibility were undertaken, amongst others, by Fortuin (1951), Balder and Fortuin (1955), Blackwell et al. (1959), and later by Blackwell and Blackwell (1971).

In 1951, Fortuin investigated the relation between the size of an object, its contrast, and the field luminance, for threshold visibility of the subject. The viewing time was not limited.

The method of examination adopted by Fortuin was to ask a large number of test subjects, covering all ages, to view a test chart composed of Landolt rings of different sizes and contrasts. A Landolt ring is a two-dimensional ring with a gap, the width of the gap and the thickness of the ring each being equal to one-fifth of the ring's outer diameter (see figure 1.1). Each ring on the chart had one of eight possible orientations viz. gap pointing N, NE, E, SE, etc. Each test subject in turn was asked to view all the rings on the chart, in an order determined by the examiner, indicating for each the direction in which he thought the gap to be pointing. The correctness of the answers received indicated to the examiner which of the gaps had, in fact, been visible.

In his investigations, Fortuin determined for every subject the smallest visible object size at a number of different combinations of contrast and field luminance. It was found, for unlimited time of observation, that the equation
$$\log D + 0.791 = -2.17 \frac{\log C - 1.57}{\log L + 3.96} \tag{1}$$

described fairly accurately the relation between the field luminance L and the values of object size D (i.e. gap size) and contrast C, for all results taken together.

This relationship corresponds to a surface – the boundary surface between visible and invisible objects – in the three-dimensional D, C, L space, figure 1.1. A point in this figure above this surface represents an object that is visible. It was found that with increasing age of the test subject this surface was displaced in the direction of higher values of D. (Figure 1.2 shows a two-dimensional representation of equation (1) with L as parameter. This figure makes quantitative evaluation easier.)

The greater the values of D and C of an object become, at a given value of the field luminance L, with respect to the values corresponding to a given point on the threshold surface (figure 1.1), the better the visibility of the object. Further, the better the visibility of an object, the shorter becomes the time of observation required. In other words, as the time of observation t becomes shorter, the farther is the D, C, L threshold surface displaced in the direction of increasing values of D, C and L.

This influence of the time of observation on the visibility of stationary objects, i.e. its influence on the position of the D, C, L threshold surface described above, was measured by Balder and Fortuin (1955). Again, a large number of test subjects, covering all ages, were asked to view a series of different-sized Landolt rings. The experimental set-up used is shown in

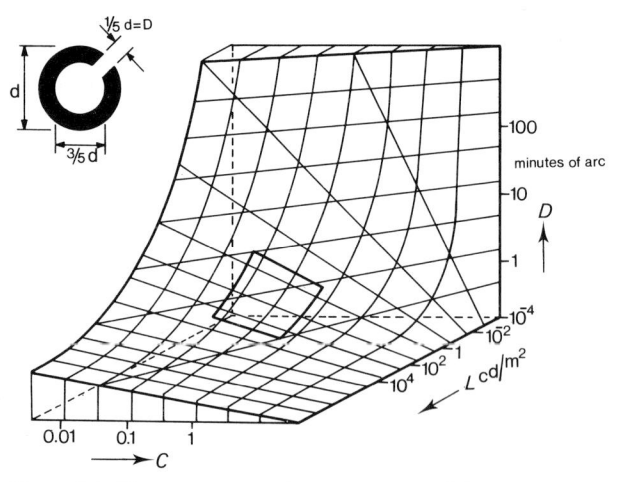

Figure 1.1 Diagram representing an equation of the type $y = x/z$, in this case $\log D + g = p(\log C + m)/(\log L + n)$, giving the threshold size D of the gap in a Landolt ring (top left in figure) as a function of contrast C and field luminance L. The 'square' in the centre of the surface represents the range of the investigation (viz. contrast 0.094–0.94 and luminance 1.2 cd/m² – 1200 cd/m²). Viewing time was not limited (Fortuin).

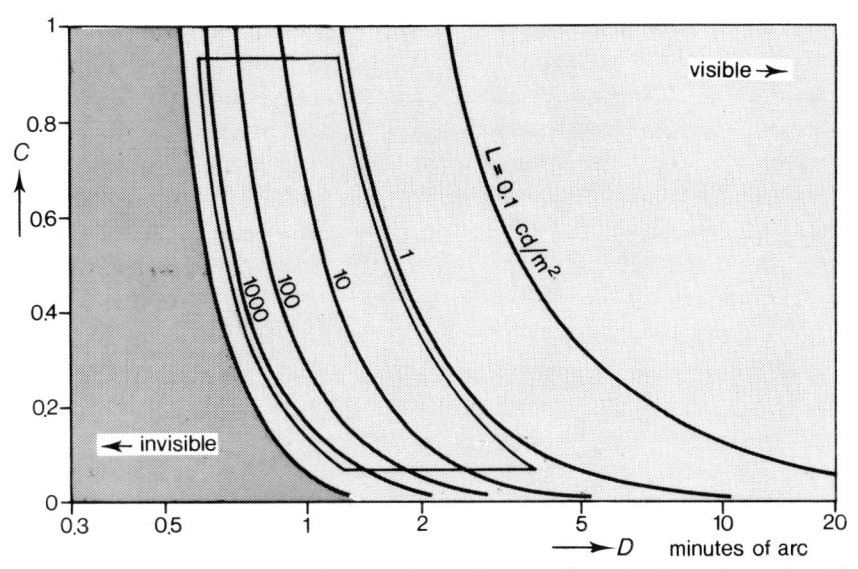

Figure 1.2 Ring contrast C on a linear scale as a function of gap size D on a log scale, with field luminance L as parameter. The 'parallelogram' represents the range of the investigation (viz. contrast 0.09–0.94 and luminance 1.2 cd/m²–1200 cd/m²).

figure 1.3. With ring size D held constant, the contrast C between the ring and its surroundings, the luminance of these surroundings L, and exposure time t were each varied over a range of four values to give a total of 64 C, L, t combinations. This was repeated for a range of ring sizes.

After each exposure, the test subject was given adequate time to signal to the test leader in which of eight possible directions he observed, or thought he observed, the gap in the ring to be pointing. From the answers received, the threshold value of D was determined for each test subject for a number of C, L, t combinations.

For each of the 64 C, L, t combinations the individual log D values were averaged for all observations carried out by test subjects of all ages represented (approximately 100 observations per C, L, t combination). These average threshold values of log D were plotted, for each of the four observation times employed, as a function of log C and log L. This gave four threshold surfaces in the D, C, L space, with t as the parameter – figure 1.4. The work carried out by Blackwell has led to the development by the CIE (see ref. CIE, 1977) of a general method, based upon visual performance criteria, by which task performance can be related to lighting variables (see Sec. 1.1.3).

Blackwell conducted basic experiments on the threshold detection of a small luminous disc flashed against the centre of a large luminous screen viewed by observers. The disc appeared briefly during one of four time intervals and the observers had to indicate afterwards during which of the intervals the disc had appeared. Test parameters varied were disc size and luminance, presentation time and task background luminance (i.e. screen luminance). From the results of more than eighty thousand observations one particular contrast/luminance relationship was extracted as a reference – the 99 per cent probability-of-seeing for a disc of 4 minutes of arc exposed for a period of 0.2 seconds, figure 1.5. This and more recent data have been

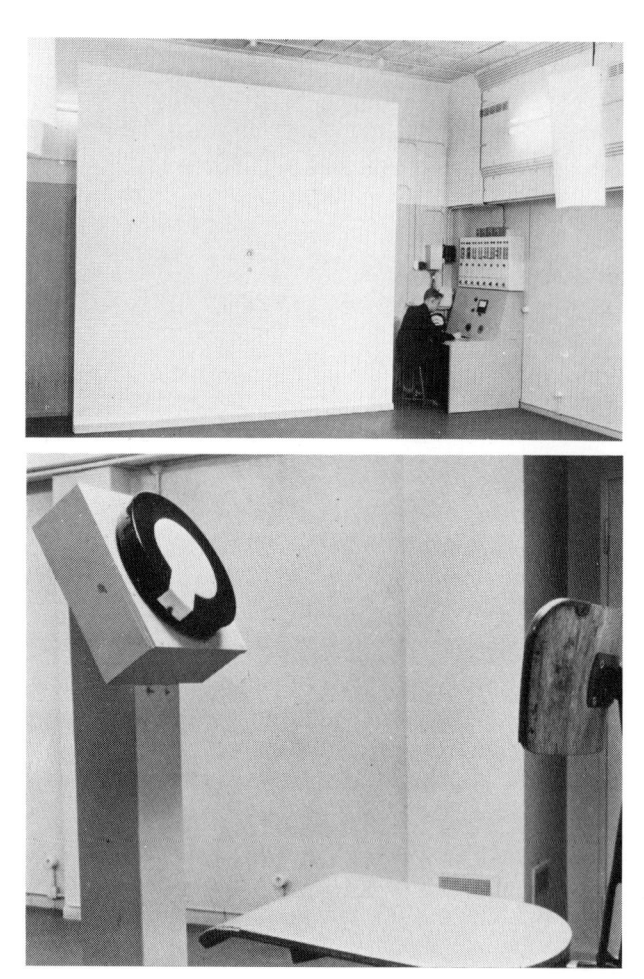

Figure 1.3 Two views of the experimental set-up for measuring threshold visual performance. The photo above shows a uniformly lighted screen in the middle of which Landolt rings of different size and different contrast could appear for an adjustable presentation time. The observer was positioned behind a model Landolt ring at a distance of six metres from the screen (photo below) and had only to turn the ring into the position of the ring being viewed.

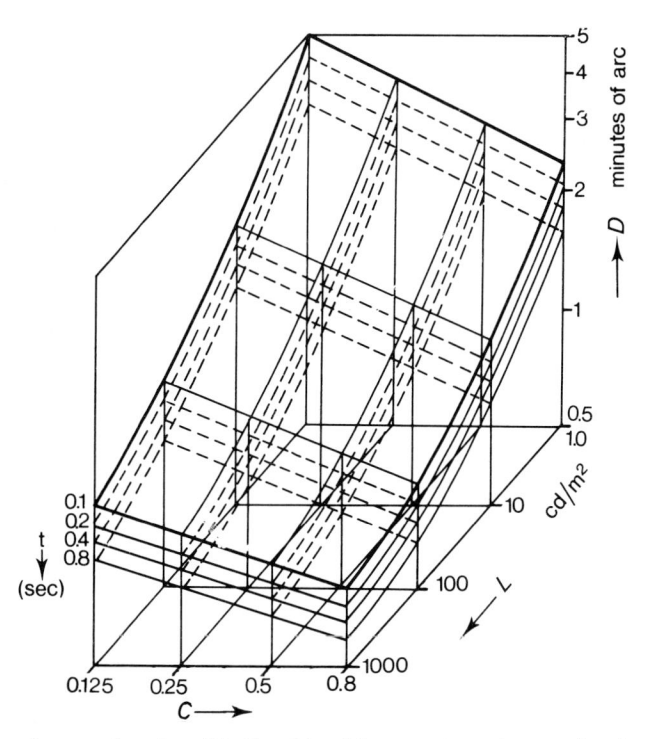

Figure 1.4 Threshold surface as a function of D, C and L, with parameter t. Average for all ages from 15 to 64 years inclusive. The surfaces have been smoothed to fit the measurement averages. (Balder and Fortuin)

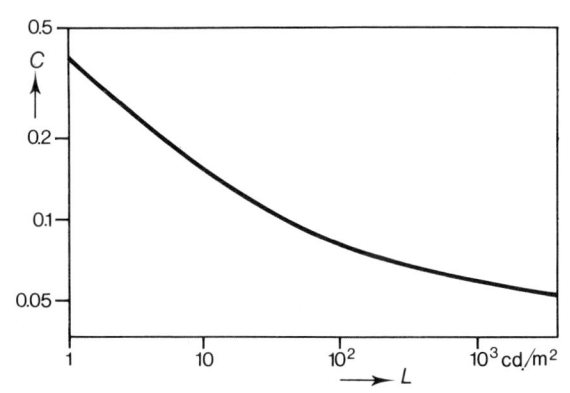

Figure 1.5 Threshold contrast C, as a function of task background luminance L needed to achieve threshold visibility for a 4-minute luminous disc exposed for 0.2 seconds. (Blackwell)

17

combined to give the following empirical function suggested by Bodmann (Bodmann, 1973):

$$C_1 = 0.05936 \left[\left(\frac{1.639}{L_{\text{ref}}}\right)^{0.4} + 1\right]^{2.5}$$

where C_1 is the threshold contrast at a given level of background luminance, and L_{ref} is the background luminance (cd/m²) produced by *reference lighting conditions*. These are defined by the use of completely diffuse and unpolarized task illuminance and a task surround of uniform luminance, each having correlated color temperature of 2856 K. The terms *reference illuminance* and *reference luminance* connote their values for the reference lighting conditions so defined. The function is valid for the average observer in a *reference population* of age 20 to 30 years. This functional relationship is called the *visibility reference function* and is based on the *visibility reference task* being the above mentioned circular disc of 4-minute diameter, which is presented in a continuous pulse train consisting of a 0.2-second presentation approximately once per second.

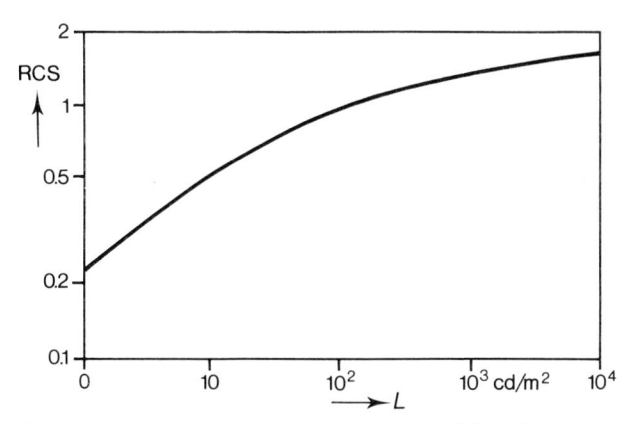

Figure 1.6 The Relative Contrast Sensitivity (RCS) Reference Function. (CIE)

The CIE recommends using the reverse of the visibility reference function, which defines values of *relative contrast sensitivity* or RCS (figure 1.6) by setting it arbitrarily equal to unity at a value of $L = 100\,\text{cd/m}^2$. The function so obtained is called the *relative contrast sensitivity reference function of luminance*. It can be described adequately by the following empirical function (Bodmann, 1973):

$$\text{RCS} = 1.555 \left[\left(\frac{1.639}{L_{\text{ref}}}\right)^{0.4} + 1\right]^{-2.5}$$

1.1.2 Visual Performance at Supra-threshold Levels

Investigations into threshold visibility can provide no more information with respect to the problem of the lighting level required for certain visual performances than the insight that in general a better visual performance is possible at increasing lighting levels. The results of such investigations cannot give information, therefore, on what lighting levels, in an absolute sense, are necessary for usual, or possibly for demanding visual tasks, as performance at those tasks is always far beyond the visual performance possible at threshold situations.

The term 'visual performance' is used in this connection to indicate quantitatively what an observer 'performs' in terms of speed and accuracy when detecting and identifying details in his visual field. Such performance is required in almost every human activity and in particular in such activities as reading, writing, driving, playing music at sight and in many types of sports such as hockey and tennis. Visual performance is then that part of activity which deals with the visual perception of details in the visual field and their detection and identification as far as necessary for the total human activity.

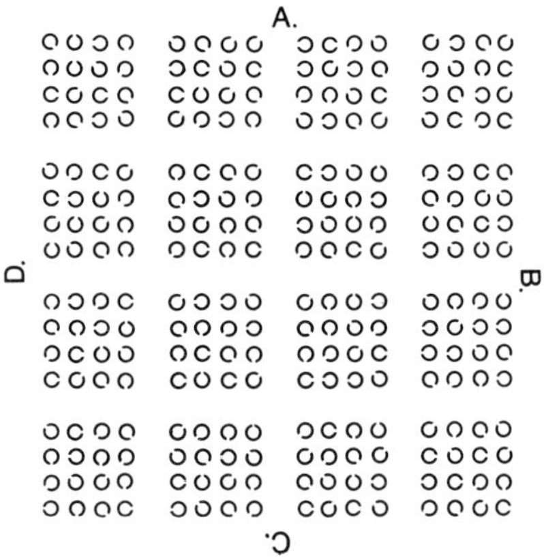

Figure 1.7 A test sheet with Landolt rings as used by Weston.

Quite a number of investigations on visual performance at supra-threshold conditions have been carried out over the years in various countries. The first broad-scale investigation with objects of different size and contrast was that of Weston (1953). He presented his observers with test sheets on each of which was printed Landolt rings of certain size and contrast and random orientation (figure 1.7). The subjects, working along each line of rings from left to right, had to identify within a fixed time of one minute as many rings as possible from those having a particular orientation of the gap.

Parameters varied were the illuminance, size and contrast of the rings. The results were presented in terms of visual performance which for this purpose was defined by Weston as the product of recognition speed, expressed by the reciprocal of the time to recognize a ring, and accuracy, expressed by the number of correctly marked rings as a fraction of the total number of rings on one sheet showing the specified orientation. The time to recognize a ring was reduced in this case by taking into account the measured time (in a special study) required for marking the rings.

Part of the results of these investigations has been given in figure 1.8. It appears from these results that the loss in visual performance associated with large reductions in size and contrast cannot be fully made up for by an increase in the lighting level. Performance approaches a 'saturation' value, and the more difficult the visual task (the smaller the size D or the lower the contrast C) the lower is this value. A relative visual performance P_{rel} can therefore be introduced representing for each task determined by D and C the fraction of the 'saturation'-value to be obtained with the task

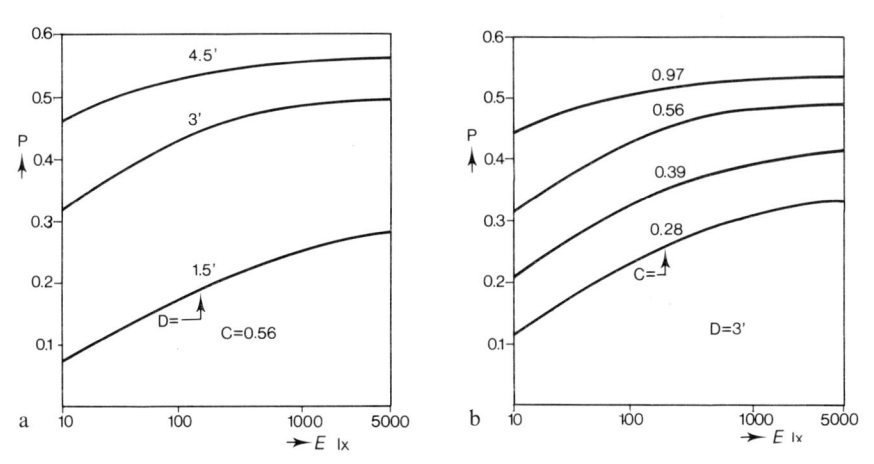

Figure 1.8 Performance P (speed × accuracy) as a function of illuminance E with (a) detail size D as parameter and (b) contrast C as parameter. (Weston)

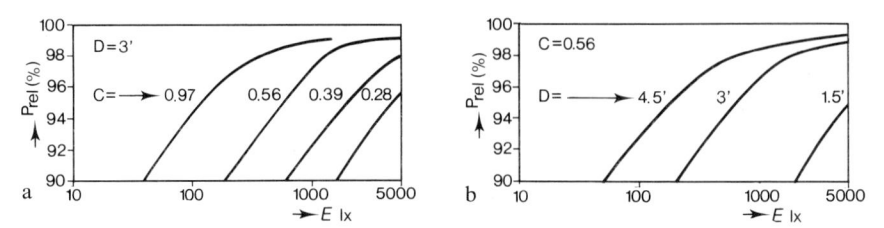

Figure 1.9 Relative visual performance P_{rel} as a function of illuminance E with (a) contrast C as parameter and (b) detail size D as parameter. (Weston)

under consideration. By way of example figure 1.9 has been derived in this way from Weston's results.

When reading normal printed texts, details of 3′ and smaller must be perceived. The speed and accuracy of these perceptions correspond for an average reader to a value of P_{rel} of at least 90%. It follows then, from figure 1.9a, that in order to offer the possibility of a visual performance of, say, 95% when reading printed text of good quality (e.g. $D = 3'$ and $C = 0.9$) a lighting level of about 150 lx is required. When the contrasts become lower and/or the details become smaller the lighting level needed to maintain performance will increase rapidly.

Muck and Bodmann (1961) gave the observers in their investigations on visual performance at supra-threshold conditions the task of searching for a given number on test sheets containing a random distribution of all integer numbers from 1 to 100. Figure 1.10 gives an example of such a test sheet. The subject held a metal pointer which, when placed on the correct number, completed an electrical circuit and stopped a timing device. The task appeared to be such that the time necessary for the search was long compared with that needed to respond with the pointer, so that the observer's task was almost exclusively a visual one. Several test sheets were used showing a size of 4′ or 6′ of the critical detail of the numbers and a contrast of 0.9 or 0.6 of the luminance of the numbers with respect to their background.

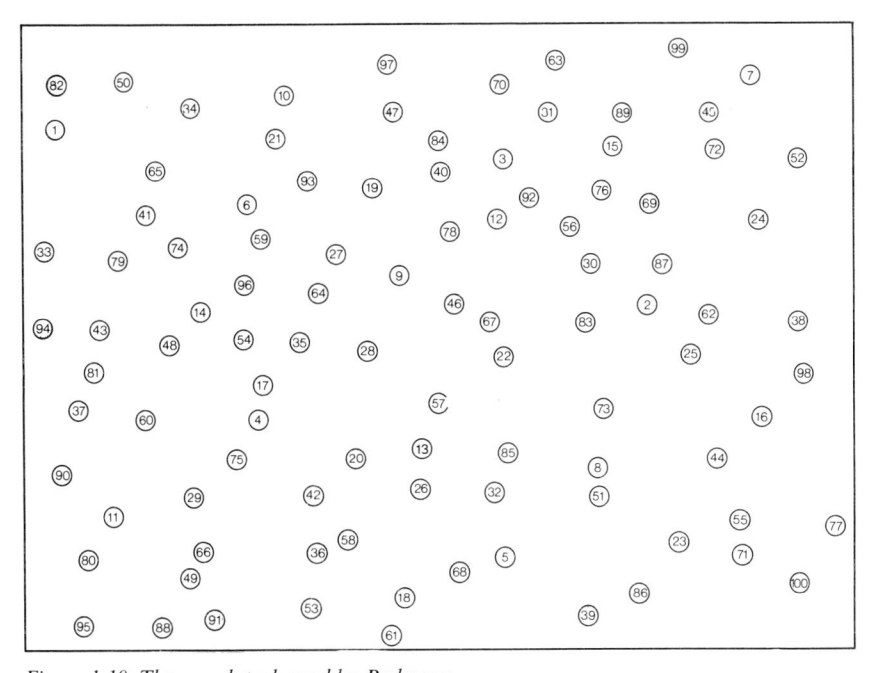

Figure 1.10 The search task used by Bodmann.

The search times varied from about 0.5 to 250 seconds. An observer was in total occupied during 25 to 30 minutes with his observations.

The reciprocal value of the search time $1/t$ can be taken as a measure of visual performance and has been plotted in figure 1.11 as a function of the illuminance E on the test sheets. In this way visual performance curves are obtained which show great similarity with the curves found by Weston. A significant influence of age is apparent from Bodmann's results.

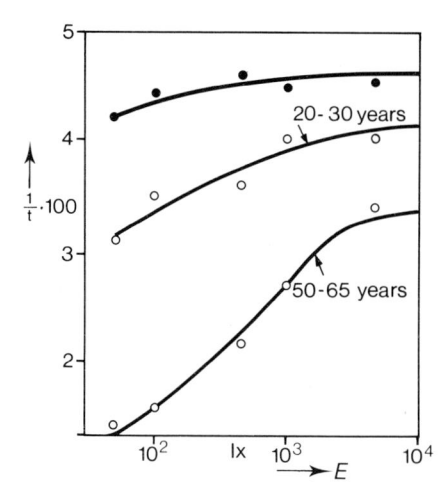

Figure 1.11 Visual performance $1/t$ achieved when searching for a given number on the test sheet of figure 1.10, as a function of illuminance E:
- ●   *black numbers on a white background, $D = 4'$ and $6'$, $C = 0.9$*
- ○   *black numbers on a grey background, $D = 4'$, $C = 0.6$*

Investigations of the Studiengemeinschaft Licht (1956) are of special interest because they included not only the relation between visual performance and lighting level but also the fatigue trend and number of errors in relation to illuminance level. They examined the effect of the change in illuminance level on the sorting of differently coloured and shaped pearls. As a measure of performance, the number of pearls sorted in 30 minutes, at each illuminance level, was expressed as a percentage of the number sorted at 1000 lx. Figure 1.12 shows the results and the close agreement found to exist between these results and those obtained by Bodmann for black numbers on white background ($C = 0.9$).

Investigations into the fatigue trend and number of errors in relation to illuminance level have also been carried out in an extensive study by Boyce (1970). The experimental task devised by Boyce was that of reading the position of meter pointers relative to two fixed black lines on a grey background.

Methods used to examine fatigue trend are of two types: physiological and psychological changes in the observer, and changes in some aspect of work performance.

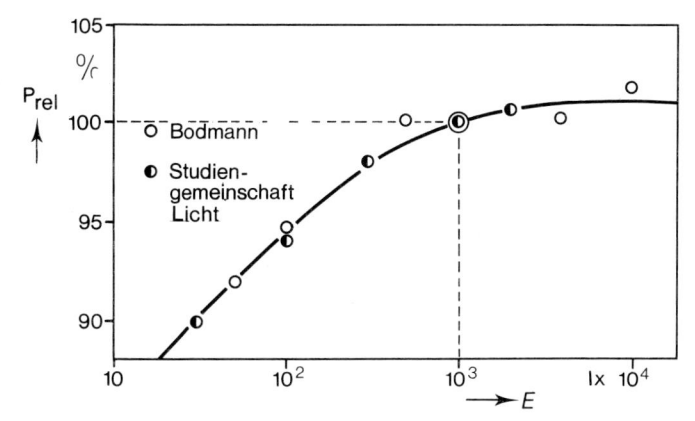

Figure 1.12 Results from two studies showing the effect of illuminance level E on visual performance P_{rel}. The performance at 1000 lx is arbitrarily set to 100%.

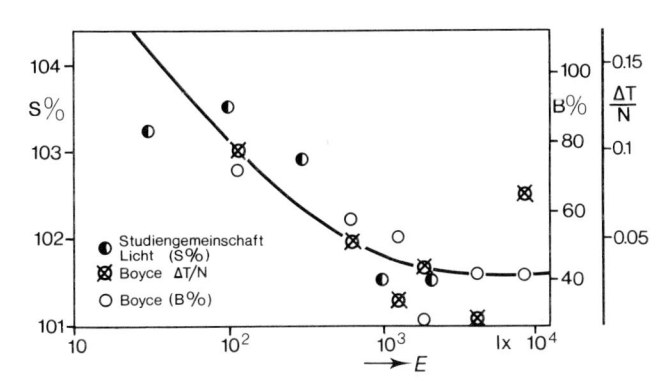

Figure 1.13 Mental fatigue as a function of illuminance E.

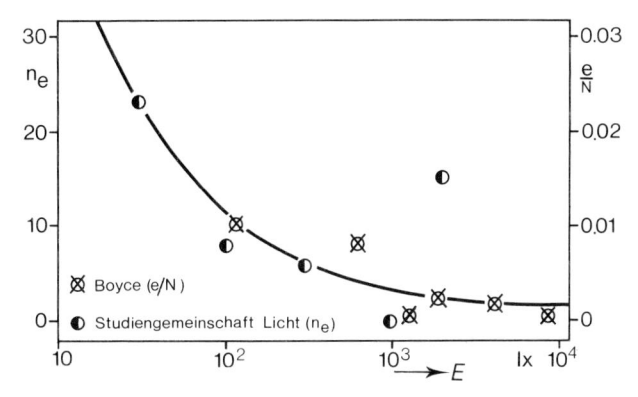

Figure 1.14 Error in visual performance as a function of illuminance E.

Boyce used both of these methods in his investigations. From his results, he plotted the percentage of subjects experiencing mental fatigue after a working period, and the mean slope of the fatigue trend as a function of illuminance level.

Mental fatigue, in the former case, was assessed according to replies made by the subjects on a questionnaire, which had to be completed at the end of each work period. The question asked was 'How would you describe your present mental state?', and the choice of answers given was (a) fatigued, (b) normal, and (c) fresh. The percentage B of subjects giving the answer 'fatigued' gave a subjective measure of the fatigue experienced.

The mean slope of the fatigue trend was defined by $(T_n - T_1)/N$, where $T_n - T_1$ was the change in block time T (T being the time needed for 200 presentations) occuring over n sessions (i.e. $n \times 200$) and N the total number of assessments made during the n sessions.

The index of fatigue used by the Studiengemeinschaft Licht was the change in the upper auditory frequency limit of the observer, measured before and after the work period, as a percentage of the frequency limit before the work period. The reciprocal of this index, S, was also plotted as a function of illuminance level. The three sets of results have been combined in figure 1.13. The relationship between fatigue and illuminance has been approximated by the solid curve.

Figure 1.14 shows the number of errors found during these tests with change in illuminance level. Boyce counted the number of errors over a set of 200 presentations (e/N), whereas Studiengemeinschaft Licht states the total number of errors (n_e) found during the sessions.

As figures 1.12, 1.13 and 1.14 show, the trend in visual performance, fatigue, and error is towards optimum values with increase in illuminance. At low levels of illuminance, the slope of each curve is rather steep. Above about 500 lx, an increase in illuminance begins to pay off until, above about 1000 lx, there seems little to be gained from increasing the illuminance any further.

It can be concluded from the results of these investigations therefore, that an illuminance in the range 500 lx to 1000 lx will prove adequate for most types of working interior in which continuous work has to be carried out.

1.1.3 CIE Methods for Evaluating Visual Performance Aspects of Lighting

In the draft, June 1977, of CIE Report 19 (CIE 1977) the results from threshold measurements (as mentioned already in Sec. 1.1.1) as well as the results from investigations on visual performance at supra-threshold conditions (examples of which have been described in Sec. 1.1.2) have been applied to develop a quantitative procedure to relate task performance to lighting variables. In this respect allowance is made for three aspects of luminous environments which influence task detail visibility. These are (a) the level of task background luminance, (b) the relative task luminance contrast, which depends upon the geometry and polarization of each light ray reaching the task detail and the task background, and (c) the spatial distribution of luminance throughout the visual field.

Visibility in supra-threshold conditions can be described by introducing the term *visibility level* VL which is the ratio of the actual luminance contrast of the reference task (see Sec. 1.1.1) and the luminance contrast of this task in the threshold situation at the same luminance of the surround. The visibility level, and thus the visibility, can be improved by increasing either the luminance contrast or the luminance of the task surround.

As in actual lighting situations we have different tasks seen under other than reference conditions the *equivalent contrast* $\tilde{C}$ has been introduced as a measure of difficulty of an arbitrary task in an arbitrary lighting situation. $\tilde{C}$ equals the luminance contrast of the reference task at equal VL as that of the arbitrary task at the considered lighting conditions.

The equivalent contrast $\tilde{C}$ of a practical task is evaluated using a contrast-reducing visibility meter, an instrument specially developed for this purpose, the design and use of which is described in CIE (1978). The contrast reduction is to be achieved over the necessary range without introduction of noticeable changes in overall luminance.

It is now necessary to establish a relation between task performance and visibility level. Analysing the results of many investigations on task performance at supra-threshold conditions it was found that, under all circumstances, the data were well covered by one or another member of a family of analytical functions, when task performance was plotted as a function of the logarithm of the visibility level. This basic function is the familiar 'ogive' or integral of the normal frequency distribution. The inclination of these S-shaped curves depends on a single parameter, α, describing the task difficulty. As α increases, the curves become flatter and the value of maximum task performance becomes smaller.

As $\tilde{C}$ and VL are interrelated (this relationship includes certain allowances for the influences of disability glare and strong luminance non-uniformities in the visual field) it is now possible to establish charts or tables representing the functional relationships between relative task visibility and reference luminance for various values of $\tilde{C}$. Such tables are included in CIE (1978). An example based on a medium value of α is shown in figure 1.15. These data illustrate the fact that the method described by the CIE can be used to calculate the relative task performance RTP to be expected at a given level of reference luminance L_{ref} provided that $\tilde{C}$ and α can be specified.

Information on the values of $\tilde{C}$ which may be expected to occur in offices has been reported in a survey by Henderson, McNelis and Williams (1975).

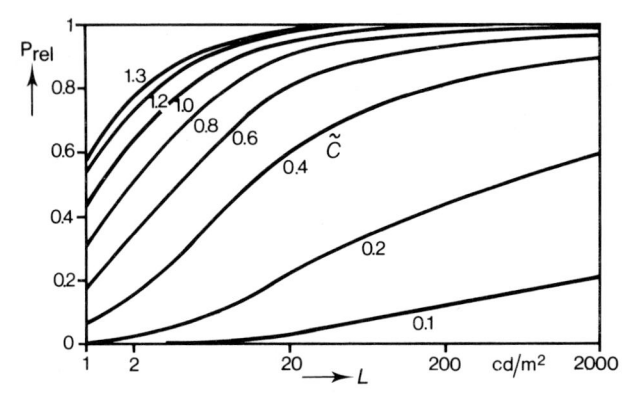

Figure 1.15 Relative visual performance P_{rel} as a function of task luminance L, with equivalent contrast $\tilde{C}$ as parameter.

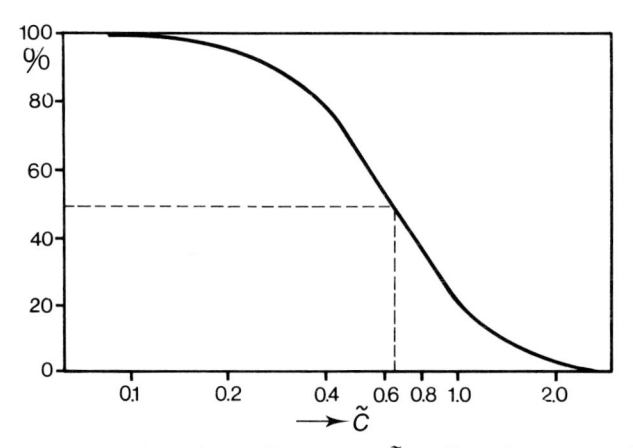

Figure 1.16 Values of equivalent contrast $\tilde{C}$ in offices. Percentage of tasks with equivalent contrast greater or equal to the selected value plotted as a function of $\tilde{C}$.

Values are shown to vary from about 0.1 to greater than 1.3, the majority (more than 70 per cent) lying between 0.4 and 1.0 with an average value of $\tilde{C} = 0.654$ (figure 1.16). Combining this information with the CIE curves of figure 1.15 gives a plot of visual performance as a function of task illuminance and luminance for a range of office tasks, figure 1.17. In this figure a task reflectance of 0.628 has been assumed, which means that $L = 0.2E$ (e.g. a task luminance of 100 cd/m² corresponds to a task illuminance of 500 lx). An illuminance of between 500 lx and 1000 lx would appear to give an adequate level of visual performance for most office tasks.

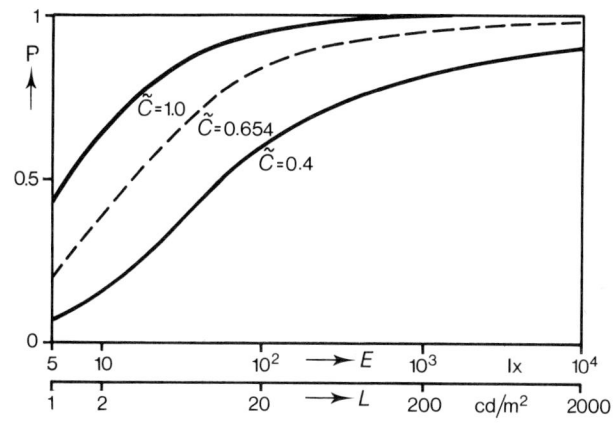

Figure 1.17 Visual performance P as a function of task illuminance E and luminance L for a range of office tasks, each defined by its equivalent contrast $\tilde{C}$.

1.2 Lighting for Visual Satisfaction

Experience gained while attempting to interpret the results of visual performance measurements for use in practical situations has shown that, in many cases, it is impossible to establish lighting recommendations for working interiors from this type of measurement alone. The 'standard' visual task simply does not exist. Most practical visual tasks are complex and differ from one working interior to another. Moreover, lighting recommendations are not confined to working areas; the circulation and recreational areas in an interior must also be considered, and here the visual performance criterion cannot be applied at all.

As a result of investigations into the *subjective* assessment of the illuminance level, which are described on the following pages, it is now recognised that the degree of visual satisfaction produced by the lighting is an important, additional criterion in all types of environment.

1.2.1 Working Areas

Preferred illuminance values: The first investigations based on the criterion of visual satisfaction in working interiors were carried out with the object of establishing preferred horizontal illuminance levels.

Balder (1957) and a number of other workers – those whose work is known to the authors are listed in table 1.1 – requested their test subjects to perform simple tasks in the test rooms concerned. After completion of the tasks, the subjects were asked to indicate whether they found the overall lighting in the rooms too dark, satisfactory or too bright. The test rooms, all of which

Table 1.1 Investigations into preferred illuminance levels in working interiors

Author and reference	Year	Number of observers	Range of illuminance (lx)	E^*_{opt} (lx)	Notation in figure 1.21
Balder	1957	296	280– 2100	1800	A
Muck and Bodmann					
(investigation a)	1961	152	50–10000	1300	B
(investigation b)	1961	152	50–10000	1800	C
Söllner	1966	15	200– 3800	1750	D
Riemenschneider					
(investigation a)	1967	432	500– 4400	2100	E
(investigation b)	1967	813	600– 4300	2500	F
Westhoff and Horeman	1963	6	300– 5000	2250	G
Boyce	1968	14	116– 8393	1550	H
Bodmann, Söllner and Voit	1963	50	257– 6075	1600	I

* Value of illuminance corresponding to assessment 'good'.

were windowless, differed both in size and furnishing. Included, were a scaled-down model of a room (Söllner – figure 1.18), an average-sized room of 4 m × 6 m (Bodmann, Söllner and Voit – figure 1.19) and a large room measuring 7 m × 14 m (Balder – figure 1.20). All rooms were lighted by fluorescent lamps in such a way that they were free from glare and showed the usual ratios of luminance, avoiding on the one hand dullness caused by too great a uniformity and on the other, hindrance caused by harsh luminance contrasts.

A basic assumption has been made in order to compare, numerically, the results of the subjective appraisals (Fischer, 1970 a/b). This is that the percentage of a group of observers judging a given lighting level as 'satisfac-

Figure 1.18 The one-third scale model of a test room used by Söllner, which could be adjusted to represent varying room sizes.

Figure 1.19 The test room, measuring 4 × 6 metres, used by Bodmann et al.

Figure 1.20 Balder's test room, measuring 7 × 14 metres.

tory' will follow a Gaussian distribution over a logarithmic scale of illuminance – thus following the laws of sensory perception. The results of the above investigations can therefore be shown as in figure 1.21a. A mean curve (thick curve in figure 1.21a) has been determined by applying the common laws of statistics. It is seen that the maximum of the mean curve lies at approximately 2000 lx and that at least 50 per cent of a group of observers should find an illuminance between 1000 lx and 4000 lx satisfactory. The calculated mean of the curves in figure 1.21a is shown again in figure 1.21b. From it has been plotted the trend of the assessments 'too dark' and 'too bright'. As can be seen, there is no illuminance level at which all people are satisfied; even at the point of optimum satisfaction there will be those who would prefer an increase in illuminance and those who would prefer the illuminance to be reduced. But practical experience has shown that lighting levels a little below rather than a little above the optimum of 2000 lx are less likely to give rise to complaints by the worker of unsatisfactory lighting. Because of cost and energy considerations, an illuminance in the order of 1000 lx would appear to offer a reasonable compromise.

In order to obtain an idea of the task luminance preferred, the preferred illuminances found in the various investigations listed in table 1.1 (results, figure 1.21) have been converted into luminance values and plotted as a function of the corresponding task reflectance as given in the publications. The result is shown in figure 1.22. As may be expected from the rather equal values of preferred illuminance in the various investigations, the preferred

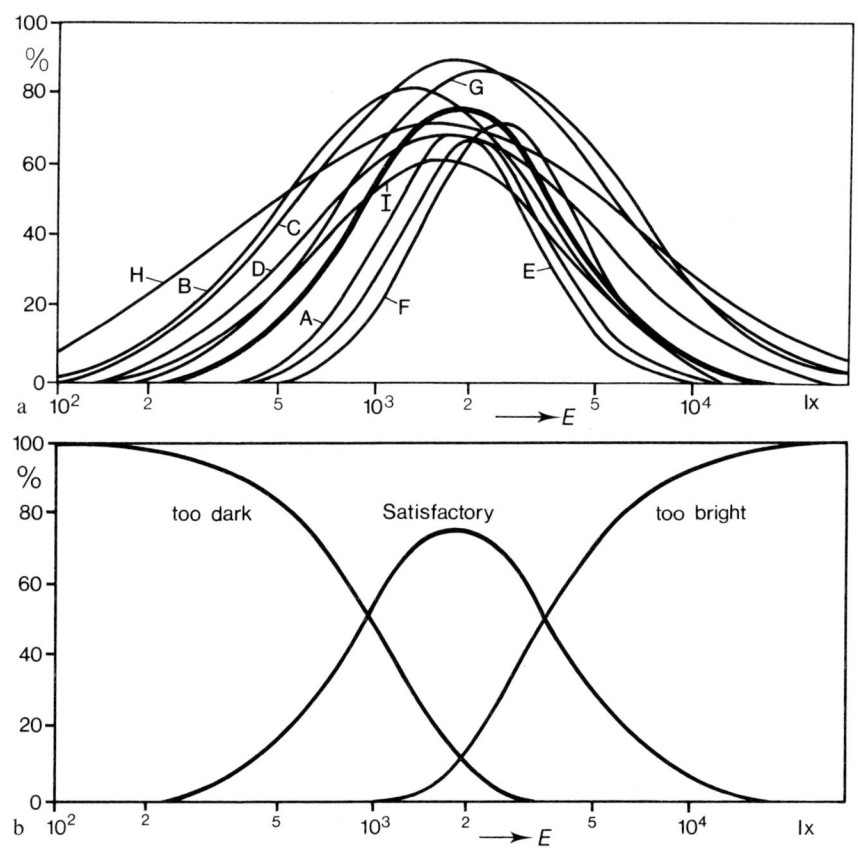

Figure 1.21 Preferred illuminance in working interiors: (a) Normal distribution curves representing the results of the investigations listed in table 1.1. The thick curve represents the calculated means of all investigations. Legends correspond to those given in column 6 of table 1.1 (b) Combination of answers 'too dark', 'satisfactory' and 'too bright'.

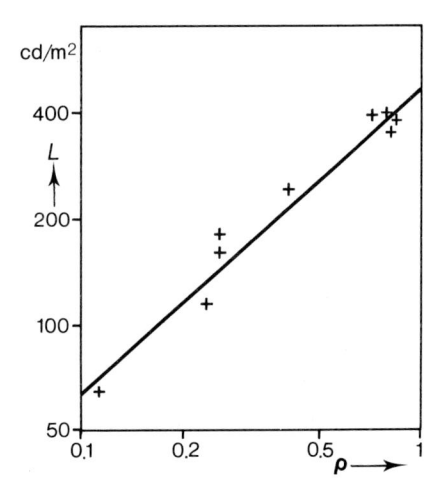

Figure 1.22 Preferred task luminance L as a function of task reflectance ρ.

31

task luminance is not constant but is related to the reflectance of the task; if the reflectance is low, the luminance judged as satisfactory is lower than for tasks with higher reflectances. Thus the theory, frequently put forward in the past, that if the reflectance is reduced to half of its value the illuminance has to be doubled, appears not to be valid in the case of the optimum range of illuminance. The values of preferred task luminance lie between about 100 cd/m² for $\rho = 0.2$ and 400 cd/m² for $\rho = 0.8$. The illuminances needed to produce these luminance values lie in a relatively narrow range below 2000 lx.

Saunders (1969) carried out a number of experiments with the object of studying some of the factors affecting a worker's preference for a given visual environment in offices. The lighting was rated on a ten-point numerical scale with extremes labelled: 10 = *very good lighting* and 1 = *very bad lighting*. Thirty-three observers participated in the experiment.

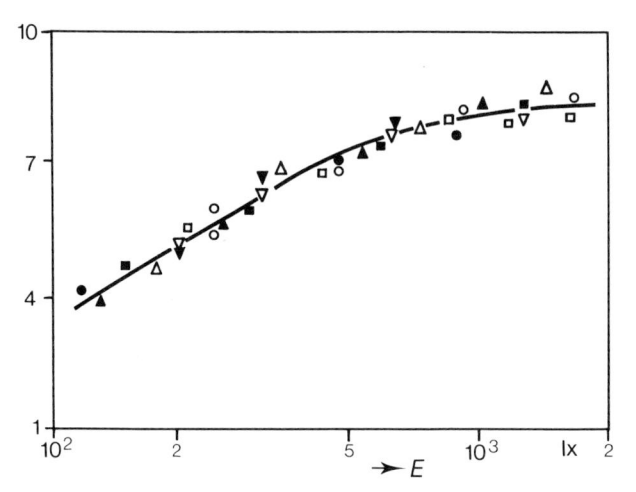

Figure 1.23 Mean numerical rating of lighting level (1 = very bad, to 10 = very good) as a function of desk illuminance E. (Saunders)

It appeared from the results that the main factor affecting a worker's judgement of the lighting was the illuminance level on the desk (or alternatively, the luminance of the task area). Further, that as the desk illuminance was increased (figure 1.23) the appraisal of the lighting level by the 'mean observer' increased considerably with increasing lighting level until a value of some 800 lx was reached. Above 800 lx the rate of increase of the subjective appraisal tended to level off, and above 1000 lx, where the mean observer was quite satisfied, any further increase produced a relatively small increase in the rating. There was an indication, in fact, that for some observers 1000 lx may be an optimum level for normal office tasks.

An alternative to presenting a test subject with predetermined illuminance patterns is to leave him free to adjust the lighting in any way he wishes. This was the technique adopted by Tregenza et al. (1974) in an experiment aimed at studying the consistency of subjects over a number of trials, and the effect of initial (i.e. adaptation) lighting conditions on lighting preference. Two groups of female subjects – sixteen in each group – participated in the study, which took place in a full-size experimental office. Each subject attended six sessions spread over a period of two weeks. The lighting was set before a subject entered the office at one of two levels, a desk illuminance of either 435 lx or 4600 lx. Half of the subjects began the first session at the lower level, the remainder at the higher level, and the conditions were alternated for each subject in subsequent sessions. After an initial work period of 15 minutes spent in the office at the preset level, the subject was asked to describe the changes she wanted in the lighting. A second 15-minute work period followed under the new lighting conditions and this was followed in turn by a second adjustment period.

The level of lighting chosen was found to vary with the initial lighting in the office, figure 1.24. As can be seen, where the initial illuminance was 435 lx the preferred level was in the order of 1000 lx, while for an initial

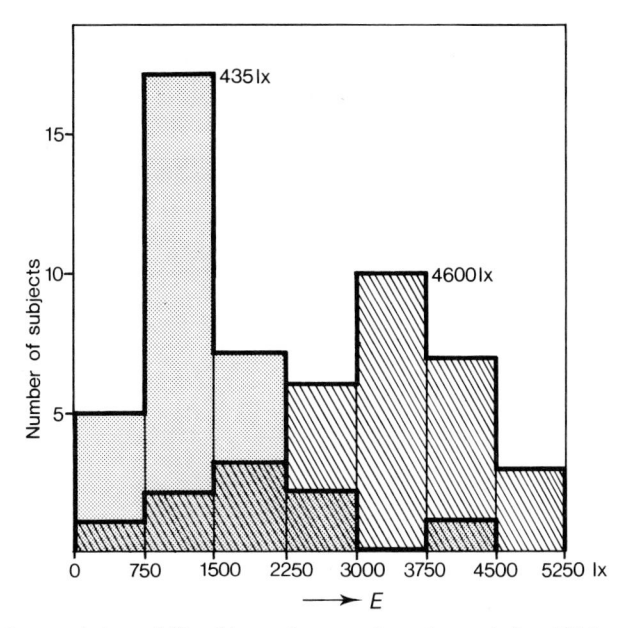

Figure 1.24 Desk illuminance choices of 32 subjects after an adaptation period at 435 lx and of the same subjects after an adaptation period at 4600 lx. (Tregenza et al.)

illuminance of 4600 lx a level in excess of 3000 lx was preferred. These values are in agreement with the findings of other authors described earlier (see table 1.1 and figure 1.21a).

At this point the reader may well find himself wondering why it is that a worker does not prefer lighting levels more in line with the very high levels prevailing out of doors. It was this thought that prompted the following experiment, which was carried out by Range (1971).

An office desk was placed out of doors facing north (figure 1.25). On the desk was placed a sheet of typewritten paper. Forty-five observers were each in turn asked to state whether they found the sky, the surroundings (grass and trees in the foreground, houses in the distance) and the typewritten paper 'too bright', 'agreeable' or 'too dark'. The observers were

Figure 1.25 Office desk placed out of doors showing observer, questionnaire and measuring equipment.

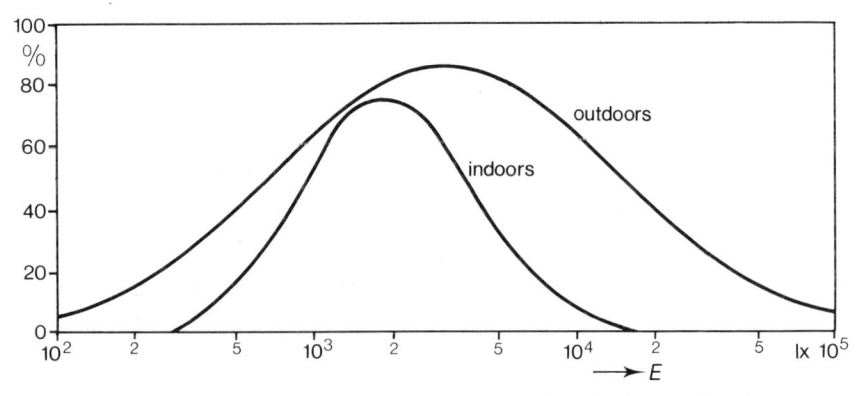

Figure 1.26 Comparison between task illuminances E preferred indoors and outdoors.

34

instructed to imagine that the desk and its surroundings were to constitute their working environment for some considerable length of time. The sky was overcast at all times during the experiment.

The results showed that the range of illuminance over which the various brightnesses were judged to be 'agreeable' by 75 per cent of the observers extends from about 1400 lx to 7000 lx. Figure 1.26 illustrates how these results compare with those obtained from the investigations outlined for working interiors (figure 1.21).

Since an illuminance of 20 000 lx under an overcast sky at noon is quite common, it will be realized that the lighting levels chosen for performing office work out of doors are considerably lower than those generally prevailing. They are, in fact, a factor of approximately only 2 higher than the levels recommended for working interiors.

Minimum illuminance values: For establishing the minimum illuminance level needed in working interiors where the visual tasks are not particularly exacting it would seem reasonable to take the perceptibility of the human features as the lighting criterion.

Investigations have been carried out (Fischer, 1973) into the perceptibility of the human features as a function of the facial and background luminances. A test subject was seated in a large, near-spherical test chamber (figure 1.27), the inner walls of which were formed by panels of opalescent glass. The chamber was equipped with two independently controlled types of light source: fluorescent tubes mounted behind the glass panelling, and spots pointing downwards towards the centre of the chamber from above. Both types of light source could be dimmed, the former to give a scale of background luminance chosen to simulate the range of sky luminance likely to occur in practice, and the latter to give a predetermined scale of facial luminance. The observer could view the face of the test subject from a position outside the chamber. For each value of background luminance presented to him, the observer was asked to state when, in his opinion, the dimmer controlled lighting of the face gave

(a) A face that was optimally (i.e. very agreeably) lit;
(b) A face that was just acceptably lit (i.e. features recognisable without any special effort on the part of the observer); and
(c) Features that were just recognisable.

The results are shown in figure 1.28, in which the facial luminance L_F needed to satisfy each of the above criteria is plotted as a function of background sky luminance L_S. As can be clearly seen, in each case the facial luminance remains constant with increasing sky luminance up to a certain value of the latter above which it must begin to increase.

Taking the horizontal portions of these curves (the oblique portions are

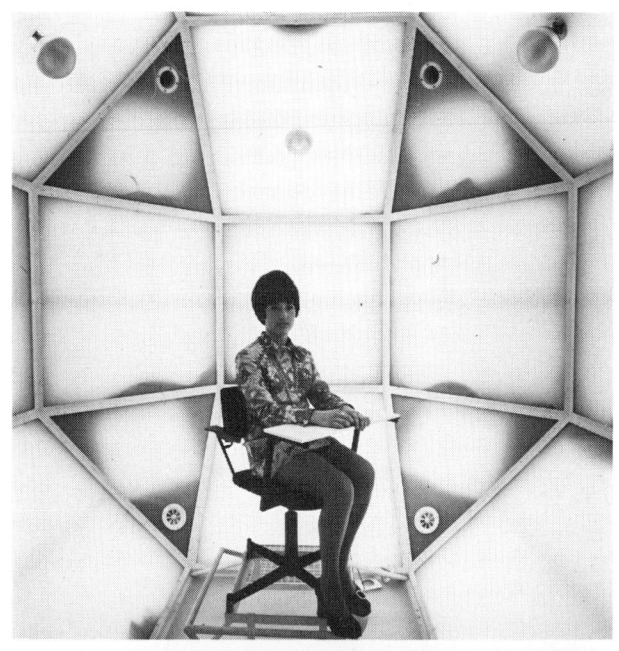

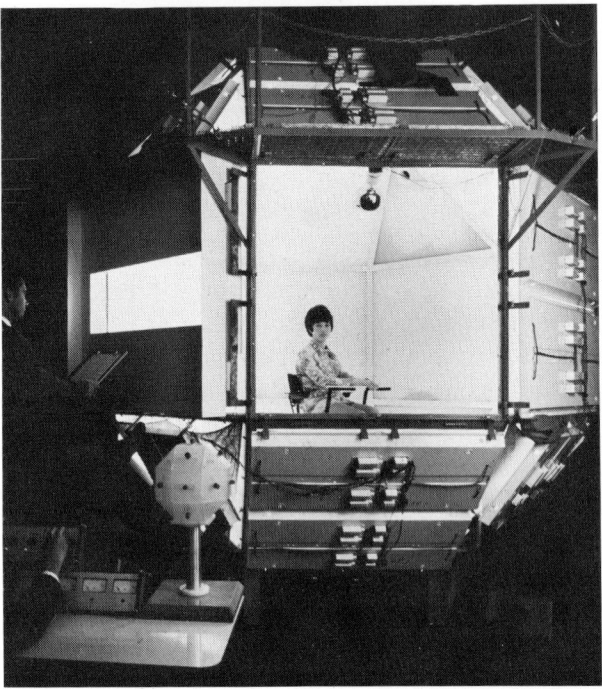

Figure 1.27 The test chamber used by Fischer in determining the perceptibility of the human features as a function of facial luminance and background luminance. (Panel removed to show test subject seated at the centre of the chamber.)

discussed in Chapter 2, Sec. 2.5, where objects seen against a very bright sky are considered), it would seem reasonable to apply the results depicted by curve B ($L_F = 17$ cd/m^2) to working interiors and those of curve C ($L_F = 1$ cd/m^2) to circulation areas.

Assuming a reflectance of the human skin of about 0.4, one needs a vertical illuminance on the face of more than 100 lx (and a horizontal illuminance of about twice this) to yield a facial luminance of 17 cd/m^2 and so make the features reasonably easy to discern. Therefore, 200 lx is regarded as the minimum value for rooms where people stay for long periods, and for all working areas.

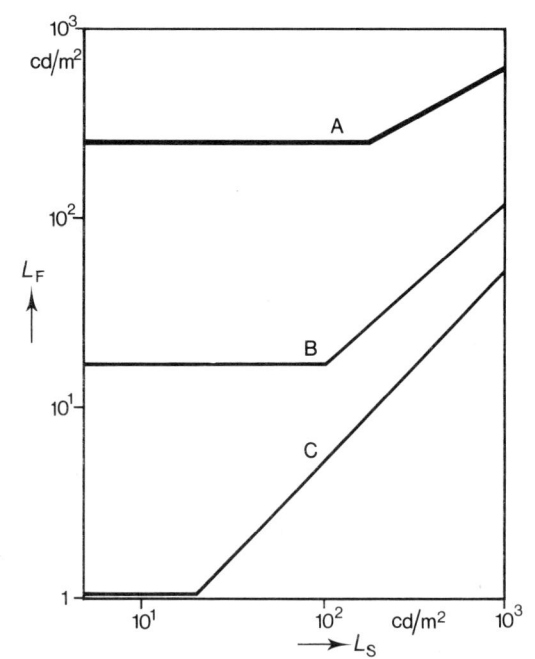

Figure 1.28 Relation between facial luminance L_F and background, or sky, luminance L_S needed to make: A-face optimally lit, B-face just acceptably lit and C-features just recognisably lit.

1.2.2 Circulation Areas

Preferred illuminance values: In circulation and similar areas the adequacy of the lighting is often judged by the general appearance of the people and objects illuminated. The fact that horizontal illuminance seemed not to offer the most appropriate measure of lighting level in such areas, led to two alternative quantities being proposed
(a) the mean cylindrical illuminance, and
(b) the mean spherical illuminance.

Mean cylindrical illuminance at a point in space in an interior is defined as the mean illuminance on the cylindrical surface of a small vertical cylinder placed at that point. Mean spherical illuminance, or scalar illuminance, at a point in space in an interior is defined as the mean illuminance on the surface of a small sphere placed at that point.

In an investigation carried out in the USSR (Epaneshnikov and others, 1971) in which observers were asked whether they found the lighting adequate in each of twenty-five different types of circulation area in public buildings, the assessment of lighting level has been found to correlate best with the mean cylindrical illuminance. Parameters measured, in each case, were horizontal illuminance, mean spherical illuminance and mean cylindrical illuminance.

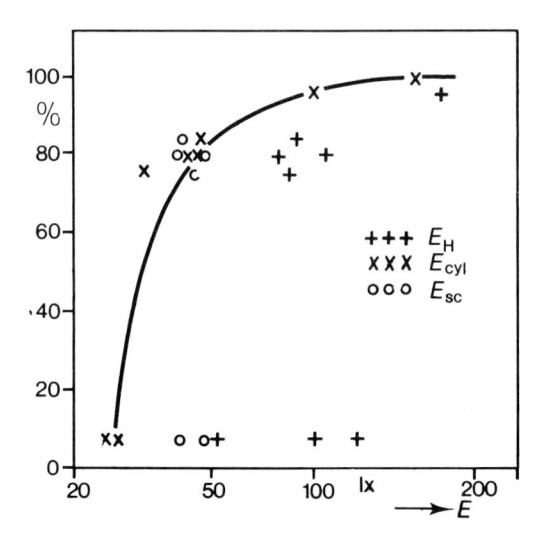

Figure 1.29 The subjective assessment of lighting level in circulation areas, showing the correlation between the percentage of observers satisfied and mean cylindrical illuminance, where E_{cyl} = mean cylindrical illuminance, E_H = horizontal illuminance and E_{sc} = mean scalar (or spherical) illuminance. (Epaneshnikov)

The correlation between mean cylindrical illuminance and the subjective assessment of the lighting level can be seen from the results of the experiment plotted in figure 1.29. It would seem that 100 lx, the level of mean cylindrical illuminance at which 95 per cent of observers considered an interior well lighted, could be taken as an acceptable level for interiors of this type. The horizontal illuminance corresponding to this value will lie in the range 100 lx to 200 lx.

Minimum illuminance values: The question of what minimum illuminance value to recommend for circulation areas leads us back to the investigation conducted by Fischer, which has been described in Sec. 1.2.1. The results of this investigation (figure 1.28) showed that a facial luminance of about 1 cd/m² was needed to render the human features 'just recognisable'. This corresponds to a horizontal illuminance of approximately 20 lx. This value is, therefore, regarded as the minimum horizontal illuminance for circulation areas and rooms of secondary importance.

1.3 Age, Visual Performance and Visual Satisfaction

The bearing that age might have on the relationship between illuminance and visual performance on the one hand, and between illuminance and visual satisfaction on the other, has been the subject of several investigations.

Bodmann (1962) took into account the possible effects of age when conducting the investigation into the effect of illuminance level on visual performance (see Sec. 1.1.2). In this investigation, in which subjects in two age groups were required to search for a given number from a random distribution of the integers 1 to 100, speed of detection and visual satisfaction were recorded at each level of illuminance.

Figure 1.1 (Sec. 1.1.2) shows the performance results obtained for each age group for different visual tasks. It indicates that performance in each group increases with increasing illuminance, with older persons benefiting more from the increase than the younger. Figure 1.30 shows the subjective assessments of the illuminance level made by these same age groups. It would seem, in this case, that there is a point (at approximately 1800 lx) beyond which a further increase in illuminance is appreciated by older people but not by the young.

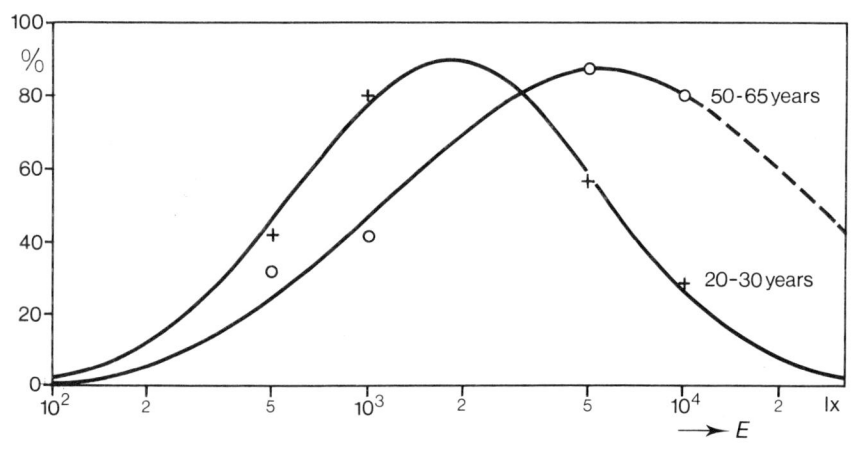

Figure 1.30 Subjective assessments of illuminance level E for two age groups (Bodmann).

Boyce (1973) was motivated by the fact that previous studies (including that of Bodmann) were insufficiently comprehensive to be used as a basis for estimating the age effect. He therefore conducted an extensive study with this object in mind.

A large number of subjects, previously selected as having sound eyesight, were divided into three age groups and requested to perform four tasks. Two of these tasks were of an analytical nature involving the self-paced and externally-paced identification of Landolt rings. The other two tasks were simulations of jobs likely to occur in practice (nulling a meter reading and sorting discs on a conveyor belt) both involving eye-hand co-ordination.

Boyce found from the results that the most difficult of the analytical tasks showed performance to be very significantly affected by both age and illuminance. He went on to derive equations to provide a quantitative estimate of the effect of the former. The performance of the visually easier, simulated tasks he found was not affected by a change in illuminance. In all cases, Boyce noted an absence of any age effect on visual satisfaction.

Bodmann and Boyce are thus basically in agreement as regards the effect of age on visual performance. The differences in their findings concerning the effect of age on visual satisfaction may perhaps be explained (as suggested by Boyce himself) by differences in the design of the experiments and by the vision screening (i.e. rejection of subjects having unsound eyesight). But these differences are of little importance in connection with the performance of practical tasks, they being apparent only at unnaturally high levels of illuminance.

1.4 Summing Up

The results of research into the effect of lighting level on visual performance and visual satisfaction can be summarised as follows.

For laboratory tasks, in which object size, contrast and viewing time are controlled, there is a visibility threshold which is dependent upon the luminances of task and background. This threshold value of luminance can cover a range of about ten decades. Further research, however, employing lighting levels well above those needed to produce threshold visibility and embracing the criterion of visual satisfaction, shows that the range of luminance values needed for both working and non-working interiors covers no more than three decades, table 1.2.

In circulation areas, where the degree of satisfaction produced by the lighting is more important than visual performance, the concept of mean cylindrical illuminance would seem to be more appropriate as a means of describing

Table 1.2 Lighting levels for different requirements in interiors

Lighting requirement	Luminance (cd/m^2)	Horizontal illuminance (lx)
To make features of human face just discernible	1	20
To make features of human face satisfactorily discernible	10–20	200
To obtain optimum viewing conditions in normal working interiors	100–400	2000
To perform critical tasks of low contrast and fine detail	1000	20000

the lighting effect than would the more familiar one of horizontal illuminance.

Finally, it has been shown that older workers can perform the majority of tasks commonly found in offices and workshops at normal levels of illuminance, but that for the more difficult of the analytical tasks some increase in the level of illuminance is called for if visual performance is not to suffer.

Chapter 2

Preferred Luminances

Our visual environment is defined in terms of a variety of patterns of brightness and colour. It is necessary, therefore, to have control over both these parameters if we are to have any say in determining the visual comfort and pleasantness of an interior. This control can be exercised by lighting engineer and interior designer working in close collaboration. We shall be taking a close look at the importance of colour and how it relates to the work of the interior-lighting engineer in a later chapter devoted to that subject. The present chapter reviews the more important factors that serve to establish the luminance values and ratios, and thus the brightnesses, preferred for the main surfaces in interiors.

The luminance of an object, as we know from the previous chapter, is a function of illuminance and reflectance; an increase in the reflectance of an object, or an increase in the amount of light falling on that object, or both, will increase its luminance. The limits to the range of luminance over which our eyes can respond without there being any serious loss of sensitivity to brightness discrimination or any feeling of discomfort have, as we shall see, been found by research. The luminance values of the various objects in an observer's field of view – e.g. luminaires, walls, ceiling – must, therefore, be arranged to fall within this range.

In a working interior the luminance in the area of the visual task and of the main surfaces in the field of view has a direct bearing on the comfort, which may also influence the performance, of the person performing that task. The same is true for the possible glare sources, that is windows and luminaires. These can give rise to a feeling of discomfort even when the other luminances in the interior are within recommended limits.

The success or otherwise of a proposed lighting installation is often judged by the effect the lighting has on the rendition of the human features. In a room lit partly by daylight, for example, the artificial lighting must be designed to prevent the possibility of faces being thrown into silhouette by backlighting from a window.

Modelling – the ability of light to reveal form and texture by creating a brightness contrast – is particularly important with regard to the human features and other three-dimensional objects. Good modelling can also help to reveal the detail in many types of industrial task.

This chapter develops each of the above points and surveys the various luminance recommendations arrived at. The chapter closes with two illustrations of how these recommendations have been applied in practical lighting installations.

2.1 Luminance Limits

Daily experience and laboratory investigation show that our eyes can respond to a certain range of luminance without serious loss of brightness discrimination or any feeling of discomfort. The limits of this luminance range are set by the adaptation luminance of the eye. For a given adaptation luminance the object luminance that is just indistinguishable from black is called the 'black limit'. Similarly, the object luminance just below that which produces a sensation of discomfort is called the 'bright limit'.

The way in which the human eye evaluates and grades luminance values in terms of brightness levels was studied by Bodmann and Voit (1962).

In the first of two investigations a number of observers were asked to give their subjective assessment of the brightness of a number of objects in an office. The office had windows in the north wall only. The observers were each given a sketch of the office (figure 2.1) on which they were asked to record their assessments using a 100-point scale of brightness. The investigation was carried out using natural daylight and repeated using artificial lighting. A total of forty-three observers, aged 20 to 30 years, participated.

The results, in which the subjective brightness assessment has been plotted against the measured object luminance, are shown in figure 2.2. The slope of the S-shaped curves in this figure is greatest for values of luminance at or around the corresponding adaptation luminance. The sensitivity to a change in luminance, which extends over roughly three decades, is therefore greatest at luminances near to these points. That the limits of the luminance range over which brightness discrimination takes place are, as stated above, determined by the adaptation luminance of the eye can be seen from the fact that the curve shifts horizontally with change in average field luminance.

In the second investigation each observer in turn was seated 1.4 metres from, and facing, a light-coloured wall in which was recessed a horizontal row of small (60 mm diameter) translucent discs. The luminance of all but the first and last discs could be varied. The first and last disc in the row were of fixed luminance and formed the maximum and minimum values in a scale of luminance. The observer was asked to adjust the luminance of each of the remaining discs to form a brightness scale that was assessed to have equal

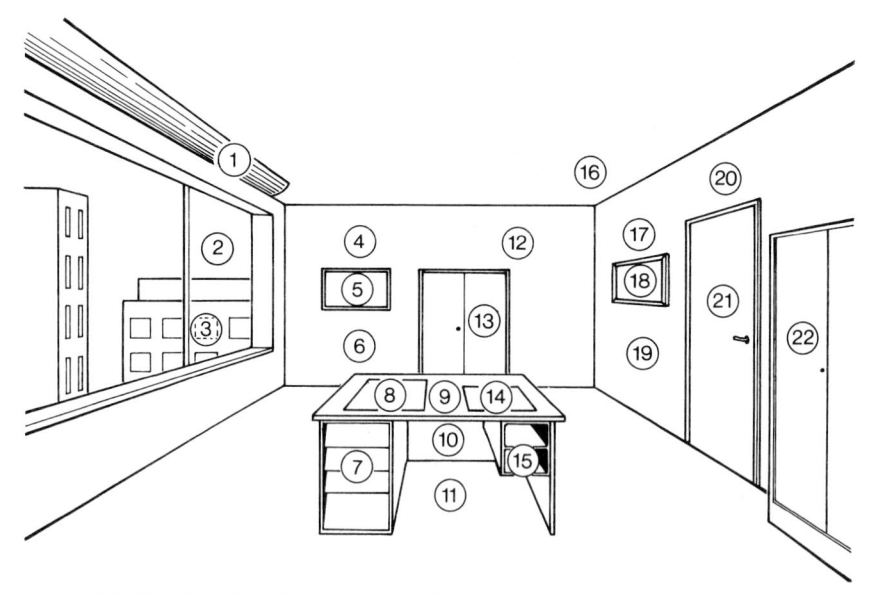

Figure 2.1 Sketch of the office as seen by the observer and used by him for recording his assessments of the brightness at each of the points indicated by a circled number.

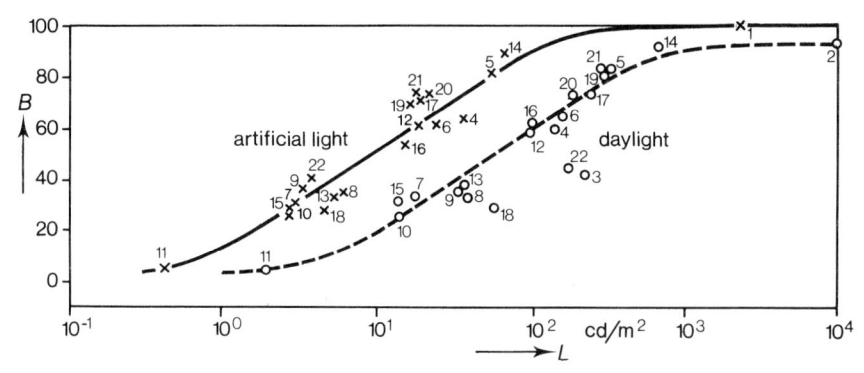

Figure 2.2 Brightness assessments B of photometric surface luminance L under artificial light and daylight. The numbers refer to the numbered surfaces in figure 2.1. (Bodmann and Voit)

steps. No time limit was stipulated and the observer was permitted to adjust the brightness of any disc as many times as he liked.

It was found that within the luminance range of interior lighting all the results could be represented by one curve, that shown in figure 2.3. This curve, which is again S-shaped, relates the subjectively assessed brightness difference between a small object and its surround to the corresponding luminance ratio. The brightness scale is in arbitrary units. It starts with −1.0

chosen for blackness which, under practical circumstances, is reached at approximately 0.4 per cent of the background luminance. This distribution function was found to apply within the luminance range of background between 65 cd/m² and 750 cd/m², which covers the normal range of luminances occurring in well-lit working interiors. (The curve in fact represents the Munsell-value function relating lightness (value) and reflectance of the colour samples in the Munsell Book of Color.)

A general brightness sensation curve, figure 2.4 (with shape similar to that of the curves in figures 2.2 and 2.3) can be described by the formula

$$B = k \frac{L_o}{L_o + L_b} \qquad (2.1)$$

where
B = brightness in arbitrary units
L_o = object luminance
L_b = background luminance
k = factor of normalisation

Figure 2.3 Subjective impression of the brightness difference ΔB (arbitrary units) between a small object and a uniform background as a function of luminance ratio of object luminance L_o to background luminance L_b. (Bodmann and Voit)

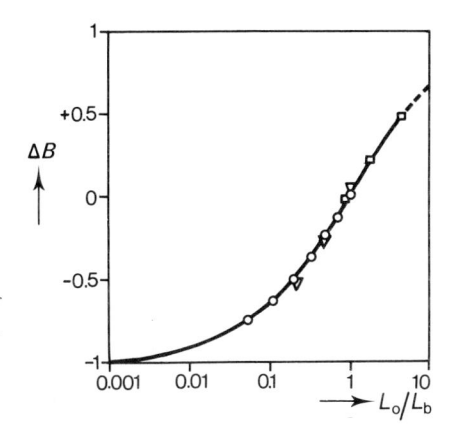

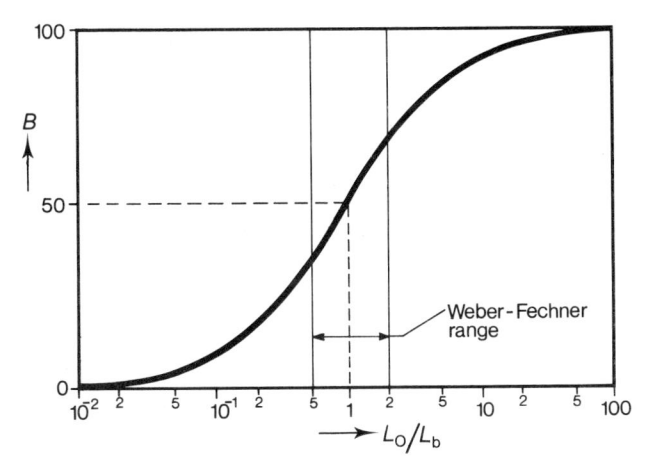

Figure 2.4 General representation of the brightness sensation function $B = kL_o/(L_o + L_b)$.

45

For values of L_o/L_b around unity ($1/2 \leqslant L_o/L_b \leqslant 2$) the brightness increase of the object varies proportionally to log L_o/L_b (the ratio of variable object luminance to constant background luminance), which is the so-called Weber-Fechner rule. Within this range the sensitivity to perceive the brightness difference produced by a given contrast $\Delta L/L$ is at a maximum and the loss of information at a minimum. At luminance ratios L_o/L_b equal to $1/5$ and 5 this sensitivity has decreased to about half of the maximum value.

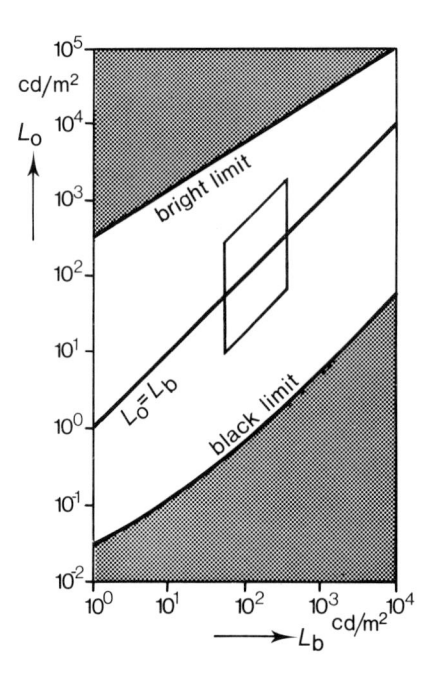

Figure 2.5 Range of object luminance L_o within which brightness difference between object and background is perceptible, as a function of background luminance L_b, showing the bright limit and the black limit. The parallelogram defines the range of lighting conditions for good seeing in interiors.

The black and bright limits of a luminous object have been measured by several groups of observers (Arndt, Bodmann and Muck, 1959a; Bodmann and Voit, 1962). The results are shown in figure 2.5. The black limit was measured by twenty-five subjects as the threshold for light on-off discrimination with a target disc of 2.4° angular subtense. The bright, or discomfort glare, limit was fixed by sixty-seven subjects using a square-shaped source of 4.15° angular subtense. This limit increases less rapidly than the background luminance; thus, the higher the background luminance the nearer is one to the glare limit. This basic effect has been confirmed in all glare studies.

The parallelogram in figure 2.5 defines the range of lighting conditions needed for good visual performance in interiors.

2.2 Preferred Luminance Ratios – Task: Task-Surround

It has been shown by Touw (1951) that there is a preferred ratio for the luminance of a task area to that of its immediate surroundings. Further, that this preferred ratio is a function of task luminance.

Touw conducted his experiment in a large room containing six desks. The desks had been painted a matt-grey colour to give six different reflectances. The room was illuminated by fluorescent lamps mounted above seats placed behind the desks. Approximately forty observers were asked to perform a simple task (copying figures using white paper) at each desk in turn stating, for each desk, which of four illuminance levels (50, 100, 500 or 1000 lux) they preferred.

It was found, as had been anticipated, that as the illuminance level increased so the preferred reflectance for the task surrounds decreased, this decrease being from 0.4 at 50 lx to 0.3 at 1000 lx. The corresponding reduction in preferred luminance ratio between task and surround, L_t/L_s, with increase in task luminance is shown in table 2.1.

Table 2.1 Task luminance L_t and its effect on the preferred luminance ratio L_{task} to $L_{task\ surround} - L_t/L_s$

L_t (cd/m^2)	10	100	1000
L_t/L_s	0.55	0.46	0.35

2.3 Veiling Reflections and Reflected Glare

Light from a bright source reflected by a glossy or semi-matt surface into the eyes of an observer can produce feelings ranging from mild distraction to considerable discomfort. Where this reflection occurs in a task it is referred to as a 'veiling reflection', where it occurs outside the task, the more general term 'reflected glare' is used.

Veiling reflections, apart from creating a disturbance, reduce task contrasts and result in a loss of detail. Consider what happens in the case of pencil writing on matt paper, figure 2.6. The luminance of the shiny-black pencilled characters is normally low in comparison with that of the paper, but this luminance is increased much more in the presence of veiling reflections than is that of the matt paper itself. The result is twofold, in the first place the reduction in contrast mentioned above and secondly an increase of the average luminance of the visual task and its immediate surround. This increase causes an increase also of the contrast sensitivity of the observer. However, the reduction of the contrast overrules by far the improvement of the contrast sensitivity and the total effect is a reduction in visibility. Similar reductions in contrast and visibility are common with printed text and illustrations on glossy paper.

The decrease in visibility of a sample of printed text in the presence of veiling reflections is thus dependent on the reflection characteristics of the task details, on the luminance and size of the light source causing the veiling reflections, and on the average luminance of the task area. Visibility is also influenced by the different patterns of reflections, the pattern for a particular surface being determined by the structure of that surface (see again figure 2.6).

Figure 2.6 Pencil text on matt paper showing (bottom photo) the reduction in contrast and visibility brought about by the presence of veiling reflection.

The first system for evaluating numerically the influence on task contrast – and hence on task visibility – of a given lighting installation was developed in the United States of America. A similar line of thought has been followed by the CIE when their concepts on the relation between visual performance and visibility level (as mentioned in Sec. 1.1.3) are applied to the conditions of veiling reflections. Using the American system, the contrast rendering properties of the installation are described by the Contrast Rendition Factor (CRF), which is defined as the ratio of the task visibility in a given lighting environment relative to that under sphere illumination, expressed in terms of a ratio of equivalent luminance contrasts. Sphere illumination is defined as the illumination on a task from a source providing equal luminous intensity from all directions, such as a sphere with uniform luminance of the inner surface with the task located at the centre.

The effectiveness of a given lighting installation with regard to task visibility is then given by the 'Equivalent Sphere Illuminance' (ESI). This is the level of sphere illuminance that would produce task visibility equivalent to that produced by a specific lighting installation. It is not to be confused with E_{sc}, or scalar illuminance.

For certain lighting application in the USA – principally those involving school and office tasks – the ESI, based on a standard pencil task, has been recommended in place of the minimum task illuminance. The ESI of a specific installation is normally calculated with computer aid for an observer looking at the task at an angle of 25° from the vertical and using the reflection characteristics of the standard pencil task, which have been published in tabular form (IES 1970, IES 1973).

A drawback of the CIE concepts for evaluating the lighting situation under conditions of veiling reflections, and of the American ESI concept – and thus of the American recommendation – is that it is based solely on a consideration of visual performance and takes no account of the typical disturbances that are bound to occur when reading under conditions of veiling reflections. For this reason, the influence of veiling reflections on both visibility and comfort has been investigated by Uitterhoeve and Kebschull (1973) – (see de Boer, 1976 and 1977) – using printed and hand-written visual tasks.

The aim of the investigation was twofold. First, to ascertain whether or not the CIE concept and the American system describe the influence of veiling reflections in a satisfactory manner, and second, to find a way of evaluating visual comfort in the presence of veiling reflections.

The question to be answered in pursuing the first of these aims was whether or not a reduction in contrast produced by veiling reflection would give the same change in visibility, and hence visual performance, as would a reduction in contrast brought about in some other way, as for example, that produced by superimposing a homogeneous veiling luminance between eye and task.

The experiments carried out to answer this question consisted of measuring visual performance using blocks of Landolt rings by recording the time T taken to observe the orientation of the 100 rings in a block. The gap in the rings subtended an angle of 1.25′ at the observer's eye.

Performance is proportional to $1/t$, where t equals the observation time per correctly observed ring averaged over a block of 100 rings (i.e. $t = T/100$).

The observations were carried out under the lighting conditions indicated schematically in figure 2.7. The desk with the visual task was lit from a luminous ceiling, an additional, ceiling-mounted luminaire being positioned in such a way that the block of Landolt rings, as viewed by the observer, was covered by a bright veil. The luminance of the luminous ceiling and that of the luminaire could be adjusted independently of each other.

The observations were made at each of the four values specified in figure 2.8 for the luminance of the task outside the region covered by the bright veil. The relative visual performance of the observer, as defined above, has been plotted in this figure as a function of what has been called here 'degree of visibility' being the product of the actual contrast C ($C = \Delta L/L$) of the task and the relative contrast sensitivity RCS of the observer.

The RCS of the observer was in fact measured under the actual working conditions prevailing. The visual task was viewed through a pair of partly regularly reflecting, partly neutrally and also regularly transmitting filters.

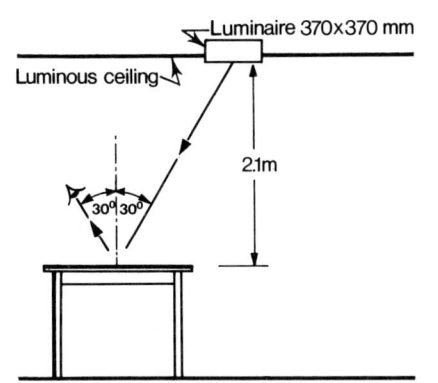

Figure 2.7 Basic test set-up used to investigate the influence of veiling reflections on visual comfort and visibility.

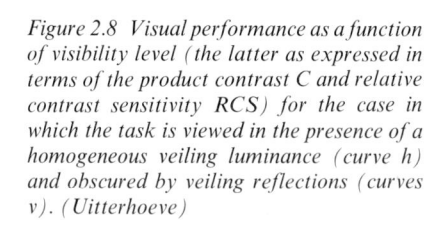

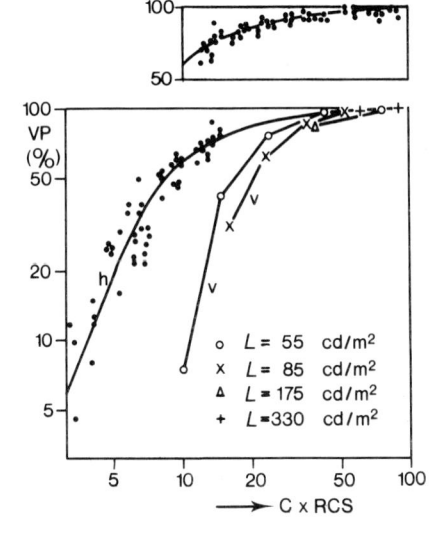

Figure 2.8 Visual performance as a function of visibility level (the latter as expressed in terms of the product contrast C and relative contrast sensitivity RCS) for the case in which the task is viewed in the presence of a homogeneous veiling luminance (curve h) and obscured by veiling reflections (curves v). (Uitterhoeve)

The observer saw reflected in these filters a screen of adjustable luminance superimposed on the task area. This device enabled the experimeter to change the contrast of the visual task and at the same time, by an appropriate adjustment of the luminance of the reflected screen, to maintain the average luminance of the task area at a number of preselected values.

The smooth curve in figure 2.8 has been fitted to the direct results of the visual performance measurements for the situation without veiling glare (luminaire in figure 2.7 switched off) for a range of task luminance between 10 cd/m² and 330 cd/m². The contrasts of the Landolt rings used in these tests were varied between 0.07 and 0.9.

The broken lines in this figure give the results for the four values of the luminance outside the area covered with a bright veil. The upper right corner of the figure represents, for all four luminances, the situation with switched-off luminaire. The lowest point on each broken line represents the situation where the ratio of the luminance in the area covered by the bright veil to that outside this area amounted to 3.1, 2.2, 1.6 and 1.3 for 55 cd/m², 85 cd/m², 175 cd/m² and 330 cd/m² respectively.

If the concept of the CIE regarding the description of lighting standard in terms of visual performance is universally applicable, one would expect that it should be possible to represent all results given in figure 2.8 by a single curve, allowing of course for the usual deviation with respect to the accuracy of the investigations. This is not in fact possible, as figure 2.8 shows. The fact that the actual contrast has been applied in the product $C \cdot RCS$ representing the degree of visibility, plotted along the abscissae and not the equivalent contrast of the relevant task detail as taken by CIE is probably insufficient to account for there being more than one curve.

The reason for the discrepancy between the results to be expected from CIE publication No 19 and those represented in figure 2.8 has been looked for in the structure of the task details, as observed in the presence of veiling glare. Two things can be said concerning veiling glare (see also figure 2.6):

a) bright spots caused by reflections of the glare source appearing in minute facets of the not completely even surface of task detail diminish the contrast and

b) these minute facets form the contours of the task symbol and thus break them up, making them unsharp.

For these reasons, a given task detail is made less conspicuous and less easily visible even when the contrast between the average luminance of the Landolt ring and that of its surrounding is made equal to that existing when veiling glare is absent. This luminance contrast does not account for the blurred edges prevailing under veiling reflections as mentioned under b.

These effects can be taken into account by introducing a structure-factor S, which is defined as the factor by which the degree of visibility under conditions of veiling glare $(C \cdot RCS)_{vg}$ has to be multiplied in order to find the degree of visibility under the condition where veiling glare is absent $(C \cdot RCS)_o$, visual performance being the same for both cases. In figure 2.8 where the degree of visibility is plotted along the axis of the abscissae on a logarithmic scale, the structure-factor S, for each situation, corresponds to the distance over which the curve for the situation considered has to be shifted horizontally in order to bring it onto the smooth curve representing the conditions without veiling glare.

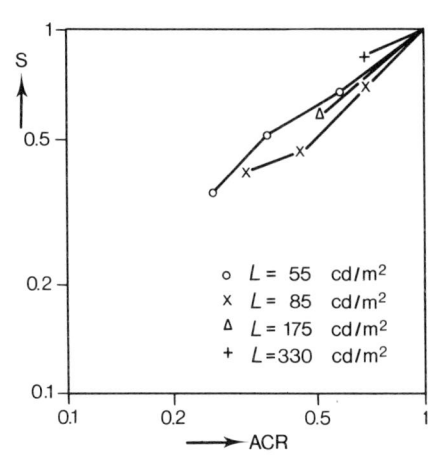

Figure 2.9 Correlation existing between structure factor S and actual contrast ratio ACR with luminance L of the task background around the area of the glaring veil as parameter.

A close relationship exists between S and the actual contrast ratio ACR for the situations investigated as shown in figure 2.9. ACR is the ratio of the contrast of a certain detail when measured under diffuse illumination by the luminous ceiling (equal luminance in all directions from the task detail in the space around the detail) and the contrast of the task detail when illuminated under the actual conditions prevailing (e.g. with veiling glare).

The conclusion to be drawn from what has been presented in this section must be that it is doubtful whether the degree of visibility – defined as the product of the actual contrast of the task detail and the contrast sensitivity of the observer under the lighting conditions considered – is the only factor determining visual performance as one would expect from the considerations given in the publication No 19 of the CIE. Under conditions in which veiling glare is present, the structure of the task will have an additional influence on visual performance.

Visual comfort in the presence of veiling reflections – the second aim of the investigations – was evaluated using tasks more representative of those likely to occur in practice: two journals (one printed on glossy paper and the other on semi-matt paper) and a sheet of pencilled text. The measurement set-up used is that depicted in figure 2.7.

Ten observers were called upon to read the three samples of texts and to assess their legibility and the degree of disturbance experienced as the actual contrast ratio was varied. This factor, which was always determined by contrast measurements in the area of the reflected brightness of the glare source, could in fact be varied from unity to almost zero by varying the luminance of the adjustable luminaire. Other lighting conditions specified were the illuminance on the task (500, 1000 and 2000 lx) and the luminance of the glare source (3420 cd/m², 6700 cd/m² and 12000 cd/m² at the 500 lx and 100 lx levels, and 18000 cd/m² at 2000 lx).

The assessment of the degree of disturbance experienced was made on a five-point scale on which the principal points were 1 (not disturbing), 3 (just disturbing) and 5 (very disturbing).

The results as given in figure 2.10 show the average appraisal as a function of the actual contrast ratio ACR that was prevailing in the worst situation lightsource-task-observer, i.e. the situation wherein the bright veil in the task was most intense. The figure is valid for the three kinds of text used in the appraisals. The figure shows a clear correlation between the subjectively appraised degree of disturbance and the contrast rendition.

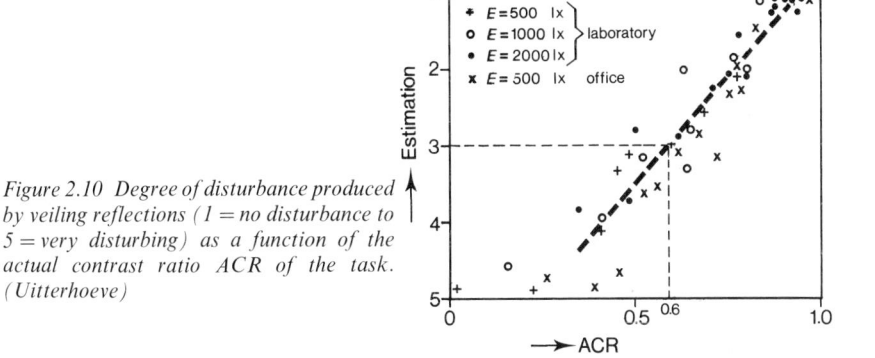

Figure 2.10 Degree of disturbance produced by veiling reflections (1 = no disturbance to 5 = very disturbing) as a function of the actual contrast ratio ACR of the task. (Uitterhoeve)

A further important conclusion to be drawn from the results of the appraisals is the fact that in the range of illuminance on the task between 500 lx and 2000 lx the degree of discomfort under conditions of veiling glare is independent of illuminance level. This fact represents a fundamental difference between these results and those dealing with visual performance.

Lighting quality determined on the basis of visual performance is dependent on the combination of the illuminance level and the prevailing contrast.

When determined on the basis of visual comfort it is, in the situations involved in the present experiments, the contrast rendition only that determines the lighting quality, independent of illuminance (within the range investigated).

The results of these tests, which were made under laboratory conditions, were later confirmed by field tests carried out in a landscaped office using the same journals to represent the task (see again figure 2.10). As can be seen from this figure, in order to remain on the 'safe' side of the assessment 'just disturbing' the actual contrast ratio should be at least 0.6. (An exact analysis of the laboratory results yields a value of 0.5 for the pencilled text and 0.6 for the printed text.) This value is confirmed by the results (figure 2.11) of the test in which the legibility of the texts was assessed as the actual contrast ratio was varied. The assessments were made on a nine-point scale ranging from 1 (poor legibility) to 9 (excellent legibility). A contrast rendition factor of 0.6 should, therefore, be used as a starting point when formulating recommendations for avoiding disturbing veiling reflections.

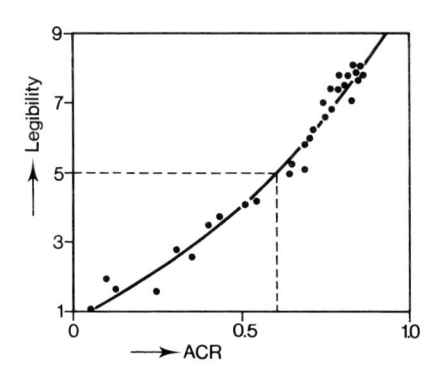

Figure 2.11 Legibility of texts ($1 = poor$, $5 = fair$, $9 = excellent$) as a function of the actual contrast ratio ACR of the task. (Uitterhoeve)

For offices and schools – areas in which tasks similar to those used in the above investigation prevail – the admissible luminance of the luminaires in the critical direction can be found using the curves given in figure 2.12. In this figure, the ratio L_L/E_T in $cd/m^2/lx$ of the luminance of the luminaire in the offending zone (see figure 2.13) to the illuminance on the task is given as a function of the actual contrast ratio. As can be seen, the ratio L_L/E_T may be as large as 15 (ACR $= 0.6$) for texts printed on semi-matt paper, but should be restricted to 7 (ACR $= 0.6$) for texts printed on glossy paper and even somewhat lower for pencilled texts on matt paper (ACR $= 0.5$). It would seem reasonable to choose texts printed on glossy paper and pencil writing as the standard task objects for this case. This means that the maximum permissible luminance of a luminaire as seen reflected in the

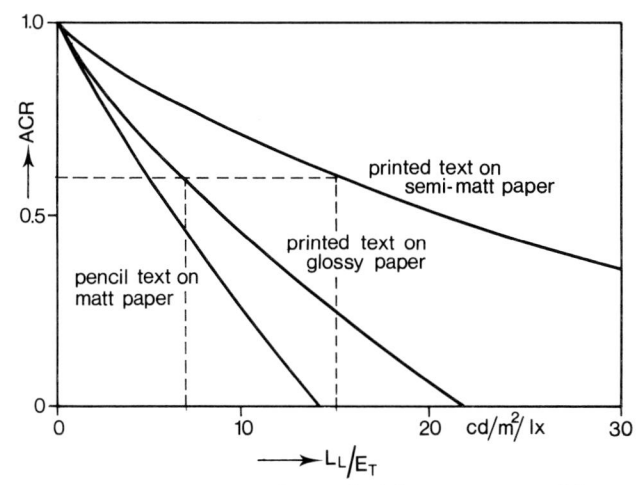

Figure 2.12 Actual contrast ratio ACR, as measured using the laboratory set-up of figure 2.7, as a function of the ratio L_L/E_T of the luminance of the luminaire in the offending zone to the illuminance level at the task. (Uitterhoeve)

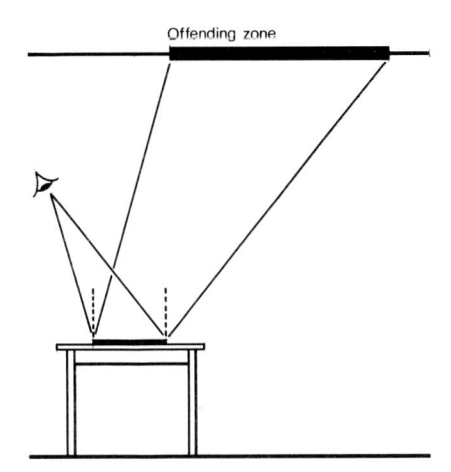

Figure 2.13 Offending zone within which reflections from luminaire will degrade the contrast of a flat task.

task should be approximately 7000 cd/m² for a 1000 lx installation and 3500 cd/m² for a 500 lx installation.

These limits of luminaire luminance should be met for the angle α corresponding to the common viewing zone, which covers (as has been shown by Allphin, 1963) the area around 25° from the vertical, figure 2.14.

Reflected glare, that is to say glare produced by specular surfaces in the near vicinity of the task area, can also prove troublesome. The problem here is that the attention is involuntarily drawn towards the area of brightness and thus away from the task, so resulting in a loss of concentration.

In practical installations, therefore, the occurrence of veiling reflections, and reflected glare in general, is dependent not only on the luminance of the luminaires, but also on their light distribution and arrangement. Ideally, the layout of the lighting should be such that no part of a task or its surround is at or near the mirror angle with respect to the eye and a source of light of high brightness. Objects at or near the task area can also give rise to reflected glare unless their surface finish is chosen with care.

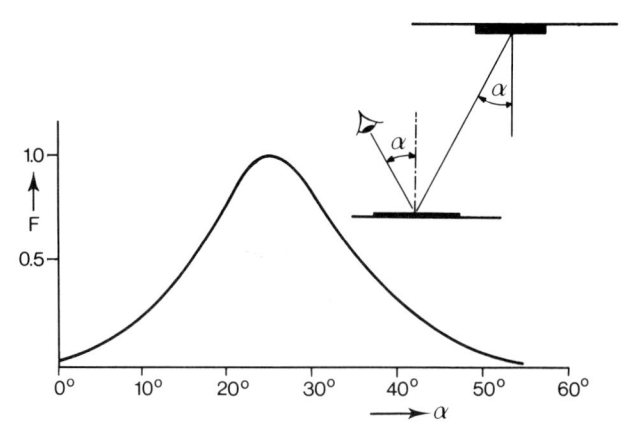

Figure 2.14 Frequency of viewing F as a function of viewing angle α showing that peak viewing occurs around an angle of 25° to the vertical. (Allphin)

2.4 Preferred Wall and Ceiling Luminances

2.4.1 Wall Luminance

There have been two studies made into the preferred luminance range for walls in interiors, those by Balder and by Barthès and Richard.
Balder (1957) dealt both with the wall facing the occupants of a room and with those to their left and right, that is, the side walls. He used for his studies the room mentioned in Sec. 1.2.1 and shown in figure 1.18. The colour of the walls was grey, with a reflectance of 0.5.
More than 21 000 observer assessments were analysed statistically to yield the results shown in figure 2.15. Figure 2.15a shows the preferred luminance of the wall facing the observers and figure 2.15b the preferred luminance of the side walls, both plotted in relation to the average horizontal illuminance on the desk tops and the corresponding task and background luminances (i.e. luminance of paper L_p and desk L_d respectively). The central line in each figure shows the luminance values preferred by the greatest number of observers (approximately 83 per cent of the observers satisfied). The

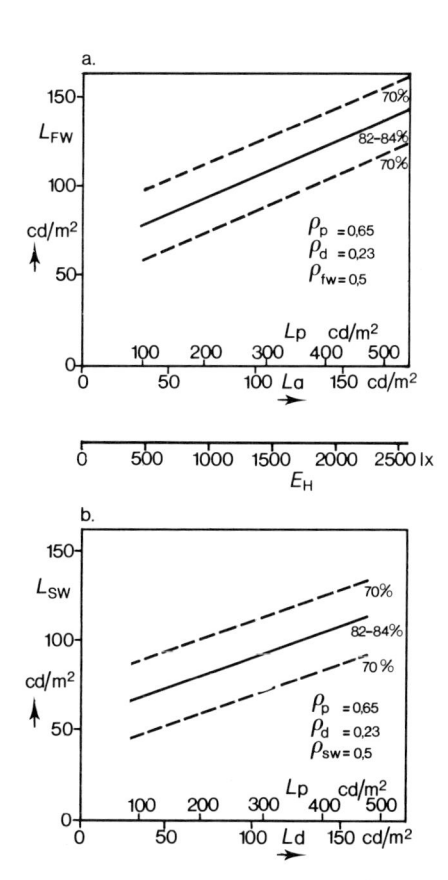

Figure 2.15 (a) Preferred facing-wall luminance L_{FW} as a function of paper luminance L_p, desk-top luminance L_d and horizontal illuminance E_H; (b) Preferred side-wall luminance L_{SW} as a function of paper luminance L_p, desk-top luminance L_d and horizontal illuminance E_H. (Balder)

vertical distance between the dotted lines at each illuminance value, which gives the range of luminances for at least 70 per cent of satisfied observers, is referred to as the 'range of comfort'.

Barthès and Richard (1969) assessed the preferred luminance of the facing wall. They used for their studies two identical one-third-scale models of a room. The facing walls in the models could be given any of five colours and three reflectances. The luminance of the visual task (reading a text) could be varied by selecting any of six illuminance values. The models could be studied simultaneously. Thus, assuming equal task illuminance in the two models, the optimum facing wall luminance could be found by a process of comparison. In all cases, the situations to be compared were adjusted by the experimenter. Six observers participated in the experiment.

The assessments of the observers showed that the value preferred for the facing wall luminance depended not only on the task luminance, but also on the colour and reflectance of the wall. For example, the luminance preferred for grey, blue, blue-green and red walls was found to increase with the value of reflectance whereas for a yellow wall this situation was reversed. The results of the assessments relating to grey walls are shown in figure 2.16. The optimum wall luminance for each level of illuminance has been made to correspond to a value of 100 on a scale of comfort.

In order to be able to compare these results with those of Balder referred to above (figure 2.15), who used a wall reflectance of 0.5, some interpolation is necessary. The outcome of this interpolation is shown in figure 2.17. (The results obtained by Barthès indicated in this figure have in fact been confirmed in more recent research carried out along similar lines by Tregenza, *et al.*, 1974). It is not usual, however, in lighting recommendations to distinguish between facing walls and side walls. What is needed is a recommendation for the luminance of the walls in general, and this is given by

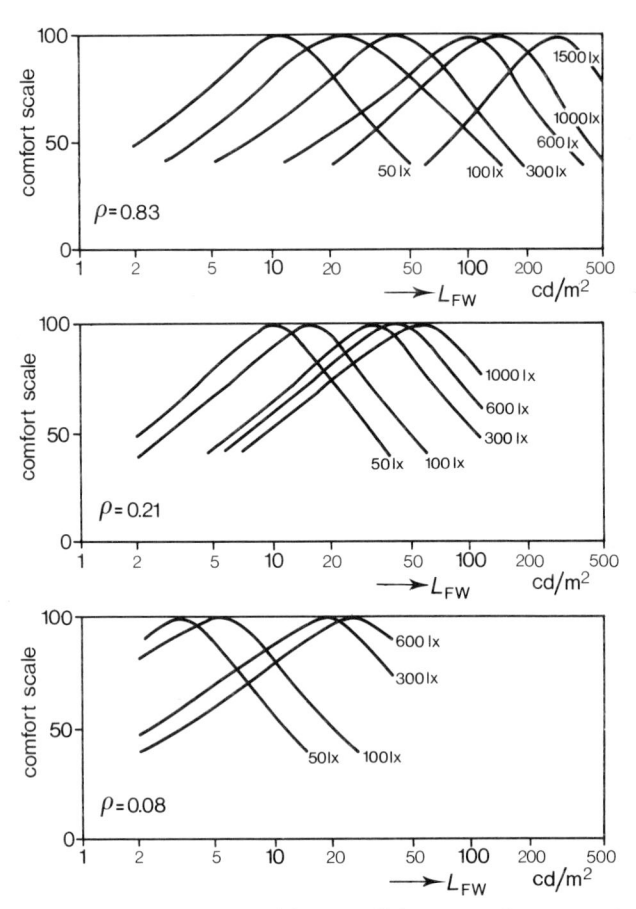

Figure 2.16 Assessment of facing-wall luminance L_{FW} on a relative scale of comfort at various levels of illuminance on the task for three values of wall reflectance ρ. (Barthès and Richard)

the dotted line of figure 2.17 which represents a compromise between the results of the two investigations outlined above. It can be seen from this line, that for the most commonly used range of illuminances, 500 to 1000 lux, the general wall luminance should lie between approximately 50 cd/m² and 100 cd/m².

A given value of preferred wall luminance could, in theory, be produced by an almost infinite range of combinations of vertical (wall) illuminance and wall reflectance. But experience, calculation and research (Jay, 1968) all indicate that satisfactory conditions are most likely to be achieved when the

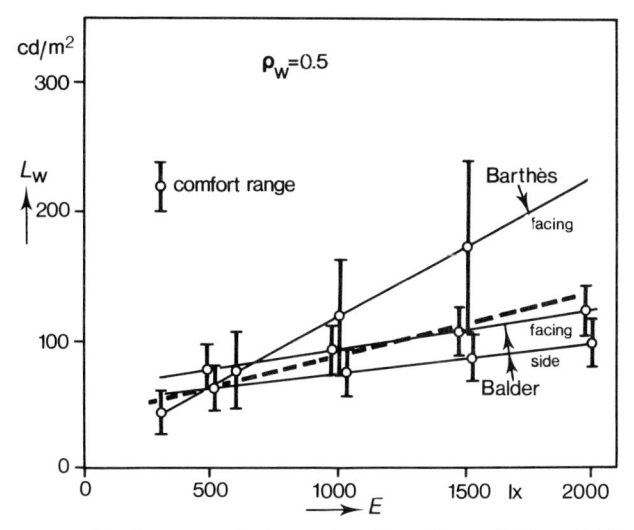

Figure 2.17 Preferred luminance L_w, for grey walls, interpolated from figures 2.15 and 2.16 as a function of task illuminance E.

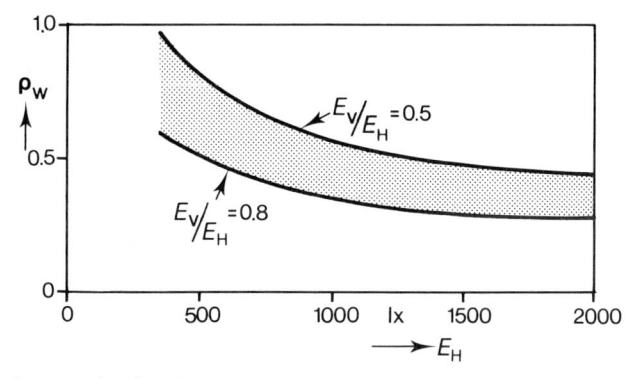

Figure 2.18 Recommended range of wall reflectance ρ_w as a function of horizontal illuminance E_h, with relative wall illuminance (E_V/E_H) as parameter.

59

relative wall illuminance – the ratio of the vertical to the horizontal illuminance – has a value lying between 0.5 and 0.8. Using this information and working from the dotted line of figure 2.17 it is possible, for a given horizontal illuminance, to specify directly the recommended range of wall reflectances. This has been done graphically in figure 2.18. As can be seen, wall reflectances for 500 lx installations may be relatively high (0.5 to 0.8) whereas for 1000 lx installations rather lower values are indicated (0.4 to 0.6). No problems will arise, in practice, if the relative wall illuminance falls just below the lower limit of 0.5 (as is often the case with narrow beam luminaires) because wall luminances slightly less than those recommended will still be acceptable.

2.4.2 Ceiling Luminance

The preferred luminance for a ceiling is governed principally by the luminance of the ceiling luminaires. That this is, in fact, so can be seen by combining the results of investigations made by Balder (1957), Collins and Plant (1971) and Fischer (1973) as has been done in figure 2.19. Below a luminaire luminance of approx. 100 cd/m^2 the luminance of the ceiling is preferred to be even higher than that of the luminaires and this is clearly unlikely to be achieved in practice. The experiments have been executed up to luminaire luminances that are felt to be already glaring. The upper limits for ceiling luminances in practical applications, however, will thus be determined by the corresponding glare limit of the luminaire used.

For this point the value specified in quality class A of the Luminance Curve Method of glare evaluation (see Sec. 3.2.1), which should be used for lighting design in offices, seems appropriate. These upper limits for ceiling luminances have been determined for the lighting levels 500, 1000 and 2000 lux and are indicated by circles in figure 2.20.

2.4.3 Wall/Ceiling Luminance Ratios

The range of preferred luminances for both ceilings and walls are shown combined in figure 2.20 where luminance is plotted as a function of illuminance. The above investigations point to rough guide values for comfortable ceiling and wall luminances of 200 cd/m^2 and 100 cd/m^2 respectively at an illuminance of 1000 lx. At the lower end of the illuminance range (500 lx) the preferred ceiling luminance is about four times the preferred wall luminance. At the upper end (2000 lx) these preferred luminance levels are nearly equal. In the latter case, a lighting scheme in which ceiling luminance and wall luminance were made equal could prove monotonous to the eye unless differences in colour were employed to give a sense of variety.

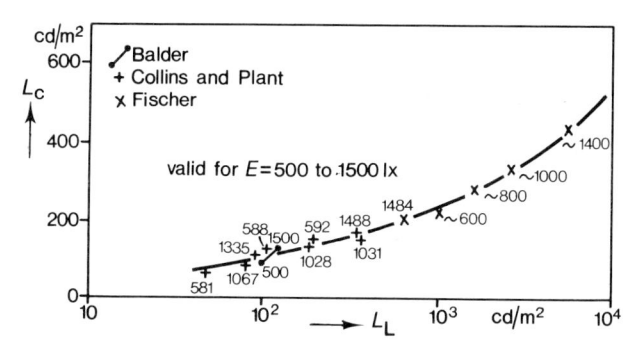

Figure 2.19 Preferred ceiling luminance L_c as a function of luminaire luminance L_L. The numbers adjacent to the points along the curve refer to the horizontal illuminances prevailing on the working plane in the various investigations.

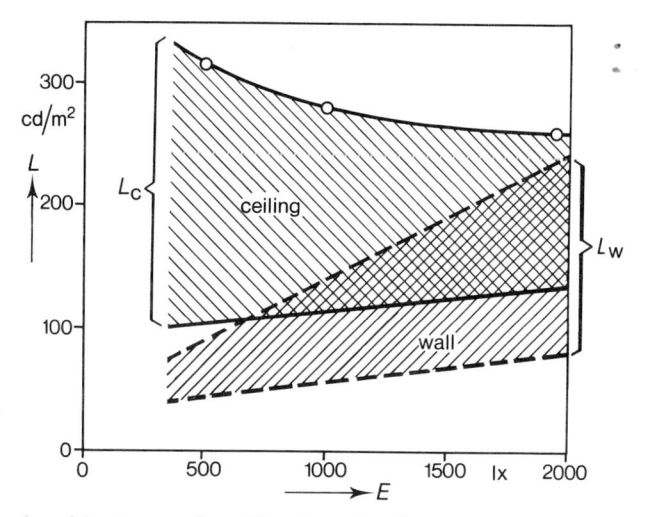

Figure 2.20 Range of preferred luminances for ceiling L_c and wall L_w as a function of illuminance E, on working plane.

2.5 Daylight and Artificial Light – Brightness Balance

In deep, windowed rooms the outer zones receive sufficient daylight for the efficient performance of a task, but the inner zones have to be provided with permanent artificial lighting. Such lighting must perform a double function. It must provide an adequate level of illuminance – this has already been discussed – whilst at the same time creating a satisfactory brightness balance with the daylight. A lack of experimental data prompted Hopkinson and Longmore (1959) to study this second point in some detail.

A model room was constructed. Daylight could enter the room via a window, the design of which could be easily altered for the purposes of comparison. Artificial lighting was provided at the back of the room in the form of a diffusing luminaire extending the full width of the ceiling. Opaque white eggcrate louvres flush with the ceiling prevented a direct view of the luminaire, which was fitted with two 3-ft 30-watt 'Daylight' type fluorescent lamps connected to a dimmer circuit. A small inspection aperture in one side wall enabled the interior of the model to be examined. Each of the ten observers participating in the study was asked to adjust the level of the artificial lighting to give the best brightness balance between it, and daylight.

The results suggested that the level of permanent artificial lighting necessary to give an acceptable brightness balance is directly proportional to the level of exterior daylight. Further, that the level of artificial lighting necessary for an overall satisfactory solution may be high because on dull days there is an additional load placed upon it, that of enlivening the appearance of the whole room.

The decision was made to base the level of permanent artificial lighting on that giving a satisfactory brightness balance at an average sky luminance of approximately 5000 cd/m^2. This level occurs very frequently throughout the working day at most times of the year. Inspection of the experimental data suggested that for this level of average sky luminance the level of lighting should fall within the range 200 lx to 500 lx. However, these levels are often exceeded when meeting the night-time requirements of modern industrial and commercial premises. In such cases, therefore, the concept of designing for a separate level of permanent supplementary lighting is no longer valid.

The most critical need for brightness balance in deep rooms occurs when looking at a face seen against the bright sky outside (figure 2.21). It will be recalled that the vertical illuminance needed on the face to avoid throwing it into silhouette has been the subject of an investigation (Fischer, 1973a) described in the previous chapter (Sec. 1.2.1).

As can be seen by referring back to figure 1.28, the luminance of the face should not be less than about one-twentieth that of the background, or sky, luminance for the human features to remain visible (curve C). Sky luminances of greater than 2000 cd/m^2 were regarded as glaring by most of the observers. It is assumed, therefore, that sky luminances in excess of this figure will be avoided by using curtains, blinds or other shielding devices. Thus, taking this value of 2000 cd/m^2 for the sky luminance, a facial luminance of at least 100 cd/m^2 would be needed, and this would necessitate a horizontal illuminance of 2000 lx in the window zone.

Some thought should also be given to the light distribution of the luminaires providing the lighting. Two possibilities exist. The artificial light can be

Figure 2.21 A face seen against a bright background will be thrown into silhouette if brightness balance is neglected.

directed into the room from the direction of the windows (asymmetrical light distribution), or it can be directed both away from and towards the windows (symmetrical light distribution). The only advantage of the first method is that an observer looking into the room with his back to the window will see a well-lighted area free from glare. Looking towards the windows, however, reinforces the silhouette effect already mentioned. The second approach, with the artificial light directed both away from and towards the source of daylight, is better in two respects. First, it gives good seeing conditions in all directions of view and second, the luminaires used can have the same symmetrical distribution as those already in use for lighting at night.

2.6 Modelling

Modelling, the balance between diffuse and directional light, is a valid criterion of lighting quality in virtually all types of interior. It is understandable, therefore, that attempts should have been made to quantify the modelling effect of lighting in a 'modelling index'.

Cuttle *et al.* (1967), who strongly questioned the validity of illuminance recommendations when applied to non-working interiors, set out to examine various other criteria, including modelling, that would enable illumination in these areas to be specified more in terms of the subjective satisfaction of the typical observer. He introduced the concept of the vector/scalar ratio to quantify the effect of directional lighting and showed how this ratio could serve as an index of modelling.

The vector/scalar ratio depends on two concepts, those of the illuminance vector and scalar illuminance. The illuminance vector indicates the directional nature of illumination at a point. Its magnitude ($\vec{E}$) is the maximum difference in illuminance that can be measured between the two sides of an infinitesimally small disc at that point, while the line perpendicular to and away from the side of the disc having the lower illuminance is its direction. The scalar illuminance (E_{sc}) – or mean spherical illuminance – at a point is the mean illuminance on the surface of an infinitesimally small sphere placed at that point. The vector/scalar ratio thus defines the directional strength of the lighting at a point. Its range of values is from zero, when the incident illumination in every direction is equal to the incident illumination in the opposite direction, to a maximum of 4.0, which would be achieved in a collimated beam in a darkened interior.

Cuttle conducted experiments on the effect of lighting with different directional strengths in which the human head was chosen as being a suitable, familiar object on which to base observer appraisals. The experimenter, who also acted as 'object', was seated in the middle of a framework of fluorescent lamps in the form of a cube (figure 2.22). The lamps forming the edges of the cube produced diffuse, or vectorless, lighting and any of those mounted across the top and down one side could be selected to give directional lighting. The experimenter had controls with which he could adjust the intensity of the diffuse lighting and select the vertical angle given to the directional lighting. The observer was seated facing the experimenter and had a control with which he could adjust the intensity of the directional lighting selected by the experimenter.

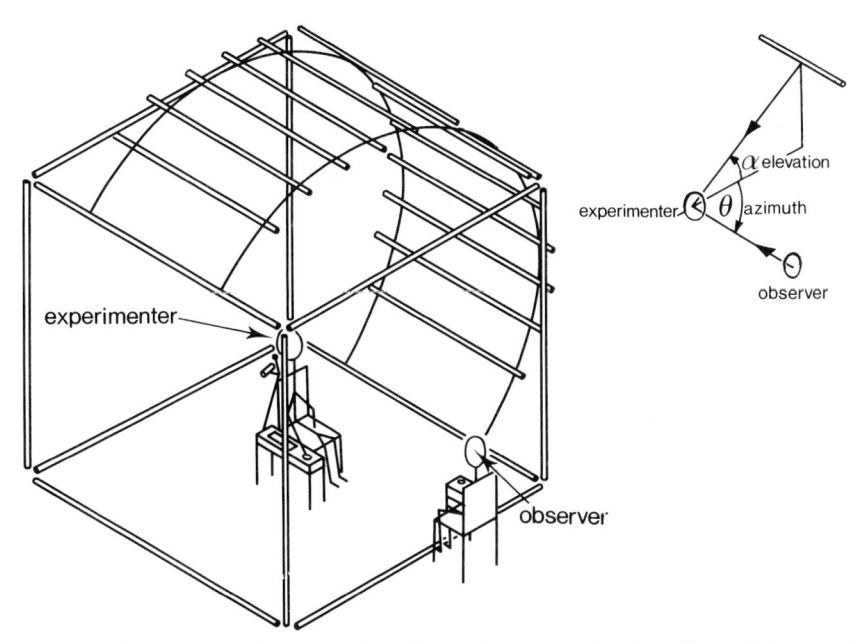

Figure 2.22 Experimental set-up used by Cuttle for investigating the validity of the vector/ scalar ratio as an index of modelling.

The procedure was for the experimenter to first select one of the lamps giving directional lighting. The observer was then asked to adjust the intensity of this lighting to identify three modelling criteria in turn:
1. Modelling just too soft to adequately define the features;
2. Preferred modelling effect;
3. Modelling just too harsh to be acceptable.

The scalar illuminance at the experimenter's head was all the time kept constant by the experimenter adjusting the intensity of the diffuse lighting. This procedure was repeated for directional lighting ranging from side lighting to overhead lighting (angles of elevation α, figure 2.22, 0° to 90°). Any influence that a change in the azimuth of the vector direction might have on the results was allowed for by rearranging the seating positions over an arc centred on the experimenter's position, a face-to-face direction of view being maintained at all times. The results, for four values of azimuth (angle Θ, figure 2.22; 30° to 120°), were averaged and combined to give the preferred and acceptable ranges of modelling shown in figure 2.23.

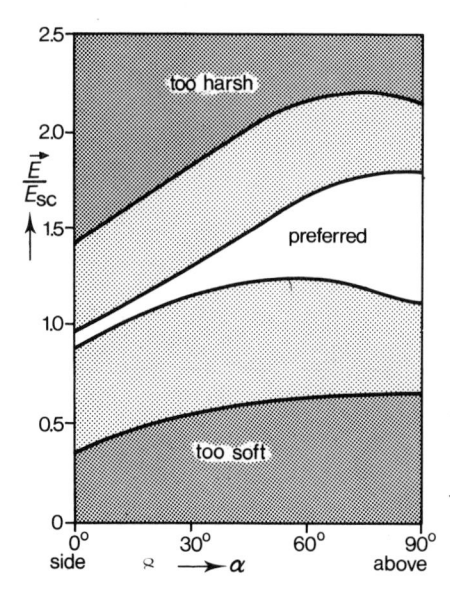

Fig. 2.23 Preferred, acceptable and too harsh ranges of modelling as a function of α (see figure 2.22) when principal direction of view in azimuth cannot be defined (valid for angles of azimuth 30° to 120°). (Cuttle)

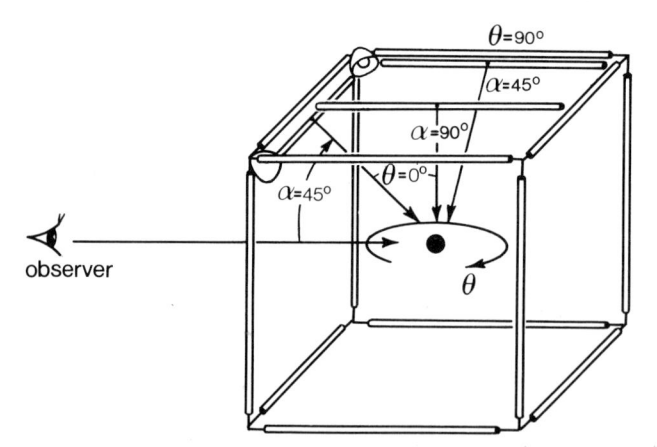

Figure 2.24 Experimental set-up used by Fischer for assessing the modelling effect of light from both fluorescent and incandescent lamps on a range of objects. The angles (Θ azimuth, α elevation) indicate the vector direction of the incident light relative to the direction of view.

Fischer (1970a) and (1970b) extended the scope of the research by assessing the modelling of the human face and of lifeless objects lit by the directional light from incandescent lamps.

The set-up used by Fischer was similar to that used by Cuttle above. The test object – the human face, flowers, a tennis ball and an unlighted incandescent lamp were used – was situated at the centre of a cube having black walls. It received vectorless illumination from twelve fluorescent lamps mounted along the edges of the cube.

Additional, directional lighting was supplied by fluorescent lamps or by incandescent lamps mounted round the top of the cube, figure 2.24. The observers looked at the objects through an aperture in the front wall of the cube (figure 2.25) and assessed each modelling situation using a specially prepared questionnaire. Each modelling situation was assessed on a ten-point scale having extremes marked 0 = unpleasant and 10 = pleasant. The modelling was specified photometrically in terms of the vector/scalar ratio as defined by Cuttle and his co-workers.

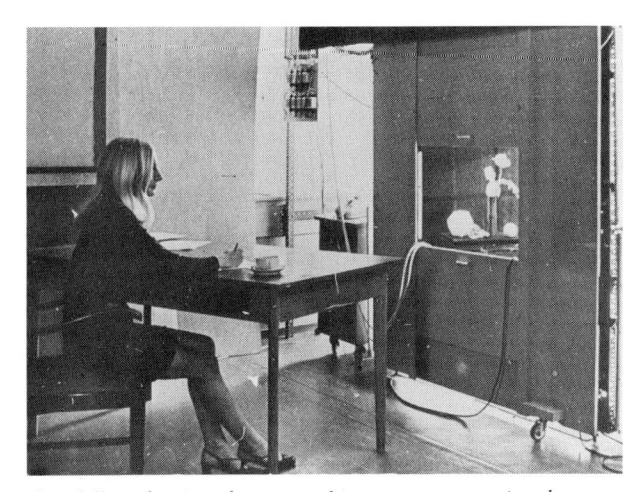

Figure 2.25 Assessment of modelling showing observer making assessments using the set-up of figure 2.24.

The preferred ranges of vector/scalar ratios found for $\Theta = 0°$, $\alpha = 45°$ and for different light sources and objects, along with that arrived at by Cuttle, are summarised in figure 2.26. As can be seen, Fischer's results relating to the modelling of the human face using fluorescent lamps are in agreement with those of Cuttle. By comparison, the results for the modelling of lifeless objects using fluorescent lamps indicate that, for such objects, a stronger directional effect of the lighting is required in order to obtain the

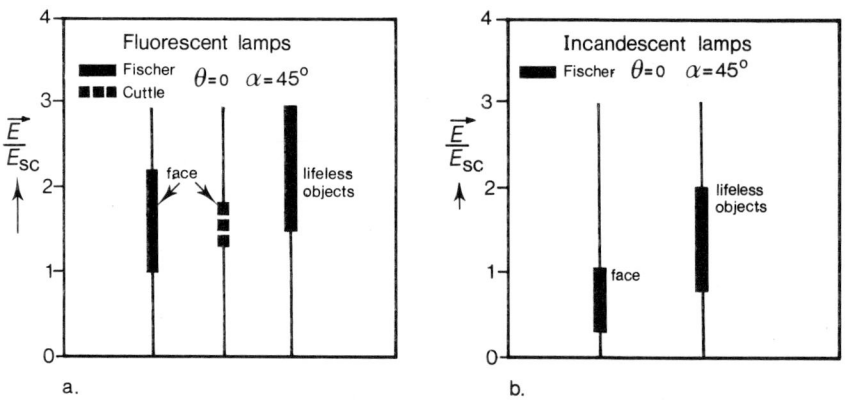

Figure 2.26 Preferred ranges of modelling using (a) fluorescent lamps and (b) incandescent lamps, in the set-up of figure 2.24. The result of Cuttle is included for the purposes of comparison.

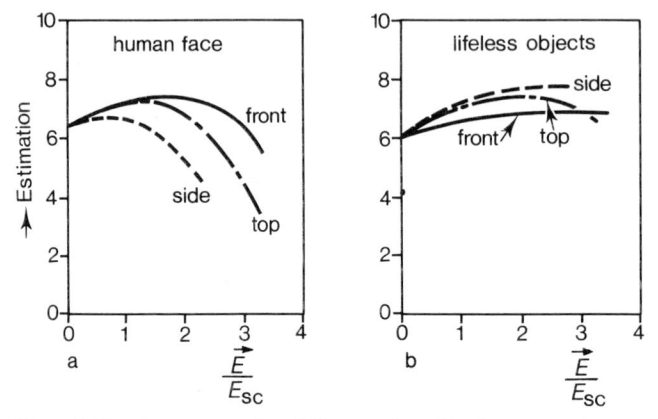

Figure 2.27 Assessment of modelling produced by fluorescent lamps for (a) the human face and (b) lifeless objects. (Fischer)

same assessment. The vector strength of the lighting produced by incandescent lamps should, for good modelling of both the human face and lifeless objects, be less than that produced by fluorescent lamps. This lessens the unpleasant hard shadows that would otherwise result from the use of incandescent 'point' sources.

The influence of the direction of the light on modelling quality in the case of fluorescent lamps is shown in figure 2.27.

Lighting from the front ($\Theta = 0°$, $\alpha = 45°$) was judged to give the best modelling of the human face, side lighting ($\Theta = 90°$, $\alpha = 45°$) being preferred for the other objects. It would seem that generally speaking more dramatic lighting is acceptable for these objects than for the human face. The preference curve for top lighting ($\Theta = 0°$, $\alpha = 90°$), which in each case lies between those for front and side lighting, indicates an optimum vector/scalar ratio of around 1.5 for the human face and 2.0 for lifeless objects.

From this it can be concluded that lighting with ceiling luminaires (top lighting) will give good results for inanimate objects and satisfactory results for the human face provided that the vector/scalar ratio, or index of modelling, lies between 1.5 and 2.0. In a typical office lighted with narrow beam luminaires, and having a medium floor reflectance, the index of modelling is in fact about 2.0. The floor must have a relatively high reflectance in this case in order to ensure that sufficient light is reflected diffusely in all directions to brighten the disturbing shadows that might otherwise occur e.g. shadows under the eyebrows of people in the area. If luminaires having a more wide-spread light distribution are employed, modelling may improve but care must then be taken not to increase glare at the same time.

In a recent investigation of Noguchi, Ejima, Nagai and Nakano (1977) the psychological meaning of the influence of direction of light on the appearance of objects (four kinds of one-piece dress were used) was studied to find better scales for the assessment. The experimental enclosure was similar to those used by Cuttle (figure 2.22) and Fischer (figure 2.24). It was found that the factors determining the appreciation of the object appraised were optimum at azimuth angles Θ between 0° and 30° and angles of elevation α between 45° and 67.5°.

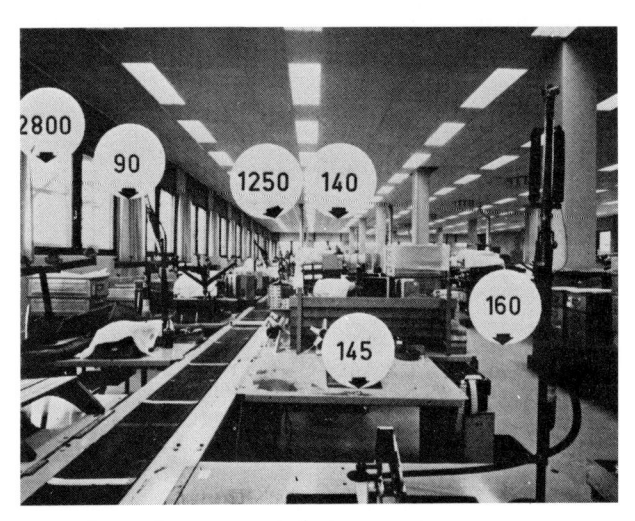

Figure 2.28 Luminance pattern in a radio-components factory.

2.7 Practical Examples

Before closing this chapter on preferred luminance distribution, let us take a brief look at how the recommendations arrived at have been applied in practice. Two examples of lighting installations will be considered.

2.7.1 A Factory Hall

The first example is a factory hall used for the manufacture of radio components, figure 2.28. The hall is lighted by mirror luminaires which, in the absence of daylight, give an illuminance of 1800 lx. The reflectance of the work surface (bench top) is 0.23 which, according to figure 1.20, calls for a task luminance of at least 135 cd/m². This is, in fact, achieved during the hours of darkness. (The increased illuminance during daylight hours can contribute as much as 50 cd/m² to this value, in fact an extra 10 cd/m² at the moment when the photograph was taken.)

The luminaire luminance of 1250 cd/m² is lower than would be permitted for quality class B (see Chapter 3, Glare), which is the quality class used for high quality factory lighting. The preferred ceiling luminance corresponding to this value of luminaire luminance (see figure 2.19) is 260 cd/m². During the hours of darkness this value is not reached, a ceiling luminance of only 70 cd/m² being recorded. The situation is, however, improved during the daytime, the ceiling luminance sometimes increasing to as much as 300 cd/m² (140 cd/m² at the time the photograph was taken).

The wall luminance of 90 cd/m² lies well within the preferred range given by figure 2.17.

Taken all round, this installation may be said to give a well-balanced luminance distribution. The interior is, therefore, most pleasant from the lighting point of view.

2.7.2 A Landscaped Office

The second example is of a landscaped office, figure 2.29. The office is lighted by recessed luminaires equipped with prismatic diffusers.

The illuminance level in the absence of daylight (figure 2.29a) is 900 lx, which gives a luminance at the task (white paper) of 200 cd/m². This is less than the 350 cd/m² which, according to figure 1.20, is preferred. The luminaire luminance of 1300 cd/m² at an illuminance of 900 lx is better than quality class A (see Chapter 3, Glare), which is the highest class recommended for schools and offices. The ceiling luminance of 30 cd/m² is much too low in comparison with the recommended value of 270 cd/m² (figure 2.19).

The photograph of the daytime situation (figure 2.29b) was taken during

Figure 2.29 Luminance pattern in a landscaped office (a) at night (b) during the daytime.

the winter at noon. The sky was overcast and the external illuminance about 10 000 lx. Under these conditions, the ceiling luminance increased to 70 cd/m², which is still far below the recommended value. It is, in fact, only during the summer months that the ceiling luminance becomes as high as it should be in order for it to produce a pleasant luminance distribution. The situation could be improved at all times of the year by increasing the lighting level to bring it within the optimum range of between 1500 lx and 2000 lx. But even then, the luminance distribution during the hours of darkness would not be entirely satisfactory.

2.8 Summing Up

An observer's field of view in an interior may include some or all of the following: faces, a task area, walls, ceiling, sky (seen through a window), luminaires. When recommending luminance values for each of these objects or areas it is customary to quote

Minimum values when referring to the luminance of the human features: 1 cd/m² for the features to be just recognisable, or 10 cd/m²–20 cd/m² for the features to be just acceptably lit, i.e. recognisable without any special effort.

Optimum values when referring to the luminance of walls, ceiling, task area and the human features:
50 cd/m²–150 cd/m² for walls,
100 cd/m²–300 cd/m² for ceilings,
100 cd/m²–400 cd/m² for the task area, and about
250 cd/m² for the human features

Maximum values when referring to the luminance of sky and luminaires:
2000 cd/m² marks the beginning of glare from the sky
1000 cd/m²–10000 cd/m² (depending on illuminance level, type of luminaire, and room conditions) is the maximum luminaire luminance (see Chapter 3, Glare).

These recommended values can be arranged to form a scale of luminance for interiors. This has been done in figure 2.30. As might be expected, the luminances occurring in a satisfactorily lit interior cover three decades, as was the case with the illuminances recommended in Chapter 1.

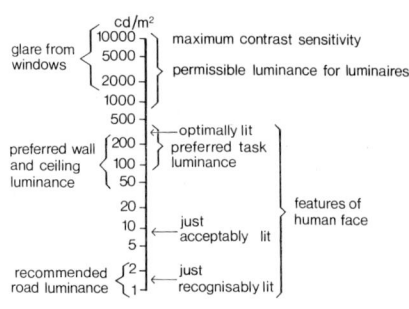

Figure 2.30 Recommended scale of luminance for interiors.

Chapter 3

Glare

Glare can be direct or reflected. Direct glare can be caused by a bright light source appearing in the normal field of view of an observer. Reflected glare will result if the observer sees the reflection of such a source in a glossy surface.

Direct glare may take either of two forms. Glare that impairs the vision is known as disability glare; it can be measured in terms of deterioration of visual performance, that is to say of contrast sensitivity. Glare that induces a feeling of discomfort is termed discomfort glare; the degree of discomfort can only be assessed subjectively. In interior lighting practice, discomfort glare is more likely to present problems than is disability glare and measures taken to control the former will normally take care of the latter also. Therefore only direct discomfort glare will be dealt with here. (Reflected glare has been discussed in the previous chapter, Sec. 2.3)

3.1 Basic Work on Evaluation of Discomfort Glare

The development of a practical system for evaluating and controlling discomfort glare has occupied research workers in several countries for a number of years. The majority of this research has been channelled along three basic lines

(a) Investigations into the fundamental mechanisms involved in experiencing glare, and its effect on the human organism.
(b) Investigations into the empirical relation between the glare sensation and the photometric and geometric characteristics of a lighting installation with a view to arriving at a phenomenological glare formula.
(c) Development of systems involving practicable rules and data for use by the lighting engineer in the control of glare.

The first line of research has so far yielded no successful understanding of what discomfort glare really is.

The formulae resulting from the second line of research (Vermeulen and de Boer 1948, and Bodmann, Söllner and Senger 1966) which are valid for

single sources, are of the type
$$G_M = \frac{L_S^m \times \omega^n}{L_A^r \times p^q}$$
where G_M = glare mark describing the degree of the glare sensation
L_S = luminance of the glare source
ω = solid angle of the glare source subtended at observer's eye
L_A = luminance of the observer's field of view determining his adaptation
p = position factor of the glare source

Such formulae describe, approximately, the influence of the most important variables on the glare sensation within a limited range of experimental conditions. The empirical exponents m, n, r and q are somewhat different as expressed by several authors; it appears that the test procedure itself influences the results.

Further complexities are raised with respect to the summation effect of multiple glare sources. As Arndt, Bodmann and Muck (1959b) have shown in an experimental investigation using several sources of light, the additivity of glare figures of single sources follows a course that, due to interaction between luminance differences within the field of vision, deviates from the two different summation methods that have been proposed by Hopkinson (1957) and by de Boer (1958) respectively.

As to the results of the third line of research, a number of glare evaluation systems have in fact been developed. The British IES Glare Index System, The American VCP Method and The Australian SAA Code System, which are briefly described further on in this chapter, make use of formulae of the type mentioned above, whereas the Luminance Curve Method used in Europe (Sec. 3.2.1) is based solely on the results of subjective appraisals made in interiors.

3.2 Systems for Evaluating Discomfort Glare in Working Interiors

3.2.1 The Luminance Curve Method

In order to overcome the unsolved problem of having to add the glare effects of single sources by means of summation formulae, Söllner (1965) (see also Bodmann, Söllner and Senger, 1966) carried out an extensive investigation with the object of establishing an empircal glare evaluation system.

The basic experiments were conducted using a number of one-third-scale models of offices in which various real-life situations could be realistically simulated (figure 3.1). Colours and reflectances in the model rooms were essentially constant in all experiments: white ceilings (70 per cent), beige walls (50 per cent), brown floors (20 per cent) and light-brown furniture

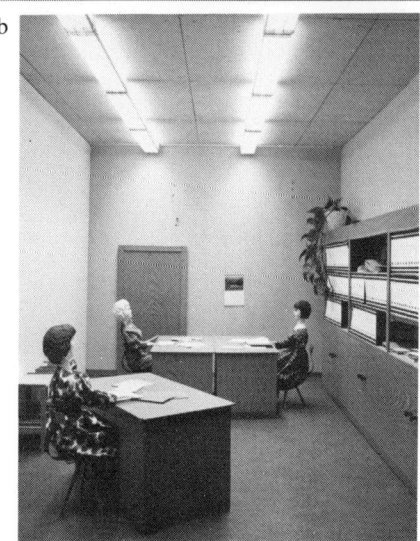

Figure 3.1 An observer's view of the model rooms used for the assessment of discomfort glare. The room in (b) was made to appear twice its actual length through the use of a mirror.

75

(30 per cent). Five models of common types of fluorescent-lamp luminaires were employed. Lighting levels and room dimensions were both varied. Glare was assessed subjectively by a laboratory team of observers using a six-point scale for the glare rating G on which the principal points were marked: 0 – no glare, 2 – slight glare, 4 – severe glare and 6 – intolerable glare.

Analysis of the results showed that only four factors have sufficient effect

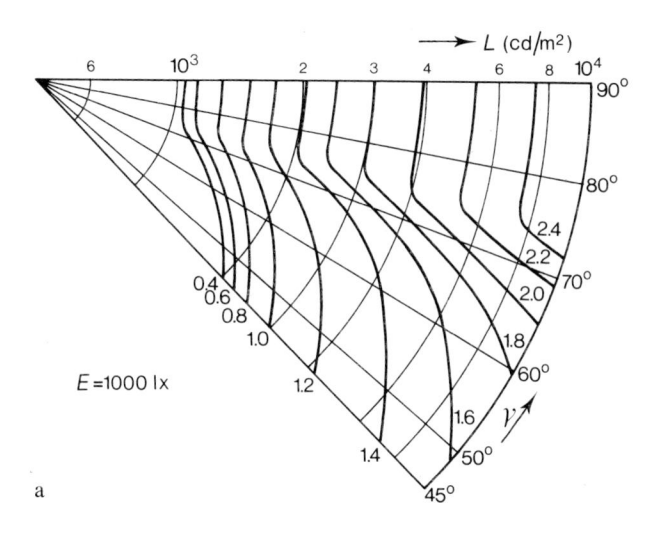

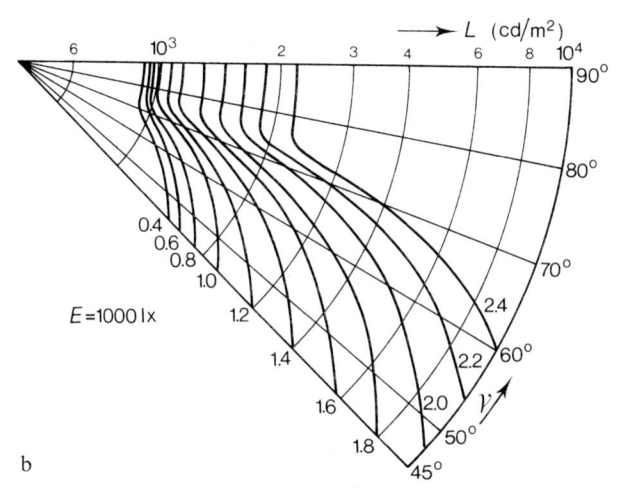

Figure 3.2 Limits of luminaire luminance L as a function of the emission angle γ with glare rating G as parameter for a lighting level of 1000 lx under standard conditions for luminaires viewed (a) parallel to the longitudinal axis and (b) at right angles to the longitudinal axis.

in practice on the degree of glare experienced to warrant consideration. These factors are
(1) The luminance of the luminaire.
(2) The room length and mounting height.
(3) The adaptation level, which can be represented by the average horizontal illuminance.
(4) Type of luminaire, viz. luminous side panels, or otherwise.

The results, for a fixed value of illuminance and for a regular distribution of identical ceiling-mounted luminaires, could be represented by sets of curves in which the luminance of the luminaire is indicated as a function of the emission angle γ for given degrees of glare experienced.

Examples of the diagrams constructed to define the luminance limits – as determined by 50 per cent of the observers – for lengthwise and breadthwise viewing of the luminaires are reproduced in figure 3.2. These diagrams are valid for an illuminance of 1000 lx only.

For a given type of luminaire, an increase in illuminance brought about by increasing the number of luminaires used was found to produce an increase in the degree of glare experienced.

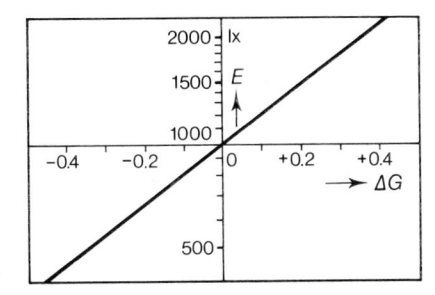

Figure 3.3 Diagram for determining the shift ΔG in the glare rating G with change in illuminance, E.

Figure 3.3 shows the chart used for finding the shift in the degree of glare for lighting levels other than 1000 lx. In mathematical terms, the initial glare rating G must be modified by adding or subtracting the amount ΔG as given by

$$\Delta G = 1.16 \log \frac{E}{1000}$$

This system of glare evaluation was subsequently shown from observations in a number of existing lighting installations to be capable of yielding reasonably accurate glare predictions in real-life situations (Söllner, 1968).

Fischer (1972) approximated the system by a mathematical frame and standardised stepped scales of glare ratings and illuminance. The curves of the basic diagrams of the system (examples of which have been shown in figure 3.2 above), redrawn in Cartesian coordinates, were approximated by point-to-point straight lines. The equations of the points determining these lines could be written

(a) for lengthwise directions of view

$$\log L_{75°-85°} = 3.0 + 0.15 \left(G - 1.16 \log \frac{E}{1000}\right)^2$$

and

$$\log L_{45°} = 3.176 + 0.40 \left(G - 1.16 \log \frac{E}{1000}\right)^2$$

(b) for breadthwise directions of view

$$\log L_{75°-85°} = 2.930 + 0.07 \left(G - 1.16 \log \frac{E}{1000}\right)^2$$

and

$$\log L_{45°} = 3.105 + 0.26 \left(G - 1.16 \log \frac{E}{1000}\right)^2$$

Using these equations, 'curves' for any glare rating and illuminance and for lengthwise and breadthwise directions of view could be constructed.

The glare evaluation system was then adapted to practical use by confining it to a stepped scale of six glare ratings ($G = 0.8, 1.15, 1.5, 1.85, 2.2$ and 2.55) corresponding to six quality classes (S, A, B, C, D and E respectively), and to a stepped scale of four levels of illuminance (250, 500, 1000 and 2000 lux). The luminance curve diagram thus evolved and the numerical values of the luminance limits used in its construction are shown in figure 3.4 and table 3.1 respectively.

The reason for the choice of the above values (glare ratings with a difference of 0.35 between steps and illuminance levels doubling with each step) was to simplify the presentation; it means that a single curve can serve for several combinations of glare rating G and illuminance E. In figure 3.4a, for example, the luminance limits for $G = 1.15$ with $E = 500$ lx, $G = 1.5$ with $E = 1000$ lx and $G = 1.85$ with $E = 2000$ lx are all specified on the one curve, c.

This method of glare evaluation, known as the Luminance Curve Method (sometimes also referred to as the European Glare Limiting Method), is being adopted by an increasing number of European countries with variations according to the glare ratings and illuminance levels chosen by these countries.

The method is valid for ceiling reflectances of not less than 0.5 and wall reflectances of not less than 0.3.

The first step in the application of the Luminance Curve Method is to determine the average luminance of the luminaire type in use over a range of viewing angles. For the vast majority of luminaires the luminous intensity distributions in the two vertical planes mutually at right angles and passing

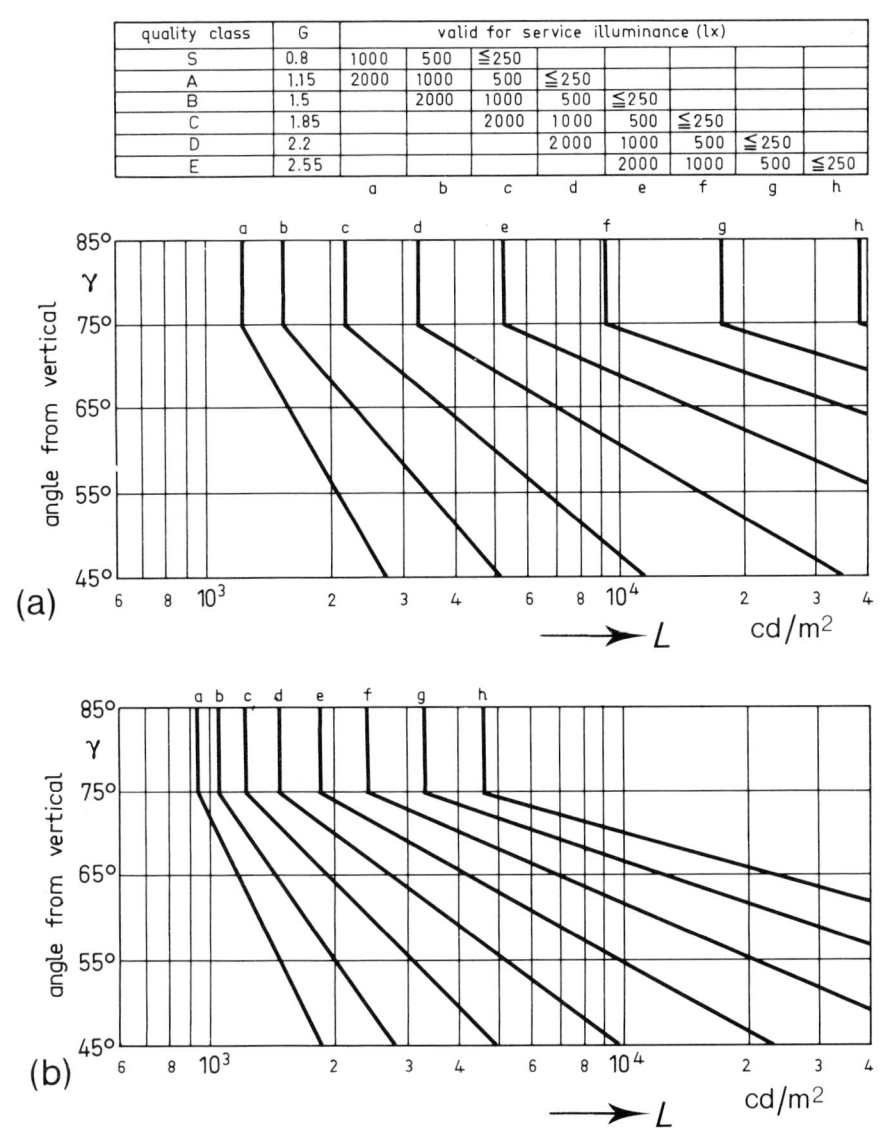

quality class	G	valid for service illuminance (lx)						
S	0.8	1000	500	≦250				
A	1.15	2000	1000	500	≦250			
B	1.5		2000	1000	500	≦250		
C	1.85			2000	1000	500	≦250	
D	2.2				2000	1000	500	≦250
E	2.55					2000	1000	500	≦250
		a	b	c	d	e	f	g	h

Figure 3.4 Luminance Curve diagrams for directions of view (a) parallel to the longitudinal axis of any elongated luminaire and for luminaires not having luminous side panels viewed from any direction, and (b) at right angles to the longitudinal axis of any luminaire having luminous side panels.

through the luminaire centre are not equal, and the luminance in both these planes will be required. Where the luminance distribution of the luminaire is not supplied by the luminaire manufacturer, this can be calculated. (See Chapter 13 Sec. 13.1.3 Luminance Calculations.)

Having determined the average luminance distribution of the luminaire the

Table 3.1 Numerical values of the luminance limits for the curves of figure 3.4 (a) and (b)

Figure	Angle γ	Luminance values (cd/m²) for curves							
		a	b	c	d	e	f	g	h
3.4 (a)	45°	2.71×10^3	5.08×10^3	1.19×10^4	3.49×10^4	1.29×10^5	5.96×10^5	3.44×10^6	2.46×10^7
	75°–90°	1.25×10^3	1.58×10^3	2.18×10^3	3.26×10^3	5.31×10^3	9.44×10^3	1.82×10^4	3.81×10^4
3.4 (b)	45°	1.87×10^3	2.82×10^3	4.90×10^3	9.88×10^3	2.30×10^4	6.24×10^4	1.95×10^5	7.00×10^5
	75°–90°	9.40×10^2	1.05×10^3	1.22×10^3	1.47×10^3	1.85×10^3	2.42×10^3	3.29×10^3	4.64×10^3

next step is to plot the luminance values on the reference diagram of figure 3.4. The plot can then be compared with the reference curve corresponding to the desired quality class and illuminance. The plot for a specific type of luminaire is shown in figure 3.5.

quality class	G	valid for service illuminance (lx)						
S	0.8	1000	500	≦250				
A	1.15	2000	1000	500	≦250			
B	1.5		2000	1000	500	≦250		
C	1.85			2000	1000	500	≦250	
D	2.2				2000	1000	500	≦250
E	2.55					2000	1000	500	≦250
		a	b	c	d	e	f	g	h

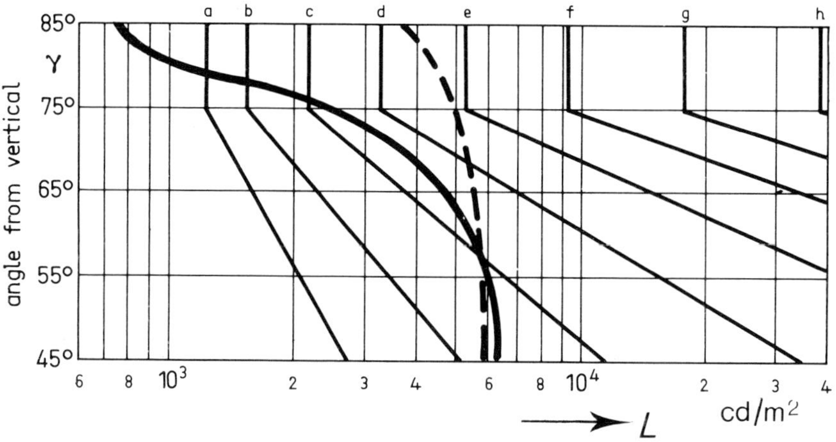

Figure 3.5 Evaluation of the degree of discomfort glare using the Luminance Curve Method for a fluorescent luminaire not having luminous side panels. The luminance distribution of the luminaire is plotted on the luminance curve diagram of figure 3.4a (distribution in the vertical plane passing through the centre of the luminaire and parallel to the lamp axes – dotted curve, distribution in plane at right angles to this plane – continuous curve).

The comparison will indicate the course of action to be taken. For example, if the luminance plot lies to the left of the chosen reference curve over the whole or a substantial part of the range of viewing angles, then the luminaire under examination comes up to requirements. If, on the other hand, the plot lies to the right of the reference curve over a substantial part of the range of viewing angles, then a different type of luminaire is called for.

Some further possibilities for presenting the glare-evaluation data of luminaires in catalogues are discussed in Chapter 11 of this book.

3.2.2 The British IES Glare Index System

The British IES Glare Index System is based on the formula mentioned in the previous section (Sec. 3.1), which defines the glare mark G_M of a luminaire. A summation of the glare marks of all luminaires gives a measure of the degree of glare of the total installation. The IES has used this formula to prepare sets of tabulated data for deriving a Glare Index for installations in which the luminaires are arranged in a substantially regular pattern.

The reader interested in obtaining details of this system is referred to IES (1967) and to Bedocs and Simons (1972).

3.2.3 The American VCP Method

The American Visual Comfort Probability (VCP) Method IES (1966) provides ratings of visual comfort in terms of the percentage of people who will consider a given lighting system to be acceptable. It takes into account the key factors that influence visual comfort, and is applicable to the usual types of interior lighting.

A standard procedure is employed to obtain ratings from VCP tables covering a wide range of room sizes and four luminaire mounting heights. The procedure can also be used for non-standard installations. Direct glare will not arise if the VCP is 70 or more and if certain maximum luminaire luminances are not exceeded.

An alternative, simplified procedure derived from the VCP Method can also be used. It is based on a weighted average luminance of a luminaire in the three viewing directions endwise, crosswise and diagonally, at angles γ between 40° and 85° from the nadir. The weighted average luminance L, which for glare to be avoided must be less than 1100 cd/m^2, can be calculated by summing the values obtained from the product of the luminaire luminance and a multiplier T. Thus

$$L = \Sigma L_\gamma \cdot T_\gamma$$

The value of the multiplier T_γ, which is dependent on the viewing direction and the angle of view from the nadir, can be found from a tabulated worksheet. Full details of this method are given in reference IES (1972).

3.2.4 The Australian Code System

The Australian system distinguishes between luminaires of the cut-off and non-cut-off types. Cut-off luminaires (units incorporating shades and louvres) are catered for in a table that specifies shielding angles. Non-cut-off luminaires (units incorporating translucent diffusing materials) and bare fluorescent lamps are dealt with in tables that specify limiting luminance values for various room dimensions. For further details see Australian Standard 1680–1975 of the Standards Association of Australia.

3.3 Comparison of Discomfort Glare Evaluation Systems

A simple qualitative comparison of the various glare evaluation methods can be made (Fischer and Hendriks, 1973) by noting the attention paid in each method to the parameters controlling glare in interiors. This has been done in table 3.2.

The quantitative comparison of these methods is made difficult by the fact that they have been based on different starting points and developed to meet differing requirements. Nevertheless, in the case of the British and European methods comparisons have been made – by Fischer and Hendriks (1973) and by Bellchambers, Collins and Crisp (1975).

Table 3.2 Qualitative comparison of glare evaluation systems

	British method	European method	Simplified American method	Australian method
Luminance distribution of the luminaire between 45° and 90°	–	+	+	–
Illuminance level	–	+	(+)	–
Reflectances of ceiling, walls and floor	+	(+)	(+)	–
Room dimensions or room index	+	+	(+)	+
Choice of quality classes available	yes	yes	no	no
Method of use	complicated	simple	simple	simple

Key: + = taken into account
 (+) = applicable only for fixed values of parameter
 – = not taken into account

Fischer and Hendriks established a sound relationship between the British IES Glare Index and the European Quality Class for luminaires classified as BZ3 or BZ4 (viz. medium-spread direct-lighting luminaires, see Chapter 8 Luminaires) used in interiors having ceiling, walls and floor of medium reflectance (viz. 0.7, 0.5 and 0.3 respectively).

With these restrictions in force (necessary because of the relatively small spread for these light distributions), they calculated the glare figures in both glare evaluation methods for rooms of various dimensions (room index

$k \geqslant 1.2$) and illuminance levels. From the results of these calculations a simple equation was derived giving, for those luminaires having no luminous sides, the British IES Glare Index in terms of the European Quality Class as indicated by the European Glare Rating, G: thus

$$\text{IES Glare Index} = 26 + 4.3\,G - 5 \log E \qquad (3.1)$$

where E is the illuminance level considered.

This equation does not give the real average of the results, but was derived in such a way that each European Quality Class always corresponds with an integer of the IES Glare Index, thus making a simple conversion possible. The error involved in its use is ± 1.5 units.

Bellchambers, Collins and Crisp extended the comparison to include luminaires emitting a certain amount of light in the upward direction and to rooms having differing room-surface reflectance values. They chose some 17 luminaires, from the vast number available, to give a broad range of BZ classifications. The glare rating for each of these luminaires was calculated for a range of room dimensions for each of the two glare evaluation systems. Good correspondence, for fluorescent luminaires classified as BZ2 to BZ7, was obtained between the British IES Glare Index and European Quality Class for a given illuminance within the limits of the reflectance of the walls and ceiling covered by the original German experimental work (Söllner, 1968). It was found that the correspondence could be extended to luminaires having differing flux fraction ratios and to other values of room reflectance

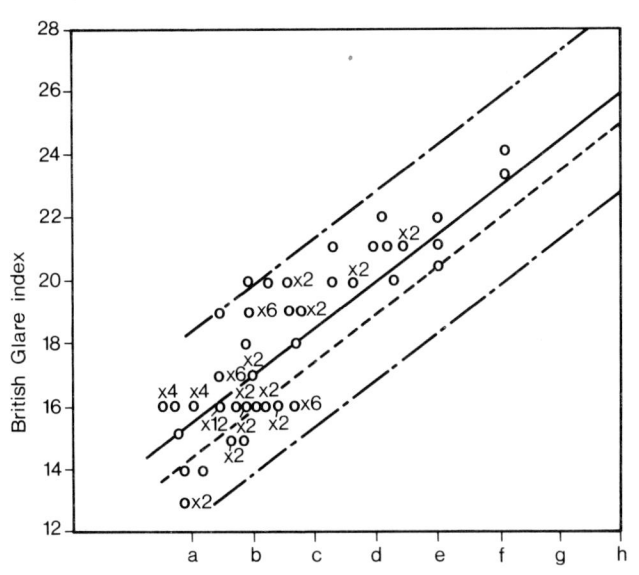

Figure 3.6 British Glare Index plotted against limiting curve (including the basic linear relationship for no upward light and reflectances of 0.7/0.5) after applying the conversion factors of table 3.3. Valid for all luminaires without significant luminous sides and all elongated luminaires viewed end-on.

Table 3.3 Conversion factors for various flux-fraction ratios (the ratio of the upward flux to the downward flux from a luminaire) and surface reflectances, applicable to the conditions of figure 3.6

Flux fraction ratio		0	0.33	0.5	1.0
Reflectances					
Ceiling	Walls				
0.7	0.5	0.0	+0.5	+0.75	+1.5
0.5	0.3	−1	−0.5	−0.25	+0.5

within a tolerance of ± 3 units in IES Glare Index by the use of appropriate 'conversion factors'.

This correspondence, for all luminaires except those with luminous sides viewed breadthwise, can be seen from figure 3.6 where the IES Glare Index for each luminaire is plotted against the Limiting Luminance Curves a to h. The straight line in this figure is defined by the equation

$$\text{IES Glare Index} = 27 + 4.3\,G - 5\log E$$

This is almost the same equation, in fact, as was derived by Fischer and Hendriks (Eq. 3.1), the only difference being that the first constant is 27 instead of 26. The equation of Fischer and Hendriks is represented by the dotted line in figure 3.6.

The conversion factors referred to above, which must be applied when using figure 3.6, are given in table 3.3. The figures in this table indicate how many limiting curves to the right (positive sign) or left (negative sign) of that indicated by the straight line relationship of figure 3.6 will lead to the same Glare Index for a luminaire of 'non-standard' upward light ratio or an installation with certain 'non-standard' surface reflectances. Specifically, a luminaire with more upward light than standard will give a smaller Glare Index than envisaged by the corresponding curves, so that a higher illuminance can be accepted. This means that one or more curves to the right can

Table 3.4 Equivalent glare indices valid for BZ3 and BZ4 luminaire classifications

IES Glare Index	Illuminance (lx)					
26						250
23				250	500	1000
20			250	500	1000	2000
17		500 1000	1000	2000		
		USA				
14		2000				
European Glare Rating	0.8	1.15	1.50	1.85	2.20	2.55
European Quality Class	S	A	B	C	D	E

be used to specify the limiting luminance to correspond to a particular Glare Index.

Using the two equations given above it is possible to draw up a table of equivalent glare indices, table 3.4. The table includes the simplified American VCP Method. For a luminaire to be acceptable according to this method, its glare index in the British Method must be not greater than 15. This corresponds to a European glare rating of 0.8 or less at an illuminance of 1000 lx.

The correlation between the two systems for luminaires with luminous sides viewed breadthwise was found by Bellchambers, Collins and Crisp to be not as good as that shown in figure 3.6.

3.4 Discomfort Glare from Luminous Ceilings

Conventional glare evaluation techniques are derived from the results of experimental work using relatively small sources. Such techniques cannot, therefore, be applied with any certainty to the evaluation of glare from luminous ceilings. It is possible, however, to investigate the tolerable levels of luminance of a luminous ceiling by direct experiment. Such was the nature of the work undertaken by Hopkinson and Collins (1963) and later, by Söllner (1972).

The primary causes of glare discomfort, in the case of a luminous ceiling, are known to be the high brightness of the ceiling itself, the contrast between the ceiling and adjacent wall surfaces, and the high brightness of these surfaces and the floor illuminated by the ceiling.

Hopkinson and Collins used a one-sixth scale model of a large unfurnished room that allowed the effect of varying each of these parameters to be studied in detail. The model was equipped with a diffusing luminous panel to represent the luminous ceiling, which could be dimmed to give luminances (measured from the observer's viewing position) ranging from approximately 100 cd/m^2 to 7000 cd/m^2. The floor and three sides of the model room were covered with detachable boards, painted in a range of neutral greys, so that the effect of different wall and floor reflectances could be studied.

Five observers participated in the study. Each observer made four sets of judgements on each of seven room arrangements using the four criteria: glare just perceptible, glare just acceptable, glare just uncomfortable and glare just intolerable. The model room was viewed from one side at one-third ceiling height.

The findings of these workers can be summarised as follows (*Note:* luminance values, originally quoted in ft-L, have been converted into cd/m^2.)

1. A luminous ceiling with a luminance in excess of about 500 cd/m^2 is likely to cause perceptible discomfort glare and a luminance in excess of about 1500 cd/m^2 intolerable glare when room-surface reflectances are

'average'. To eliminate glare entirely, the luminance of the ceiling must not exceed 140 cd/m².
2. Where the floor (and the lower hemisphere of the visual field in general) is of moderately low reflectance ($\rho = 0.20$), light-coloured walls give the greater comfort.
3. Where the floor is light (or where, for example, white papers on desks increase the effective reflectance of the lower visual field), darker walls give the greater comfort.
4. It is a disadvantage, and not an advantage, to have all the room surfaces very light in colour, since the room surfaces themselves can give rise to some degree of discomfort.
5. On the other hand, if the ceiling luminance is only moderate (100 cd/m²–170 cd/m²) the lightness of the room decorations has only a small effect. The only exception is that with very dark surfaces ($\rho = 0.04$) some discomfort will always arise no matter what the ceiling luminance.

Although these and other findings were consistent with the theories of adaptation and glare, it was not found possible to deduce a formula suitable for practical application.

Söllner carried out his experiments in a test room measuring four metres by six metres with a ceiling height of 2.8 metres. The room surfaces were given reflectances of 0.2, 0.5 and 0.15 for the facing wall, side walls and floor respectively. The luminosity of the luminous ceiling could be adjusted to give three levels of illuminance (700, 2000 and 3200 lx) independent of the luminance of the ceiling as seen by the observers; the latter could be changed by the use of neutral filters at the observation point. By this means, the relation between glare and illuminance could be investigated while the ceiling luminance was held constant at a predetermined value.

Glare, which was assessed on a seven-point scale with endpoints numbered 0 (glare non-existant) and 6 (glare intolerable), in fact decreased with an increase in illuminance. For example, at a ceiling luminance of 500 cd/m² (the figure proposed by Hopkinson as being the upper limit for ceiling luminance when surface reflectances are average) glare decreased from 3 on the scale of assessment at 700 lx, to 1 at 3200 lx (i.e. from between noticeable and disagreeable to between non-existant and noticeable).

It is in fact allowed to increase the luminance of the ceiling with increasing illuminance – although not in the same proportion – without increasing the amount of glare. For example, were the above increase in illuminance from 700 lx to 3200 lx to be accompanied by an increase in ceiling luminance from 500 cd/m² to 1200 cd/m², the degree of glare would remain constant.

Söllner also found that the ceiling luminance as measured at 45° to the vertical could be about twice as high, for the same degree of glare, as when measured at an angle of 75°.

3.5 Summing up

The fundamental mechanisms involved in experiencing the phenomenon of direct discomfort glare are as yet little understood. Much work has nevertheless been done in establishing and perfecting glare control, or evaluation, procedures.

Four systems of glare evaluation are currently in use. Three of these are tailored to meet national – British, American and Australian – requirements. The fourth system, known as the Luminance Curve Method (although sometimes still referred to using its former title of the European Glare Limiting Method), which is perhaps more concise than any of the other three, has gained wide support within Europe as well as within the CIE.

Simple qualitative comparison of all four systems of glare evaluation is perfectly straightforward (see table 3.2), but quantitative comparison, made difficult by the differences in approach adopted from one system to another, has so far been confined to the British and European systems. The results of two such quantitative comparisons have been expressed in the form of two almost identical equations giving, in each case, the British IES Glare Index in terms of the European Glare Rating, from which a table of equivalent glare indices can be derived (See table 3.4).

The glare evaluation systems referred to above can only be used in those cases where the glare phenomenon arises as a result of discrete ceiling mounted luminaires entering the field of view. Glare from continuous luminous ceilings has proved difficult to evaluate outside of the laboratory and at present there is no convenient or recognisable method of establishing what is acceptable in terms of ceiling luminance; all that can be done is to rely on a system of trial and error based on a roughly established rule of thumb value of 500 cd/m^2 for average room reflectances and illuminance levels.

Chapter 4

Colour

The lighting engineer is not fully equipped to deal with the many and varied problems that can arise during the course of designing an indoor lighting installation unless he has at least a basic understanding of colour and the role played by colour in interiors.

Colour begins at the light source. The phenomenon of the colours of objects appearing to change when they are viewed under the light from different sources is familiar to everyone. It is the difference in the spectral distribution of the radiant power emitted by the different types of source that, in part, is responsible for this apparent change in object colour.

These colour rendering properties of a light source cannot be assessed from its colour appearance. Two sources may have the same colour appearance and yet have entirely different colour rendering properties. Equally, two sources may exhibit a marked difference in colour appearance and yet, under certain circumstances, be capable of giving equally acceptable colour rendering. An understanding of how such a paradox can arise will take the reader a long way towards reaching an understanding of what colour is all about.

The preferred colour appearance of both sources and objects is often important in connection with the lighting level in an interior. Experience, backed up by research, shows that the atmosphere created in an interior is greatly influenced both by the colour of the light used and the brightness impression created by that light.

The colour rendering properties of a source are particularly important in those special purpose lighting applications in which fine differences in colour must be easily discernible; colour grading and matching are just two examples of such applications. Here, the need to have some idea of the kinds of light source suitable for different applications will have to be reckoned with.

The lighting engineer must also be able to combine his knowledge of the colour rendering properties of different light sources with an understanding of the use of object colour in interior decor, the choice of light source and object colour being mutually dependent. It is here that the roles of the lighting engineer and interior designer overlap; it is only by each being aware of some of the problems of the other that an interior lighting installation can be designed to give the highest lighting efficiency without it detracting from the overall appearance of the environment.

These and other related aspects of colour form the basis for discussion in the pages that follow.

4.1 Systems of Colour Specification

Over the years a great number of systems for specifying and classifying colour have been proposed (Bouma, 1971). Many of these systems were developed with rather narrow, specialised fields of application in mind. They can be divided into two main groups. The first group comprises systems based on a classification in accordance with three dimensions: the so-called dominant wavelength, the saturation and the brightness. The second group contains those systems working on the principle that a given colour can be created by a specified mixture of three primary colours.

Systems belonging to the first group are termed monochromatic colour classification systems. Many such systems consist of a standardised series of colour samples arranged and named so as to facilitate identification. The colour requiring specification is simply matched with one of the many colours in one of these systems. The best known and most widely used system of this kind is the Munsell system.

Systems belonging to the second group are referred to as trichromatic colour classification systems. The most prominent system in this group is that adopted by the CIE. In 1931 this body recommended the chromaticity diagram, or colour triangle, for the mathematically exact specification of colour. Later, in 1960, the CIE introduced an extension of this system – the uniform chromaticity scale (UCS) diagram – for the specification of colour differences.

4.1.1 The Munsell System

The Munsell system is used in lighting engineering for specifying object colours under daylight conditions. The three dimensions used in this system are termed hue, value and chroma. In the Munsell system each of these dimensions is given a scale of values. The hue scale contains five Principal Hues: Red (R), Yellow (Y), Green (G), Blue (B) and Purple (P), and five Intermediate Hues: YR, GY, BG, PB, and RP. Finally, each of the ten hues is subdivided into ten gradations indicated by a number from 1 to 10 before the name of the nearest hue; for example, 4R or 7BG. The number 5 always denotes one of the Principal or Intermediate hues. Value, which is the lightness of the hue, is indicated on a grey scale ranging from 0 (black) to 10 (white) – the value of a sample is related to its reflectance by the curve of figure 2.3 (Chapter 2). Chroma, the saturation of the colour or, conversely, its freedom from dilution with white, is indicated by a number of steps from the totally unsaturated sample.

The division of the scale is chosen in such a way that for daylight conditions an approximately uniform spacing of colour is obtained resulting in equivalence of the subjective impression of colour change when changing value one step, chroma two steps or hue three steps. This is the reason why the number of steps of the chroma scale is different for different hues; the number of distinct colour steps which the human eye can observe between white and a completely saturated colour of the same brightness (value) being dependent on its hue – it is, for example, far greater for yellow and red colours than for blue colours. As, furthermore, the Munsell system deals with surface colours only, the number of steps on the chroma scales is also dependent on the value.

Collections of carefully standardised colour chips can be obtained in different arrangements according to the scales for hue, value and chroma. A usual collection is edited in the form of a book of colour charts, each chart with the hue held constant. Thus, in the Munsell system, any colour can be specified by the use of three symbols. For example: saturated vermilion 5R 5/12; non-saturated pink (same hue as above) 5R 8/4; black N 1/0; and white N 9/0. The notation, in each case, is written in the order hue, value/chroma. A typical page from the 'Munsell Book of Color' is shown in colour plate 1.

4.1.2 The CIE System

In 1931 the CIE recommended a system of a purely physical nature for the numerical definition of colours. The system, termed The CIE 1931 Standard Colorimetric System, is based on one of the basic laws of colour theory, namely that a colour can be created by mixing three primary colours in a certain ratio. This system has since found general application as a basis for colour measurement and for the indication of the chromaticity of light sources.

The system is derived from the so-called RGB colorimetric system, a system based on the use of the three primary colours monochromatic Red, Green and Blue. All colours can be presented in a two-dimensional representation – in other words in a plane – if a whole family of colours are each represented by one point in this plane. In the RGB system the points defined by the corners of an equilateral triangle are used to represent the three primary colours chosen, i.e. red, green and blue (R, G and B in figure 4.1). Any colour can then be defined using a system of coordinates.

This triangle is in fact a two-dimensional cross-section through a three-dimensional figure, the so-called colour space of the RGB system. The two-dimensional representation cannot deal with differences in colour brightness (which corresponds to the lightness of the hue, or Value, in the Munsell system) – this would necessitate the use of the three-dimensional figure. But for the purposes of practical application this form of representation is sufficient, since differences in perceived colour brightness can, if necessary, always be dealt with by measuring the luminance and indicating this separately.

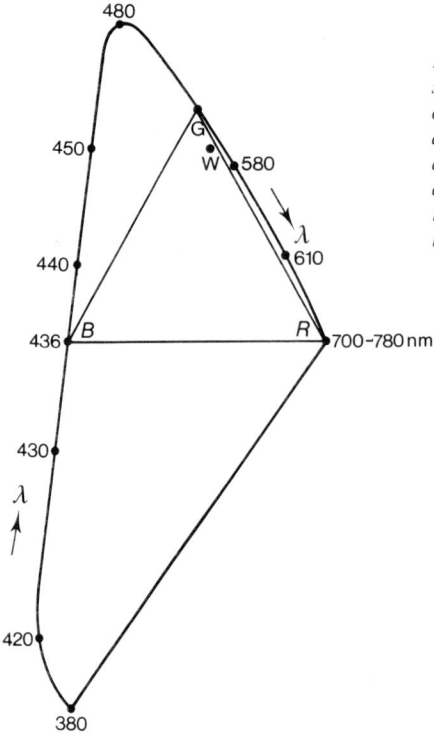

Figure 4.1 RGB colour triangle showing the spectrum locus (curve enclosing triangle) and line of purple colours (line joining 380 and R). The distance between the line G-R and the spectrum locus has been grossly exaggerated for the purposes of this illustration. W = colour point of achromatic stimulus.

Considerable changes were required to the RGB system as a result of inconveniences experienced in its application. In the first place, it was found that the colours along the sides of the triangle, which are the most saturated colours obtainable from a mixture of the monochromatic red, green and blue chosen as primary colours, were, in fact, less saturated than their spectral counterparts. These lay on a curve outside the triangle. This meant that there were many colour points that could be described only by subtracting one primary colour from the addition of the other two. Furthermore, the point representing the colour white lay very near to the side RG of the triangle, and this meant that all colours that are mixtures of red, green and white would be confined to a very small area of the triangle.

These problems were solved in the CIE 1931 standard colorimetric system by adopting a colour triangle that encompassed this curve of monochromatic colours. The three primary colours located at the corners of this triangle are the hypothetical colours, or stimuli: X (red), Y (green) and Z (blue).
The tristimulus values, X, Y and Z for a given colour can be calculated from

$$X = \int \Phi(\lambda)\bar{x}(\lambda)d\lambda$$
$$Y = \int \Phi(\lambda)\bar{y}(\lambda)d\lambda$$
$$Z = \int \Phi(\lambda)\bar{z}(\lambda)d\lambda$$

where $\Phi(\lambda)$ is the spectral distribution of the light source and where the so-called spectral tristimulus values $\bar{x}(\lambda)$, $\bar{y}(\lambda)$ and $\bar{z}(\lambda)$ are given in tables to 4 decimal places at 5 nm intervals. These tables have been represented by figure 4.2 from which the values of $\bar{y}(\lambda)$ are identical with the spectral luminous efficiencies conforming to the $V(\lambda)$ curve of a standard observer.

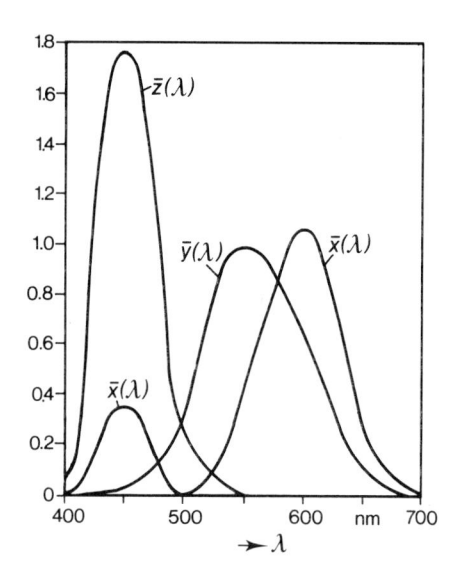

Figure 4.2 The CIE 1931 spectral tristimulus values $\bar{x}(\lambda)$, $\bar{y}(\lambda)$ and $\bar{z}(\lambda)$.

The tristimulus values X, Y and Z are transformed into the chromaticity coordinates x, y and z, thus

$$x = \frac{X}{X+Y+Z} \qquad y = \frac{Y}{X+Y+Z} \quad \text{and} \quad z = \frac{Z}{X+Y+Z}$$

The three chromaticity coordinates x, y and z together are equal to unity, so that if two of them are known, the third can be derived. Normally, the x and y chromaticity coordinates are the ones used. In this way the most frequently used rectangular colour triangle representing the 1931 CIE XYZ system of figure 4.3 is obtained. The system is depicted in colour in colour plate 2.

Colour points can be measured using three light-sensitive cells for which the sensitivity as a function of wavelength is proportional to the $\bar{x}(\lambda)$, $\bar{y}(\lambda)$ and $\bar{z}(\lambda)$ functions (figure 4.2). To measure colour, therefore, three accurately established photocell/filter combinations can be employed to supply currents proportional to the tristimulus values X, Y and Z of the light,

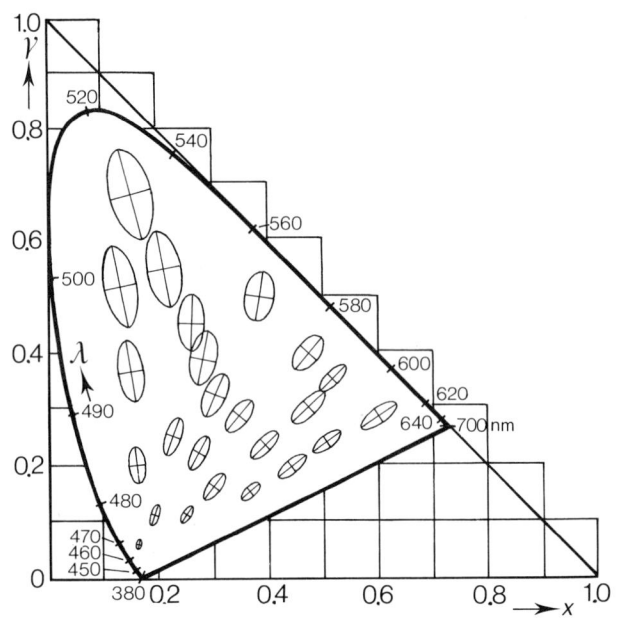

Figure 4.3 CIE 1931 standard chromaticity diagram with colour discrimination ellipses calculated by Stiles (on an enlarged scale).

reflected by the surface colour to be measured, that strikes them. The x and y chromaticity coordinates can then be calculated using the transformation formulae given above. In practice, however, the chromaticity coordinates of a light source are rarely determined in this way, it being more usual to calculate them from a knowledge of the spectral composition of the source using the formulae given above.

A serious disadvantage of the chromaticity diagram for certain applications is that chromaticity spacing is not uniform, that is, equal steps in x and y do not represent visually equal colour differences. This can be seen from figure 4.3 in which the locus of equal steps in perceived colour difference away from a point in any direction takes the form of an ellipse – the colour discrimination ellipses calculated by Stiles (1929) – the size and the orientation of the ellipse varying with its position in the diagram. Thus, in 1960, the

CIE recommended that a uniform chromaticity scale (UCS) diagram, figure 4.4, based on that described by Stiles, be used wherever it is desired to specify colour differences. As can be seen, the ellipses have almost become circles, which differ little in size. The u, v coordinates in the UCS diagram for a particular colour can be found from its x, y chromaticity coordinates using simple transformation formulae (Bouma, 1971).

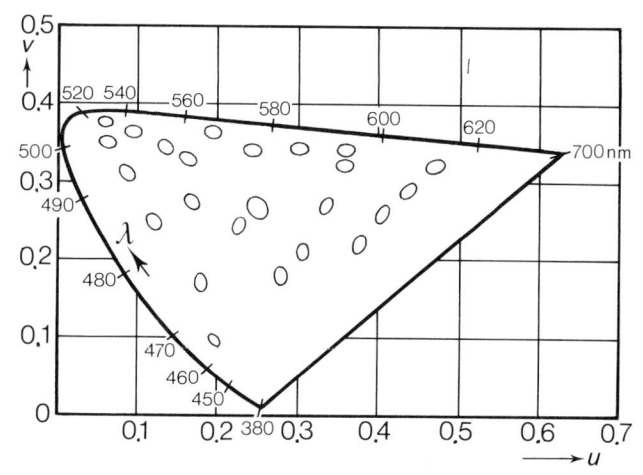

Figure 4.4 CIE 1960 UCS diagram with colour discrimination ellipses of Stiles (on an enlarged scale).

4.2 Colour Temperature

4.2.1 Colour Temperature and Colour Appearance

Colour temperature is a term used to describe the colour appearance of a light source by comparing it with the colour of a black body radiator, or full radiator. The temperature of the black body at which a colour match is obtained is said to be the colour temperature of the source.

The black body is a special form of thermal radiator and the spectral distribution of its radiation can be calculated, for each temperature, using a formula known as Planck's law. The colour of a black body would be red at a temperature of 800 K to 900 K, yellowish-white at 3000 K, white at about 5000 K and a pale bluish colour between 8000 K and 10000 K.

The curve formed on the CIE chromaticity diagram by plotting the chromaticities of a black body at various temperatures is known as the Planckian locus, figure 4.5 and colour plate 3. Any source that has a chromaticity on this locus may be specified by a colour temperature, table 4.1. The source need not be a thermal radiator for its chromaticity to lie on the Planckian locus and for it to be awarded a specific colour temperature. But only if a source is a thermal radiator, e.g. an incandescent lamp, does its colour temperature give information on its spectral energy distribution, this distribution being virtually identical to that of a black body at the same temperature. For other, non-thermal sources, such as fluorescent lamps, it should be clearly understood that colour temperature serves only as a convenient guide to colour appearance.

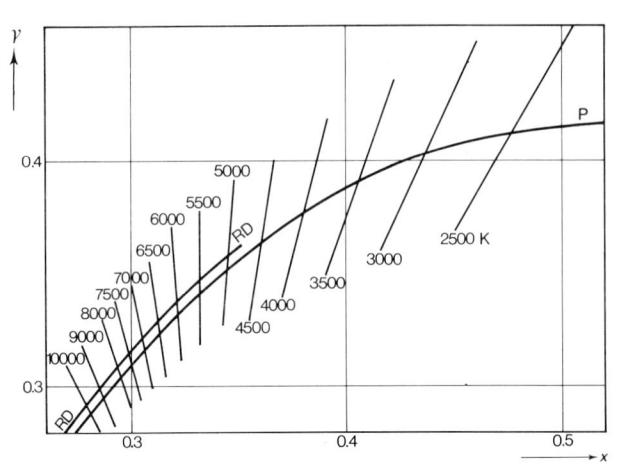

Figure 4.5 Part of the CIE chromaticity diagram showing the Planckian locus (P), lines of constant correlated colour temperature and the curve of reconstituted daylight (RD).

Table 4.1 Colour temperatures of a selection of natural and artificial light sources

Light Source	Colour Temperature (K)
Candles	1 900 – 1 950
Carbon filament lamps	2 100
Tungsten filament lamps:	
40 W	2 700
150 W – 500 W	2 800 – 2 900
Film and projection lamps	2 850 – 3 200
Carbon arc lamps	3 700 – 3 800 and above
Moonlight	4 100
Sunlight	5 300 – 5 800
Daylight (sun + clear sky)	5 800 – 6 500
Overcast sky	6 400 – 6 900
Clear blue sky	10 000 – 26 000
Fluorescent lamps	3 000 – 7 500

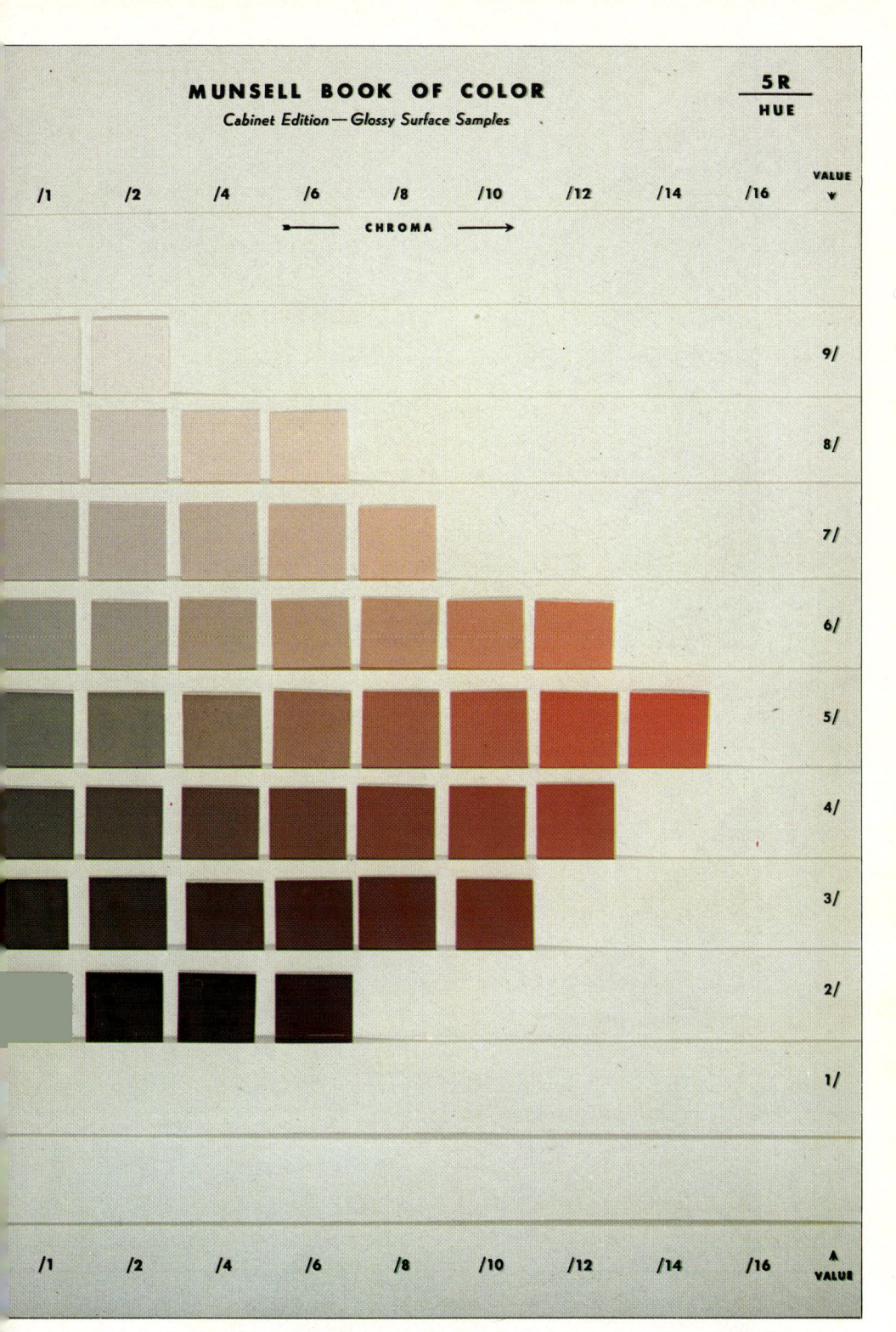

MUNSELL BOOK OF COLOR
Cabinet Edition — Glossy Surface Samples

5 R
HUE

Page 5R/HUE from the Munsell Book of Color showing, amongst others, the colour chips 'saturated vermilion' 'non-saturated pink' mentioned in the text.

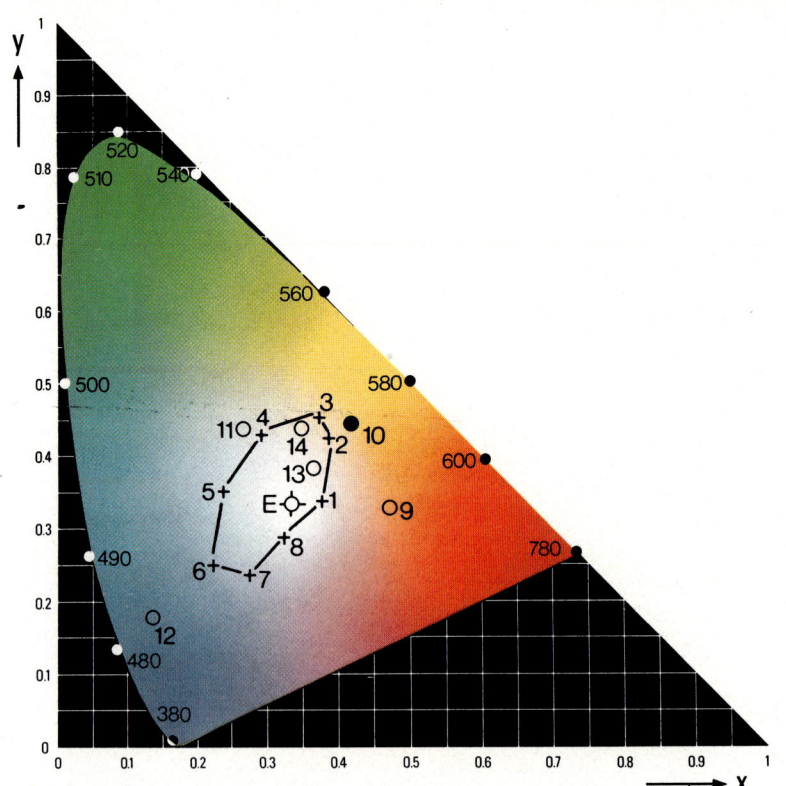

2 Colour points of CIE test colours under reconstituted daylight of correlated colour temperature 6500 K.

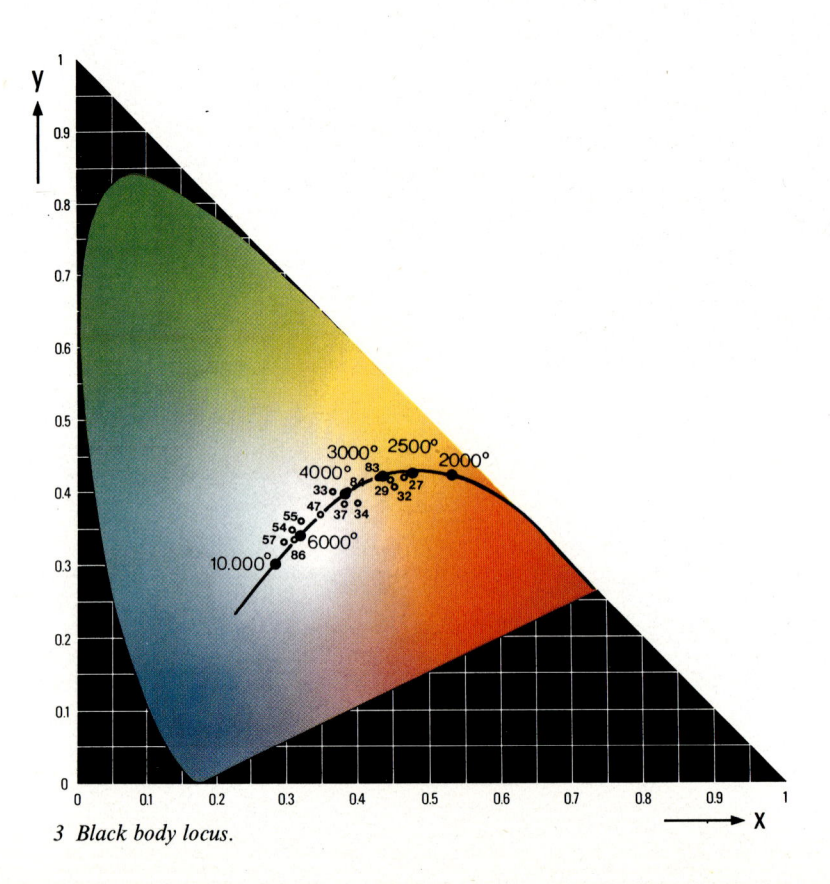

3 Black body locus.

Strictly speaking, colour temperature should not be used to specify a chromaticity that does not lie on the Planckian locus. However, a source not on the Planckian locus can be described by means of its correlated colour temperature, that is the temperature of the black body at which the body's colour resembles most closely that of the source. Lines of constant correlated colour temperature, figure 4.5, (or iso-colour-temperature lines) may be used as an approximate means of locating the point of correlated colour temperature on the CIE chromaticity diagrams provided this is not too far away from the Planckian locus. The correlated colour temperature is found on such a diagram by moving from the chromaticity point of the light source, in a direction parallel to the nearest iso-colour-temperature line, towards the Planckian locus, where the correlated temperature can be read. Table 4.2 gives an indication of the change in colour appearance over a range of correlated colour temperature.

Table 4.2 Correlated colour temperatures and colour appearance

Correlated Colour Temperature (K)	Colour Appearance
> 5 500	cool (bluish white)
3 300 – 5 500	intermediate (white)
< 3 300	warm (reddish white)

4.2.2 Colour Temperature and Lighting Level

It is known from experience that a relaxing atmosphere in an interior can be created by low-level lighting from 'warm' (low colour temperature) sources and that for working interiors, where a more lively atmosphere is preferred, the desired conditions can be created by high lighting levels using 'cool' (high colour temperature) sources.

The first laboratory investigations aimed at establishing the relationship between source colour and lighting level were carried out by Kruithoff (1941). Kruithoff confirmed, in quantitative terms, what had been found from past experience. However, his findings, which were published in the form of a diagram indicating the upper and lower limits of the preferred illuminance for lamps of specified colour temperature, were based on the results of pilot studies in which only two observers had participated and so allowed no general conclusions to be reached.

Some years later, Bodmann, Söllner and Voit (1963) and Bodmann (1967) undertook a more extensive series of studies along the same lines. The studies were carried out in a conference room (see figure 1.19) lit solely by artificial light. The lighting was provided by 24 recessed ceiling luminaires fitted with matt-white louvres, each luminaire containing three 65 watt fluorescent lamps. The lamps could be selected from a range of eight different types to give a range of colour appearance corresponding to colour temperatures from 2800 K to 7400 K.

A total of more than 400 observers, divided into groups of five, participated in the study. Each group remained in the test room for a period of about 30 minutes. They were free to occupy themselves by reading, writing or entering into conversation with one another. At the end of 20 minutes the observers were asked to complete a questionnaire giving, in their own words, their assessment of

(a) the general atmosphere in the room as created by the lighting level and colour,
(b) the brightness of the room in general, and
(c) the brightness on the working plane, (viz. on the conference table)

The lighting level was changed during the times that the group was out of the room to give illuminances ranging from 220 lx to 6000 lx. The colour of the light sources was similarly changed during the periods that the room was vacated.

Table 4.3 shows the breakdown of the answers given to question (a). The terms used in this table were carefully chosen to describe accurately the many assessments given by the observers. Generally speaking, an illuminance range of about 700–3000 lx seems to be acceptable for all types of fluorescent lamps, provided that no other displeasing factors are involved.

Table 4.3 Impressions associated with different levels and colours of fluorescent lighting in a conference room

Average illuminance (lx)	Colour of light		
	warm white	white	daylight
< 700	not unpleasant	dim	cool
700–3000	pleasant	pleasant	neutral
> 3000	excessive, artificial	pleasant, lively	pleasant

The results were obtained under climatic conditions that were typical for mid-European countries. It is known, however, that extremes of climate can influence these findings. In warmer countries, sources with a somewhat cooler colour appearance are preferred, and vice versa.

The observer assessments concerning room brightness, questions (b) and (c), were performed using the terms 'too bright', 'good' and 'too dark'. The assessments are shown graphically in figure 4.6. As can be seen, the desired illuminance levels lie within the middle range of table 4.3. Furthermore, it can be concluded that people prefer illuminances in this desired range, even if the general atmosphere created in a room by a particular lamp is capable of improvement.

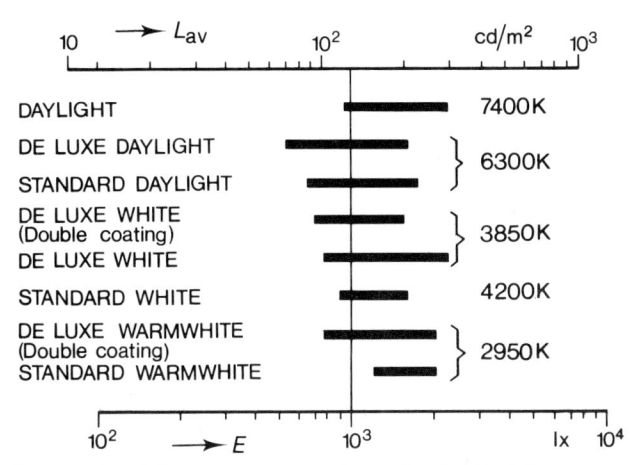

Figure 4.6 Subjective evaluation of satisfactory average luminance levels (L_{av}) in a conference room illuminated by different fluorescent lamps, where E is the illuminance at table height. (A maximum percentage of 'good' ratings – based on a probability rate of 90% – occur within the indicated ranges.)

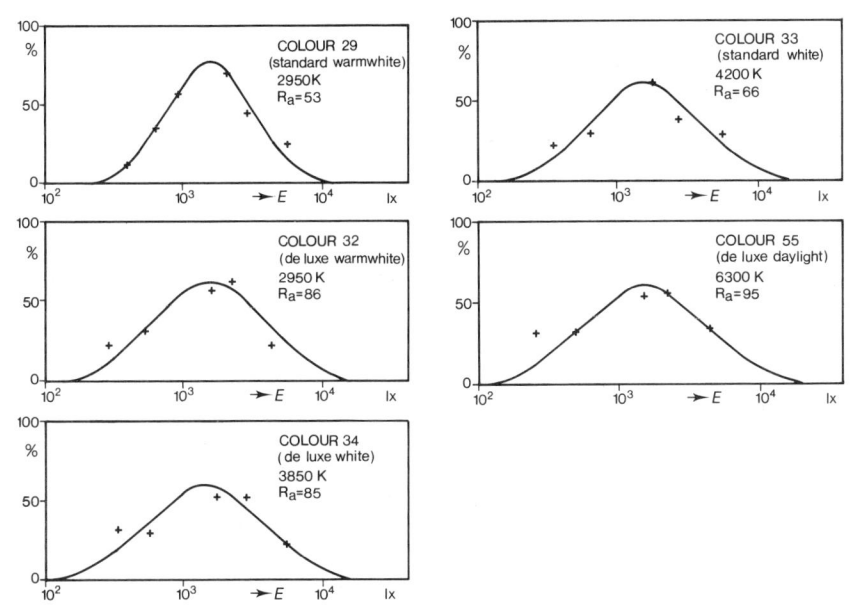

Figure 4.7 Percentage of observers assessing the level of illuminance E at the working plane as 'good' for fluorescent light sources of differing colour appearance and colour rendering.

The results relating to the illuminance on the working plane are given in figure 4.7. (as compiled by Fischer, 1970b – from the originally unpublished results of Bodmann, Söllner and Voit). The curves show the percentage of observers giving the assessment 'good' for five lamp types. The fact that the preferred lighting level was not influenced by the colour temperature of the source seemed to indicate that, where a visual task was concerned, more stress was placed on achieving comfortable viewing conditions than on creating a pleasant atmosphere.

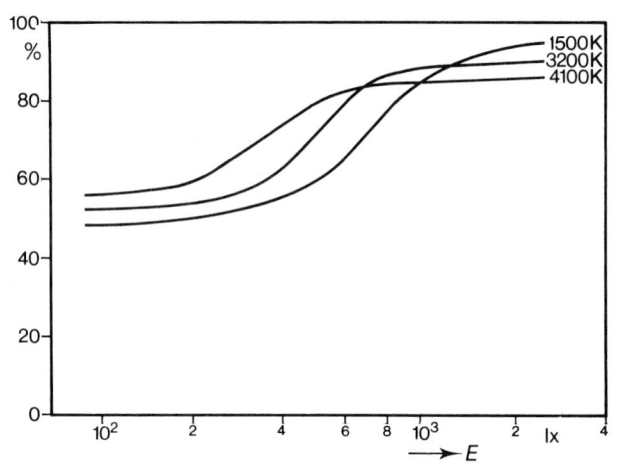

Figure 4.8 Percentage of observers answering 'yes' to the question 'Are you satisfied with the colour of the lighting in this room?' plotted as a function of illuminance E for fluorescent light sources of differing colour temperature.

This last finding was confirmed by Schröder and Steck (1974). These workers used a test room that could be illuminated by three types of fluorescent lamp (3200 K, 4100 K and 5400 K) to give lighting levels ranging from 90 lx to 2400 lx. The results, in which the percentage of observers who found the 'colour of the light' in the room pleasant were plotted against lighting level, figure 4.8, showed that, independent of lamp type used, the illuminance necessary to give an optimum positive response was at least 700 lx.

4.3 Colour Rendering

The colour qualities of a light source of the type usually employed in interior lighting are characterised by its colour appearance – which as we have seen may be defined by its colour temperature – and its colour rendering properties, which describe its ability to affect the colour appearance of objects illuminated by the source. Light sources of like colour appearance can have completely different spectral compositions and, consequently, can display great differences in colour rendering. Thus, it is impossible to draw any conclusions regarding the colour rendering properties of a source from its colour appearance.

4.3.1 Reference Sources

In every-day life we say that the colour rendering of a light source is either 'good', 'poor' or, in some cases, 'flattering'. Consciously or subconsciously we are comparing the colour rendering of the source in question with that of a familiar reference source; that is, a source that we believe shows objects in their 'true' colours.

The best known and most widely used reference source is mid-day daylight. Although the spectral composition of daylight varies considerably, its correlated colour temperature ranging over several thousand kelvins, the corresponding variations in the colour of an object seen under changing daylight conditions are, in practice, hardly noticed. (This is because the variations in the spectral composition of the light are largely compensated by chromatic adaptation in the eyes of the observer.) So, notwithstanding the wide variation in spectral composition of daylight, it seems logical to take this as the reference source for judging the colour rendering properties of artificial light sources, the only proviso being that the colour temperature is similar in both cases.

In order to be able to compare the colour rendering properties of a light source with that of a reference source, the spectral power distribution of both must be known. Information relating to the power distribution of daylight is contained in a report prepared by Judd, MacAdam and Wyszecki (1964). These workers analysed 622 different energy distributions of daylight in various places around the world and then derived a standardised set of formulae and tables for use in calculating the appropriate spectral power distribution corresponding to any given correlated colour temperature from 4000 K to 25000 K. The colour points of this so-called reconstituted daylight lie on a curve on the green side of the Planckian locus. (See figure 4.5.)

The CIE has decided to take as a reference source for light sources with colour temperatures above 5000 K, daylight with a correlated colour temperature nearest to that of the source under consideration – assuming that the spectral power distribution of this daylight is in accordance with the formulae given by Judd, MacAdam and Wyszecki. The majority of artificial light sources – particularly those used for interior lighting – have correlated colour temperatures in the low end of, or even far below, the range 25 000 K to 4000 K mentioned above. For light sources such as these, specifically for those with correlated colour temperatures below 5000 K, the CIE has decided that the Planckian radiator at a colour temperature nearest to that of the light source shall be taken as the reference source.

The recommendation of the CIE to use Planckian radiators has met with some criticism, not everyone being convinced that such radiators are, in fact, ideal for this purpose. But the recommendation is well supported by experience gained in the lighting of museums, colour inspection rooms, doctors' consulting rooms and hospitals. In all these areas the light sources are chosen to show either objects or patients in their true colours, that is to say, they are chosen to obtain a colour rendering that is best described by the word 'natural'. The fact that the lamps, or combinations of lamps, chosen come nearest in spectral composition to the Planckian radiators would seem to indicate that, for the time being at least, the Planckian radiators are the best reference sources when it comes to specifying natural colour rendering at colour temperatures below 5000 K. The spectral energy distributions of a number of CIE reference sources are shown in figure 4.9.

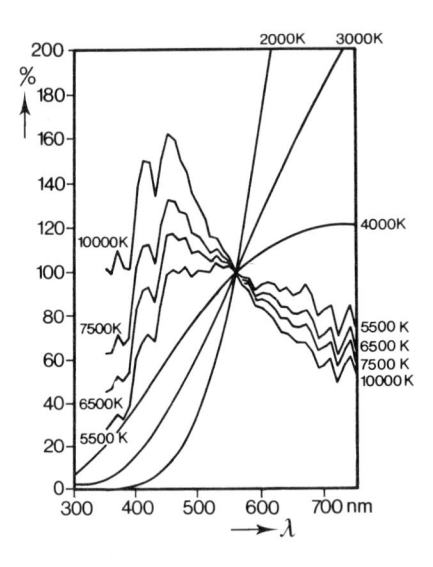

Figure 4.9 Relative spectral energy distribution of some CIE reference sources, showing the Planckian radiator of 2000 K, 3000 K and 4000 K, and reconstituted daylight of 5500 K, 6500 K, 7500 K and 10 000 K.

4.3.2 The CIE General Colour Rendering Index R_a

In 1948, the CIE recommended a Spectral Band Method for specifying the colour rendering properties of lamps. This method was based on work carried out by Bouma (1939). Bouma divided the visible spectrum into eight bands, the amount of light in each band being compared with that in the corresponding band of the reference source. But Ouweltjes (1960) showed that this method was far from satisfactory. The CIE Technical Committee on colour rendering therefore developed a method that rates lamps in terms of a general colour rendering index, R_a (CIE 1965 and 1974). The method is based on the average colour shift of a number of test colours that takes place when changing from test to reference illuminant and has built-in correction for chromatic, or colour, adaptation.

The question of how many test colours are needed in order to arrive at a dependable measure of the colour rendering of lamps was studied by Ouweltjes (1960). Using fluorescent lamps, Ouweltjes compared the average colour shift of a series of 19 specially selected test colours with the shift produced in a smaller series of eight test colours taken from the series of 19, and with that produced in an even smaller series of five colours. This was done for 164 hypothetical spectral energy distribution curves of fluorescent lamps as calculated from the most important phosphors used.

It was shown that the colour shifts for the series of eight test colours correlated well with those for the larger series of 19, figure 4.10. It was concluded, therefore, that a series of eight test colours could be considered sufficient for use in describing the general colour rendering properties of the lamps. The eight finally selected test colours (Nos. 1 to 8) together with their Munsell notation are the first eight listed in table 4.4. These colours are evenly distributed over the complete range of hues, are moderate in saturation and are approximately the same in value. The colour points of these eight test colours when lighted by reconstituted daylight of 6500 K correlated colour temperature are given in colour plate 2.

In order to obtain a more informative picture of the colour rendering properties of a source the colour shifts of additional test samples may be

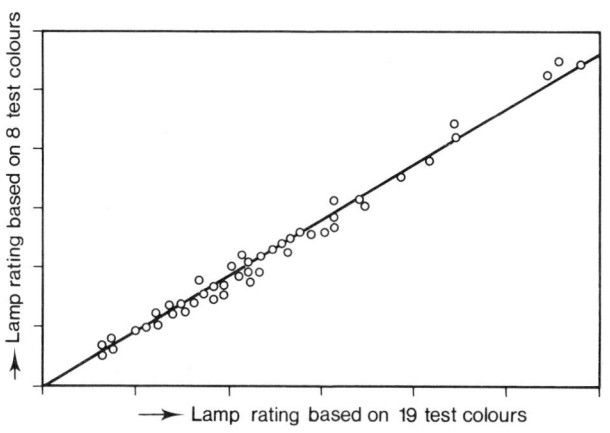

Figure 4.10 Correlation between lamp ratings for a set of 8 test colours and a set of 19 test colours for 'cool white' lamps.

evaluated. For this purpose, the CIE has recommended the addition of some strongly saturated test colours and some test colours representing the complexion of the human face and foliage (Nos. 9 to 14, see table 4.4) to make a total of fourteen. No. 13 is the colour of Caucasian skin. It is the colour used in those cases where good colour rendering of flesh tones is desirable.

Table 4.4 Test colours from the Munsell system

No.	Approximate notation	Colour appearance under daylight
1	7.5R6/4	Light greyish red
2	5Y6/4	Dark greyish yellow
3	5GY6/8	Strong yellow green
4	2.5G6/6	Moderate yellowish green
5	10BG6/4	Light bluish green
6	5PB6/8	Light blue
7	2.5P6/8	Light violet
8	10P6/8	Light reddish purple
9	4.5R4/13	Strong red
10	5Y8/10	Strong yellow
11	4.5G5/8	Strong green
12	3PB3/11	Strong blue
13	5YR8/4	Light yellowish pink (human complexion)
14	5GY4/4	Moderate olive green (leaf green)

The first step in the CIE colour-shift method, which was accepted internationally as a standard method (CIE, 1965), is the determination of the chromaticity of the source under test, that is, its colour point on the UCS diagram. A reference light source (a black body, or Planckian radiator, for colour temperatures below 5000 K, or a particular spectral energy distribution of daylight for correlated colour temperatures above 5000 K) is then chosen whose colour temperature is the same or nearly the same as that of the test source. The chromaticities of the test samples in the UCS system are then computed under both the light of the test source and that of the reference source. (In theory the chromaticities may be measured direct, but this is seldom done in practice.) The difference between the two chromaticity values obtained for each coloured test sample denotes a specific colour shift. The average colour shift in the UCS diagram, corrected for chromatic adaptation, is a measure of the colour rendering quality of the light emitted by the source under test: the smaller the shift, the better the colour rendition. The correction for chromatic adaptation is obtained by subtracting vectorially the difference in colour points of reference source and source to be tested from the average colour shift.

The General Colour Rendering Index, R_a, is calculated from the arithmetical mean $\overline{\Delta E_a}$ of the eight values $\Delta E_{a,i}$ of colour shift for each of the eight test colours in the CIE UCS diagram according to the formula

$$R_a = 100 - 4.6\,\overline{\Delta E_{a,i}}$$

Similarly, a Special Colour Rendering Index, R_i, describing the colour shift for an individual colour may be described as

$$R_i = 100 - 4.6\,\Delta E_{a,i}$$

Table 4.5 *Colour rendering indices of fluorescent lamps*

Colour rendering index R_a		Source
100		Reference illuminant (reconstituted daylight, Planckian radiator)
	(92–97)	'Special de luxe white' fluorescent lamps
90	(92 95)	Xenon lamps
		'De luxe white' and 'New generation' fluorescent lamps
80		
70		
		'Standard white' fluorescent lamps
60		
50		'Standard warm-white' fluorescent lamps
90–100		'True' colour rendering
70– 90		Good colour rendering
50– 70		Moderate colour rendering

By definition, therefore, the R_a and R_i of the reference illuminant are fixed at 100. Table 4.5 gives a rough indication of the position of a number of different types of fluorescent lamps on the scale of R_a values. The higher the R_a value, the better the colour rendering properties of the source. In a direct comparison, a difference of five points in the value of R_a corresponds to a colour difference that is just noticeable. But colour difference alone is not a true indication of the suitability of a particular light source; the direction in which an object colour is shifted is needed to complete the picture. For example, whereas a greenish distortion of the human flesh tones is disagreeable, a similar distortion, but towards the red, often makes people look healthier and will, therefore, frequently be accepted or even preferred.

4.3.3 Use of the General Colour Rendering Index

Since the reference illuminant used must be of the same colour temperature as the lamp to be tested, it is clear that a direct comparison of colour rendering properties is only possible between lamps in the same colour temperature category. Each lamp is, therefore, identified in relation to its own Planckian radiator or reconstituted daylight counterpart. In the CIE testcolour method both a Planckian radiator with a colour temperature of 3000 K and daylight with a colour temperature of 7500 K are rated at 100, although their colour rendering properties are different. Consequently, the fact that a warm-white and a daylight lamp have equal colour rendering indices does not imply that they will have identical colour rendering properties. The lamps will be at least as different in this respect as their related reference sources. The colour rendering indices are not, therefore, absolute figures as is, for example, a lumen output measured under specified conditions.

It should be appreciated that the R_a value is based on the average of eight colour distortions and gives no direct information on the colour rendering of individual objects. Only in the case of a very high R_a value, say 95, can it be stated that the lamp will very probably give true colour rendering for all kinds of object colour. As the numerical value of the R_a decreases, however, the variations in the value for the individual test colours are likely to become greater and it becomes increasingly difficult to predict the colour rendering of specific object colours. All that can be said about a lamp with an R_a of 70 or lower is that noticeable colour distortions are likely to occur for various objects colours. This is illustrated in table 4.6, where the colour rendering R_i of individual test colours are compared for four types of fluorescent lamp: a 'standard' white lamp, a 'de luxe' white lamp, a 'new

Table 4.6 *Colour rendering of individual test colours for four types of fluorescent lamp*

Test colour sample (Munsell notation)	'standard' white (colour 33)	'de luxe' white (colour 34)	'new generation' series (colour 84)	'special de luxe' white (colour 37)
1 7,5 R 6/4	$R_i = 58$	$R_i = 90$	$R_i = 96$	$R_i = 98$
2 5 Y 6/4	$R_i = 78$	$R_i = 85$	$R_i = 95$	$R_i = 97$
3 5 GY 6/8	$R_i = 99$	$R_i = 79$	$R_i = 52$	$R_i = 94$
4 2,5 G 6/6	$R_i = 56$	$R_i = 84$	$R_i = 90$	$R_i = 97$
5 10 BG 6/4	$R_i = 59$	$R_i = 89$	$R_i = 90$	$R_i = 99$
6 5 PB 6/8	$R_i = 68$	$R_i = 78$	$R_i = 81$	$R_i = 97$
7 2,5 P 6/8	$R_i = 76$	$R_i = 81$	$R_i = 89$	$R_i = 97$
8 10 P 6/8	$R_i = 40$	$R_i = 86$	$R_i = 97$	$R_i = 95$
	$R_a = 67$	$R_a = 84$	$R_a = 85$	$R_a = 97$

generation' lamp and a 'special de luxe' white lamp.

By relating the light source to a reference, the colour rendering of which is said to be natural, the R_a value becomes a measure for the degree of natural colour rendering. But it does not necessarily mean that the colour rendering of a lamp with an R_a value of 100 is ideal for all circumstances. Neither does it imply that a lamp with a lower R_a value is always poorer in colour rendering than the reference source. Indeed, in the latter case, the lamp may even be 'richer' than the reference source in the sense that skin colour and other object colours (meats, salads, etc.) are shown more attractively than in daylight. This is especially true of the 'new generation' series of fluorescent lamps which do indeed render most colours more vividly than do daylight or Planckian radiators. It may be that in the future an additional index will be developed – a Colour Preference Index, or whatever – that has as starting points not the 'true colours' of objects, but the 'preferred colours' for specified fields of lighting.

4.3.4 Interchangeability of Lamps of Equal R_a Value

There has been a good deal of confusion about the use of the R_a value for standardising purposes. One of the goals of standardisation is to guarantee interchangeability. Can it be said that two lamps of equal colour appearance are interchangeable with respect to colour rendering when they have the same R_a value? The answer, in most cases, is clearly 'no' when we recall that the R_a value is derived from the average colour distortion for eight test samples. It says nothing about the colour distortions of the individual samples, nor does it say anything about the direction of the distortion, or colour shift.

4.3.5 Colour, Colour Rendering and Lighting Level

It has been mentioned above (see table 4.3) how the illuminance in an interior can influence the impression associated with lamps of differing colour appearance. More recent research (Bellchambers *et al.*, 1969 and 1972) has shown that another colour property of a lamp, namely its colour rendering index, is linked with illuminance in determining what has been called the visual clarity of our surroundings. This expression, visual clarity, was used by Bellchambers to describe the balance found to exist between illuminance and colour rendering index for equal satisfaction with appearance.

Later research by Boyce (1977) confirmed the existence of this balance and showed that it is in fact present over a wide range of interior colourfulnesses. Boyce used for his research a 1/12 scale model of a large open-plan office divided into two identical halves by a wall. The subject sat with his head inside the model and viewed each office by turning his head to the left or to the right of the dividing wall. Three experimental variables were employed: tubular fluorescent lamp type, illuminance, and colourfulness of the office furnishings.

The general conclusion reached from an analysis of the results obtained was that the office interior lit by lamps giving good colour rendering ($R_a > 90$) could be matched for satisfaction with appearance to an interior lit by lamps giving poorer colour rendering ($R_a < 60$), but at an illuminance some 25 per cent lower.

Boyce felt that it should be possible to optimise the colour properties, the luminous efficacy and the illuminance so as to produce a good visual appearance at minimum energy cost. Table 4.7 shows some estimated installed loads for a range of different fluorescent lamps.

Boyce stressed that his finding only concerns satisfaction with visual appearance – it says nothing about visual performance. He specifically warned that it would be a mistake if, in the search for energy economies, the illuminance of an interior were reduced to a level where performance is likely to be worsened.

Table 4.7 Estimated installed loads for a typical commercial interior lit to 500 lux, for a range of different fluorescent lamps using White as a base lamp

Lamp name	Luminous efficacy (lm/W)	Installed load for equal satisfaction with visual appearance (W/m^2)	Installed load for equal illuminance (W/m^2)
White	69	31	31
Daylight	64	31	33
Natural	53	33	40
Warm White	68	34	31
Nortlight	41	37	52
'Kolor-rite'	45	38	47
'Grolux'	21	42	101
'De Luxe Natural'	37	42	57
'De Luxe Warm White'	45	45	47
Artificial Daylight	27	57	78

The interior is 20 m × 20 m × 3 m, the luminaire used is a recessed opal diffuser, utilization factor = 0.

For the 'TL' 84 having the same luminous efficiency as the white lamp, and therefore needing also 31 W/m^2 for equal illuminance, approximately 24 W/m^2 only are needed for equal satisfaction.

4.3.6 Chromatic Adaptation

Chromatic adaptation is the term used to describe the facility of the eye to adapt itself to the colour of the ambient light. The result of this adaptation can be that two light sources of different spectral composition and different colour appearance can appear to produce practically no difference in the appearance of object colours. Surfaces that are lit by incandescent light, for example, usually create almost the same colour impression as they do in daylight, despite the fact that great differences are found in the coordinates of the colour points of the same surface when it is first measured in incandescent light and then in daylight. This difference, however, is clearly seen if two samples of the same colour are placed in two directly adjacent compartments, one lit by incandescent light and the other by daylight. Normally, however, the observer is in a room lit by either one or the other type of light, or a mixture of both. He is, therefore, completely adapted to the colour of the light prevailing.

Other factors, such as a memory for colours and the ability to associate certain objects and surfaces with certain colours (e.g. the green of grass, the blue of the sky) do, of course, play a part in this phenomenon. But chromatic adaptation is primarily brought about by changes in the retina under the influence of the type of light applied.

For light sources of similar type, such as the various Planckian radiators – which, as far as the spectral energy distribution is concerned, are not essentially different – adaptation is virtually complete. This is true for all object colours. If the spectral compositions of the illuminants differ from one another, adaptation is limited to white and neutral shades of grey. For example, a piece of paper that is white in daylight will also look white in the light of a warm-white fluorescent lamp. For other object colours, however, colour distortion will occur to a greater or lesser extent.

4.4 Metamerism

Metamerism is the name given to the property whereby spectrally different radiations may produce the same colour impression under the same viewing conditions. There is surface-colour metamerism, where a pair of samples may match under one illuminant but not when viewed under another, and there is observer metamerism, where the match occurs due to differences in the colour vision of individual observers. The term metamerism may also be used to describe light sources that evoke the same colour impression, although their spectral compositions are different.

Surface-colour metamerism is most easily detected when the comparison between a sample and a reference standard is made under each of two widely different light sources each having a continuous energy distribution. Light sources such as incandescent lamps, which are predominantly reddish, and blue or daylight type fluorescent lamps are often used as the two dissimilar sources. The metamerism of light sources will usually be revealed by looking at a spectrally selective object and noting that the object is of different colour under the two sources.

4.5 Special Purpose Applications and Colour

4.5.1 Colour Grading

Colour grading is the judgement of equality or difference in the colour of surfaces or objects. Typical products that are colour graded before appearing on the market are raw cotton, tobacco and furs. In some instances such products are accepted or rejected on the basis of colour specifications or standards.

Daylight is often used for colour grading purposes. But it is known that the intensity and colour temperature of daylight vary over a wide range with changing sun and sky conditions. It is generally preferable, therefore, to use artificial light with colour rendering properties approximating to a particular phase of daylight. Artificial light with a colour temperature of around 7500 K is generally used for this purpose.

There are cases, however, where large departures from the daylight spectrum are desirable for colour grading. For example, if yellow samples are to be examined a light source rich in the blue portion of the spectrum will enable an observer to detect differences in colour more easily than when he uses a source deficient in blue light.

4.5.2 Colour Matching

Colour matching, in which samples of a material are selected as being identical in colour to a reference sample, is more exacting in its requirements than colour grading. For precise colour matching, spectrophotometric curves should be compared and matched.

A subject that requires special attention is the use of artificial daylight sources for colour matching, such as is done, for example, in the paint and textile industries. It may happen that the samples to be examined match under natural daylight, but not under artificial daylight. As the customer will usually compare the two samples under natural daylight, the demands placed on artificial daylight sources are very severe. In such cases, it is recommended that the behaviour of the saturated test colours be included in the evaluation of artificial daylight. Not because their behaviour should necessarily be exactly the same as that of the metamers likely to be found in practice, but in order to make use of their larger discriminative power as compared with the unsaturated ones.

To be satisfactory for colour-matching purposes artificial daylight lamps should have an R_a value of at least 90, which is also the recommended minimum value for the R_i of the individual saturated test colours. Rooms used for colour matching should be painted in neutral colours.

4.5.3 Colour Shading

Colour shading is the adjustment of the proportions of the ingredients, or colorants, in a mixture to improve colour conformity to a standard. It is a form of colour matching and requires the same type of lighting or spectrophotometric curves as colour matching. The mixing of pigments, dyes, and inks are examples of tasks in which colour shading is employed.

4.5.4 Colour Reproduction

Colour reproduction is generally taken as meaning the making of pictures that reproduce the colours of the original surface or scene as faithfully as possible. Colour reproduction processes are used in such activities as colour printing, colour photography and colour television.

Colour reproduction processes carried out under artificial light demand the use of lamps with good colour rendering capabilities. But the decisive factor in achieving a satisfactory end result is the proper matching of the lamps to the medium. In this respect, the colour temperature of the lamps is of prime importance. In the case of colour printing, for example, it is important that the light source used for preparing the photographs from which the blocks are to be made, and those used for viewing and matching colour transparencies and colour prints, should all have excellent colour rendering properties. The light source commonly used in the graphics arts industry for the inspection of colour prints, colour transparencies, etc., is a fluorescent tube with a colour temperature of 5000 K and a colour rendering index R_a of at least 90.

4.5 Colour Schemes for Interiors

Another aspect of colour that influences the visual comfort and pleasantness of a room is the colour scheme used for the room surfaces. Generally speaking, in order to achieve a high efficiency for the lighting, rather light colours should be used for the main surface areas. Ceilings are normally white, or nearly white, while all other surfaces are usually coloured in one way or another.

Although personal taste in colour varies with personality, age, sex, climate, fashion and even ethnic group, it is possible to formulate a number of general rules regarding surface colours and the colour appearance of light sources. (Helson and Lansford, 1970.)

- Surfaces with 'warm' colours are judged as being more pleasant to look at under 'warm-coloured' light than under 'cool' light. Conversely, the lack of short-wave energy in warm light tends more or less to 'kill' cool surface colours.
- The best all-round light sources, so far as the judgement of a range of object colours is concerned, are those having a colour appearance between cool and warm. Sources of this type can, therefore, be called 'safe' sources in this respect.
- The surface colour most preferred for backgrounds (walls, ceilings and objects having a large area) is either white, or pale colours with very low saturation (i.e. pastel shades). Such colours can, therefore, be called safe background colours.

  Very dark background colours are acceptable when it is desired to create contrasts, but wall colours of medium lightness and medium saturation are rated lowest of all.
- The question as to whether or not a surface colour is rated as pleasant, is dependent more on the colour of the background than on the colour of the light used. Thus, a good choice of background colour may counteract, to a greater or lesser extent, a 'bad' colour of light source. Conversely, the background colour, may, if badly chosen, spoil the effect of a 'good-coloured' light source.
- Independent of the colour appearance of the light source and the colour of the background, the most widely preferred object colours are the blues, blue-greens, and greens. These colours can, therefore, be regarded as safe object colours. Following these colours, in order of preference, come red and orange, with yellow ranking lowest of all.
- Whereas the best colours for large areas are light but desaturated, the best-liked colours for small objects are those that are highly saturated.
- Women generally tend to prefer warm colours (red, yellow-red, yellow), in contrast to men who generally prefer green or blue hues.
- Colours of foodstuffs are generally rated as being more favourable when seen under a warm light than under a cool one.
- Two adjacently situated colours having the same or similar hue are judged to be more harmonious than colours lying further apart on the colour scale.
- A coloured environment will satisfy only if it is designed to look both vivid and varied. Extensive repetition of a design, although accepted as pleasant in itself, may lead to displeasure and monotony and thus to the opposite of the effect desired.

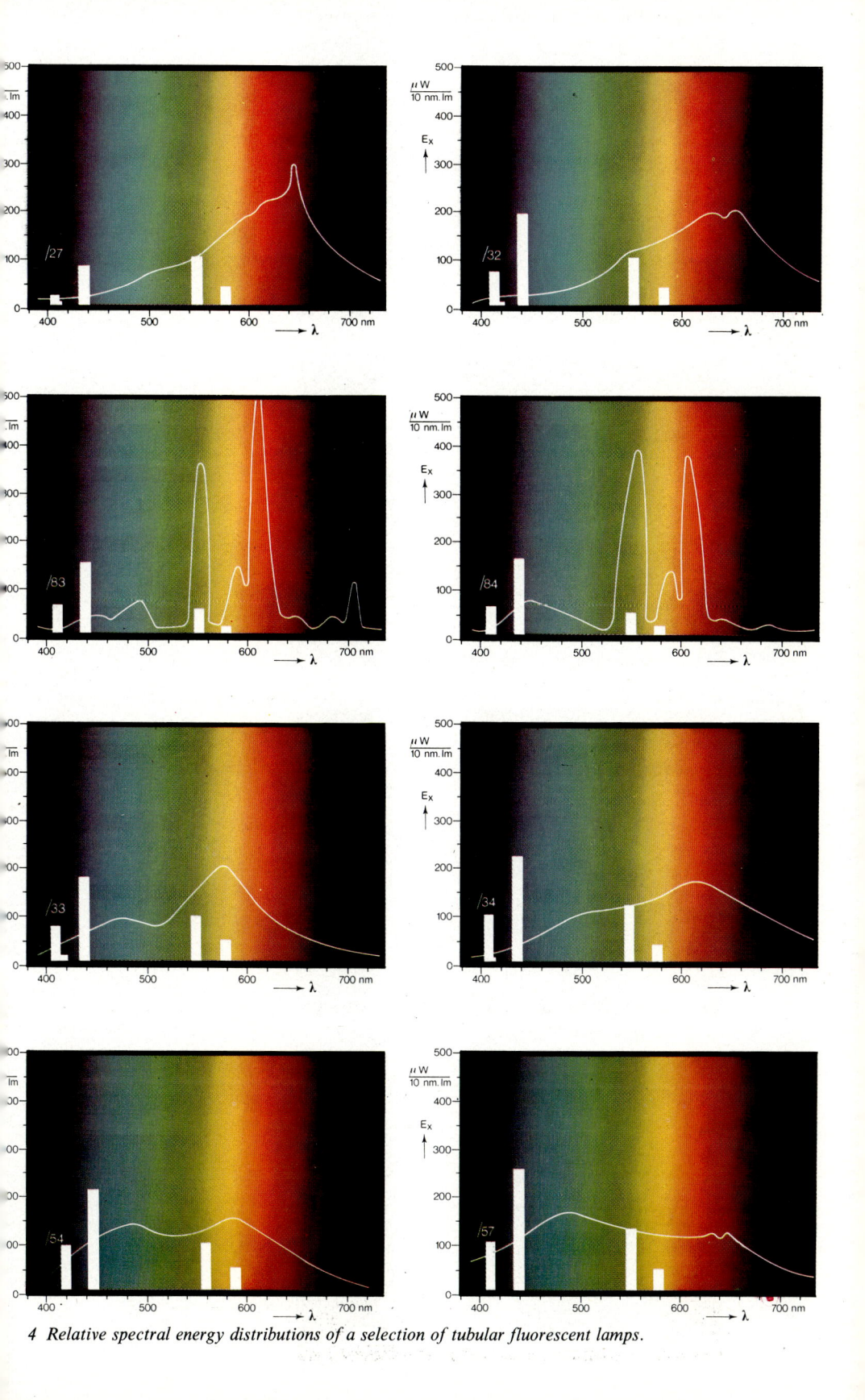

4 *Relative spectral energy distributions of a selection of tubular fluorescent lamps.*

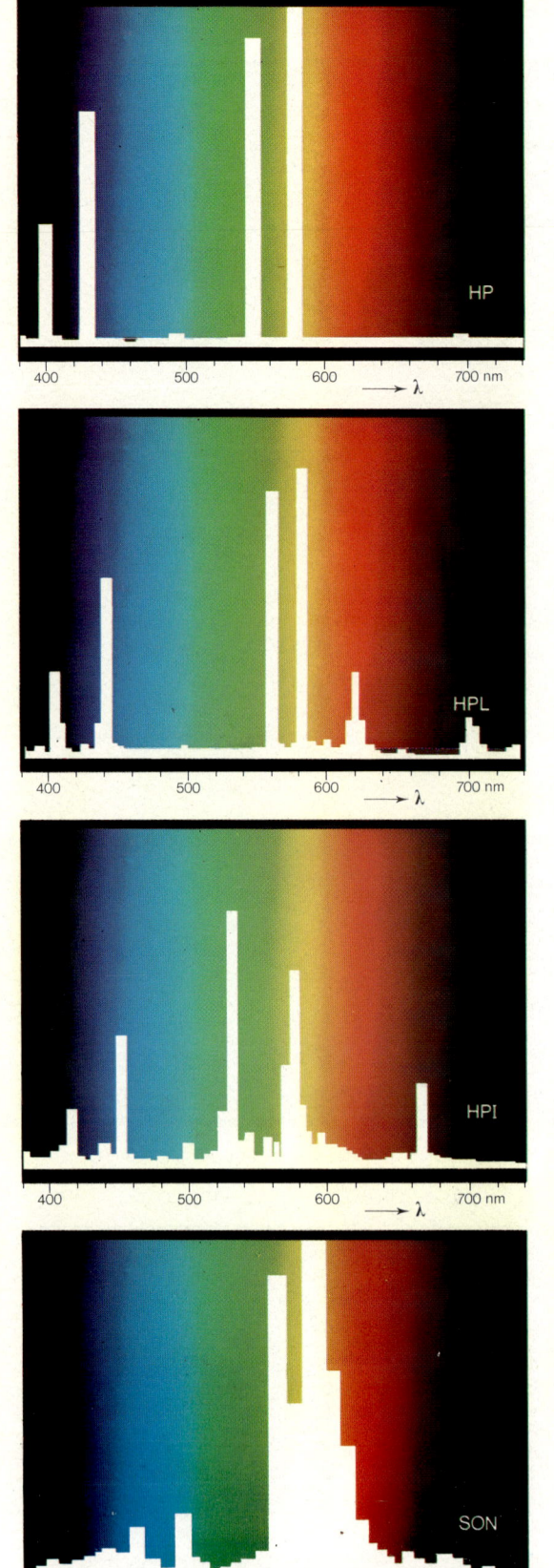

5 Relative spectral energy distributions of a selection of high-pressure discharge lamps.

Chapter 5

Ventilation, Air Conditioning and Acoustics

There is a growing trend towards larger working areas in many fields, particularly in production, administration, education and health. As a consequence, the quantity of heat produced by the lighting, machinery and occupants in areas such as these is often such as to warrant the installation of a ventilation or air conditioning system. (The choice of system is largely dependent on the outside temperature normally prevailing in the country concerned: forced ventilation alone may be satisfactory in temperate zones but where the temperature of the air outside a building is equal to or higher than that planned for the interior there is a clear need for air conditioning.)

Where it is possible to combine the ceiling-mounted air-handling elements of such systems (viz. air supply and air exhaust openings) with the lighting hardware it is, as will be shown in this chapter, generally advantageous to do so, chief among the benefits to be gained being a saving in installation and running costs for the lighting and an overall increase in worker comfort. Such integration can be satisfactorily brought about through the use of specially designed false ceilings in which are mounted special air-handling luminaires and air supply elements, the space above the ceiling serving to house the necessary runs of air ducting and power cabling. The three basic types of integrated ceiling system are described in this chapter.

Another possible complication associated with large space interiors is that of noise. Generally, some background noise – such as that produced by the rush of air through the ceiling mounted elements of a ventilation or air conditioning system – can serve to mask noise in adjacent areas by overriding these weaker sounds, thereby affording a certain degree of acoustical privacy. The level of this background noise must, however, be carefully controlled so as to produce a balanced noise environment – too little background noise will prove ineffectual while too much will draw attention to itself. It is also possible to tackle the noise problem by attenuating the noise transmission along the path between source and receiver. The false ceilings referred to above afford a certain degree of control in this respect by virtue of the acoustically absorbent materials used in their construction.

These and related topics form the subject of this chapter. No attempt has been made to delve into the intricacies of air handling and acoustical control theory; only those aspects of these subjects relevant to lighting and to the establishment of a satisfactory interior environment in general are discussed.

5.1 Ventilation and Air Conditioning

5.1.1 Ventilation

Natural ventilation is frequently insufficient to keep the temperature in an interior down to an acceptable level. An alternative to natural ventilation is of course forced ventilation in which a large fan forces air through a distribution system to bring about an increase in the volume of cooling or refreshing air circulated. Such a system can continue to function effectively, however, only so long as the temperature of the incoming air is lower than that planned for the interior. In the case where the outside air temperature is consistently above this value, forced ventilation as described above would have an effect opposite to that desired.

During cool periods the situation is reversed. Where the winter is severe, the volume of incoming, fresh cold air must be limited so as not to overload the building's heating system. As a result, the ventilation cannot be fully effective.

Ventilation systems not having provision for cooling or heating the incoming air are thus to be found chiefly in buildings not subjected to the extremes of temperature indicated above.

5.1.2 Air Conditioning

Air conditoning may be defined as the control of air temperature, speed, humidity and purity.

The first air-conditioning installations arose out of a need to exercise close control over the atmosphere surrounding certain industrial production processes. Examples of industrial air conditioning are the moistening and cooling needed in many textile and food-processing factories. Comfort air conditioning – that is to say air conditioning designed to improve personal comfort – developed rapidly in the wake of industrial air conditioning once the advantages in terms of increased worker efficiency and satisfaction that could be gained from its use had been realised.

General requirements. The function of a comfort air-conditioning installation is, in conjunction with a suitable system of ventilation, to supply an interior, in a draught-free manner, with fresh, clean air; to cool or heat an interior so as to maintain the desired air temperature and temperature uniformity; and to moisten or dry the supply air so as to maintain the atmosphere at the desired relative humidity.

In an office, for example, the interior climate created by the air-conditioning should, ideally, satisfy the following requirements
(a) Fresh air – 30 m³/h per person (minimum)
(b) Air speed ⩽ 0.25 m/s.
(c) Air temperature 20°–25°C (depending on heat radiated by walls)
(d) Air-temperature differences in the living zone (viz. the zone extending from floor level to head height):
when heating $T_{max} - T_{av} = 2°C$
when cooling $T_{av} - T_{min} = 1.5°C$
(e) Relative humidity – between 30 and 70 per cent

It should be appreciated, however, that it is impossible to be dogmatic with regard to the specification of the interior climate. The requirements (a) to (e) listed above should be seen merely as guide lines exerting, as they do, a mutual influence one upon the other. In the assessment of the climate, such factors as the nature and duration of the work performed there, and the type and style of clothing worn, all play their part. What would constitute a comfortable atmosphere for all people, in all places and at all times is, therefore, rather difficult to define.

Thermal Load. Before an air-conditioning installation can be designed, the maximum total thermal, or heat, load in the interior has to be calculated. The thermal load is expressed in watts per square metre of floor area. Contributary factors include solar radiation transmitted through windows, walls and roof, heat generated by people and machines in the interior and, of course, heat generated by the lighting.

The heating effect of solar radiation, when absorbed by the walls and roof of a building, is expressed in watts per square metre for the surface concerned. Tables are available that specify the heating produced by solar radiation for several angles of incidence, at a number of geographical locations and at various times of the day and year.

Solar radiation transmitted through windows and incident upon objects within the interior can add considerably to the thermal load.

The human body dissipates heat to its surroundings according to the degree of body movement involved. This varies from about 100 watts for sedentary office tasks to more than 300 watts for heavy physical work.

The amount of heat produced by machines can usually be determined from the technical data supplied by the manufacturer of the machines concerned. When calculating the total heat load produced by machines allowance should, of course, be made for the case where not all machines are in use at any given time.

The total amount of heat generated by the lighting will depend on the lamp load that must be installed per square metre of area illuminated in order to obtain the required mean illuminance on the working plane. The expression relating these two quantities lamp load P and mean illuminance E, is given in Chapter 13 'Calculations and Measurements'.

It should not be forgotten that electric lamps and their associated control gear are efficient converters of electric power to heat energy. For example, a typical 40 watt fluorescent lamp with a light output of 2400 lumens (which represents a luminous efficacy halfway between excellent and poor) has an energy dissipation when working at its optimum ambient temperature (25°C) as follows (See also table 5.1)

Lamp:	light	8 W
	radiant heat (infrared + ultraviolet)	16 W
	conduction	1 W
	convection	15 W
		40 W
Ballast:	radiant heat + conduction + convection	10 W
Total input		50 W

The conduction and convection components of the heat energy dissipated by the lighting can, as will be shown below, largely be prevented by the air-conditioning from entering the room being lighted and therefore from having a direct influence on the physical comfort of the occupants. Of the energy radiated, a portion will be felt as heat by the occupants.

Investigation (Schröder and Steck, 1973) and experience have shown, however, that so long as the heat energy dissipated in this way does not amount to more than 20 W/m^2 of room floor area there will be little chance of the occupants experiencing any feeling of discomfort, figure 5.1. The situation becomes critical when sensitive individuals begin to complain, and this point is reached at an irradiance of some 40 W/m^2. (For a typical 1000 lx installation in a large room approximately 30 W/m^2 has to be installed of which – depending upon the type of air-conditioning system employed – some 8 W to 15 W will penetrate into the working space.)

5.1.3 Air Supply, Circulation and Extraction

The general pattern of the circulatory air currents created during the ventilation or air-conditioning process is influenced more by the design and location of the air supply inlets than by the design or position of the outlets.

Table 5.1 Percentage energy distribution of the most important lamp types (without ballasts)

Source	Conduction and convection heat	Total radiation	Radiation in various wavebands						Efficacy lm/W
			UV-B	UV-A	Visible	IR-A	IR-B	IR-C	
Incandescent lamp 100 W	7	93	–	0.03	9.0	36.0	32.0	16.0	13.8
Tubular fluorescent lamp 65 W	ca. 40	ca. 60	0.06	0.5	18.0	0.6	0.12	ca. 41	58.5
High-pressure mercury fluorescent lamp (HPI) 400 W	25	75	0.12	2.0	14.8	5.5	6.1	47.0	53
Blended-light lamp (HPL) 250 W	19	81	0.02	0.8	7.6	19.2	21.2	32.0	21
High-pressure sodium lamp (SON) 400 W	23	77	–	–	30.0	16.0	8.0	23.0	95

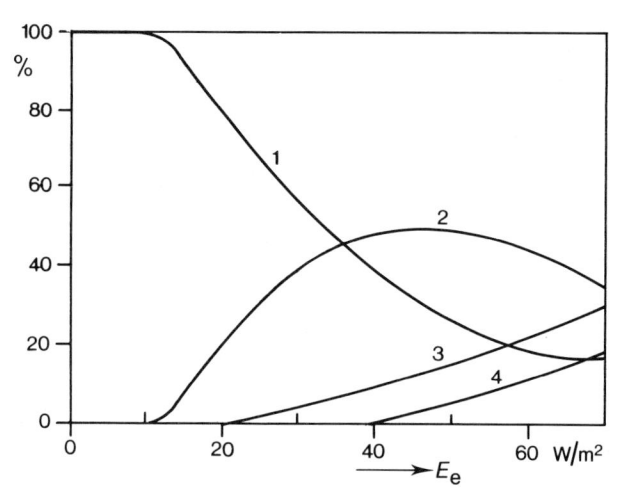

Figure 5.1 Percentage assessment of the effect of heat radiation from lamps and luminaires on personal comfort as a function of the irradiance E_e at a room temperature of 22°C. (Schröder and Steck). Scale of assessment:
1 = not noticeable
2 = noticeable
3 = very noticeable
4 = disturbing

It is by no means an easy matter to predict the probable paths of these air currents. Take the case of a large empty interior with cool air entering through slots in the ceiling. Air warmed by contact with the room surfaces will rise, and the cool air entering from above will fall. But research (Söllner, 1968b) has shown that the effect is not, as might be assumed, that of a regular pattern of upward and downward moving air streams, it is rather that of one or more huge rotating air cylinders filling the whole room and creating high air speeds near the floor, walls and ceiling, with a turbulent zone of lower speeds in the middle of the room. The air rises at the warmest wall of the room and falls on the opposite side thus causing considerable draughts both in these areas and near the floor.

The presence of people in the interior will modify this pattern of air flow considerably. As was mentioned earlier, the human body acts as a heat source. Part of the heat dissipated will rise and, in so doing, will alter the temperature distribution within the interior so helping to create a new, less disturbing pattern of low-speed movements. The effects described above are illustrated in figure 5.2. Figure 5.3 gives an impression of the sort of measurement set-up used for gathering this kind of information.

The disturbance can be still further reduced by giving the injected air a high degree of turbulence. This can be achieved by special air supply diffusers,

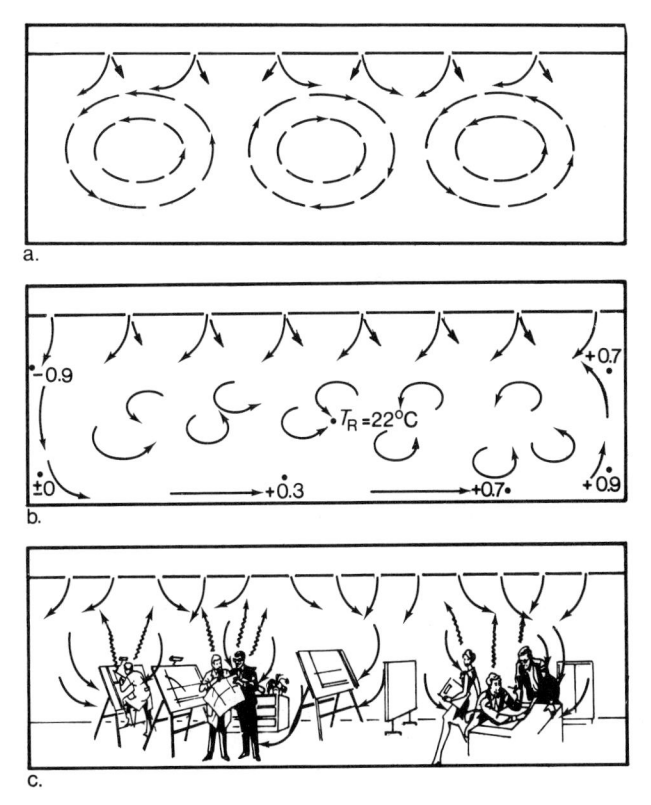

Figure 5.2 Schematic sketch of the air movements prevailing in a large interior in which cool air enters through slots in the ceiling. (a) The rotating cylinder effect created by the mixing of cool and warm air when the interior is unoccupied (b) The resultant temperature distribution indicating the temperature differences above and below room temperature (T_r). (c) The modified pattern of air flow brought about by the presence of 'human' radiators.

some of which permit the speed and the direction of the incoming air to be controlled locally.

It is difficult to specify a maximum permissible speed for the circulating air currents. Air travelling at a speed of 0.5 m/s out of doors, for example, would be barely noticeable whereas air travelling at the same speed across an interior could be experienced as a draught. The maximum will depend on the temperature and humidity of the surroundings, on the sensitivity of the individual to local changes in temperature (the thermal insulation properties of the clothing worn will exert an influence here) and on whether the occupants of the interior are sitting, standing or moving about. Generally speaking, however, it can be said that the speed should not exceed 0.2 to 0.25 m/s, depending on the temperature, where people are seated, with higher speeds permitted where they are moving about.

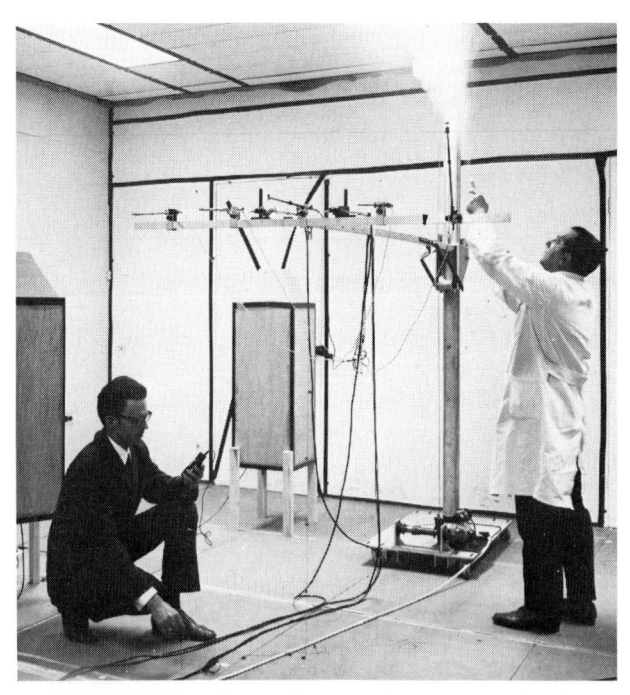

Figure 5.3 Test room equipped for measuring the speed, path and temperature distribution of the air currents produced by a system of air conditioning. The smoke trail is used to reveal the path of the circulating air currents. The photo shows the dummy human radiators used to create the sort of conditions prevailing in an occupied room.

5.2 Integration of Lighting and Air-Handling Equipment

In a large modern building electric lighting supplements daylight or replaces it entirely and forced ventilation or air conditioning takes over from natural ventilation. Such technical facilities as these can only be designed to work together efficiently, however, if they are considered from the outset as forming one coherent, or integrated system.

It will be shown in the following chapter how the integration of ceiling-mounted lighting and air-handling equipment can lead to a more effective use of energy. But integration can bring together a number of largely independent benefits, none of which have anything to do with energy conservation directly.

Cost saving is one. A feature common to each of the three basic systems of integration (which are described below) is that the return, or used, air is extracted from the interior via slots in the luminaires and not, as would be the case in the absence of integration, only through separate grills in the ceiling. The lamp cooling that takes place can, where standard types of fluorescent lamp are concerned, give an increase in the light output and a corresponding reduction in the number of lamps needed to produce a given level of illuminance. In a large installation, nine of these so-called air-handling luminaires can give as much light as roughly ten luminaires of the closed or unventilated types, with economies both initially and in running costs. There may also be some saving on maintenance costs, since the fall in light output due to dirt accumulation is generally less than is the case with any of the unventilated luminaires.

Increased comfort is another. The fact that the return air is exhausted through the luminaires means that heat dissipated by the lamps is largely prevented from entering the interior. The heat disspated by the luminaires themselves in the form of radiation will also be reduced since their operating temperature will be held low by virtue of the cooling effect of the exhaust air passing through them. Air flow rates can therefore be kept lower with this form of air handling in the interests of reducing not only noise and draughts but also the cost of the installation.

Flexibility can also be improved as a result of integration. It is more than likely that an interior designed today for one specific activity will be used at some time in the future for something quite different. It is often quite impossible to foresee the nature of these future activities. This means that the lighting, along with the other building services, should contain a certain degree of built-in flexibility. This flexibility can easily be built into a fully integrated system of lighting and air handling by employing a ceiling of the integrated type; the hardware, viz., luminaires, supply-air diffusers and ceiling panels, being then dimensionally related, it is a simple matter to reposition individual units – or redesign the entire layout if needs be – to suit the needs of the moment.

No less important than any of the benefits mentioned above is the visual coordination that the use of dimensionally related hardware makes possible.

5.2.1 Integrated Ceiling Systems

The physical integration of the ceiling mounted elements of the lighting and air-handling equipment commonly involves the use of special air handling luminaires assembled along with air supply diffusers and acoustic panels to form an integrated ceiling system.

There is no unique system of integrated air handling. The truth of this can be illustrated by examining the main features of each of the three basic types of system in turn.

Common to all three is the use of the space between a suspended (or false) ceiling and the permanent ceiling – the so-called plenum – for housing the air supply and/or air exhaust ducting. The systems differ in the method adopted for supplying and extracting the air. (See figure 5.4.)

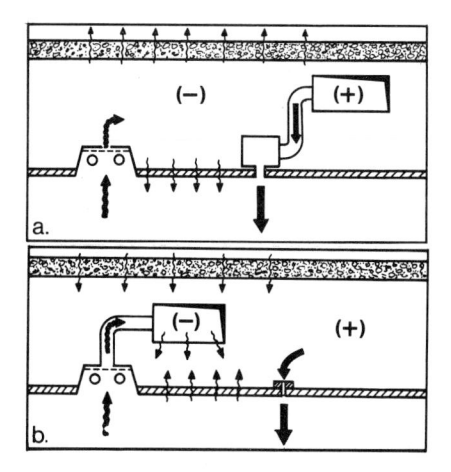

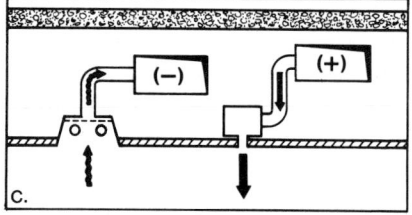

Figure 5.4 Integrated ceiling systems. (a) Ducted-supply/plenum-exhaust. (b) Plenum-supply/ducted-exhaust. (c) Ducted-supply/ducted-exhaust. The direction of the heat flow into and out of the plenum is indicated by the small arrows.
(+) *positive pressure.*
(−) *negative pressure.*

a. Ducted-supply/plenum-exhaust. In this system the supply air is ducted in through a distribution network to individual air supply diffusers built into the ceiling. The plenum, which is at a lower pressure than the room, acts as a duct for the return air, which is extracted through slots in the luminaires.

The ceiling should, ideally, be sealed against air leakage. Leaks in the ceiling will allow the return air to pass direct from the room to the plenum. This will result in a reduced current of cooling air passing through the luminaires, thereby increasing very slightly the heat load produced by the lighting. (See Sec. 5.2.2.) But perhaps more important, is the fact that the airflow through the ceiling at a point of leakage will inevitably produce fouling of the ceiling at this point due to the local accumulation of dirt.

With the plenum exhaust system described above, there is the problem of heat transfer from the warm air extracted from the room to the bounding surfaces of the plenum. Part of the heat absorbed by these surfaces is returned to the room below by conduction through the suspended ceiling, and part is transmitted in a similar way to the room above. There is a similar heat transfer from the warm air in the plenum to the cooler air in the air-supply ducting, although this can be kept to a minimum by thermal insulation of the ducts. There will, nevertheless, be a twofold heat transfer and because of this the heat load in the room will not be reduced to a minimum.

The advantage of the sealed-plenum system is that it saves on return-air ducting. Moreover, since there is no return-air ducting, there is no need for plenum boxes – the joining pieces normally needed on each luminaire for interface with the ducting. There is thus an additional saving on the cost of the luminaires.

b. Plenum-supply/ducted-exhaust. The positive-pressure plenum used in this system acts as a duct for the supply of incoming air to the interior, the air entering the room via air supply elements (e.g. specially perforated ceiling tiles or strip diffusers mounted between the ceiling tiles). The return air is extracted through slots in the luminaires and led away through ducting.

The supply air will be warmed to a certain extent on its passage through the plenum by contact with the warm exhaust ducting. However, unlike as is the case with the 'sealed' plenum system, the average temperature of the air in the plenum will be below that of the air in the rooms above and below. There will thus be a net heat flow into the plenum rather than out of it.

Again, there is a saving on the amount of ducting needed. In this case, there is no requirement for ducting to connect the air supply elements to the main air-supply duct. The primary consequence of this is the obvious saving in materials and installation. Needless to say, these air-supply elements must not be mounted so close to the luminaire that the incoming air is drawn away before it has had a chance to do its job.

c. Ducted-supply/ducted-exhaust. This system contains two ducting networks, one for distributing the supply air to individual air diffusers and the other for extracting the return air via slots in the luminaires.

The advantage of a system such as this in which air supply and air exhaust are kept separate is that, by preventing the heat transfer that would otherwise occur, it allows the heat produced by the lighting and entering the space below to be reduced to a minimum for a given air exhaust rate.

There is no need, of course, for the plenum to be sealed. This means that a ceiling panel can be removed to gain access to a luminaire without disturbing the functioning of the system.

The obvious drawback of the system is the extra amount of ducting required. As can be seen, if it were simply a question of choosing say the least costly or most efficient system for a given application the choice would not be too difficult. More often than not, however, cost must be balanced against efficiency, and the balance judged as proper will be greatly influenced by the many technical considerations prevailing in the greater context of building design and appointment. The average lighting engineer is rarely equipped to make decisions concerning the choice of system and the matter is normally decided by a team in which the air-conditioning consultant plays the major role.

5.2.2 Characteristics of Air-handling Luminaires

Thermal characteristics. Söllner (1968b) showed that the downward flow of heat from fluorescent luminaires could be effectively reduced with a relatively low rate of air extraction (figure 5.5), but that higher extraction

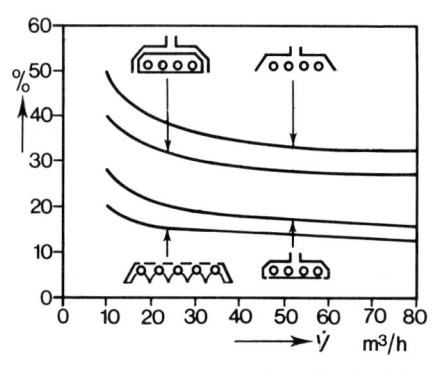

Figure 5.5 Return-air cooling of air handling luminaires showing how downward heat flow, which is plotted as a percentage of the total heat generated, decreases with increase in air flow rate $\dot{V}$ m³/h per lamp. Temperature of the air entering the luminaires, 25°C.

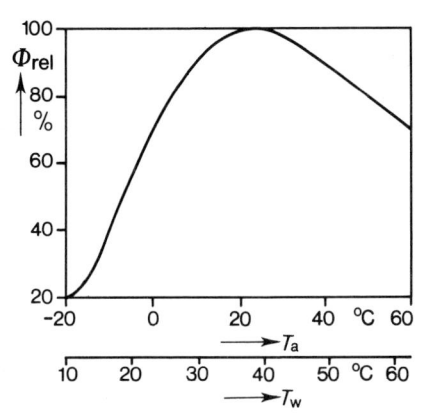

Figure 5.6 Variation of relative luminous flux Φ_{rel} for a tubular fluorescent lamp in still air as a function of ambient temperature T_a and wall temperature T_w.

rates, although reducing still further the downward heat flow, could lead to overcooling of the lamps causing their light output to fall (figure 5.6).

The difference between one luminaire and another in the amount of heat removed at a given rate of air extraction is due to the way in which differences in luminaire construction can alter the path taken by the air. To effect

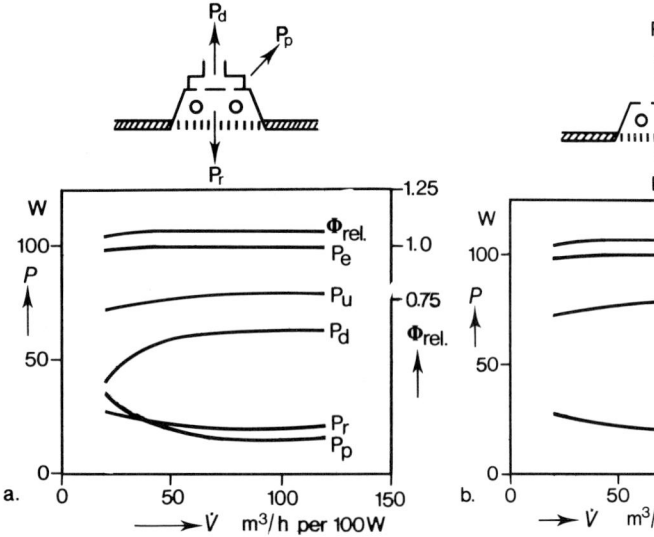

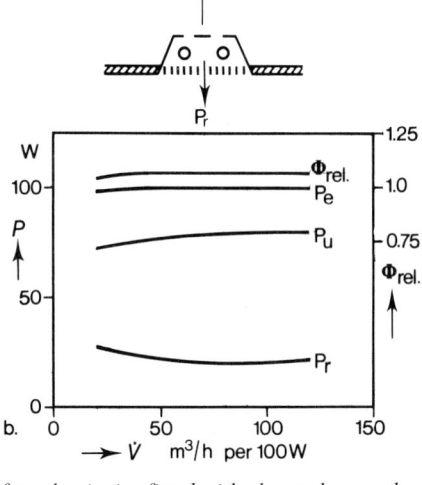

Figure 5.7 Characteristics of a typical air handling luminaire showing distribution of heat watts P and change in relative luminous flux Φ_{rel} as a function of air flowrate $\dot{V}$: (a) for a luminaire fitted with plenum box, and (b) for the same luminaire without plenum box. Nominal installed load in both cases 100 watts.

optimum heat removal, the air passages should be designed to allow maximum contact between the return air and the lamps and their ballasts.

The information needed by the user for the prediction of luminaire performance is obtained by calorimetric measurement. (See Hentschel *et al.*, 1972.) This information can be presented for general use in the form of a set of characteristic curves (figure 5.7), for each luminaire type, in which the various quantities of interest are plotted as a function of air flow rate. A typical measurement set-up is shown in figure 5.8.

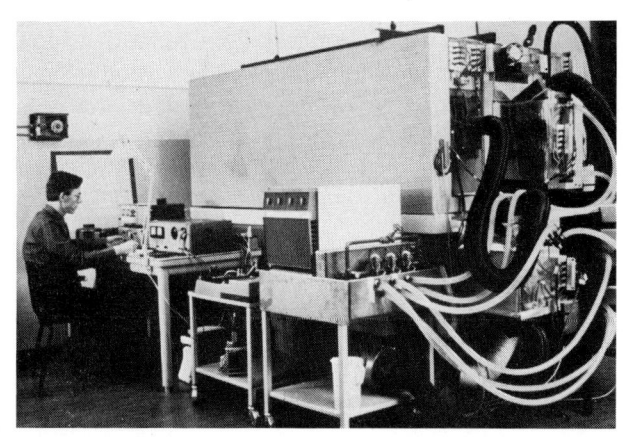

Figure 5.8 Calorimeter for determining the power distribution characteristics of air handling luminaires.

Pressure characteristics. The inner surfaces and channels of luminaires present a frictional resistance to the flow of air through them, and this causes a pressure difference to exist between inlet and outlet. As the flow rate is increased, the pressure difference will increase also (figure 5.9).

Figure 5.9 Pressure diagram for a standard type air-handling luminaire showing the increase in pressure drop ΔP across the luminaire (S1 with plenum box and S2 without plenum box) with increasing air flow rate $\dot{V}$.

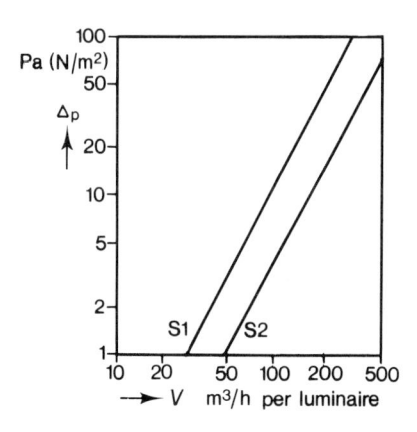

The relationship existing between air-pressure difference and air flow rate is specified by the luminaire manufacturer for each type of air handling luminaire in his programme. This information, together with similar information relating to the other components of the air handling system (e.g. ducts, air supply diffusers) is used by the air-conditioning engineer when approaching the design of the system as a whole.

Noise characteristics. Air travelling through the various sections of the distribution system e.g. luminaires, pressure regulating valves, bends and branches in the ducting and other discontinuities or obstructions to the smooth flow of air, cause noise. With low air flow rates and good system design, the noise produced is minimal and may be safely neglected. However, as air speeds are increased, a point is reached where the corresponding increase in noise can become a problem.

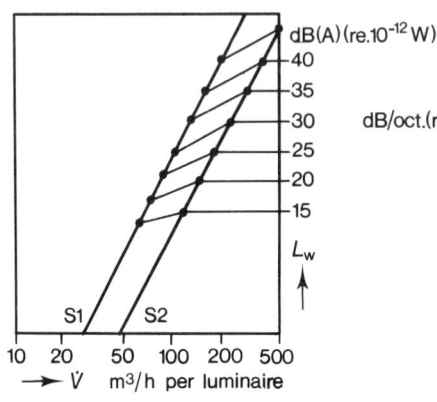

Figure 5.10 Sound power diagram for a standard type air-handling luminaire showing the increase in sound power level L_w with increase in air flow rate V. (Reference power 10^{-12} W).

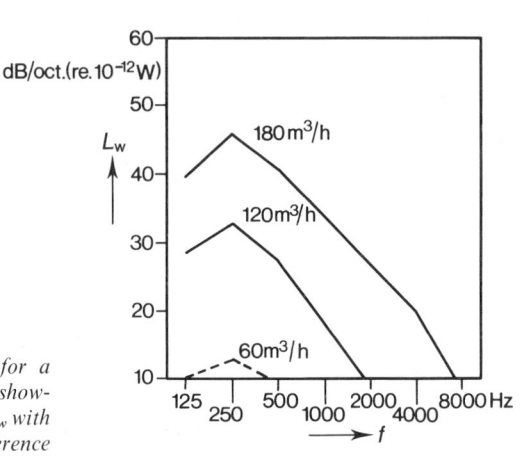

Figure 5.11 Sound power spectrum for a standard type air-handling luminaire showing sound power level L_w as a function of mid-octave frequency f for three air-flow rates. (Reference power 10^{-12} W.)

Amongst the information required for the prediction of the noise level in a room is a knowledge of the sound power level, L_w (see Sec. 5.3 Acoustics), of the luminaire as a function of air flow rate. This relationship is given in the form of a sound power diagram, figure 5.10. Where the luminaire is equipped with an air flow control valve, the sound power level for the main positions of this valve must be indicated.

In many cases, the spectral distribution of the sound power level is also required. This information is presented in the form of a sound power spectrum, figure 5.11, on which sound power level is given as a function of the mid-octave frequencies for various air flow rates.

A typical measurement set-up employed for the determination of the above relationship is shown in figure 5.12.

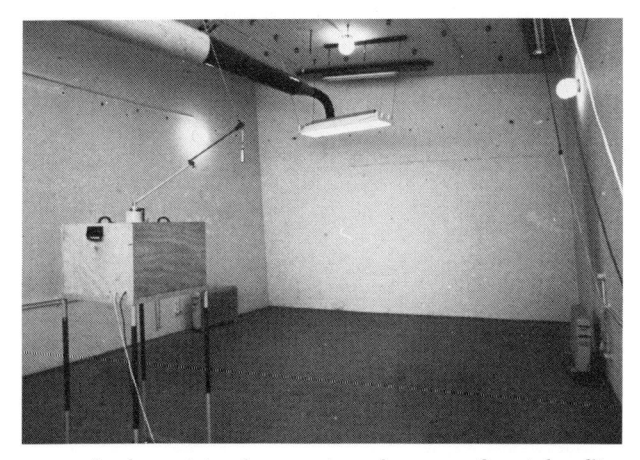

Figure 5.12 Measurement set-up for determining the acoustic performance of an air handling luminaire.

5.3 Acoustics

Just as the interior environment can be improved by a well designed system of ventilation or air conditioning so too can it be improved by careful attention paid to the room acoustics.

5.3.1 Sound Absorption and Insulation

There is a need here to distinguish clearly between two forms of acoustical control: sound insulation and sound absorption. Sound insulation is the prevention or marked reduction of sound transmission. Sound absorption is the reduction of sound reflection.

The ceiling and the permanent dividing walls in a building interior provide, by virtue of the weight and structure of material used, a fair degree of sound insulation between adjacent areas. Local noise is reduced to a certain extent by the sound absorbent nature of the normal room furnishings e.g. carpets, curtains, chairs and so forth. Transmitted and reflected noise can both be reduced still further by the use of free-standing screens designed for the purpose. But it is wisest to place most of the acoustical control treatment on the ceiling since this is often the surface nearest the source of the noise and the one most exposed to it.

Where the reduction of sound reflection is the aim, an acoustically 'soft', or sound absorbent, material must be employed. There are many lightweight, sound-absorbent materials to choose from. The choice of material may be affected by its fire resistance, maintenance characteristics and appearance, but its absorption characteristics have a particular importance. Efficiency in sound absorption varies with frequency. Ideally, therefore, the frequency characteristic of the absorbent chosen should match that of the local noise being generated. Porous materials give sound absorption at mainly high frequencies whereas resonant panels give absorption at low frequencies.

5.3.2 Decibels and Levels

In the field of acoustics, a number of specialised terms are used for convenience and clarity. Particular note should be made of the following terms, which are used when discussing criteria for noise in buildings.

Sound power level. A useful quantity for characterising the loudness of a noise source is the acoustic power of the source expressed in watts.

The range of sound power covered by even common sources of sound is tremendous. A very soft whisper, for example, involves a total radiated power of about 10^{-9} watt, a blaring radio radiates about 10^{-1} watt, while for a large jet aircraft taking off, the power radiated can be as much as 10^5 watt.

It is convenient to be able to compare the power of a source with that of a standard, or reference, source. This is done using a logarithmic, or decibel, scale of sound power levels. The sound power level L_w of a source is the ratio of the power W of that source to the power W_o of a reference source, expressed in decibels

$$L_w = 10 \log \frac{W}{W_o}$$

The reference power chosen for international use is 10^{-12} watt. The acoustic powers mentioned above, i.e. 10^{-9} W, 10^{-1} W and 10^5 W then correspond to sound power levels of 30 dB, 110 dB and 170 dB respectively.

Sound pressure level. Most acoustic measurements are made in terms of effective sound pressure. The effective sound pressure created by different sources has been found to vary greatly, viz. from about 2×10^{-5} N/m² at the threshold of hearing under ideal conditions, to around 2×10^2 N/m² for noises that can cause pain or permanent damage in the ear – the so-called pain limit. A scale such as this, where extremes differ by a factor of 10^7, is not really suitable for use in acoustics. Use is therefore made of a decibel scale of sound pressure levels. The sound pressure level L_p is derived from the effective sound pressure P_{eff} using

$$L_p = 10 \log \frac{P^2_{\text{eff}}}{P_o^2}$$

where P_o is the reference sound pressure. Using an agreed reference pressure of 2×10^{-5} N/m², the effective sound pressure at the threshold of hearing (2×10^{-5} N/m²) corresponds to a sound pressure level of 0 dB, while at the pain limit (2×10^2 N/m²) the level is 140 dB.

Table 5.2 Typical sound pressure levels

L_p (dB)	Example
0	Threshold of hearing
20	Rustling of leaves
40	Whispering at 1 metre
60	Conversation at 1 metre
80	Blaring radio
100	Klaxon from nearby
120	Machine-gun
140	Pain limit

Table 5.2 gives a few examples of noise sources, with a rough indication of the corresponding L_p values.

Sound pressure levels should not be confused with sound power levels which, as has been shown, are also expressed in decibels. The sound power level describes the total acoustic power radiated by a source (i.e. its potential for making noise), whereas the sound pressure level, which depends upon the distance from the source, losses in the intervening air, room effects, etc., describes the measured effect of that source at a point.

Sound pressure levels, which are measured with the aid of a sound-level meter, are often specified in terms of the 'weighted' decibel, in particular decibel A (dBA). The weighted decibel is a single number giving the total sound pressure level weighted by an approximation to the loudness sensitivity of the human ear for pure tones. The sound power level of a source can be derived from the measured sound pressure level and can also be expressed in terms of the weighted decibel (as has been done, for example, in figure 5.10 above).

5.3.3 Noise Rating Curves

The ear is not equally sensitive to all frequencies: a tone of 20 Hz at 80 dB will sound as loud as a tone of 1000 Hz at 20 dB. However, it has been found that high frequency tones cause more irritation than do tones of high sound level, and this is a good reason for being careful when deciding whether or not a particular tone is permissible in a given situation.

In order that a criterion may be applied to the sound pressure level, the International Organisation for Standardisation (ISO) has published a set of noise rating (NR) curves. These curves (NR 0 to NR 70, figure 5.13) indicate the sound pressure level in decibels as a function of frequency. The number of a particular curve corresponds to the sound pressure level indicated by that curve for an intermediate frequency of 1000 Hz.

Table 5.3 Recommended NR values for various areas

Building Interior	Recommended NR value
Studios	10
Concert halls	20
Conference rooms	25
Lecture rooms	25
Auditoria	25
Hospitals	30
Private offices	30
Offices	35
Landscaped offices	40

A number of NR values for various areas have been recommended. These recommendations are shown in table 5.3. The curve corresponding to the recommended NR number for a particular area may be used to rate the frequency or sound pressure-level components of any tone occuring there. For a landscaped office, for example, an NR value of 40 is recommended. It can be seen from figure 5.13 that a tone of, say, 4000 Hz at 40 dB falls in the area above the NR 40 curve. Such a tone would therefore not be permissible; to become so, the sound pressure level of the tone would have to be reduced by at least 5 dB.

5.3.4 Acoustical Control

In the three systems of integration described earlier, the luminaires, the ducting and the air control elements are housed above a false ceiling which is suspended from the permanent ceiling. Since such false ceilings add nothing to the strength of the basic structure of the building, they tend to

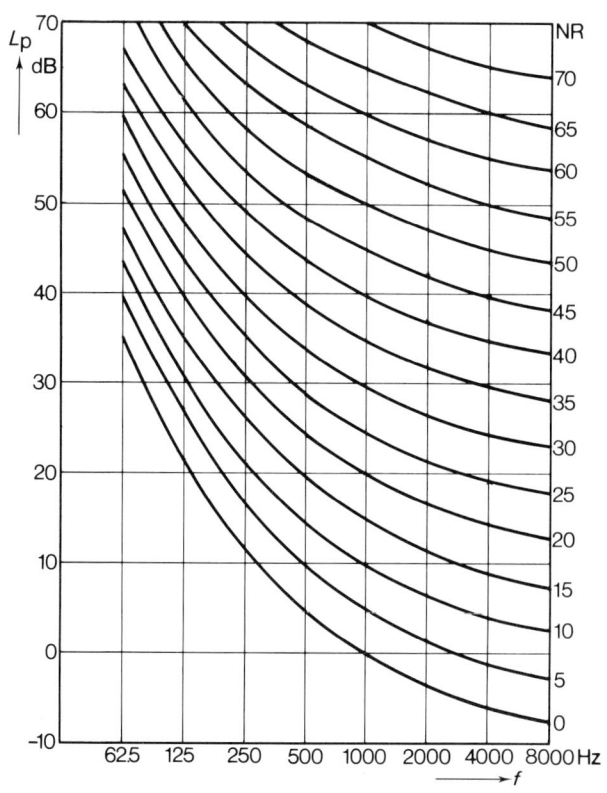

Figure 5.13 Noise rating curves indicating the sound pressure level L_p as a function of frequency f. (Reference pressure 2×10^{-5} N/m^2.)

be kept as light as possible. The use in these ceilings of the necessarily heavy materials needed to provide sound insulation is thereby effectively ruled out. This means that noise that could be produced by the rush of air through the ducting concealed in the plenum must be kept to the desired level by routing the ducting to avoid bends and discontinuities in the air flow, by the addition of stiffening materials to the duct walls, or both. Stiffening materials increase the absorption at low frequencies but produce negligible change at high frequencies. This approach does, however, have the advantage that it serves also to insulate the ducting thermally, thereby lessening the problems caused by heat exchange between return air and supply air mentioned earlier.

But to come back to the ceiling itself. What the suspended ceiling can readily provide is sound absorption, that is to say the absorption of sounds generated in the room proper, which would otherwise be reflected across the room via the ceiling.

Porous materials e.g. mineral wool (slag wool or rock wool), glass wool, foamed plastics, soft asbestos, give sound absorption at mainly high frequencies whereas resonant panels give absorption at low frequencies. Where a porous material is used, this can be compressed to form a thick, self-supporting tile or panel which can be mounted direct in the ceiling framework. Alternatively, it can form an inlay to a metal tray, the tray being perforated to allow the sound to pass through it to the absorbent.

Where space permits, it is possible to increase the attenuation of noise transmitted via the ceiling by the addition of specially contoured baffles.

Chapter 6

Energy Considerations

The present world focus on energy conservation, brought about initially by the recent awareness of the fact that the world's fuel supplies are dwindling and heightened by subsequent increases in the cost of fuel, has had – and will no doubt continue to have – a profound effect on the building industry. All those concerned with building design and appointment are having to find ways of keeping energy requirements to a minimum.

Included among those factors having an indirect influence on the amount of energy consumed during a building's lifetime are its shape, the insulation properties of its outer walls, and the size and number of windows. Directly energy consumptive, and of particular interest to the lighting engineer, are such technical services as the ventilation or air conditioning and, of course, the lighting. These factors are, to a certain extent, interactive. It would be remiss, therefore, to conclude our treatment of lighting fundamentals without placing lighting in the greater context of energy-effective building design.

6.1 Buildings

6.1.1 Building Shape

Personal opinions regarding the advantages and disadvantages of the conventional office building versus those of the deep-plan type vary widely, and will no doubt continue to do so, but the rising cost of energy, and the inevitable constraints being placed upon its use, have made subjective choice in the matter of building shape and interior layout almost a thing of the past. In-depth analysis, particularly in connection with building economics and energy conservation, is now becoming a familiar aspect of building design, and this frequently comes out in favour of the low-rise deep-plan office building, the tower block being both more costly to build and more wasteful in the use of energy.

In the simplified analysis of figure 6.1 (Wyatt, 1973), the calculations are based on a building having a gross floor area of 3300 square metres, a square floor plan and a glazed surface area equal to 10 per cent of the total. The preference is clearly towards the three-storey building, which is both cheaper to keep cool in the summer (low heat gain from surroundings) and cheaper to heat in the winter (low heat loss to surroundings) since it has maximum space enclosed by minimum envelope.

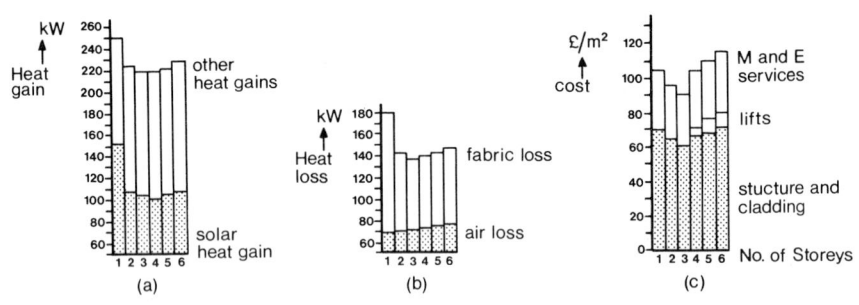

Figure 6.1 Effects of building shape on thermal performance and costs: (a) Total heat gain, (b) Total heat loss, (c) Total cost (1973). The number of storeys of a building having a square floor plan is plotted on the horizontal axes. Calculations for all building types are based on a gross floor area of 3300 m^2 and a glazed area of 10% of room wall areas. (Wyatt)

However, in view of the many variables involved in this type of analysis, such studies must be undertaken for each project; no general conclusion can be reached from this example alone.

6.1.2 Cladding Materials – Glass versus Brick

Tables 6.1 and 6.2 (Wyatt, 1973) show an example comparison of the capital costs and costs-in-use of two alternative types of cladding material, namely glass and brick. The glass cladding is seen to have almost eight times the capital cost of the brick cladding and very nearly 11 times the cost-in-use of the latter. The fact that adequate thermal comfort and freedom from glare inside large areas of glass cladding is only possible with further expenditure on louvres, blinds or special glass would seem to indicate, from the point of view of costs at least, that the surface area of a building taken up by windows should be kept to a minimum.

6.1.3 Window Size

Ordinary window glass admits daylight into a building almost unaffected. Most of the admitted energy is absorbed by the room surfaces and converted into heat, which is trapped in the interior due to the low transmittance of

Table 6.1 Comparison of capital costs for glass and cavity wall claddings used in an air-conditioned building

	Cladding material	
Item	window glazing	cavity walls
Basic construction cost	19	9
Proportion of air-conditioning plant installation cost attributable to cladding material	80	3
Total construction cost	99	12

Table 6.2 Comparison of annual costs in use for glass and cavity wall claddings used in an air-conditioned building

	Cladding material	
Item	window glazing	cavity walls
Capital cost (assume 10% of total construction cost)	9.9	1.2
Window cleaning	0.9	0
Decorating	0.18	0.14
Air-conditioning and heating running cost inc. fuel, maintenance of plant etc.	4.95	0.13
Total cost in use	15.93	1.47

glass for this long-wave radiation. An ideal sun protective glass, on the other hand, would reflect all energy beyond the visible spectrum and would not reflect or absorb any of the visible radiation. In practice, however, sun-protective glass migh reduce the energy flow per lumen of light to about half that of ordinary glass, but this is the maximum improvement that choice of window glass makes possible without affecting the visible spectrum and causing colour distortion. Sun shields, and heat reflective coatings applied to the glass hinder the view out or reduce the influx of daylight.

Various studies (Hardy, 1972), however, have demonstrated the reduction in solar heat penetration, in conduction losses and in sound penetration that can result from building with smaller windows. In-use studies show, as was illustrated above, that windows cost nearly 11 times more than the wall they replace. These considerations together have led to the conclusion that there would be both environmental and economic advantages if windows were reduced in size to cover about 20 per cent of the facade area. Although the contribution made by daylight to the horizontal illuminance in a building would be small, these smaller windows would still provide visual contact with the outside world. In this respect, narrow vertical windows appear to be preferable to long horizontal ones. With a vertical window the view provided will contain a large variety of scale from foreground to distance and sky. In addition, because it will admit only a narrow shaft of sunlight which will track across the room, the area insolated will be smaller with a vertical window than with a horizontal one.

Small windows might be thought to lead to objections on the grounds of inadequate view out. This idea led to a study (Hardy, 1972) of 12 offices in which 950 workers were asked to rank 12 environmental factors in order of importance. 'Good lighting' was found to be the most important and 'view out' the least. Further analyses of the findings revealed that the importance attached to the view was related to the 'information content', that is to say, the more information and the more variety in the view, the more the view was appreciated. An overriding design consideration results from this study, namely that it is wrong to provide an extensive view as the resultant large window is detrimental to the lighting, thermal and acoustic conditions in the interior.

6.2 Lighting

6.2.1 Daylight versus Artificial Light

Because of the influence of building shape and window size on both the daylight level in the interior and the need for supplementary artificial light, it has been suggested that consideration of the lighting should take place at a very early stage of the building design. Experience confirms this, as it has shown an interrelationship to exist between the lighting system and the cost and energy factors. Decisions made on daylighting, artificial lighting, lighting level and quality, and even on the dimensions and arrangement of luminaires, have far-reaching effects on the overall design, layout, appearance, economics and the resulting energy consumption of the building as a whole.

A building design team must therefore undertake a careful study of the matters relating to lighting at a very early stage in the design process. Such a study will often show that daylight, although costing nothing in terms of the direct expenditure of energy, is an expensive commodity to use.

Figure 6.2 (Wyatt, 1973) illustrates this. It shows the energy requirements resulting from two alternative designs for a given building. Design I has

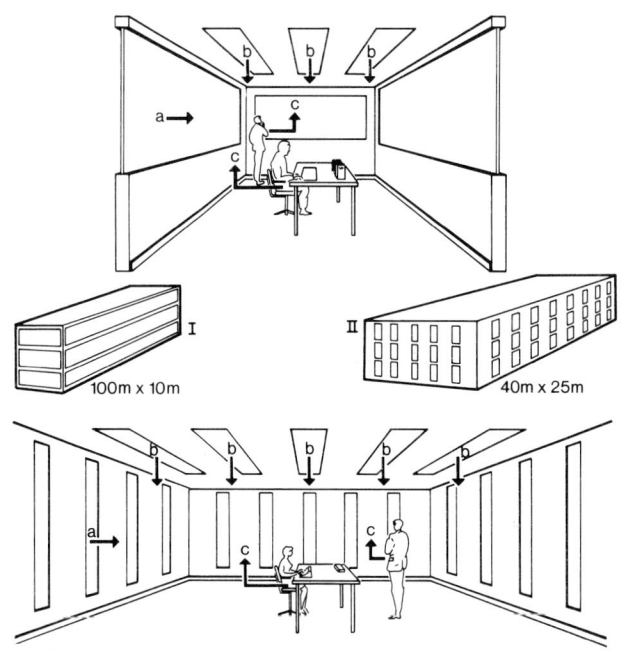

Figure 6.2 Energy requirements resulting from two alternative building designs, each with three floors of 1000 m² area, 3 metre height, and lighting to 1000 lx. (Wyatt)

	Design I	Design II
a. Energy required to counteract climatic fluctuation	95.2 W/m²	29.5 W/m²
b. Energy required to provide lighting and compensate for heat generated by lighting	49.3 W/m²	49.3 W/m²
c. Energy for cooling and ventilation air and machinery	22.8 W/m²	22.8 W/m²
Total	167.3 W/m²	101.6 W/m²

windows to a daylight factor of 2 per cent involving 66 per cent glazing, whereas design II has narrow, floor to ceiling windows amounting to 22 per cent glazing for amenity only. It can be seen that the 2 per cent daylit building requires substantially more energy – what little is saved on artificial lighting is more than lost in the heating and cooling due to the poor thermal qualities of glass. Similarly, a building shape chosen from the viewpoint of affording good daylighting will usually be one that is uneconomic from an energy conservation viewpoint.

6.2.2 Utilisation of Lighting Heat

It has been shown in the previous chapter how the amount of lighting heat from fluorescent lamps entering the interior can be kept to a minimum by removing the heat at source using special air-handling luminaires connected to the return air duct of the air-conditioning system. Extracting heat in this way also ensures that the lamps will operate at optimum efficacy, but how does it affect the total energy requirements of the building?

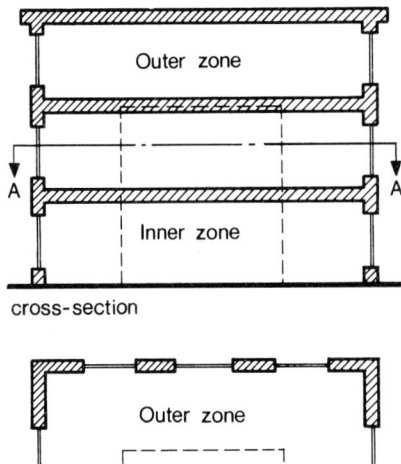

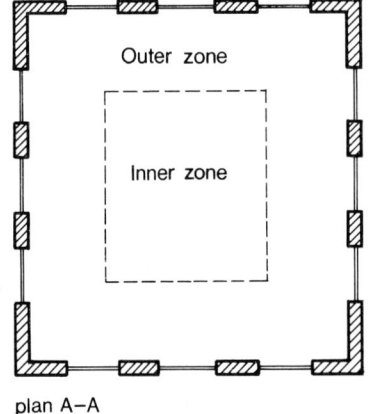

Figure 6.3 Plan and cross-section of building showing the inner and outer zones referred to in the text.

The outer zone of a building (figure 6.3) is much affected by the outside temperature – gaining heat in the summer and losing it in the winter – and may frequently require heating (Bodmann, 1970). At first sight, one may be inclined, at least during the cold season, to apply the opposite of the system described above, i.e., to discharge the supply air through the luminaires into this outer zone. This is possible in theory, but the method is not used in practice principally because warm air supplied to the outer zone is mainly required at the window sill to counteract the downward flow of cool air at this point. A ceiling mounted luminaire is clearly not ideal for this purpose.

The answer, of course, is to utilise the lighting heat generated in the inner zone of the building. The inner zone provides an excess of heat throughout the year. This excess, extracted via the luminaires, can be transferred to the outer zone where it is needed. With return air luminaires the temperature of the exhaust air is higher than that in the room, so allowing more efficient heat exchange with the fresh air supplied to the outer zone.

So far, we have considered how locally available excess heat, notably that from the lighting, can be used to compensate for heat losses elsewhere. There is still the problem of temporal compensation for intervals during which a building is unoccupied. During the night and at weekends the building may cool down unless supplementary heating is provided. This can be done by pumping a portion of the heated air via insulated water storage tanks. These tanks absorb heat during the day and release it during the night to the outer zone. The same tanks can also be used in the hot season to store cold water which is chilled during the night and circulated during time of peak heat gain.

Part 2

LIGHTING EQUIPMENT

Chapter 7

Lamps

Electric lamps may be divided into two main groups: incandescent and discharge. The light from an incandescent lamp is generated by bringing a filament to a high temperature by passing an electric current through it. Discharge lamps have no filament, but produce light by excitation of a gas contained between two electrodes.

Discharge lamps may be further divided into two groups according to whether the gas is contained at low or high pressure. The final lamp classification is shown in figure 7.1.

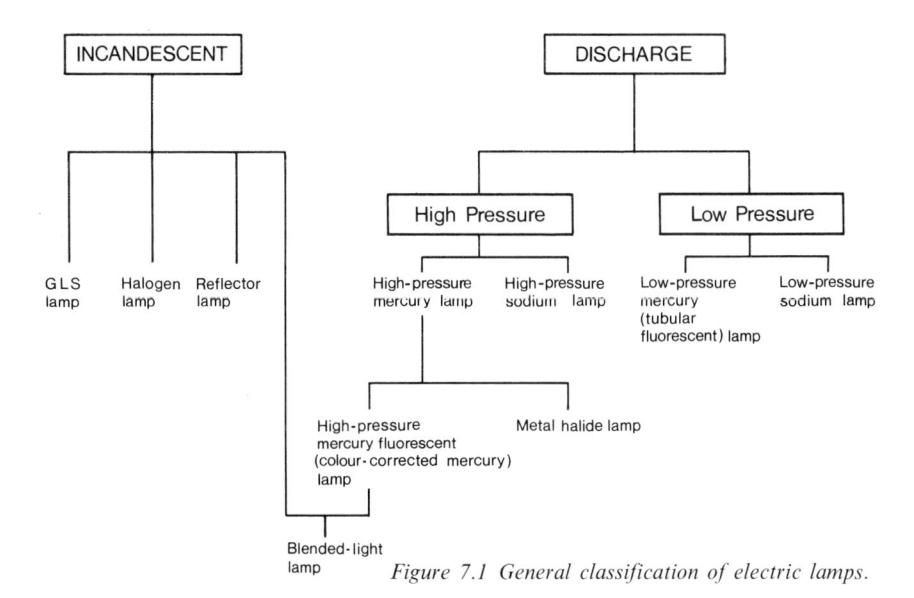

```
INCANDESCENT                              DISCHARGE
    |                                         |
    |------|------|                    |--------------|
    |      |      |              High Pressure    Low Pressure
   GLS  Halogen Reflector              |                 |
   lamp  lamp    lamp           |------|------|    |------------|
                          High-pressure  High-pressure  Low-pressure  Low-pressure
                          mercury lamp   sodium lamp    mercury       sodium lamp
                                |                      (tubular
                                |                      fluorescent) lamp
                         |------|------|
                   High-pressure      Metal halide lamp
                   mercury fluorescent
                   (colour-corrected mercury)
                   lamp
                         |
                   Blended-light
                   lamp
```

Figure 7.1 General classification of electric lamps.

7.1 Principal Characteristics

The principal characteristics of light sources are
(a) Luminous flux, expressed in lumens
(b) Luminous efficacy, expressed in lumens per watt (lm/W)

(c) Life, usually expressed as the number of operating hours elapsed before the lumen output falls to a certain percentage of its initial value
(d) Luminance, expressed in candelas per square metre (cd/m^2) or per square centimetre (cd/cm^2)
(e) Colour appearance. The colour impression received when looking at the light source itself
(f) Colour temperature. An incandescent lamp has a low colour temperature (approx. 3000 K), the sun has a high colour temperature (approx. 6000 K)
(g) Colour rendering properties, for which there is the colour rendering index (Sec. 4.3.2); when the index figure is in the 90–100 range, a faithful rendering of an object's colours is obtained
(h) Physical size

Incandescent lamps are characterised by their compact shape and rather low efficacy. Their colour rendering is excellent, but lamp life is relatively short. These lamps are connected direct to the mains supply.

The highest lamp efficacies are to be found in lamps of the low-pressure discharge variety. Superior to all other lamps in this respect is the low-pressure sodium lamp. Unfortunately, the monochromatic light output of this lamp, which gives it its high efficacy, means that its colour rendering is virtually non-existent, any object colours seen in its light being reduced to various shades of yellow. While this matters little in the case of, say, interior security lighting, it effectively eliminates the lamp for consideration in connection with interior lighting in general. Low-pressure mercury lamps with phosphor coating, or (to use the more common term) fluorescent lamps, have a moderate to high efficacy (see table 7.1) and lamp life is considerably longer than for an incandescent lamp. The fluorescent lamp is characterised by its relatively low luminance, variety of colour appearance (from 'warm white' to 'daylight') and by the choice of colour rendering properties offered. As with all discharge lamps, a ballast is indispensable.

High-pressure discharge lamps have a higher, sometimes much higher, efficacy than that of incandescent lamps (see again table 7.1.) and their life is considerably longer. Apart from certain exceptions (more about this later), colour rendering is inferior to that given by incandescent lamps. Luminance may be medium to relatively high. Some form of external ballast is necessary, with the sole exception of the blended light lamp to which we shall refer later.

7.2 Incandescent Lamps

Incandescent lamps form the oldest family and remain the mainstay of home lighting, basically because they are easy to work with and cheap.

Table 7.1 A comparison of representative lamp types

Lamp type (A) clear bulb (B) bulb with diffusing or fluorescent layer	Luminous efficacy (lm/W)		Colour rendering (colour rendering index)		Colour appearance	Luminance (cd/cm²)
	lamp	lamp + ballast				
Normal incandescent lamp 100 W (A)	14*		excellent	(100)	excellent	700
Normal incandescent lamp 100 W (B)	13*		excellent	(100)	excellent	3
Halogen incandescent lamp 100 W (A)	30* (100 h life)		excellent	(100)	excellent	1 500
Halogen incandescent lamp 1 000 W (A)	22* (2000 h life)		excellent	(100)	excellent	1 000
High-pressure mercury lamp 400 W (A)	52	49	modest	(20)	modest (blue)	460
High-pressure mercury lamp 400 W (B)	57	54	modest	(40)	reasonable	12
Blended light lamp 250 W (B)	22	22*	modest	(40)	reasonable	5
High-pressure sodium lamp 400 W (A)	120	110	modest	(25)	modest (yellow)	600
High-pressure sodium lamp 400 W (B)	117	107	modest	(25)	modest (yellow)	25
Metal halide lamp 400 W (A)	80	75	reasonable	(65)	good	600
Metal halide lamp 400 W (B)	75	70	reasonable	(65)	good	14
Fluorescent lamps 40 W						
Colour 27	44	35	excellent	(94)		0.4
Colour 33	79	64	reasonable	(66)		0.8
Colour 37	43	35	excellent	(96)	excellent	0.4
Colour 84	80	64	good	(86)		0.8
Low-pressure sodium lamp 180 W	180	150	poor		poor	10

* No ballast required

The limited life and efficacy of the incandescent lamp are the immediate outcome of evaporation of the tungsten filament caused by its high operating temperature. Any attempt at increasing the lamp's efficacy by increasing still further the temperature of the filament, as in done by increasing the supply voltage, will result in a shortening of lamp life, figure 7.2. The converse is equally true.

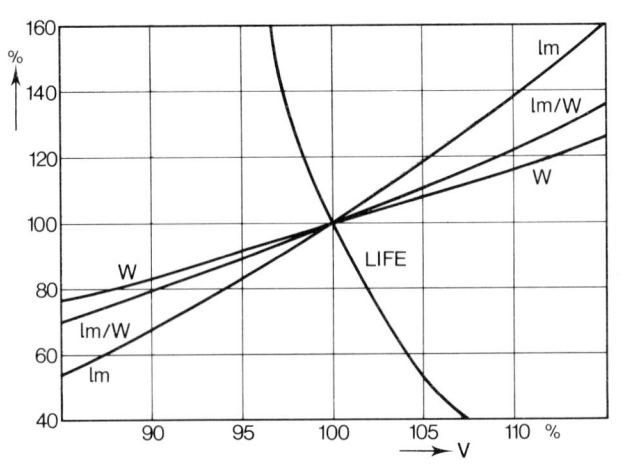

Figure 7.2 Effect of supply voltage variation (% V) on the rated operating characteristics of a GLS incandescent lamp. At 5% overvoltage, for example, the lumen output (lm) will increase by almost 20%, but the lamp's life will be shortened by some 50%.

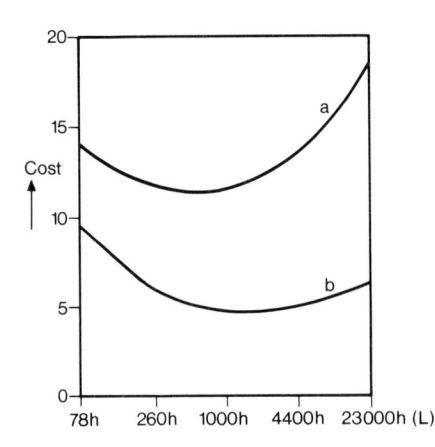

Figure 7.3 The most economic life of an incandescent lamp depends upon the cost of electricity, the price of the lamp and the cost of replacing it. The diagram shows the total operating cost per 10^6 lumen.hour with (a) a higher cost of electricity, and (b) a three times lower cost of electricity, both in relation to the relative supply voltage (V) and lamp life (L).

Taking into account the cost of electricity and the price of the lamp, one can work out the lamp's most economic life. As can be seen from figure 7.3, this is approximately 1000 hours.

Inert gas is introduced into the bulb of the incandescent lamp with the aim of slowing down the evaporation of tungsten from the filament. A mixture of nitrogen and argon gas is most commonly used for this purpose. Krypton causes less heat loss by conduction, but due to its higher price has so far been used only in certain special lamps.

7.2.1 Tungsten Halogen Lamps

In about 1960 tungsten halogen incandescent lamps were introduced. In these lamps the blackening of the lamp bulb is prevented. A halogen is added to the fill-gas so that the evaporated tungsten atoms are able to form gaseous compounds with the halogen. The bulb remains clear provided it is within the correct temperature range. In the temperature-controlled chemical cycle the compounds dissociate again near the hot filament, the released tungsten settles somewhere on the filament, and the free halogen may once again combine with free tungsten atoms. (At first the halogen used was iodine; today bromine is often used, in the form of a bromine compound.)

Use of this principle makes it necessary to adopt a smaller bulb and to increase the pressure of the inert gas. The temperature of the filament can then be higher than with normal incandescent lamps resulting in a higher luminous efficacy at the same or longer lamp life. The efficacy remains almost unchanged till end of life because of the absence of wall blackening.

The chief advantages of tungsten halogen incandescent lamps, namely their reasonably high efficacy (up to 30 lm/W), excellent colour rendering, simple connection to the mains or a battery, small size and high luminance, are well illustrated by the extensive use made of these lamps in floodlighting, motor car lights, projectors, spotlights – in short, all those applications in which an optical system demands a concentrated light source with good colour rendering. Where long lamp life is of importance – floodlighting being an example – a life of 2000 hours with an efficacy of over 20 lm/W is possible.

7.2.2 General Lighting Service Lamps

The general lighting service (GLS) lamp consists of a coiled tungsten filament surrounded by an inert gas and enclosed in a glass bulb (figure 7.4). To diffuse the light from the filament lamps may have inside-frosted bulbs, produced by etching the inner surface of the bulb with acid, or bulbs that have been given an internal white coating having the desired diffusing properties.

Generally speaking, the term general lighting service lamp refers to incandescent lamps of the shape shown in figure 7.4, this being the most familiar and widely used bulb type in general lighting service; variations on this

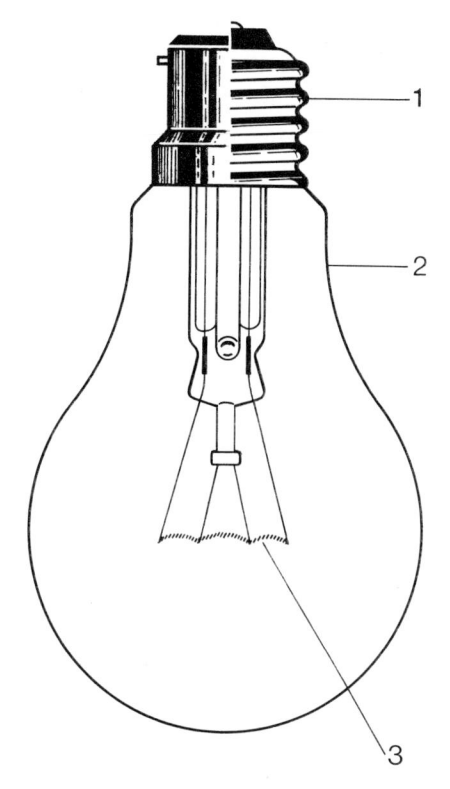

Figure 7.4 General lighting service (GLS) lamp showing 1. Cap (screw or bayonet) 2. Bulb 3. Filament

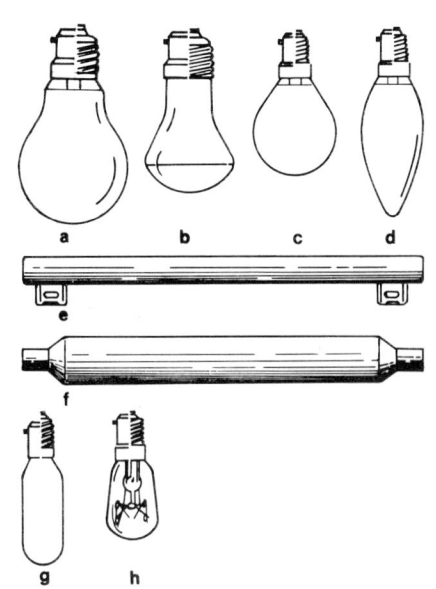

Figure 7.5 Incandescent lamps – typical bulb shapes:
a *GLS (A bulb)*   e *Linear decorative*
b *Mushroom (E bulb)* f *Show window*
c *Lustre*   g *Tubular*
d *Candle*   h *Pilot*

shape used for the purposes of decoration (figure 7.5) are generally referred to using an appropriate descriptive name (e.g. candle lamp). The majority of these decorative lamps are, like the GLS lamp itself, available in a range of bulb finishes.

7.2.3 Reflector Lamps

If the lamp bulb of figure 7.5b is partially frosted and partially provided with a thick white reflector layer it could be described as a reflector lamp since it does have a reflector, although a poor one. But the term reflector lamp specifically applies to those lamps in which the reflector part on the inside surface of the bulb is a true mirror finish.

This mirror surface, being internal, is not subject to corrosion or contamination of any form. Cleaning costs using reflector lamps are thereby largely avoided.

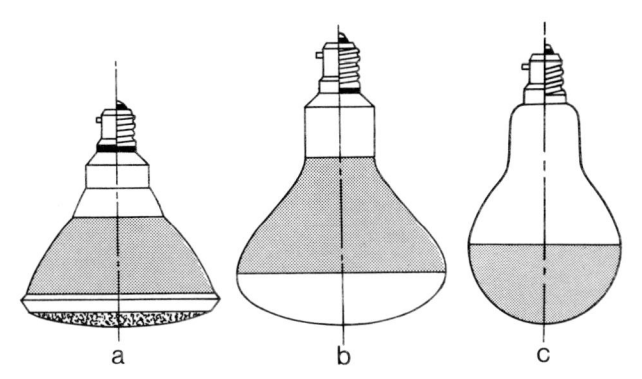

Figure 7.6 Reflector lamps (a) Pressed-glass (b) Blown-bulb (parabolic reflector) (c) Blown-bulb (hemispherical, or bowl, reflector).

Reflector lamps (figure 7.6) may be conveniently divided into two main groups according to the method of construction used, viz. pressed-glass and blown-bulb, with the lamps in the latter group being further divided into two groups according to whether the reflector is situated in the neck or in the bowl of the bulb.

Pressed-glass reflector lamps. These have a pressed, hard glass bulb. The back of the bulb, which is near parabolic in cross section, has a mirror finish and thus forms the reflector of the lamp. The front element (or lens) is patterned to give a variety of beam patterns, e.g., spot, flood, wide-flood. For decorative lighting the lens, which is normally of clear glass, is available with a coloured coating.

Blown-bulb reflector lamps. These are of two types: in one, the back of the bulb is of a specially designed functional shape and is provided with a specular reflecting layer to form the reflector of the lamp, mostly in combination with a slightly frosted front surface, or bowl; in the other type, it is the hemispherical bowl portion of the bulb that is reflectorised, the remainder of the bulb being either clear or frosted.

The former type, like pressed-glass lamps, are available in various beam patterns and colours. The fact that also small, low wattage versions are available, makes these reflector lamps ideal for a wide range of indoor lighting applications.

Reflector lamps of the bowl-reflector type, unlike other reflector lamps, are used in conjunction with an external reflector to obtain the desired light distribution.

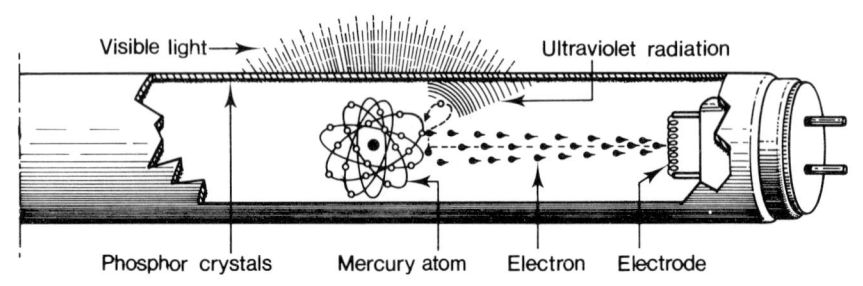

Figure 7.7 Part-section of a tubular fluorescent lamp, illustrating the mechanism of discharge.

7.3 Fluorescent Lamps

The fluorescent lamp (figure 7.7) consists of a tubular bulb having an electrode sealed into each end and containing mercury vapour at low pressure with a small amount of inert gas to aid starting. The inner surface of the tube is coated with fluorescent powders. When a current is passed through the gas mixture, predominantly ultraviolet radiation is produced. The fluorescent powders transform this radiation into visible light.

The long life, high efficacy and good colour rendering of fluorescent lamps makes them eminently suitable for numerous applications in both indoor and outdoor lighting.

Their luminance is less than that of both high-pressure gas discharge lamps and incandescent lamps. This may be an advantage or a drawback, depending on the application. The advantage is the reduction in glare; the drawback is the relatively large volume occupied by the lamps when a given illuminance is required.

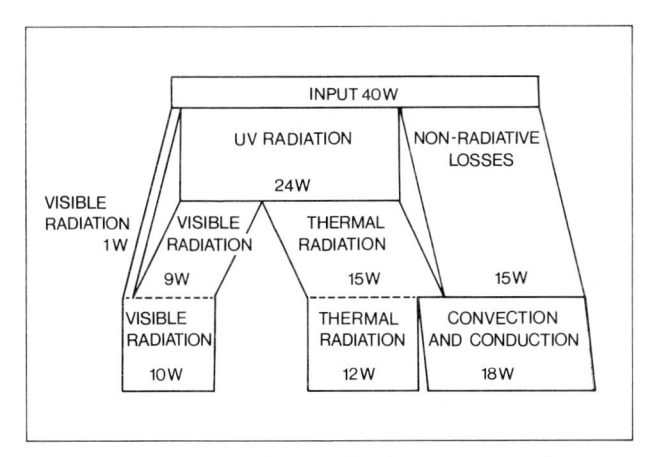

Figure 7.8 Diagram representing schematically the conversion of power in a tubular fluorescent lamp.

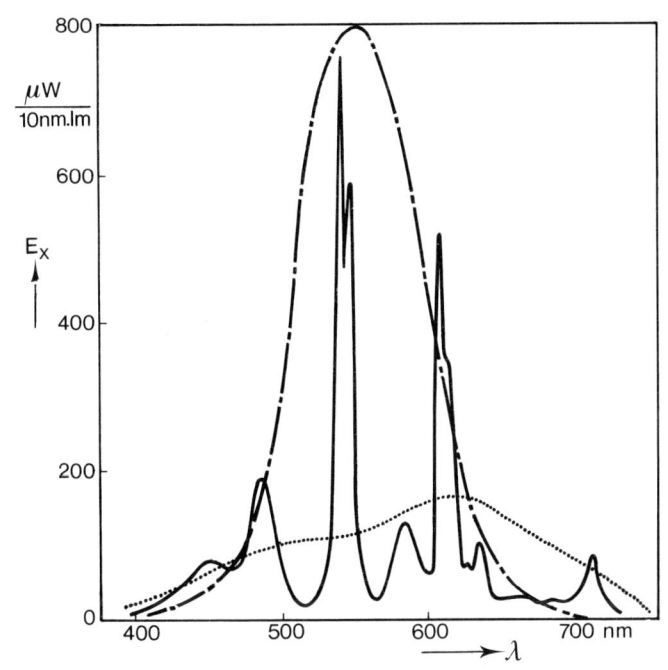

Figure 7.9 Comparison of the spectral energy distribution at 4000 K of a 'TL' 84 fluorescent lamp with that of a 'TL' colour 34 (conventional) lamp, both 40 W, with the CIE standard observer eye sensitivity curve superimposed.
—— *'TL' 84 lamp*
..... *'TL' 34 lamp*
-.-.- *eye sensitivity curve*

151

7.3.1 Efficacy and Colour Rendering

In a 40 watt fluorescent lamp of good colour rendering roughly one watt is directly converted into visible radiation and 24 watts into ultraviolet radiation. Of this 24 watts, about nine watts appear as visible radiation; the other 15 watts, plus the 15 watts of the original 40 that were not converted into ultraviolet radiation, heat the wall of the discharge tube and the electrodes (see figure 7.8). The highest efficacy of fluorescent lamps having continuous spectra is about 80 lm/W.

The mixture of fluorescent powders used in these lamps emits radiation throughout the visible range of the spectrum (see colour plate 4). Research and calculation have shown, however, that very good colour rendering can be achieved with a light source emitting radiation in only three narrow spectrum zones, viz. the red, green and blue zones, figure 7.9. The application of special fluorescent powders containing certain rare earths has now made it possible to obtain emission in these zones (see again colour plate 4) and thus to make fluorescent lamps (the so-called 'new generation' lamps) with a high efficacy combined with good colour rendering. Moreover, by varying the mixture ratio of the phosphors a wide range of colour temperatures from 2500 K upwards can be obtained. If these phosphors are applied in tubes of smaller diameter (e.g. 25 mm) an efficacy of 100 lm/W can be obtained.

7.3.2 Colour Designations

White fluorescent lamps are generally grouped according to their colour appearance and the balance existing between efficacy and colour rendering.

Table 7.2 Fluorescent lamp colour designations

Colour appearance	High efficacy & good colour rendering			High efficacy & moderate colour rendering			Moderate efficacy & good colour rendering			Truest colour rendering		
	lm/W*	Ra**		lm/W	Ra		lm/W	Ra		lm/W	Ra	
Warm ca. 3000 K	/83	80	86	/29	76	52	/32	49	85	/27	44	94
Intermediate ca. 4000 K	/84	80	86	/33	79	66	/34	51	86	/37	43	96
										/47	44	97
Cool ca. 6500 K	/86	80	85	/54	65	75	/55	50	93	/57	47	93

* Efficacy in lumen/watt
** Colour rendering index

Colour type	Colour designation	Colour temp. (K)	Colour rendering	Special charact.	Typical applications
Warm white	29	3000	Moderate		Outdoor lighting
	32	3000	Good		Suitable for use in kitchens, shops, stores, theatres, restaurants, conference rooms, private offices
	83	3000	Good		Areas covered by the colour 32 lamp calling for good colour rendering and high efficacy
	27	2700	Excellent	Very low UV output	Home lighting, restaurants, theatres, museums, art galleries, etc. where a warmer white colour and a better colour rendering than that given by the colour 32 are considered important
White	33	4200	Moderate		Factories, workshops, etc. where the demands on colour rendering are not high
	34	3800	Good		Offices, schools, display windows and shop interiors in general
	84	4000	Good		Areas covered by the colour 33 and 34 lamps calling for good colour rendering and high efficacy
	37	4200	Excellent	Very low UV output	Exhibitions, museums, art galleries, hospitals
	47	5000	Excellent		Colour comparisons in the graphics industry, general lighting in clothing and fabric retailers
Cool	54	6500	Moderate		Because of its cool appearance this lamp is used predominantly for general lighting purposes in tropical countries
	55	6500	Good		Colour comparison of raw materials, textiles, etc.
	57	7400	Excellent	Added UV output	Specially developed as a colour comparison lamp for the tobacco and textile industries
	86	6000	Good		Areas covered by the colour 54 and 55 lamps calling for good colour rendering and high efficacy.

Colour appearance, that is to say whether a particular lamp creates a warm, intermediate or cool colour impression, is denoted by one of the three type names 'warm white', 'white' or 'daylight'. The corresponding approximate colour temperature of the three types are 3000 K, 4000 K and 6500 K respectively. A warm white lamp is one that will combine well with incandescent lamps; a white lamp will combine reasonably well with both incandescent lamps and daylight, while a daylight lamp is one that will combine well only with daylight.

The differences in terms of efficacy and colour rendering between lamps falling in the same group as regards colour appearance can be denoted by the use of appropriate trade names or, as is the case illustrated in table 7.2, by the use of a numerical colour designation suffix.

The application fields of the various tubular fluorescent lamps, listed according to colour designation, may be summarised as in table 7.3.

7.3.3 Type Designations

Other factors influencing the choice of a tubular fluorescent lamp for a given application, in addition to its colour designation, are its wattage and its physical size.

Fluorescent lamps are commonly available in wattages ranging from 15 to 125 watt, depending upon type. The physical size of a given lamp type is very much dependent upon the wattage: in general, the higher the wattage the longer the tube. The outer tube diameter of most existing tube types is standard, although miniature tubes of much smaller length and diameter are also available.

Table 7.4 lists a selection of the lamp types most widely used for lighting purposes.

7.4 High-pressure Discharge Lamps

The light from a high-pressure discharge lamp is produced by passing a current through a gas under high-pressure contained in a small discharge tube. Unlike that of the fluorescent lamp, this discharge tube is enclosed in an outer bulb or tube, one of the functions of which is to protect the discharge tube from atmospheric influences.

7.4.1 High-pressure Mercury Lamps (HP)

Under normal conditions of operation the gas atmosphere of the discharge tube in a high-pressure mercury lamp (figure 7.10) consists of vaporised mercury at a pressure of between 0.2 MPa and 1 MPa. To facilitate ignition, a small quantity of inert gas is added.

The discharge tube, which is of quartz, has a main electrode sealed into each end. Adjacent to one of these electrodes is an auxiliary starting electrode. The glass outer bulb normally contains an inert gas (at atmospheric

Table 7.4 The main distinguishing features of the most widely used fluorescent lamp types

Type designation	Main distinguishing features
'TL' Standard	The most commonly used fluorescent lamp type. Suitable for the majority of general lighting applications.
'TL' Coloured	Identical as regards dimensions and electrical characteristics with lamps in the 'standard' range but available in four colours: red, blue, yellow and green.
'TL' Miniature	Short, small diameter, low-wattage lamps. Much used for concealed lighting effects, showcase lighting in galleries etc. and for decorative lighting. General lighting in boats, caravans, etc.
'TL' Slimline	Instant-start lamps giving reliable, flicker-free ignition down to $-18\,°C$. Available in 26 mm diameter version as well as the normal diameter of 38 mm.
'TL' D	Small diameter lamps much used for decorative lighting.
'TL' E	These are, in effect, 'standard' tubes bent into a ring form to give a compacter light source.
'TL' F	The F indicates 'reflector'. These lamps have an additional, highly reflective coating between the fluorescent phosphor and the inside of the glass tube. This reflective coating covers about two-thirds of the glass surface, the light being radiated at increased intensity through the remaining third of the lamp's surface.
'TL' H	These lamps give their optimum light output at a higher ambient temperature than do other fluorescent lamps. Much used in closed luminaires to increase light output at the high operating temperatures prevailing.
'TL' U	These are compact, U-shaped 'standard' lamps.
'TL' MRS	These lamps are capable of being dimmed, and ignition is flicker free.
'TL' RS	The RS stands for 'rapid start'. Ignition is almost instantaneous.
'TL' S	These are instant start lamps that can be operated either with choke ballasts or with special stabilizing incandescent lamps.
'TL' X	These lamps are designed for use in explosive atmospheres. The lamp caps have long thick pins which are so shaped as to provide maximum surface contact in special lampholders, so excluding all possibility of sparking at the moment of ignition.

pressure when the lamp is operating) which, in addition to protecting the discharge tube and its lead-in wires from atmospheric influences at the high operating temperatures prevailing, stabilises the arc discharge by maintaining a near constant temperature over the normal range of ambient conditions.

High-pressure mercury lamps are of basically two types: clear glass (HP and HP/T) and phosphor-coated (HPL, HPL-N, HPLR and HPLR-N).

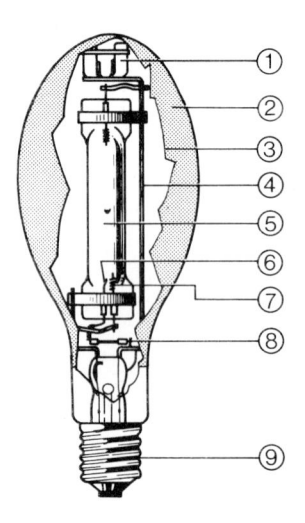

Figure 7.10 High-pressure mercury fluorescent lamp. 1. Support spring 2. Ovoid hard-glass outer envelope 3. Inner phosphor coating 4. Lead-in wire/support 5. Quartz discharge tube 6. Auxiliary electrode 7. Main electrode 8. Starting resistor 9. Screw base.

Clear-glass lamps. These are characterised by their bluish-white colour appearance, although the arc in fact produces a line spectrum (see colour plate 5) with emission within the visible region at the blue, green and yellow wavelengths, there being an absence of red radiation. Their luminous efficacy ranges from 40 lm/W for an 80 W lamp to more than 50 lm/W for a 400 W lamp (figure 7.11a).

Phosphor-coated lamps. The pure mercury arc has both poor colour appearance and colour rendering, but emits a significant portion of its energy in the ultraviolet region of the spectrum, i.e. between 100 nm and 400 nm. By the use of a phosphor coating on the inside of the outer envelope, as is done in the fluorescent versions of this lamp, this ultraviolet energy can be made to introduce a red component (see colour plate 5), which greatly improves the lamp's colour appearance.

The improvement in efficacy is slight (about 10 per cent) as the eye's sensitivity to red is low and, in addition, some of the visible radiation generated by the discharge is absorbed by the fluorescent coating.

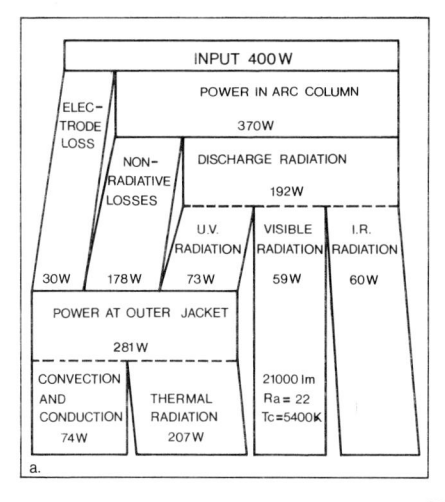

Figure 7.11 Power conversion in (a) a clear-glass mercury lamp (b) a high-pressure sodium lamp.

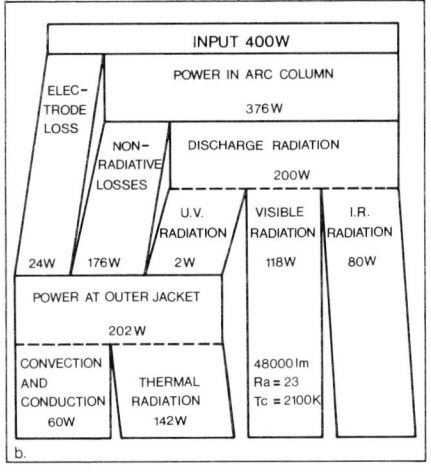

The HPLR and HPLR-N lamps, which are derived from the normal HPL and HPL-N lamps, are in fact reflectorised versions of the latter. Each has its bulb coated over part of its inner surface with a reflective powder.

The main advantages of the mercury discharge lamp are its long life and its low price in comparison with other high-pressure gas discharge lamps. These points make this type of lamp eminently suitable for the lighting of large areas in which high intensity lamps are wanted, but where colour rendering is not of primary importance, although the higher efficacy of the high-pressure sodium lamp (see Sec. 7.4.4) may well serve to tip the balance in its favour should energy costs continue to rise.

7.4.2 Blended Light Lamp (MLL-N)

The blended light lamp (figure 7.12) consists of a gas-filled bulb coated on its inside with a phosphor and containing a mercury discharge tube connected in series with a tungsten filament. The filament acts as a ballast for the discharge, so stabilising the lamp current. No other ballast is needed.

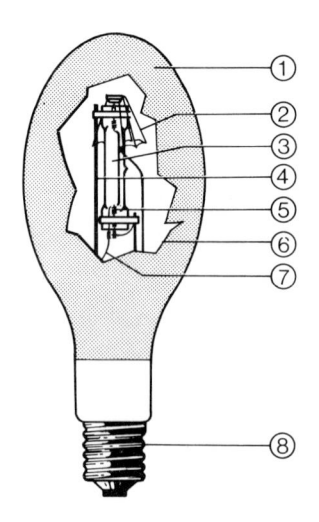

Figure 7.12 Part-section of a blended-light lamp showing 1. Ovoid hard-glass outer envelope 2. Coiled filament 3. Quartz discharge tube 4. Support 5. Main electrode 6. Internal phosphor coating 7. Lead-in wire 8. Screw base.

The blended light lamp, like the HPL-N phosphor-coated lamp from which it is derived, emits visible radiation from the mercury discharge tube plus that obtained by conversion of the ultraviolet radiation at the phosphor coating. The additional, incandescent filament of the blended-light lamp adds its own warm-coloured light to this visible radiation to give the lamp a more pleasant colour appearance.

Blended light lamps can, by virtue of the built-in ballast, be connected direct to the mains. This means that existing lighting installations employing incandescent lamps can easily be modernised using blended light lamps, which have almost twice the efficacy and five times the operating life, at no extra cost in terms of special gear, wiring or luminaires. However, compared with HPL lamps they have lower efficacy and a shorter life.

7.4.3 Metal Halide Lamps (HPI)

Metal halide lamps (see figure 7.13) are very similar in construction to the high-pressure mercury lamp, the major difference being that the metal halide discharge tube contains one or more metal halides in addition to mercury. These halides are partly vaporised when the lamp reaches its normal operating temperature. The halide vapour is then dissociated in the hot central region of the arc into the halogen and the metal, with the metal radiating its appropriate spectrum.

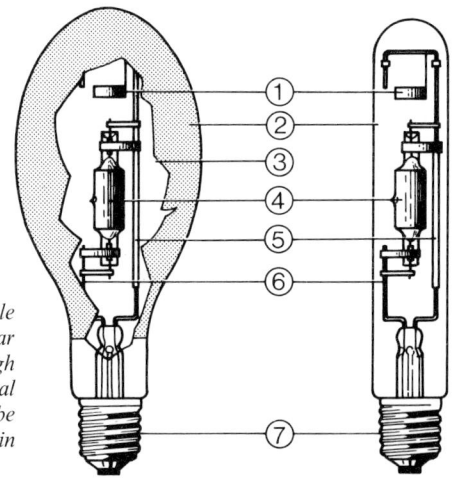

Figure 7.13 Metal halide lamps are available in two versions: diffuse ovoid and clear tubular. 1. Getter ring for maintaining high vacuum 2. Hard-glass outer bulb 3. Internal phosphor coating 4. Quartz discharge tube 5. Sleeve protecting the support 6. Lead-in wire/support 7. Screw base.

A number of different metal halide lamps have been developed. A typical combination of halides used is that comprising the iodides of sodium, indium and thallium. These halides give an increase in intensity in three spectral bands, viz. blue, green and yellow-red. Colour rendering is improved in comparison with that of the high-pressure mercury lamp. Efficacy is also increased considerably; this is because the radiation emitted lies in the region of the spectrum to which the eyes are highly sensitive. The result is a lamp with reasonable colour rendering (an R_a of 70 is possible) and an efficacy of 80 lm/W for a 400 watt lamp.

Its application remains mostly limited to floodlighting and sports-field lighting, there being an essential need here for a compact (thus easily focussed) source giving 'white' light.

7.4.4 High-pressure Sodium Lamps (SON)

A more recently developed discharge lamp having about twice the efficacy of the high-pressure mercury lamp is the high-pressure sodium lamp, figure 7.14. It has been known for a long time that sodium gives a higher proportion or radiation in the visible range than mercury. However, the presence of sodium in the discharge tube necessitates the use of wall materials resistant to sodium at relatively high temperatures. Quartz, which is used as wall material for the discharge tube of the high-pressure mercury lamp, is affected by sodium at these high temperatures and so cannot be used. Finally, translucent sintered alumina, a material resistant to sodium at high temperatures was discovered. This also transmits visible radiation well, and is, therefore, suitable as a material for a sodium discharge tube.

Whereas the energy of the visible radiation in a 400 watt lamp is about 60 watt in the case of a mercury discharge, it is double that, i.e. about 120 watt, in the case of a sodium discharge (figure 7.11b). Luminous efficacy thus rises by about a factor of 2 to over 120 lm/W.

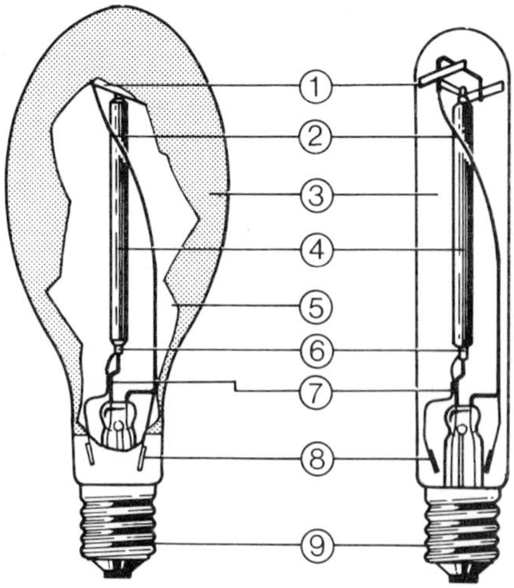

Figure 7.14 High-pressure sodium lamps are available in two versions: diffuse ovoid and clear tubular. 1 Support springs to maintain discharge tube alignment 2. Lead-in wire 3. Hard-glass outer bulb 4. Translucent aluminium oxide discharge tube 5. Inner phosphor coating 6. End cap of discharge tube 7. Lead-in wire/support 8. Getter rings for maintaining high vacuum 9. Screw base.

Colour rendering and colour appearance are at best passable; still, lighting using this lamp is usually found to be more pleasant than mercury-lamp lighting and we may expect its greater efficacy gradually to result in the sodium lamp being preferred to the mercury lamp for certain applications, such as indoor lighting in heavy industry, but primarily in outdoor lighting applications.

Special versions of the high-pressure sodium lamp have in fact been developed (SON/H) that can be used to replace the high-pressure mercury lamps in existing installations, without the necessity of changing the ballast or adding a starter system. These lamps consume less power than the mercury lamp they replace (up to 15 per cent less) for a higher luminous flux (up to 25 per cent higher).

7.5 Control gear

7.5.1 Ballasts

All discharge lamps, including fluorescent lamps, need a series impedance to limit the lamp current. Were such a device not used, there would be nothing to prevent this current from increasing to the point where lamp destruction takes place. Such an impedance is called a ballast and forms part of the control gear necessary for the operation of these lamps.

Apart from providing good stabilisation of the lamp current, the ballast must

(a) Have a high power factor to ensure economic use of the supply system.
(b) Generate a minimum of harmonics.
(c) Present a high impedance to audio frequencies.
(d) Offer adequate suppression of radio interference caused by the lamp.
(e) In many cases, furnish the correct starting conditions for the lamp concerned.

Another group of requirements is constituted by the wish of both the luminaire manufacturer and the user to have available ballasts of small dimensions, low losses, long life and very low hum level.

An effective form of ballast is the reactor, or choke, placed in series with the lamp (figure 7.15a). Inherently, the power factor of this circuit is low, viz. about 0.5 lagging. This can be increased to 0.85 or greater quite simply by connecting a capacitor in shunt across the a.c. supply (figure 7.15b).

Because of the waveform distortion produced by discharge lamps it is not possible to correct the power factor to unity by a shunt connected capacitor. An overall power factor approaching unity can be achieved, however, by combining the uncorrected 0.5 lagging circuit with a circuit that gives a 0.5 lead. A leading power factor of 0.5 can be obtained by connecting a suitable capacitor in series with the choke ballast (figure 7.15c). The resulting twin-lamp lead-lag circuit with a near-unity power factor is illustrated in figure 7.15d.

Ballasts for fluorescent lamps are grouped according to whether they are for a.c. or d.c. operation. A.C. ballasts are sub-divided into two types: those suitable for use with switch start lamps and those for use with starterless lamps (see Sec. 7.5.2). The twin-lamp lead-lag circuit described above is typical of the sort used with switch start lamps. A typical circuit for use with starterless lamps is illustrated in figure 7.16a. Figure 7.16b shows a starterless circuit that uses the so-called semi-resonant ballast. This circuit has the advantages of high power factor (0.95 or greater) and reliable starting at very low temperatures (down to −20 °C).

Fluorescent lamps can be operated from a d.c. supply using resistance stabilisers. There are, however, so many restrictions to their use that this method is rarely employed in practice. A far more convenient method of stabilisation is afforded by special d.c. transistor ballasts.

The transistor ballast converts the supply voltage from d.c. to a.c., provides for ignition of the lamp and stabilises the lamp current. Because of the high

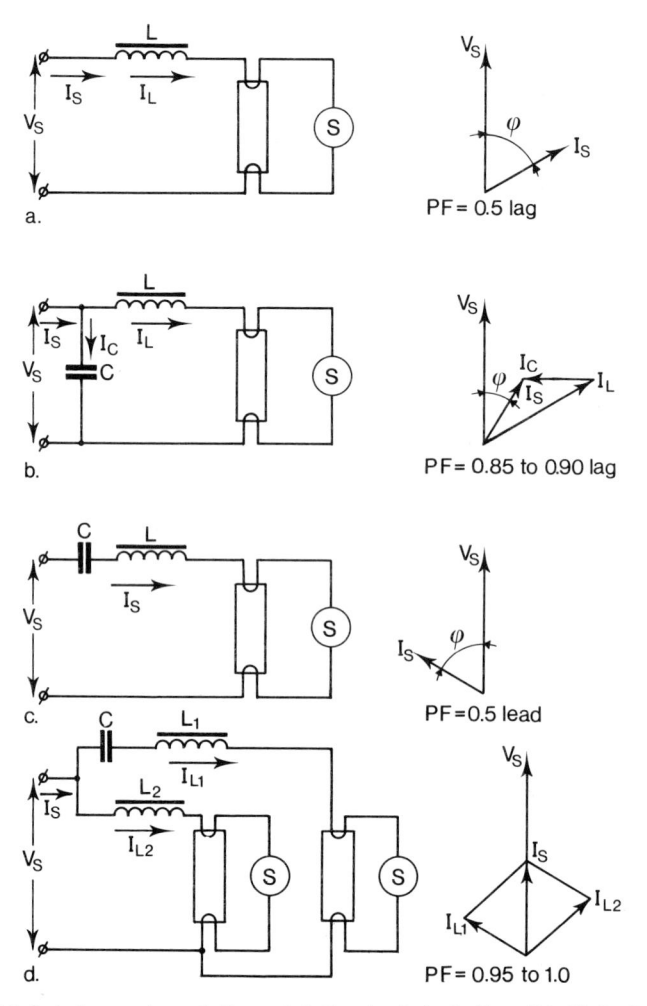

Figure 7.15 Switch-start lamp ballasts (a) Simple choke ballast (b) Choke ballast with parallel connected compensating capacitor (c) Choke ballast with series connected compensating capacitor (d) Ballasts a and c combined to obtain optimum power factor (PF) correction.

frequencies used (20 kHz or higher) the ballast is silent in operation. Transistor ballasts are employed where only a d.c. supply is available and where, in spite of this, one wishes to exploit the advantages of fluorescent lighting. This is often the case in the lighting of public transport vehicles, caravans, etc. Transistor ballasts are also much used in connection with emergency lighting.

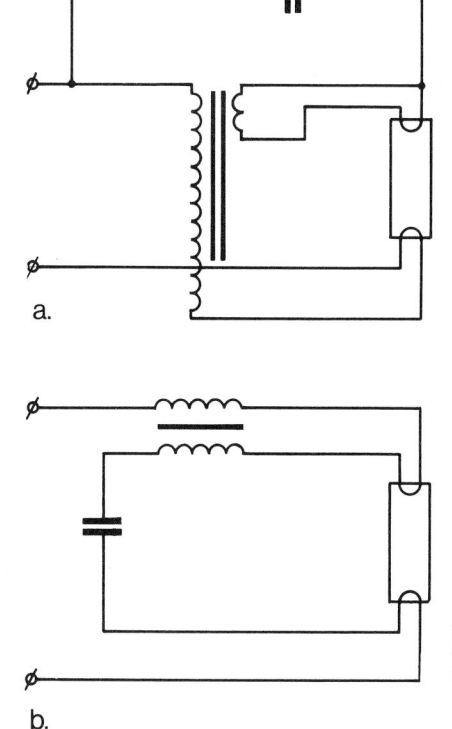

Figure 7.16 Starterless fluorescent lamp ballasts (a) Inductive ballast with preheating transformer (b) Semi-resonant ballast.

7.5.2 Starters and Ignitors

Most arc-discharge lamps need a voltage higher than that of the mains supply to initiate the discharge. In general, where this is the case, the lamp concerned must be operated in conjunction with some form of starting device. This device may constitute a separate item of control gear or it may form an integral part of the ballast, depending on the lamp type concerned.

In the case of fluorescent lamps, those of the preheat switch-start type are started by heating the lamp electrodes before application of the high starting voltage. This preheating, which may take a few seconds, is usually accomplished by a starter switch which, after short-circuiting the lamp by placing the lamp electrodes in series across the output of the ballast, then opens, applying the high choke voltage to the lamp. The transient voltage caused by the opening of the switch causes the lamp to ignite. If the lamp does not strike the first time, the process is repeated.

Starterless fluorescent lamps are of two types: rapid start and instant start. The electrodes of a rapid start lamp are heated continuously, from the moment of switch on, from low-voltage windings built into the ballast.

Since the ignition 'kick' supplied by the action of the starter is not available, these lamps are provided with an external ignition strip to aid starting. In an instant start fluorescent lamp, ignition is dependent solely on the application of a high voltage across the lamp, this voltage being supplied by the ballast. All starterless lamps are given a transparent, water-repellent coating on the outside of the tube for reliable starting under humid conditions. The efficacy of these lamps is in general lower than that of standard fluorescent lamps of the same power rating.

Of the discharge lamps, the halide and the high-pressure sodium lamps require an auxiliary starting device.

A metal halide lamp can be started with a thyristor ignitor, connected across the lamp. The ignitor generates a series of high-voltage pulses (600–700 volts peak), which cease when the lamp starts.

High-pressure sodium lamps also need a peak voltage in order to ensure ignition which, depending upon the lamp type, can be obtained from a starter device either built into the lamp itself or contained in the luminaire.

Chapter 8

Luminaires and Other Equipment

8.1 Luminaires

A luminaire is a device that controls the distribution of the light given by a lamp or lamps and which includes all the items necessary for fixing and protecting those lamps and for connecting them to the supply circuit.
The first part of this chapter takes a look at some of the basic luminaire types currently used in interior lighting, and touches briefly on the subject of luminaire classification.

8.1.1 Basic Luminaire Types

Luminaires may be conveniently divided into three groups according to the type of lamp used, viz., fluorescent, high-intensity discharge and incandescent.

Luminaires for fluorescent lamps

General-lighting types. The general-lighting luminaire housing one or more tubular fluorescent lamps is the type most frequently used in commercial lighting applications, e.g. in shops, stores, offices, etc. Is is also the preferred type for use in many industrial applications where the mounting height is less than about five to six metres.
The range of luminaires of this type is extensive. In its simplest form, the fluorescent luminaire consists of a batten mounting in which is housed the control gear for the fully exposed lamp. At the other end of the range is the multi-lamp ventilated luminaire complete with reflectors (mirror or otherwise) and metal louvre or prismatic cover. What distinguishes one type of luminaire from another is the type of light control used (and hence the type of luminous intensity and luminance distribution), the number of lamps employed, or the method of mounting. (See table 8.1.)
First the light control, the primary purpose of which is to direct the light in the required directions whilst reducing it in directions in which it might cause glare discomfort. The only luminaire commonly used without any form of

Table 8.1 Fluorescent-lamp luminaires – some basic types

Luminaire cross-section	Description	Light-control element(s)	Mounting	Typical luminous intensity* distribution
	batten luminaires and attachments	none	surface or suspended	
		single-sided reflector		
		wrap-around diffuser		
		trough reflector		
		slotted trough reflector		
		slotted trough reflector plus square-mesh louvre		
		slotted trough reflector plus transverse (lamellae) louvre		
	closed-top box luminaires and attachments	mirror reflectors with louvre shielding	surface or recessed	
		prismatic diffusing panel		
		square-mesh louvre		
		transverse louvre		
		diffusing panel	surface or semi-recessed	
		wrap-around diffusing panel	surface only	

* Distribution in the longitudinal plane is shown dotted

light control is the above-mentioned single-lamp batten. The majority of luminaires, however, incorporate reflectors (enamelled or mirrored, with or without louvre shielding), louvres, prismatic panels or opalescent diffusing panels.

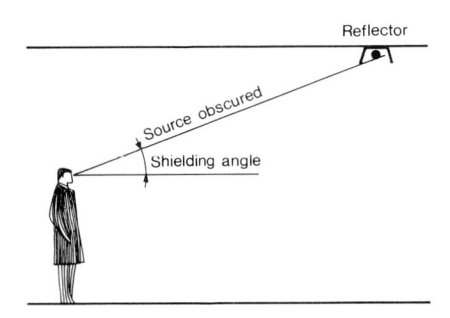

Figure 8.1 Glare control by shielding. The term 'cutt-off angle' is sometimes used in place of shielding angle. The cut-off angle is the complementary angle of the shielding angle.

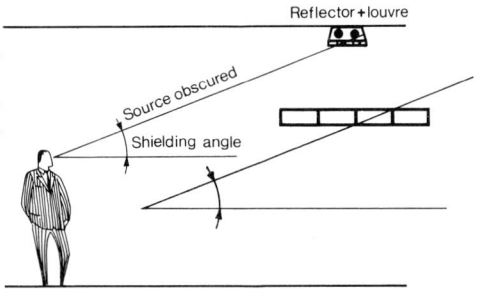

A reflector directs the light into the desired solid angle and so gives it a directional character. The shadow effect is strongest where the reflector is of the mirrored-finish type. In some cases the reflector itself is designed to provide a certain degree of lamp shielding, but where more effective shielding is required, some form of louvre is added (figure 8.1).
A louvre, in shielding the lamps from direct view, also serves to reduce the luminance of the luminaire in directions where it could otherwise cause glare.
There are basically three types of louvre: square-mesh, diamond-mesh and lamellae. Louvres of the square-mesh and diamond-mesh types, which are widely used with the reflectorless box-type luminaire, give both longitudinal and lateral screening. The lamellae louvre, in which the screening strips run at right angles to the axes of the lamps, gives longitudinal screening only; lateral screening in this case has to come either from the walls of the luminaire itself or from the lower edges of the mirror reflectors which are

often employed in conjunction with louvres of this type. The louvres may be made from thin strips of white opalescent plastics or metal. In some cases, however, the strip is given a V-shaped cross-section and a mirror finish to help reduce still further the luminaire's brightness.

A prismatic diffuser (or refractor) panel serves to give the light some slight directional character, whilst reducing the luminance of the luminaire in directions where glare could cause discomfort. These panels are generally available in a variety of patterns to offer a choice of lighting effect.

The luminace of a luminaire fitted with an opalescent diffusing panel is virtually uniform in all directions. Such a luminaire does not, therefore, afford the directional control of the light needed for efficient high illuminance installations. The lighting produced by the 'wrap-around' type of diffuser has the lowest shadow effect of all the luminaires described here.

Luminaires are either recessed into the ceiling, mounted on its surface or suspended from some part of the ceiling or roof structure. Box-type luminaires are designed mainly for recessed or surface mounting. The batten luminaire, with or without attachments, is normally mounted on or suspended from the ceiling or some part of the ceiling structure, or else suspended from special trunking erected specifically for the purpose.

Table 8.2 IEC classification of luminaires according to degree of moisture protection

Luminaire class	Symbol	Description
0		No protection against water.
2	Drip-proof	Protection against drops of liquid. Drops of liquid shall have no harmful effect when the luminaire is tilted at any angle up to 15° from the vertical.
3	Rain-proof	Protection against rain. Rain falling at an angle equal to or less than 60° from the vertical shall have no harmful effect.
4	Splash-proof	Protection against splashing. Liquid splashed from any direction shall have no harmful effect.
5	Jet-proof	Protection against jets of water. Water projected by a nozzle from any direction under stated conditions shall have no harmful effect.
7	Watertight	Protection against immersion in water. It must not be possible for water to enter the luminaire under stated conditions of pressure and time.

Luminaires for use in special areas. Two further important types of fluorescent luminaire are those suitable for use in moisture and dust-laden atmospheres and those designed for use in hazardous areas.

Fluorescent luminaires intended for use in moisture or dust-laden atmospheres are of two types. In one type the lamp or lamps are fully exposed to the surrounding atmosphere, but the connection between lamp cap and lampholder is sealed by means of a rubber gasket. In the other, the lamp or lamps are protected by a plastics cover which is sealed to the housing. The exact nature of the sealing in each case determines the degree of resistance of the luminaires to the ingress of water and dust (see tables 8.2 and 8.3). Where the danger of breakage exists, the exposed lamps of the former type can be protected by enclosing them individually in special plastics tubes.

There are two main types of luminaire used in the lighting of hazardous areas, that is to say areas where explosive gases or vapours, or volatile liquids may be present.

One type is designed to withstand the pressure caused by an internal explosion, so preventing the ignition of a potentially explosive atmosphere surrounding the luminaire. This means that the luminaire must be of sturdy construction; for example, the housing must be made of steel or cast iron and the cover of hard glass. Luminaires of this type bear the internationally agreed symbol Ex_d.

Table 8.3 IEC classification of luminaires according to degree of dust protection

Luminaire class	Symbol	Description
0		No protection against ingress of solid foreign bodies.
1		Protection against ingress of large, solid foreign bodies.
2		Protection against ingress of medium-sized, solid foreign bodies.
3		Protection against ingress of small, solid foreign bodies.
5	Dust-proof	Protection against harmful deposits of dust. The ingress of dust is not totally prevented, but dust cannot enter in an amount sufficient to interfere with satisfactory operation of the equipment.
6	Dust-tight	Protection against ingress of dust. The ingress of dust is totally prevented.

The other type makes use of a 'restricted-breathing' cover to virtually eliminate the possibility of explosive gases entering the housing. If, despite this precaution, explosive substances should find their way into the lamp compartment, special safety devices in the circuitry and the switching equipment ensure that no explosion can occur. The lamps used, either one or two in number, are of the 'TL' X type. (See Chapter 7 Lamps Sec. 7.3.3). Luminaires of this type bear the internationally agreed symbol Ex_e.

Emergency Lighting Luminaires. Emergency lighting is defined as lighting that is designed to come into operation when the normal lighting fails. (See also Chapter 9 The Electrical Installation Sec. 9.3.1) Perhaps the most reliable form of emergency lighting is that employing individual battery-powered luminaires, as opposed to that in which the luminaires derive their power from some centralised, and therefore inherently more vulnerable, source. Each luminaire has its own battery which is charged whilst 'floating' across the mains. If the mains supply (and hence the normal lighting) breaks down, the battery is automatically switched in. When power is restored the battery goes back on charge. The capacity of the battery is generally sufficient to keep the lamp alight for an hour or more.

Table 8.4 Typical High-bay Luminaires

Luminaire cross-section	Light-control element	Typical luminous intensity distribution
	vitreous enamel reflector	
	anodised aluminium reflector	
	anodised aluminium reflector	

Luminaires for High-Intensity Discharge Lamps

In those industrial interiors where the luminaires are to be mounted at heights greater than about five or six metres above the floor, use can be made of the increased luminous flux of single high-intensity discharge (H.I.D.) lamps housed in reflector luminaires (table 8.4) without the local illuminances becoming too high, as would be the case were these lamps to be mounted any lower.

These, high-bay, luminaires are often of two-piece construction for ease of maintenance. One part, the housing, to which the reflector is attached, contains the lampholder. It is suspended from a cap which contains the ballast, the power factor compensating capacitors and electrical connections. The two parts are held together by means of quick-release clips. The lamp and reflector are thus easily removed for maintenance purposes.

Luminaires for Incandescent Lamps

The vast majority of incandescent lamp luminaires used in interior lighting are designed for domestic use. Of these, spotlights and downlights are much used in interior lighting in general.

The spotlight is a small, directional lighting luminaire that is used mainly to provide accent lighting. Those available in a given range are often built up from a common basic unit, the spotlight body. The body can be fitted with different lamps and attachments to suit the needs of the application. The lamps used are of the pressed-glass, blown-bulb and bowl-reflector types. Coloured lamps, reflectors and filters can be employed to produce coloured light. Screening attachments can be used in combination with different lamp types and reflectors to provide the desired degree of beam cut-off.

The downlight is, in effect, a special type of spotlight that can be suspended from or built-into the ceiling such that all the light is distributed downward. By employing different types of lamps, reflectors, lenses, diaphragms and louvres, downlights can be made to distribute their light in a wide variety of patterns, the lamp itself being hidden for normal angles of view. The downlight mounting can be either adjustable or fixed. The adjustable type, or the appropriately angled fixed type, will allow light to be directed to walls and other vertical surfaces.

8.1.2 Luminaire Light Output Ratio

The light output ratio of a luminaire (the term used in the USA is 'luminaire efficiency') is defined as the ratio of the light output of the luminaire to the sum of the individual light outputs of the lamps operating outside the luminaire. Notice, however, that the definition says nothing about how the light from the luminaire is distributed. The light output ratio (l.o.r.) so defined is, in fact, the total l.o.r. of the luminaire and is equal to the sum of the upward and downward l.o.r.'s. The light emitted upwards from the luminaire will only contribute to the illuminance at the working plane indirectly, that is to say, via reflection from the ceiling. What is needed, therefore, for optimum utilisation of lighting energy are luminaires in which the *downward* light output ratio is as high as possible.

Luminaires with reflectors but without screening have the highest light output ratio. Where the possibility of glare arising is of minor importance, such luminaires should automatically be the first choice.

Of the luminaires with screening, those with lamellae louvres have, in general, the highest light output ratios and those with opal diffusers the lowest.

8.1.3 Luminaire Classification

Luminaires may be loosely classified in many ways. It is quite usual, for example, to prefix the word luminaire with a term describing the type of lamp used. The prefix can equally well be a reference to the application for which the luminaire was designed, e.g. industrial, commercial or perhaps more specifically high-bay industrial, commercial display lighting. The method of mounting employed can also serve as a classifying tag, e.g. recessed, semi-recessed, pendant, bracket, and so forth.

Luminaires can be more tightly specified in terms of their optical performance. Luminaires were originally classified in this way in order to simplify the specification of the utilisation factor. (See Chapter 13 Calculations and Measurements.) Using such a system of luminaire classification, the utilisation factor for a particular luminaire type could be found from a set of standard utilisation factor tables. However, there seems to be little need any more for this type of classification because luminaire manufacturers publish comprehensive tables of utilisation factors for each luminaire type in their programme.

The British IES classifies luminaires according to the distribution of the downward component. The British Zonal (BZ) System, as this system is called, classifies a luminaire's luminous intensity distribution according to one of ten hypothetical polar distributions. The system makes it possible to assign most luminaires to one of ten categories, i.e. to give it a BZ number from 1 to 10 corresponding to one of ten hypothetical distributions (figure 8.2), the number rising as the spread of downward light becomes greater.

Features of construction affording safety to the user and protection of the luminaire itself against the harmful deposit of dust and moisture – features that are frequently of even greater importance than optical performance – are also often used for classification purposes.

Luminaire class	Distribution
BZ 1	$I \propto \cos^4 \theta$
BZ 2	$I \propto \cos^3 \theta$
BZ 3	$I \propto \cos^2 \theta$
BZ 4	$I \propto \cos^{1.5} \theta$
BZ 5	$I \propto \cos \theta$
BZ 6	$I \propto (1 + 2 \cos \theta)$
BZ 7	$I \propto (2 + \cos \theta)$
BZ 8	I constant
BZ 9	$I \propto (1 + \sin \theta)$
BZ 10	$I \propto \sin \theta$

Figure 8.2 British Zonal (BZ) classification of luminaires showing the equations of the ten hypothetical polar distributions BZ1 to BZ10 and the polar curves of some common luminaire types (BZ2 to BZ7).

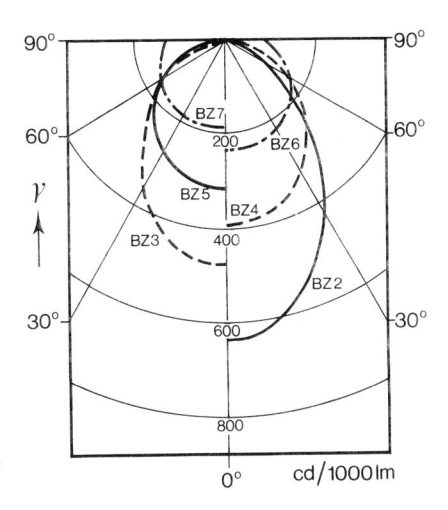

Table 8.5 CEE classification of luminaires according to type of electrical protection

Luminaire class	Electrical protection
0	A luminaire having functional insulation, but not double insulation or reinforced insulation throughout, and without provision for earthing.
I	A luminaire having at least functional insulation throughout and provided with an earthing terminal or earthing contact, and, for luminaires designed for connection by means of a flexible cable or cord, provided with either an appliance inlet with earthing contact, or a non-detachable flexible cable or cord with earthing conductor and a plug with earthing contact.
II	A luminaire with double insulation and/or reinforced insulation throughout and without provision for earthing.
III	A luminaire designed for connection to extra-low-voltage circuits, and which has no circuits, either internal or external, which operate at a voltage other than extra-low safety voltage.

A classification based on the degree of protection afforded by a luminaire against the penetration of moisture or dust is that made by the IEC. (See again tables 8.2 and 8.3 respectively.)

Finally, luminaires may also be classified, as is done by the CEE, according to the degree of protection afforded against electrical shock, table 8.5.

8.2 Other lighting Equipment

Three further items of lighting equipment, in addition to the lamps and luminaires already dealt with, are worthy of consideration here. These are integrated ceiling systems, power tracks and light regulators (or dimmers).

8.2.1 Integrated Ceilings

The physical integration of lighting, ventilation or airconditioning, and acoustics involves the use of special air-handling luminaires assembled in company with air supply diffusers and acoustic panels to form what is known as an integrated ceiling system.

The principles of ventilation, air-conditioning and acoustics are dealt with at some length in Chapter 5. The principal features of three commonly used systems – ducted-supply/plenum-exhaust, plenum-supply/ducted-exhaust and ducted-supply/ducted-exhaust – are also outlined in that Chapter. The present section takes a look at the sort of hardware employed in each of these systems.

Most ceiling systems involve a false ceiling suspended from the structural ceiling. For plenum-type air-conditioning systems the false ceiling is, of course, essential, but such a ceiling is often used even with double-ducted systems, the space above it (i.e. the plenum) in this case being used to hide the runs of ducting and so forth.

The false ceiling is built up using a suspended ceiling grid. The main function of this grid is to provide a rigid structure (figure 8.3) in which the ceiling and other components of the system, viz. air-handling luminaires, air diffusers and ceiling panels can be mounted to form the complete ceiling system, but it can also serve as a top support for partition walls.

The type of luminaire and air diffuser employed will depend on which of the three systems of air handling is chosen, figure 8.4. Where the return air is exhausted through the plenum (figure 8.4.a) the luminaires will be of the slotted-top variety. The air diffusers (figure 8.5) may be either elongated or circular. The elongated diffuser (figure 8.5a) will generally contain a baffle to create turbulence, with the air being delivered at an angle to the vertical and away from the luminaire to ensure that it produces sufficient downward penetration without being carried away via the luminaire. These

Figure 8.3 Suspended ceiling grid.

diffusers can be mounted in the ceiling separately, joined to form continuous rows (as illustrated in figure 8.4a) or combined with the luminaires (as shown in figure 8.4c).

Circular diffusers (figure 8.5b) can also provide an adjustable supply of highly turbulent air. These diffusers are installed as individual units at suitable points in the ceiling.

Where the plenum is used for the supply of conditioned air, (injection) strip air diffusers can be used – figure 8.5c. The strip diffuser is generally equal in length to the ceiling panels, between which they are mounted end to end to form continuous rows across the ceiling. The supply air is delivered vertically downward through these strips. Because of the extremely large number of openings involved, the incoming air mixes freely with the air in the room without causing discomfort to the occupants. The luminaire used in this system of air handling again has a slotted top, but in this case it is fitted with a plenum box (see figure 8.4b), that is, a sort of inverted tray covering the slots and forming an interface between these and the flexible exhaust ducting.

175

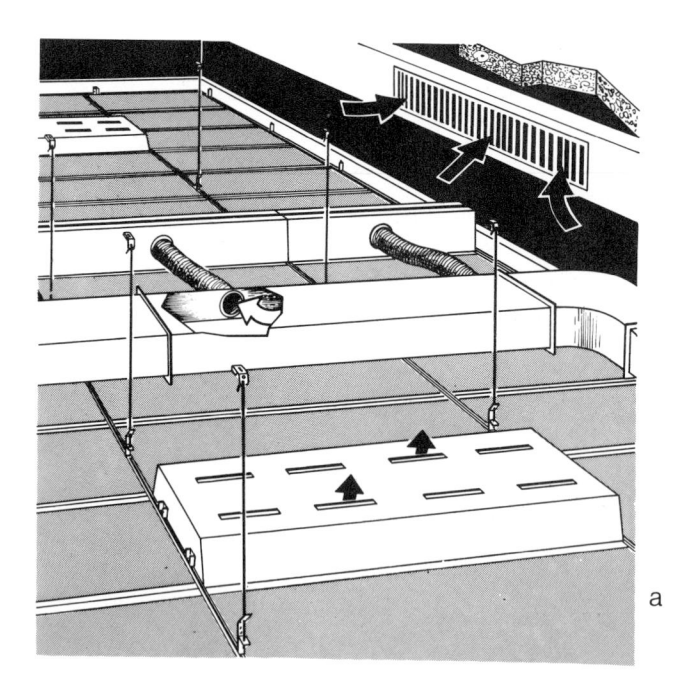

Figure 8.4 The three systems of air handling (a) Ducted-supply/plenum-exhaust (b) Plenum-supply/ducted-exhaust (c) Ducted-supply/ducted-exhaust showing, in each case, a typical layout of the luminaires and air supply diffusers.

Fig. 8.4c

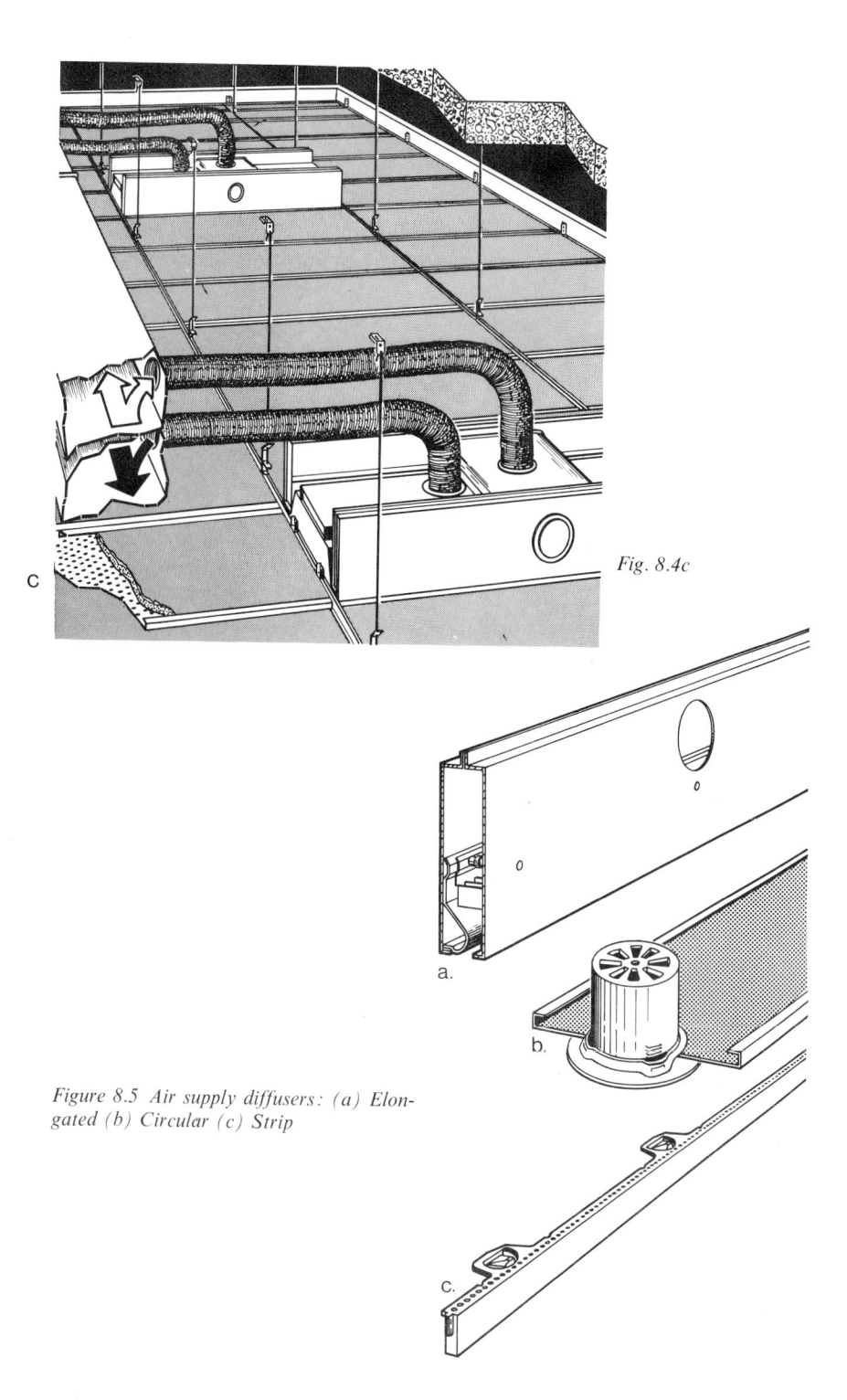

Figure 8.5 Air supply diffusers: (a) Elongated (b) Circular (c) Strip

177

The slotted-top luminaire fitted with plenum box is also used in the third system of air handling, i.e. that in which both the supply air and the return air are ducted through the plenum. The air diffusers employed can again be either of the circular or elongated types. Figure 8.4c shows the latter type combined with the luminaires. The advantage of this particular arrangement is that it allows the greatest degree of flexibility in the event of the need arising to alter the layout of the partition walls in the area below.

The ceiling between luminaires and diffusers is covered with acoustic ceiling panels. These are of two basic types. One type is made of a special sound-absorbent mineral wool compressed to form a thick, self-supporting tile. The other (see again figure 8.4) is in the form of a metal tray perforated to allow the sound to pass through it and carrying a suitable sound-absorbent material contained in a plastic bag.

8.2.2 Power Tracks

The power track system of lighting (figure 8.6) provides complete economic flexibility of lamp position over a plane. It consists of the power track itself (which is basically one or more lengths of trunking each length providing access to two or more recessed conductors), a selection of junction boxes and coupling pieces to enable the track to be assembled in various configurations, and a range of light sources each of which can be connected to the track using special adaptors.

One of the most popular types of track is that containing three conductors, viz. a neutral centre rail and two live rails (these being suitably protected, by some feature of the construction, to ensure that they cannot be accidentally touched and are therefore electrically safe). The adaptor used to connect the light source to the track has two current carrying pins. One of these

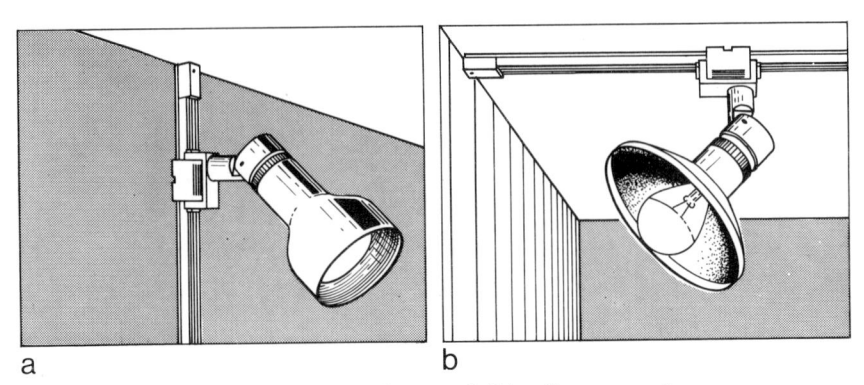

Figure 8.6 Power track shown (a) wall mounted (b) ceiling mounted.

connects with the neutral rail in the centre of the track and the other with one of the track's two live rails. Thus, depending on the orientation of a particular adaptor, it will receive power from one or other of these rails. This allows two groups of light sources connected to the one piece of track be switched individually. A typical current carrying capacity for such a track would be about 16 amperes.

8.2.3 Light Regulators

In planning certain types of lighting installations, e.g. cinemas and lecture theatres, it is evident that there is a need to provide facilities that will enable the illuminance level to be regulated continuously from between near to zero and maximum without upsetting the lighting uniformity.

Lighting control by dimming is sometimes also put forward as a possible solution to the problem of how to economise in the use of lighting energy, the idea being that as the amount of daylight increases, so the contribution made by the artificial lighting is automatically reduced.

The most practical method of controlling light output is, of course, to control the electrical input to the light source rather than to employ filters or shutters. The methods by which this may be accomplished are based on one of two principles: the input current can be varied by changing its amplitude, or it can be varied by changing the length of time during a cycle that it is permitted to flow.

Change in amplitude – a principle that, where full control is required, can only be employed in the case of incandescent lamps – can be accomplished by means of a resistance dimmer or a variable transformer. The resistance dimmer is connected in series with the lamp circuit and the voltage that appears across the lamp is equal to the supply voltage less the voltage dropped across the dimmer. The dimmer itself is relatively inexpensive, but it is also wasteful in the use of energy because at settings to give low light outputs an appreciable percentage of the power fed to the circuit is dissipated in the dimmer itself.

This waste is avoided with the continuously variable (auto) transformer. Here one pays mainly for the energy consumed by the lamp. Dimmers of this type are frequently used in such places as cinemas, where a heavy lighting load must be operated dimmed for long periods at a time.

Regulators working on the timed-flow principle can be used to control both incandescent lamps and, with the appropriate special ballasts, tubular fluorescent lamps. The basic element in modern electronic light regulators of this type is the thyristor. A typical regulator consists of a pair of thyristors connected in inverse parallel so that each one may conduct during each half cycle of the a.c. supply voltage. Drive circuits control the switching on of the thyristors at a chosen instant in the supply voltage waveform, thereby increasing or decreasing the mean power supplied to the load. The drive circuits may derive their input signal from a variety of controllers, e.g. manual or electronic potentiometers and light-sensitive cells.

Chapter 9

The Electrical Installation

The purpose of this section is to acquaint the reader with those general aspects of electrical engineering practice that are relevant to the design of lighting installations. It should be emphasised that no attempt has been made to provide solutions to all the many and varied electrical problems that might conceivably arise during the design of a lighting project. All that reasonably can be done in a book of this nature, which deals primarily with lighting technology, is to supply a framework of good engineering practice on which to build.

9.1 Electricity Supply and Distribution

Electricity generated at a large power station at a voltage in the region of 10 kilovolts is stepped up to above 100 kilovolts before being fed into the national grid for distribution to the primary and secondary sub-stations. At the sub-stations the voltage is varied by transformers to suit the needs of the area. Voltages range from the 33 kilovolts needed by heavy industry to the domestic 220/380 volt, figure 9.1.

Voltage and frequency are kept within strictly controlled limits. Although there may be a specified tolerance of plus or minus 10 per cent on voltage, this will generally be kept within 5 per cent under normal conditions of operation. Frequency limits common within Europe are plus or minus 0.2 per cent.

9.1.1 Industrial Premises

In factory and other premises where heavy currents are required it is usual for the supply undertaking to bring a high-tension supply to the premises and install one or more step-down transformers.

If large currents have to be fed from a transformer situated a long distance from the factory, heavy underground cables would be required to carry the low-tension current. It is more economical, therefore, to break down to low voltage as near to the consumer's main switch as possible. A transformer sub-station built with low-tension and high-tension switch rooms

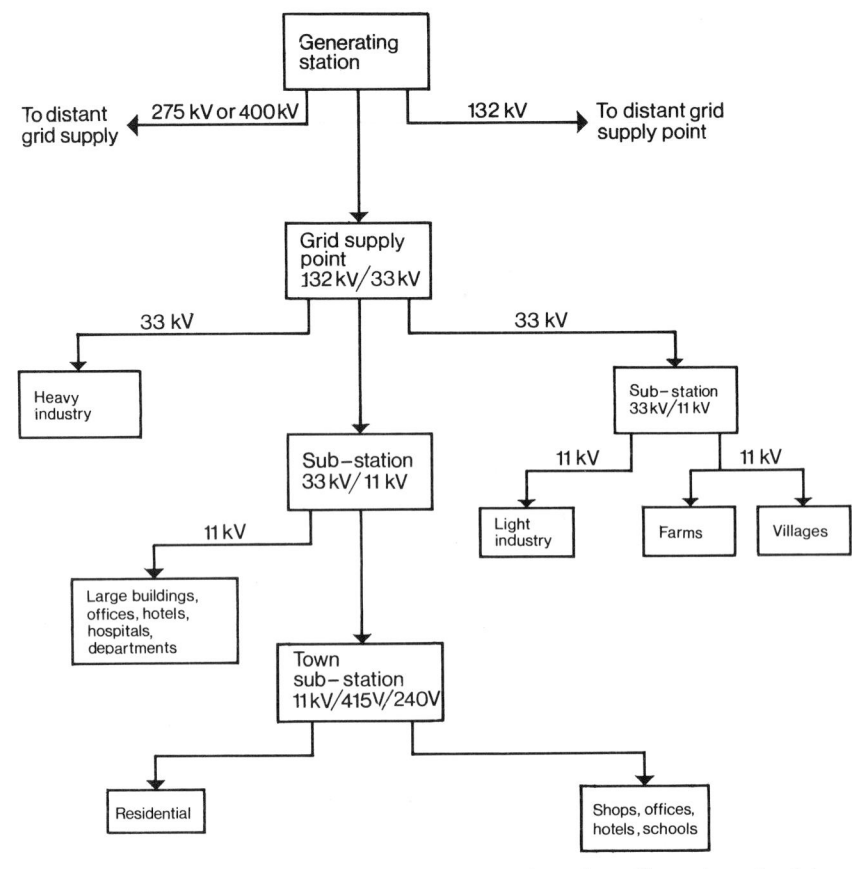

Figure 9.1 Electricity supply system. (The voltages indicated are illustrative only of those found within Europe.)

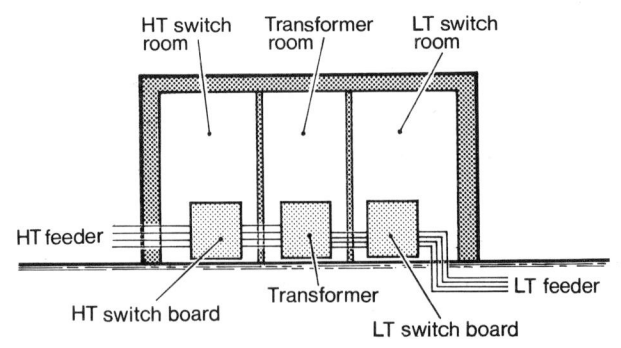

Figure 9.2 Transformer sub-station showing the L.T. switch room located as near as possible to the transformer room in order to keep the heavy, low-tension cables as short as possible.

adjoining a transformer room enables the low-tension cables from the secondary side of the transformer to the consumer's main switch to be as short as possible, figure 9.2.

The main low-tension switchboard serves to distribute the L.T. supply over the cables feeding perhaps a number of sub-switchboards located in different parts of the site. These cables are protected by fuses or by automatic circuit-breakers and can be isolated from the main switchboard for repair and maintenance purposes.

Each sub-switchboard will normally consist of a wall-mounted metal or synthetic resin cabinet containing a switch to disconnect the incoming power from the electrical installation within the building, and a number of fuses or automatic circuit breakers to protect the wiring and the various current consuming devices in the event of overload.

9.1.2 High-rise Buildings

The practice in large buildings supplied direct from the national grid has in the past been to locate the transformer sub-station in the basement, the electricity being distributed throughout the building using either low-voltage cables or bus-bars, figure 9.3a. In a modern high-rise multi-storey building, however, this method of distribution is not practicable. The electrical load is so great that were long runs of L.T. cable or bus-bars used they would have to be prohibitively thick in order to keep the voltage drop occurring along them to an acceptable size.

One solution to this problem has been found by using decentralised transformer sub-stations, each transformer serving one or more floors, figure 9.3b. Big a.c. loads can be handled by separate transformers to avoid fluctuations in the lighting circuits. A substantial saving in both costs and floor space can sometimes be obtained by using H.T. switchgear equipped with fuses instead of circuit breakers. The decentralised transformer sub-station also has obvious advantages should it ever be necessary to increase the capacity of the installation.

9.2 The Lighting Circuits

9.2.1 Minimising Costs

The labour costs involved in installing the wiring for a lighting system often form a substantial part of the total costs. Labour costs are minimised by employing ready-wired luminaires, and where fluorescent luminaires are concerned, these should be mounted in continuous rows.

Large installations normally operate on a three-phase supply. Here, the

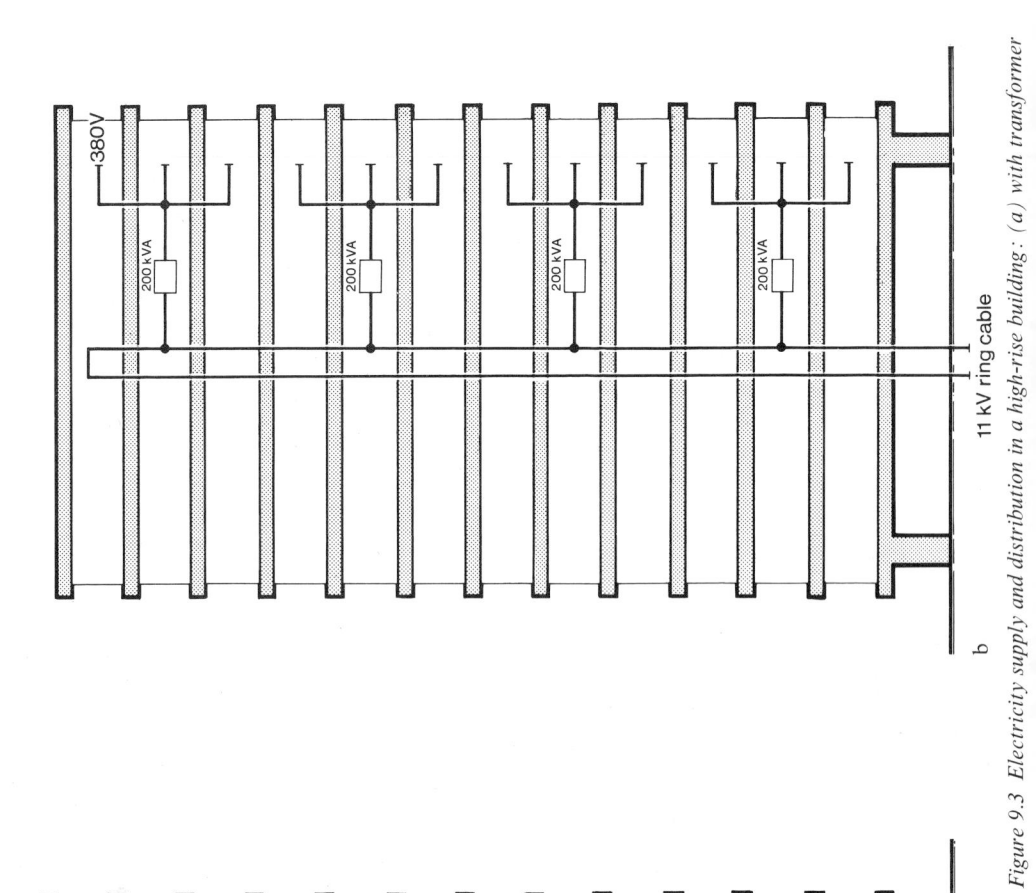

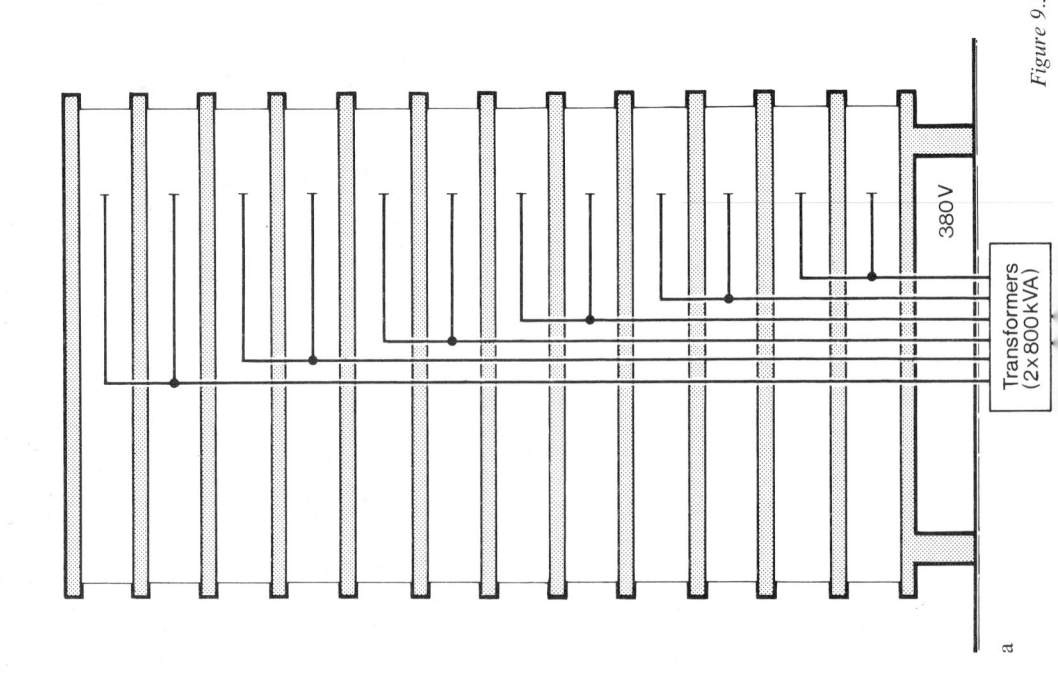

Figure 9.3 Electricity supply and distribution in a high-rise building: (a) with transformer

cable runs can be kept to a minimum length by dividing the luminaires into three groups and distributing the lighting load equally over the three phases of the supply.

In order to limit equipment costs and to obtain a high level of reliability the switches used to control the lighting in a small installation are generally kept as simple as possible, some form of direct load-carrying switch being employed for this purpose. However, where larger installations are concerned it is not usually practicable for the actual control switch to carry the heavy load current, so central relays and contactors are often employed.

9.2.2 Long-term Flexibility

The design of the lighting circuits, particularly in office buildings, is governed to a large extent by the degree of flexibility given to the area concerned. The interior of the building may be divided into a number of areas using permanent walls or movable partitions, or it may be left to form one or more large landscaped areas.

Permanently walled areas. Even the lighting circuit designed for a permanently walled area is often given a certain degree of flexibility to allow for unforseen changes in the layout of the area; for example, the addition of partition walls.

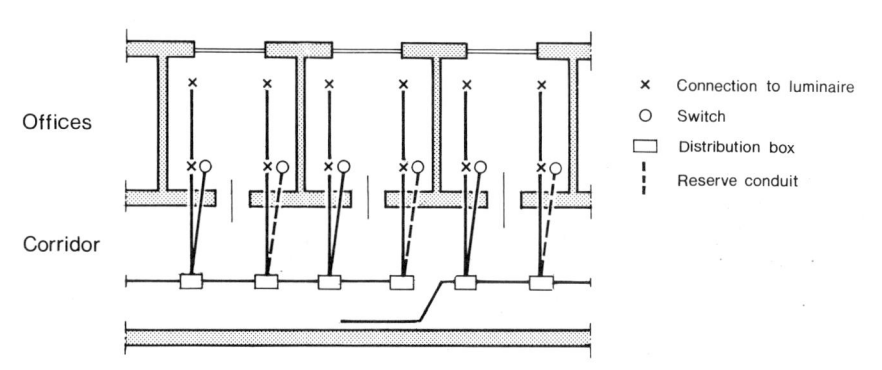

Figure 9.4 Lighting circuits can be given a certain amount of flexibility by installing some reserve conduit for use if needed at a later date.

This flexibility can be achieved by locating the supply distribution boxes in the false ceiling outside in the corridor, and by installing some reserve conduit for the addition of lighting switches at a later date, figure 9.4. The luminaires are, for this reason, often connected to the supply by means of wall or ceiling-mounted socket outlets.

Semi-permanent areas. Where the floor area is divided into a number of individual areas using movable partition walls the electrical installation must be carefully planned to permit of quick and easy modification.

Where the partitioning is too thin to permit the use of conventional low-voltage wiring, a solution may be to use relays for the mains switching. The relays are connected to the various light switches using safety-extra-low-voltage (SELV) wiring and this can be easily concealed in the partitioning. With this type of circuit it is possible to switch the lighting locally as well as from a remote control position.

Needless to say, such an installation is more costly than one designed along more conventional lines, but these costs can be kept to a minimum by cutting down on the number of individual lighting circuits employed in any one area for there is, in fact, no practical saving to be gained from group switching.

Landscaped areas. Landscaped or open-plan areas present no special problems as far as the layout of the wiring for the lighting is concerned. The lighting is generally controlled from one or more wall-mounted switches similar to those used in factory areas.

Communicating areas. The lighting for the communicating areas in a building (stairs, corridors, etc.) can best be controlled from one point, e.g. the porter's lodge. This simplifies the installation and at the same time keeps servicing costs to a minimum. The escape route, particularly in a high-rise building, should be provided with some form of emergency lighting (see Sec. 9.3).

9.3 Emergency Lighting

In certain types of building there are occupied areas that are lit only by artificial light. This artificial lighting may fail, and unless precautions are taken whole areas may be plunged into darkness. Lighting fed from more than one circuit will afford some measure of protection in the event of a local failure within the premises, but in the event of a network failure it is likely that all incoming supplies will be lost. Therefore, when the circumstances demand, a form of lighting alternative to the normal lighting should be provided, and this alternative lighting should be on when the normal lighting fails.

This alternative lighting, described here as emergency lighting, may be of basically three types according to the duty mode used: 'non-maintained', 'semi-maintained' or 'maintained'.

9.3.1 Non-maintained Emergency Lighting

A non-maintained emergency lighting system is one in which the emergency lighting luminaires are lit only when the normal mains supply is interrupted. A typical non-maintained system is illustrated in figure 9.5. During normal operation the a.c. mains voltage supplying the normal lighting installation also appears across the mains-watch relay. This relay is thereby energised and feeds the a.c. power via the rectifier circuit to charge the accumulator.

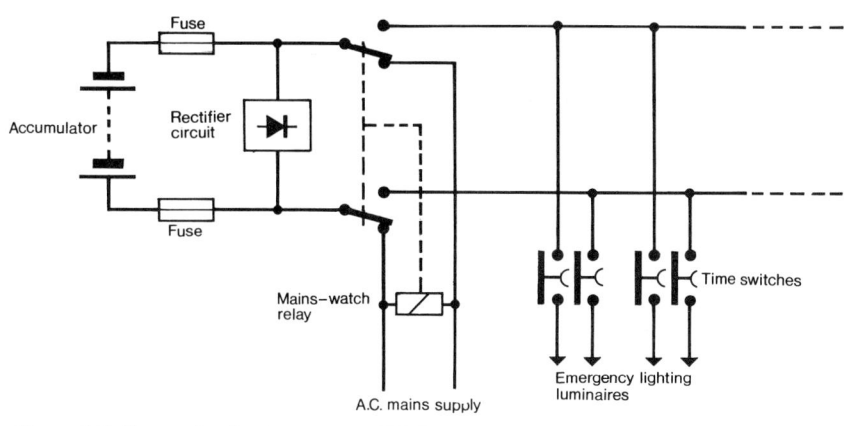

Figure 9.5 Non-maintained emergency lighting.

In the event of a failure of the normal lighting due to mains failure, the mains-watch relay becomes de-energised. This switches the accumulator across the time switches in the d.c. emergency circuit. After a predetermined time interval – sufficient to prevent actuation due to transient failure of the mains – the time switches feed this standby supply into the emergency lighting circuit. When the mains power returns, the emergency lighting switches off and the accumulator is put back on charge.

A disadvantage of systems like that described above in which the emergency luminaires receive their power from a central source, is that the internal wiring of the building is relied upon for distribution of the emergency power. In the event of a fire, structural damage, etc., such systems can easily become disrupted.

Where only a few emergency luminaires are needed, a solution to the above problem can be found by the use of luminaires equipped with their own mains-rechargeable batteries. Each battery-powered emergency lighting luminaire figure 9.6, contains, besides the battery, a battery charging unit, a transistor ballast, a mains relay and a low-wattage (e.g. 6 watt) high-efficacy fluorescent lamp. During normal operation (i.e. mains supply present) the mains relay is energised, causing the battery to be charged from

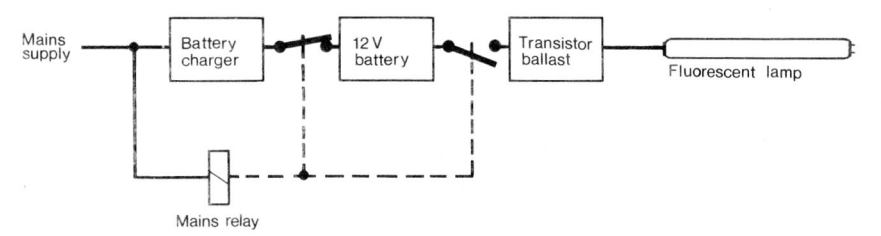

Figure 9.6 Schematic representation of a self-contained non-maintained emergency lighting luminaire. (The neutral line is omitted for the sake of clarity.)

the charging unit. In the event of a mains supply failure the relay falls out, isolating the charger from the battery and connecting the latter, via the ballast, to the lamp. (The capacity of the battery is generally sufficient to operate the lamp for an hour or more.) When the mains power is restored, the lamp is automatically extinguished by the action of the relay and the battery put back on charge. The luminaire generally contains a switch which permits the connection between battery and ballast to be broken. This allows the battery to be left in the fully charged state during prolonged periods of maintenance, holidays, etc., when no mains supply is present. There may also be a switch the operation of which, by simulating a mains failure, allows a quick and simple check to be made on the correct functioning of the unit. This system is extremely reliable, since individual lamps can go on functioning even when the mains distribution cable within a building is destroyed.

9.3.2 Semi-maintained Emergency Lighting

A semi-maintained emergency lighting system is one in which the emergency lighting luminaires are normally lit, but are extinguished momentarily during changeover to standby power.
The standby power in such an installation may be provided by a diesel, petrol, or gas-engine driven generator. Even when automatic start-up features are incorporated a delay of ten seconds or longer is quite normal before the generator unit becomes effective. However, special precautions such as keeping the engine and cooling liquid at normal operating temperature may reduce this delay to less than a second.
A semi-maintained emergency system with automatic start up is illustrated in figure 9.7. A failure in the mains-fed normal and emergency lighting systems is detected by the mains-watch relay. This relay opens switch 1, so disconnecting the mains-fed emergency lighting from the mains, at the same time giving a start command to the diesel motor. As soon as the generator reaches full load power, switch 2 is automatically closed and the

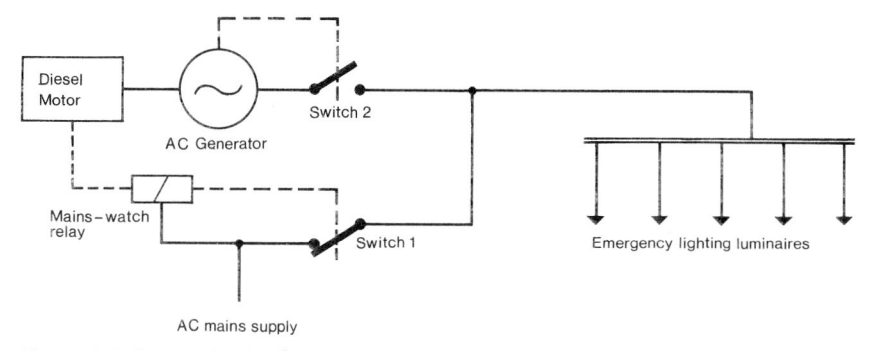

Figure 9.7 Semi-maintained emergency lighting. (Neutral line omitted.)

standby power from the generator is fed into the emergency lighting circuits. Generator shutdown and return to the mains power is initiated by the same mains-watch relay.

9.3.3 Maintained Emergency Lighting

The delay inherent in the semi-maintained emergency lighting system makes it unsuitable for use in certain areas (e.g. hospital operating theatres, escape routes) or in conjunction with discharge lamps that need a cooling off period before re-ignition can take place. In such cases a maintained, or 'no-break', emergency lighting installation is essential.

A maintained emergency lighting system is one in which the emergency lighting luminaires are lit at all times when the building is occupied. By far the simplest and cheapest maintained emergency lighting system is that in which each emergency lighting luminaire, normally fed from the mains, automatically receives its power from a battery immediately at the onset of a mains failure. The battery, which while not in use is charged from the mains via solid-state rectifiers, has a capacity sufficient to provide only escape lighting. Where standby lighting is required (as for example in a hospital operating theatre) the necessary power can be provided by a standby generator which, having reached full output, takes over from the battery, this having provided the necessary 'tide-over' service during the period of run up.

Where such standby lighting is considered imperative – as in the case of the operating theatre mentioned above – this should come on automatically. In locations where it is merely desirable, perhaps for reasons of economy, to operate a standby lighting system, manual switch-on may be acceptable.

Finally, a few words with regard to emergency lighting installations in general. Where incandescent lamps are used, they should be of the bayonet-fitting type so as to avoid the possibility of vibration causing a loose connection.

In some countries, there are strict regulations that call for the use of heat resistant cables.

The number of switches used in an emergency lighting installation should be kept to a minimum. Where switches are necessary, they should be inaccessible to the public.

9.4 Safety Regulations

National electrical safety regulations are many and varied and their inclusion is beyond the scope of this book.

Suffice it to say that such regulations fall into two groups
(a) Those dealing with the design, construction and quality of the electrical equipment e.g. switches, cables, fuses, luminaires etc.
(b) Those dealing with the installation of the electrical equipment – wiring rules.

Although the regulations in group (a) are aimed primarily at the electrical equipment manufacturer, both the lighting engineer and the electrical contractor should be fully conversant with at least the major points covered. For example, luminaires mounted up against a flammable material will have to satisfy certain requirements with respect to their permitted temperature increase both during normal operation and in the presence of a possible fault condition.

There are two international bodies concerned in the formulation of these regulations. They are: The International Commission on Rules for the Approval of Electrical Equipment (CEE), and The International Electrotechnical Commission (IEC).

National regulations concerned with the proper installation of electrical equipment differ on a number of points. However, an attempt has been made (IEC, 1973) to arrive at some degree of standardisation.

Some of the important points on which the national regulations differ are
(a) The way in which interiors are classified according to the type of materials that may be used in them;
(b) The way in which equipment must be protected to eliminate the possibility of human contact with live parts;
(c) The way in which equipment must be earthed to provide protection in the event of a short-circuit;
(d) The maximum currents permitted in the various electrical cables, according to their location, viz. ceiling mounted, wall mounted etc.

A point worth stressing with regard to protection by earthing, is that safety earthing is a supplementary, or back-up, protection requirement and is not intended to make up for deficiencies in the design or construction of the equipment itself.

Earthing is generally accomplished by means of an extra core in the wiring cable. Where power track is in use the trunking may sometimes be used for earthing purposes, but only if it is not liable to become corroded.

Chapter 10

Lighting Maintenance

A lighting installation will continue to operate efficiently only when it is well maintained. Poor maintenance can allow the effects of lamp ageing and failure, and the accumulation of dirt on lamps, luminaires and room surfaces to bring about an intolerable reduction in the amount of useful light available. This can lead not only to illuminance levels that are substantially below those required, but also to the installation assuming a dowdy appearance. Poor maintenance can also adversely effect the light distribution of the luminaires, especially where these are of the type embodying some form of optical control.

10.1 Maintenance Operations

The maintenance operations that need to be carried out during the life of an installation in order to ensure that it will remain free from these harmful effects of neglect may be listed as: lamp replacement; lamp and luminaire cleaning; and cleaning of the room surfaces.

10.1.1 Lamp replacement

Lamp replacement is carried out in order to reduce the fall off in light output of the installation due to lamp ageing and lamp failure.
The luminous output of lamps decreases with use, but the rate of decrease varies to a certain degree between lamp types. This is illustrated in figure 10.1 where the fall in light output, or lamp lumen depreciation, of the three basic lamp types viz. incandescent, gas discharge and fluorescent, is compared.
It is impossible, because of tolerances in manufacture alone, for a lamp to have a precisely defined life. One can speak only of average lamp life. For incandescent lamps, where the spread on lamp life due to tolerances in manufacture is rather limited, deviations of lamp life from the standard value (viz. 1000 h) is mainly determined in practice by the operating voltage of the specific installation considered. With discharge lamps, lamp life is influenced by several factors apart from the operating voltage. These

factors are: the frequency of the on/off switching; the type of ballast, viz. inductive or capacitive; the ambient temperature (fluorescent lamps only); the adjustment of the control gear; and the method of ignition, viz. with or without starter.

An impression of the combined influence that these factors have on the life of a particular type of gas discharge lamp, namely the fluorescent lamp, can be gained from a study of figure 10.2. From this figure which, it must be stressed, is valid only for optimum conditions of operation, it can be seen that for the first 40 per cent or so of anticipated (or average) lamp life very few failures occur. The failure rate is seen to increase sharply when the lamps have reached around 70 per cent of their anticipated life. By definition, 50 per cent of the lamps installed are still working when the anticipated

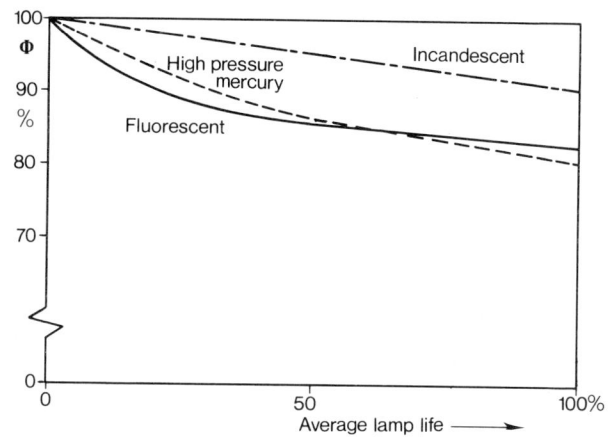

Figure 10.1 Indication of the fall in light output Φ of fluorescent, high-pressure mercury and incandescent lamps due to ageing.

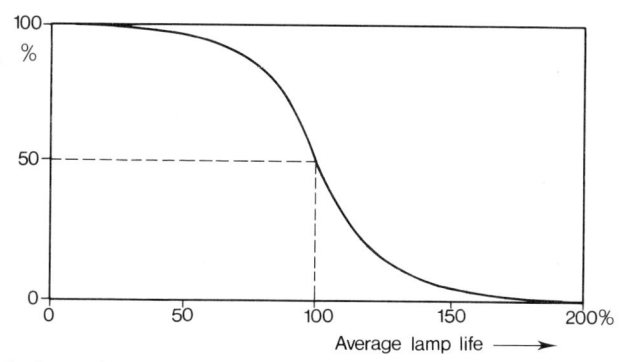

Figure 10.2 Percentage of tubular fluorescent lamps still functioning, as a function of percentage of average lamp life.

life expectancy is reached. The number of lamps continuing to function beyond this point continues to fall off rapidly, and then more slowly until, at around twice the average life, all the lamps have failed.

Lamps may be replaced individually as they burn out, or the entire installation can be relamped at one time. The latter system is commonly referred to as group replacement. Sometimes a combination of these two systems is used.

Individual lamp replacement can result in adjacent lamps being noticeably different in luminance and colour, a consequence of lamp ageing. This method of replacement can also be very wasteful in labour since, if carried out properly, it will involve making a special visit to the installation each time a lamp fails, and this means keeping a continuous check on the in-installation. Finally, the replacement operation itself can create a disturbance in the area concerned.

Group replacement obviates the problems so far mentioned, but suffers from the disadvantage that the odd lamp that fails between replacement operations may have to remain in situ for several months awaiting replacement. These systems are therefore often combined. Group replacement ensures that, say, no more than five per cent of the lamps will be burned out at any given moment, with individual replacement taking care of the re-

Table 10.1 Practical replacement and cleaning periods for discharge lamps

Type of interior	Lamp burning time (hours/year)	Lamp replacement period (years)	Cleaning period (years)
Foundries, mines etc. (heavy pollution)	3 000 (2 shifts)	1.5	0.5
Ordinary working interiors (moderate pollution)	2 000 (normal working week)	2	2
	3 000 (2 shifts)	1.5	1.5
	5 000 (continuous working)	1	1
Offices (light pollution)	2 000	2	2
Schools (light pollution)	1 000 (day school)	4	4
	2 000 (day school + evening classes)	2	2

maining failures. Because fewer lamps will have to be replaced individually, the disturbance caused by this work will be reduced to a minimum. The main group replacement operation can, of course, be arranged to take place at some convenient time outside of working hours. An additional advantage of group replacement is that since it involves all the luminaires, these can be cleaned at the same time as the lamps are replaced.

A practical scheme providing the guidelines for the group replacement of gas discharge lamps is outlined in table 10.1. The table gives the replacement and cleaning periods for a number of different areas according to the number of hours that the installation is in use per year.

10.1.2 Lamp and Luminaire Cleaning

Dirt or dust deposits on lamps and on the reflecting and transmitting surfaces of luminaires absorb light. The amount of light lost from an installation in this way can be considerable, and will naturally be greatest where pollution is heaviest.

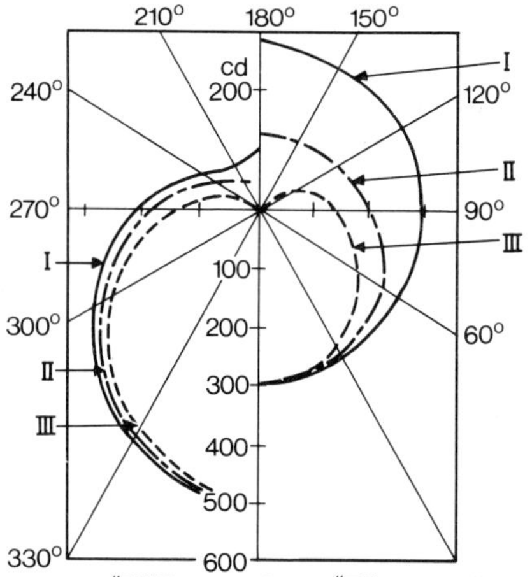

Figure 10.3 Influence of dust accumulation on light output of twin tubular fluorescent reflector lamps ('TL'F) and standard tubular fluorescent lamps ('TL') mounted in twin-lamp trough luminaires.
  I = Clean lamps
  II = Normal dust accumulation
  III = Excessive dust accumulation

The nature of the pollution, the type of lamp used and the design of the luminaires will all have a bearing on the rate at which light output decreases and therefore on the frequency with which cleaning need be carried out.

In dry, dusty areas where open-bottomed luminaires are used, dust will accumulate mainly on the upper surfaces of the lamps. It is preferable in such a situation to use a lamp having a reflective coating on its top inner surface. The output of these reflector lamps is influenced very little by such dirt deposits (figure 10.3).

If ventilated luminaires can be used, so much the better. In a ventilated luminaire the heat from the lamps produces convection currents and these carry the dust through holes or slots in the canopy or reflector and thus away from the lamps themselves. In heavily polluted atmospheres, however, protection against fouling may only be possible by using sealed luminaires of the so-called dust-tight or dustproof varieties.

Careful consideration given to measures such as these, which are aimed at lessening the effects of pollution, will go a long way to reducing the need for cleaning. It will ensure, also, that the lighting installation remains at near to optimum efficiency between cleaning operations. For the maximum economic advantage the cleaning interval should, in any case, be related to the lamp replacement interval.

10.1.3 Cleaning Room Surfaces

Dirty room surfaces reduce the amount of light reflected from them and spoil the appearance of an interior. The amount of light lost in this way will obviously depend on the size of the interior and the light distribution of the luminaires. It will be greatest in small rooms where luminaires with a large indirect component are involved and smallest in large rooms lit by luminaires having a predominantly direct light distribution. On average, however, for a medium-sized room lit by semi-direct luminaires the light lost by absorption in an interior that has not been cleaned for two years can amount to as much as 10 per cent.

10.2 Light Loss (Maintenance) Factors

When determining the number of lamps necessary to provide the required illuminance for a particular lighting installation, it is necessary to apply a light loss factor to the calculations. (See Chapter 13 Calculations and Measurements.) This factor is defined as the ratio of the recommended illuminance after a certain period of use (which will depend on the frequency of cleaning) to the illuminance obtained under the same conditions for a new installation. It takes into account, therefore, the overall depreciation caused by the various factors already mentioned.

The light loss factor depends on the type of lamp/luminaire combination used, the proportions of the room, the degree of pollution present and the effectiveness and frequency of the maintenance. Published data (IES, 1967) available for the systematic selection of light loss factors invariably assume that the lighting engineer is in possession of full information concerning each of these points. This is often not the case and, in the absence of experience to draw from, some form of rough guide to selection can be invaluable. Table 10.2 has been included with this thought in mind. The table gives light loss factors for installations using discharge lamps and for luminaires having a prevailingly direct lighting component. The table is valid for rooms of medium size. The cleaning interval is taken as 12 months.

Table 10.2 Light loss factors (for rough guidance only)

Recommended illuminance	Lamp luminous flux applied	Room pollution	Light loss factor
Service value*	100 hours value	light	0.8
		moderate	0.7
		heavy	0.6
Minimum value**	100 hours value	light	0.7
		moderate	0.6
		heavy	0.5

* The mean illuminance throughout the life of an installation and averaged over the relevant area; this area may be the whole area of the working plane in an interior, or the area of the visual task and its immediate surround

** The lowest recommended illuminance on the task at any time, irrespective of the plane on which it is located

Part 3

LIGHTING DESIGN

Chapter 11

Lighting Criteria

The investigative work carried out in connection with each of the main lighting criteria relevant to interior lighting design, viz. lighting levels, preferred luminances, glare, colour appearance and colour rendering, and modelling, is described in detail in Part One of this book.

The present chapter goes a step further and summarises the most important findings to emerge from this research as seen in the light of present day knowledge and experience.

Many of these findings are seen reflected in the recent CIE publication 'Guide to Interior Lighting'. The chapter thus forms a practical survey of lighting criteria and can be used as a check list against which both new and existing interior lighting designs can be easily evaluated.

11.1 Lighting Level

It is of fundamental importance that there should be sufficient light in an interior to allow work or other activities to be carried on effectively, safely and in comfort. The amount of light, or the lighting level, may be specified by the illuminance on the imaginary horizontal working plane or on a specific task, by the luminance of a particular surface or surfaces of interest, or both. Experience has shown that a variation in the magnitude of either of these quantities can have a profound influence on a person's work performance and his sense of well-being. This has been confirmed by research, in which the nature of these rather complex relationships – that existing between lighting level and visual performance on the one hand, and between lighting level and visual satisfaction on the other – have been investigated. (See Chapter 1.)

The findings emerging from the first line of research referred to above are, of course, extremely useful in the guidance that they can offer when planning the lighting of an interior in which some kind of visual task is to be carried out. These findings are, therefore, taken into account when drawing up national recommendations on the lighting of working interiors.

Another criterion on which to base lighting recommendations has been found to be the degree of visual satisfaction afforded by a specific lighting level. Investigations of this nature are conveniently grouped according to whether the interior concerned is classed as a working area or as a circulation area.

The findings relating to working interiors (Sec. 1.2.1) show that the visual comfort of people engaged in the performance of simple office tasks increases with increase in task illuminance up to a level of about 2000 lx, provided, that is, that the necessary precautions are taken concerning the avoidance of unpleasant luminance contrasts and glare and that due regard is paid to the colour aspects of the lighting. Levels in the order of 1000 lx would seem realistic for working interiors in which the tasks are not of a prolonged or visually very exacting nature. Research has shown that the minimum, based on the visual comfort criterion, lies at about 200 lx (Sec. 1.2.1).

For circulation areas a much lower minimum of around 20 lx had been found to be perfectly acceptable (Sec. 1.2.2).

In practice, a compromise has often to be made between the desirable illuminance and that which is related to the economic conditions prevailing. In consequence, it may be necessary to accept a lower standard of lighting than that which would be desirable from the point of visual performance, visual satisfaction, or both.

The CIE, in its report entitled 'Guide on Interior Lighting' (1975), suggests that, based on a consideration of the above requirements, three ranges of illuminance should be recommended when formulating lighting specifications, viz., 20–200 lx, 200–2000 lx and 2000–20 000 lux. These three ranges are each sub-divided by the CIE into a number of steps, each step differing by a factor of approximately 1.5 from its neighbour. The resulting scale of recommended illuminance levels is shown in table 11.1.

The illuminances recommended in this table relate to normal working conditions in rooms having at least some daylight. When circumstances make the working conditions more difficult these illuminances should be increased accordingly.

Special circumstances calling for an increase in illuminance of one or more steps are
(a) The need, for reasons of cost or personal safety, to ensure accuracy of perception;
(b) The presence of low reflectances or contrasts in the task, or the demand for a high speed of working.

An instance of where the illuminance can be safely reduced from that recommended in the table is where the area concerned forms that part of a working interior used for circulation purposes. The lighting level in such an area should be not less than one-fifth of that recommended for working, with a minimum of 150 lx.

Table 11.1 Recommended illuminances for interiors.

Range	Recommended illuminance (lx)	Type of activity
A general lighting for areas used infrequently or having simple visual demands	20 / 30 / 50	public areas with dark surroundings
	75 / 100	simple orientation for short temporary visits only
	150 / 200	rooms not used continuously for working purposes e.g. storage areas, entrance halls
B general lighting for working interiors	300 / 500	tasks with limited visual requirements e.g. rough machining, lecture theatres
	750 / 1000	tasks with normal visual requirements e.g. medium machining, offices
	1500 / 2000	tasks with special visual requirements e.g. hand engraving, clothing factory inspection
C additional lighting for visually exacting tasks	3000 / 5000	very prolonged and exacting visual tasks e.g. minute electronic and watch assembly
	7500 / 10000	exceptionally exacting visual tasks e.g. micro electronic assembly
	15000 / 20000	very special tasks e.g. surgical operations

Alternative concepts that have been considered for the specification of lighting levels in circulation areas and the like are the mean cylindrical and the mean spherical illuminance at a point in space in the area concerned (Sec. 1.2.2).

11.2 Preferred Luminances

It is generally agreed that the human eye expects surfaces with high reflectance to be considerably lighter than those with low reflectance. This is why, in general, it is more convenient for interior lighting recommendations to be based on illuminance values, the luminances being left to take care of themselves; from which it follows that it will be more convenient also to design in terms of illuminance, that is to say, to employ the lumen method of design. (See Chapter 13.)

The planned distribution of luminance in an interior – luminance design – should be regarded as being complementary to a design based on illuminance. It should be limited in application to the following:

 The task and its immediate surrounds (luminance ratios)
 Ceiling, walls and floor (luminance ranges)
 Luminaires (luminance limits)

Detailed luminance calculations may be suitable for rather special lighting projects, but for normal lighting design it is sufficient to observe certain simple rules aimed at avoiding unpleasant extremes of contrast.

First, the luminance of the task relative to that of its surround. Investigation has shown (Chapter 2 Sec. 2.2) that the luminance of the area immediately surrounding a task should, wherever possible, be lower than the luminance of the task itself but not less than about one-third of this value. Assuming the illuminance to be even throughout the area concerned, the required luminance ratio can be obtained by careful choice of the task-surround reflectance.

In offices the visual tasks mostly involve the use of matt-white paper seen against a matt or semi-matt desk-top. For tasks of this nature, the luminance ratio referred to above may be obtained by ensuring that the surface reflectance of the desks lies between 0.25 and 0.5.

In industry, the visual tasks are so varied that it is virtually impossible to formulate general recommendations concerning the preferred reflectance of the task surround. Each case must, therefore, be treated individually on a trial and error basis.

Consider now the bounding surfaces of an interior, that is to say the ceiling, walls and floor. The importance of ceiling luminance as a factor in the lighting design of an interior is dependent largely on the ceiling height involved. Where this is great enough to put the ceiling effectively out of sight its luminance will obviously have little or no direct influence on the sense of well-being of those working below; ceiling luminance may, in such a case, be chosen purely on practical grounds, e.g. so as to promote good lighting utilisation. It is impossible to specify the exact floor-to-ceiling height at which ceiling luminance becomes aesthetically important (the height at which a ceiling effectively enters the field of view is so much dependent on ceiling area), but this is generally taken to be about three metres. At or below this height (which is the norm for most working interiors) a ceiling should be visually pleasing, and its luminance chosen accordingly.

Research has in fact shown that preferred ceiling luminance is essentially a function of luminaire luminance and that as this increases so too does the luminance of the ceiling needed to avoid unpleasant luminous contrasts between it and the luminaires (See figure 2.15 Chapter 2.)

In practice, the luminance of a ceiling will invariably be less than the preferred value as indicated by the luminance of the luminaires, unless these provide sufficient upward illumination. Where the luminaires are of the fully recessed type the ceiling will be lighted purely by reflection from the floor and the difference between the actual and the recommended luminance may be considerable. In the latter case, therefore, it is essential to produce the maximum possible ceiling luminance for the luminaire type in use. The reflectance of the ceiling should, therefore, be as high as possible, and certainly not less than 0.7, with a floor-cavity reflectance in the region of 0.2 to 0.4. (Sec. 2.4.2).

The luminances preferred for the walls in working interiors has also been the subject of research (See Chapter 2 Sec. 2.4.1.) The results of the research indicate that preferred wall luminance is a function of the horizontal illuminance level and wall reflectance. The permitted range of wall reflectance is, for example, between 0.5 and 0.8 for installations in the order of 500 lx and between 0.4 and 0.6 where the illuminance is around 1000 lx.

11.3 Glare

Glare can produce a variety of sensations ranging from mild discomfort to momentary blindness. The magnitude of the sensation will depend on the size, number, position and luminance of the glare sources, and on the luminance to which the eyes are adapted.

Glare control begins at the luminaire itself by ensuring that excessively high luminances are avoided. The luminance of the luminaires used has to be limited in such a way that the glare produced by the installation as a whole is within acceptable limits. The possibility of the luminaires producing reflected glare must also be considered (Sec. 11.3.3), if necessary modifying the planned ceiling configuration of the luminaires accordingly or selecting luminaires giving a more favourable light and luminance distribution.

11.3.1 Direct Glare and Luminaire Luminance

The angular zone measured from the downward vertical axis of a luminaire at which glare is most likely to occur is defined in figure 11.1. Glare is avoided, or at least kept acceptable, by arranging that the luminance of the luminaire in this zone is kept within certain defined limits. (The calculation of luminaire luminance is described in Chapter 3, Sec. 3.2.1)

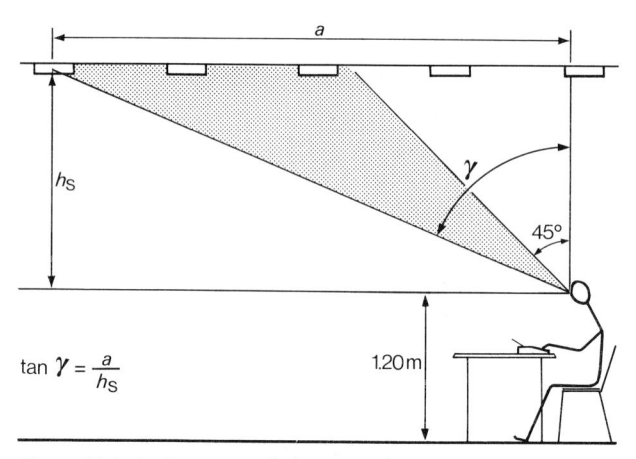

Figure 11.1 Radiant zone of a luminaire ($\gamma = 45°$ to $\gamma = 85°$) in which luminance limits have to be observed.

Luminaires are of basically two types: those in which a translucent diffusing screen or refractor panel is used to increase the luminous area of the luminaire so as to bring about a real reduction in luminance, and those in which the lamp or lamps within are shielded from direct view (for normal viewing angles) by a reflector, louvre, or reflector-louvre combination (figure 8.1).

The choice of luminaire type in a given situation will depend, to a large extent, on the luminance of the lamps being used. It is convenient, for the purpose of giving guidance on this point, to divide lamps into two main groups

(a) Those with a luminance up to about 20 000 cd/m². This group includes all the normal types of tubular fluorescent lamps.

(b) Those with a luminance of above about 20 000 cd/m². This group includes most of the 'compact' lamps viz. incandescent and gas-discharge lamps.

For lamps falling in the upper-end of group (a) or the lower-end of group (b) either of the glare control methods mentioned above may be used. For the more powerful lamps in group (b) the shielding principle is used almost exclusively.

The only lamps that may, on occasion, be used bare are the low luminance lamps in the lower-end of group (a), viz. the lower-wattage fluorescent tubes. This is permitted, for example, for certain interiors with lower quality requirements if the lighting level is less than about 500 lx but the tubes should then be mounted parallel to the main direction of view. Bare incandescent or discharge lamps should not be used at all in working interiors – the possiblity of their producing glare is too great – but in areas where the lighting has an animating function (entrance halls, foyers, etc) small sources of high luminance can be used to advantage.

Open-bottomed luminaires permit a clear view of the lamps contained within from a position immediately below. Because of this, they should not be used to light a task for which the line of sight is much above the horizontal. Neither, when housing high powered lamps, should such a luminaire be mounted low over a person's head as the heat radiated from the lamp could be extremely disturbing.

11.3.2 Evaluation of Direct Glare

The Luminance Curve Method: The CIE has recommended adopting the Luminance Curve Method of glare evaluation described in Chapter 3 of this book for the evaluation of direct glare in working interiors, but modified to include only three quality classes instead of six, and presented in table form rather than as diagrams. (See table 11.2.) Countries preferring the diagram form should use the presentation shown in figure 11.2.

The three quality classes in the proposed new method have been selected from the previous stepped scale of classes. Defined according to glare rating (G), the new classes are

Class   I, $G = 1.15$
Class II, $G = 1.5$
Class III, $G = 2.2$

Class I limits should be observed for those interiors where high quality lighting is required. Class II limits represent a minimum lighting standard for work such as that normally carried out in offices. Class III limits represent a minimum lighting standard for heavy industry and for circulation areas, viz., areas in which quality requirements in general are at a minimum.

The method does not take into account areas lit by luminaires of very large surface area, an extreme case being a luminous ceiling. Where such lumi-

Table 11.2 Luminance limits (cd/m^2) for all luminaires and bare lamps

C plane	γ	Quality class I				Quality class II				Quality class III			
C_{90}		Service Value of Illuminance				Service Value of Illuminance				Service Value of Illuminance			
		≥ 750 lx		≤ 500 lx		≥ 750 lx		≤ 500 lx		≥ 750 lx		≤ 500 lx	
		All Types		All Types		All Types		All Types		All Types		All Types	
	85°	1600		2200		2200		3300		5300		9400	
	75°	1600		2200		2200		3300		5300		9400	
	65°	2300		3800		3800		7200		15000		38000	
	55°	3400		6800		6800		16000		45000		–	
C_0		Service Value of Illuminance				Service Value of Illuminance				Service Value of Illuminance			
		≥ 750 lx		≤ 500 lx		≥ 750 lx		≤ 500 lx		≥ 750 lx		≤ 500 lx	
		Luminaires with		Luminaires with		Luminaires with		Luminaires with		Luminaires with		Luminaires with	
		Bright Sides	Dark Sides	Bright Sides	Dark Sides	Bright Sides	Dark Sides	Bright Sides	Dark Sides	Bright Sides	Dark Sides	Bright Sides	Dark Sides
	85°	1100	1600	1200	2200	1200	2200	1500	3300	1900	5300	2400	9400
	75°	1100	1600	1200	2200	1200	2200	1500	3300	1900	5300	2400	9400
	65°	1500	2300	1900	3800	1900	3800	2800	7200	4300	15000	7100	38000
	55°	2000	3400	3100	6800	3100	6800	5200	16000	10000	45000	20000	–

naires are used, the luminance at angles above 45° to the vertical should be limited to about 500 cd/m² (CIE, 1975).

Presentation of Glare Evaluation Data: The designer of an indoor lighting installation must be able to see at a glance, either from the relevant luminaire

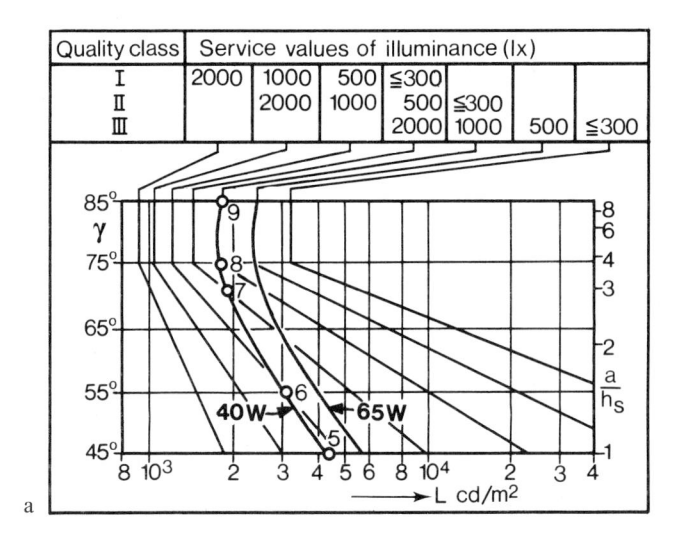

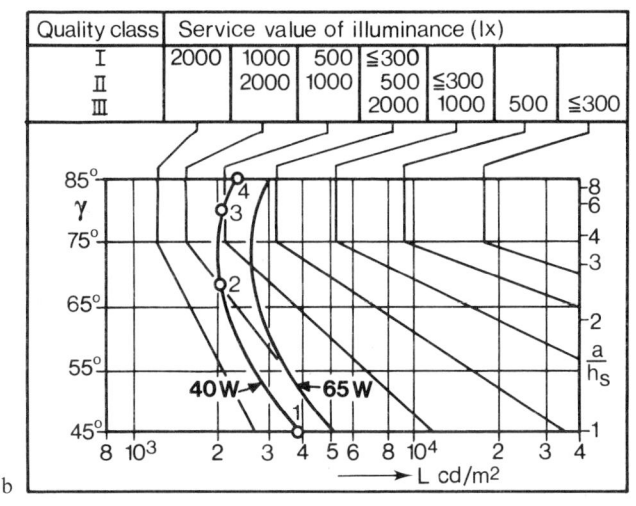

Figure 11.2 Luminance curve diagrams showing the luminance distribution (a) in the plane parallel to the lamp axes, and (b) at right angles to the lamp axes, of twin-lamp fluorescent ceiling luminaires having clear prismatic acrylic diffusers with luminous sides, one fitted with 40 W fluorescent tubes and the other with 65 W tubes. (The quotient a/h_s is defined in figure 11.1)

catalogue or from the photometric data sheet, whether or not a particular luminaire fulfils the glare limitation requirements for a given installation. It is imperative, therefore, that luminaire manufactures publish the glare limitation data concerning their luminaires in an easily understandable form. The easiest way of preparing a presentation of luminaire luminance values using this modified luminance curve system is to plot the luminance distribution of the relevant lamp/luminaire combination, as obtained from the photometric data sheet, on the standard diagrams of the system. The result, for a specific type of twin-lamp ceiling luminaire having an acrylic diffuser and luminous sides and equipped with either 40 W or 65 W fluorescent tubes, might appear as shown in figure 11.2.

This figure shows that if the 40 W luminaire concerned is mounted parallel to the line of sight (figure 11.2a), it may be used in quality class I installations up to an illuminance level of about 500 lx and in class II installations up to a level of 1000 lx, independent of room size. In smaller rooms (for example, where $a/h_s = 3$) it may be used up to 1000 lx in quality class I. As may be expected, its applicability is more restricted if it is mounted across the line of sight; in this case (figure 11.2b), the luminaire may be used for quality class II installations in rather small rooms only ($a/h_s < 3$), and even then only up to an illuminance of 500 lx.

The 65 W version of the same luminaire, if mounted parallel to the line of sight, may be used for quality class II installations up to a level of somewhat more than 500 lx. For crosswise mounting, the luminaire should only be permitted for use in rather small rooms ($a/h_s \leqslant 2$).

The presentation of luminaire glare limiting data in tabular form, which is sometimes preferred, is illustrated by table 11.3. Such a table – referred to as an admissibility table – shows, for a given quality class and illuminance level, under what conditions the luminaire concerned (in this case the luminaire/lamp combination described above) will give rise to glare.

The table contains all the information, in an easily readable form, for the designer to be able to reach a decision regarding the acceptance or rejection of a given luminaire type. It is suggested, therefore, that such tables should be the means normally employed for presenting glare limiting data in manufacturers' luminaire catalogues.

11.3.3 Reflected Glare and Veiling Reflections

The measures taken to control direct glare will not necessarily take care of reflected glare also. For example, a bright light source screened from direct view may still be visible as a reflection in specular surfaces on, or adjacent to, the work task – especially if this is badly positioned relative to the source.

Table 11.3 Specification of glare limiting data in the form of an Admissibility Table (as drawn up for the twin-lamp luminaire specified in figure 11.3)

Quality class	Service illuminance (lx)					
I	2000	1000	500	≤250		
II		2000	1000	500	≤250	
III			2000	1000	500	≤250
40 W ∥	⊠	2.5	+	+	+	+
40 W ⊥	⊠	⊠	1.5	3.0	3.5	+
65 W ∥	⊠	⊠	3.0	+	+	+
65 W ⊥	⊠	⊠	⊠	2.2	3.0	+

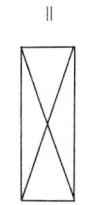

Line of sight relative to luminaire: ∥ , ⊥

⊠ $\tan^{-1} \gamma$ = glaring

= no glare up to the value indicated ($\tan \gamma = a/h_s$, see figure 11.1)

+ = no glare for any room length

Reflections occurring in the task itself that reduce task contrasts to give a loss of detail sufficient to impair visibility are termed veiling reflections. Reflected glare caused by specular surfaces adjacent to the task can result in discomfort and loss of concentration, the attention being drawn involuntarily away from the task toward the area of higher brightness.

The occurrence of reflected glare in general and veiling reflections in particular, is dependent not only on the luminance of the luminaires and their arrangement, but also on the layout of the luminaires relative to the working areas and on the illuminance level prevailing. Ideally, no part of a task or its surround should be at or near to the mirror angle with respect to the eye and any bright source of light (figure 11.3). If the light can be arranged to fall on the task from approximately the same direction as the direction of view or from the sides, so much the better; loss of task contrast will then usually be at a minimum. This condition is, however, difficult to meet in practice, especially in rooms occupied by many people. The usual approach is to aim at avoiding layouts in which the luminaires are in the same vertical plane as the observer's line of sight.

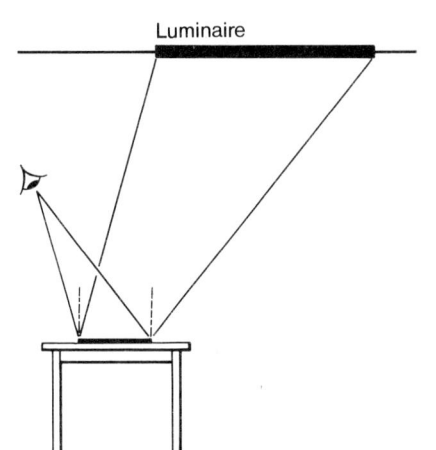

Figure 11.3 Any bright luminaire located at the mirror angle relative to the line of sight will be in danger of producing veiling reflections in the visual task.

Luminaires of large surface area and low luminance also help to lessen the chances of glare occurring. (For reading tasks, the luminaire luminance in cd/m^2 in the direction where reflected glare can occur should be limited to 7 times the illuminance value on the task in lx.)

Needless to say, glossy or high-reflectance surfaces should be avoided wherever possible.

11.4 Colour Appearance and Colour Rendering

The colour qualities of a lamp are characterised by its colour appearance and its colour rendering, that is its ability to influence the colour appearance of the objects it illuminates.

The lamps normally used for interior lighting may be divided into three groups according to their colour appearance: warm, intermediate and cool. For low lighting levels a warm colour is usually preferred. Higher illuminances are best produced using lamps of intermediate colour appearance. Cool lamp colours are used with high levels of illuminance or, in tropical countries, where a light source that gives an impression of coolness is required. The general impressions associated with different illuminances and different colour appearances have been tabulated by the CIE. (See table 11.4.)

Table 11.4 General impressions associated with different illuminances and different colour appearances of light

Illuminance (lx)	Colour appearance of light		
	Warm	Intermediate	Cool
⩽ 500	pleasant	neutral	cool
500–1000	↕	↕	↕
1000–2000	stimulating	pleasant	neutral
2000–3000	↕	↕	↕
⩾ 3000	unnatural	stimulating	pleasant

Note: The terms used above are general subjective assessments and may need modification in extremes of climate. For example, warmer countries may prefer sources with a cooler appearance

Both the colour appearance and the colour rendering properties of a light source are determined by the spectral composition of the light emitted. But a difference in spectral composition does not necessarily imply that two lamps will differ in colour appearance (they can in fact be identical in this respect) merely that they will exhibit a difference in colour rendering. It is impossible, therefore, to draw any conclusions regarding the colour rendering properties of a lamp from its colour appearance.

The colour rendering properties of a lamp are described by its colour rendering index (see Sec. 4.3.2): the higher the index, the better the colour rendering. It is convenient for the purposes of specification to divide lamps into three main colour rendering groups, the lamps in each group being those most suitable for a particular range of applications. This grouping is shown in table 11.5 (CIE, 1975). As can be seen, a distinction has been made between

Table 11.5 Lamp Colour Rendering Groups as given in the 1975 CIE 'Guide on Interior Lighting'.

Colour rendering group	Range of colour rendering index R_a	Colour appearance	Examples of use
1	$R_a \geq 85$	Cool	textile industries, paint and printing industries
		Intermediate	shops, hospitals
		Warm	homes, hotels, restaurants
2	$70 \leq R_a < 85$	Cool	offices, schools, department stores, fine industrial work (in hot climates)
		Intermediate	offices, schools, department stores, fine industrial work (in temperate climates)
		Warm	offices, schools, department stores, fine industrial work (in cold climates)
3	Lamps with $R_a < 70$ but with sufficiently acceptable colour rendering properties for use in general working interiors		interiors where colour rendering is of comparatively minor importance
S (Special)	Lamps with unusual colour rendering properties		special applications

'standard' lamps, which are those used in lighting installations where the specification of a colour rendering index is important (groups 1 to 3), and an additional group of lamps, the so-called 'special' lamps of group S. The lamps in this latter group are specially designed to give a spectral distribution that produces colour distortion, or emphasis. Examples of applications in which group S lamps may be employed are: floodlighting, garden lighting, display lighting and the lighting of certain industrial processes.

It should also be noted, in conclusion, that certain applications, e.g. colour matching, may be extremely critical with regard to the colour rendering properties of the lamps used. Here, the minimum colour rendering index should be 90.

11.5 Modelling

The general appearance of an interior is enhanced when its structural features and the people and objects within are lighted so that form and texture are revealed clearly and pleasingly. This occurs when the light comes noticeably from one direction; the shadows so essential to good modelling are then formed without confusion. But the lighting must not be too directional or it will produce unpleasantly harsh shadows, neither can it be too diffuse or the modelling effect will be lost entirely.

Modelling has long been recognised as an important qualitative factor in lighting. It is understandable, therefore, that attempts should have been made to quantify the effect of directional lighting.

Experience has shown that with direct-glare control by means of strong downward directional light, deep shadows from the eyebrows may occur on the face, or distortion may arise from multiple shadows on the task. Experience gained from high-level installations with good shielding indicate that a minimum ratio for the illuminance on vertical to that on horizontal surfaces of 0.25 is required for acceptability in this respect. Highly diffused lighting, on the other hand, as results from the use of luminous ceilings and indirect lighting, leads to flat modelling. Such lighting should, therefore, be avoided in working interiors.

Chapter 12

Lighting Codes

Quite a number of countries, in the absence of international agreement, have developed their own individual recommendations on interior lighting. The points of difference from one national recommendation to another are confined in the main to the way in which illuminance levels, luminance ratios, glare evaluation and colour rendering are dealt with for the various types of interior and activity. It can be expected that the future development of these recommendations will be influenced to some extent by the Guide on Interior Lighting prepared by the Commission Internationale de l'Eclairage, (CIE, 1975). This guide supplies general information on the many different aspects of interior lighting. The guide does not, however, include illuminance values for specific tasks.

Three different approaches may be recognised in the national recommendations. There are the very extensive and detailed recommendations of the American Illuminating Engineering Society, which appear in the IES Lighting Handbook. The handbook has chapters devoted to the fundamentals of lighting, light sources, luminaires and lighting calculation, and numerous chapters dealing with the various fields of lighting application – industrial, office, residential, roadway, sports, transport, and so forth.

Then there are the quite different Russian recommendations. Unlike other national recommendations, the information relating to industrial applications does not deal with specific areas and activities, but with dimensions of the task being illuminated, the contrast between task and background, and background reflectance. There are also differences in approach between the recommendations given for general lighting and those dealing with local lighting.

Finally, there are the various Western European recommendations. National recommendations within Western Europe reach agreement on many points (Fischer, 1973b). It is these European national recommendations that form the basis for discussion in this chapter. The discussion is restricted to the following aspects of these recommendations: lighting level, luminance distribution in the visual field, glare control, directional effects in lighting and colour.

12.1 Lighting Level

Information relating to lighting levels (illuminance values) for use in interiors can appear in a number of forms
(a) As codes issued by standards organisations and illuminating engineering societies and giving recommended lighting levels based on the criteria of efficiency and comfort;
(b) As specifications or legislation defining minimum levels as dictated by the needs of safety and welfare. These levels are in general lower than those recommended in (a) above – in Germany, for instance, they are 50 per cent lower;
(c) As specifications or legislation defining minimum levels based on the criterion of safety only. These levels are very much lower than those recommended in group (a) above. Typical levels as specified in the USA are 5 lx to 50 lx for industrial areas;
(d) As specifications, legislation and codes defining the minimum levels to be provided in the case of emergency, e.g. failure of primary power supply. (Minimum levels for escape lighting are extremely low, in the order of 1 lx)

In the discussion that follows, only those levels appearing in codes described by (a) above will be considered.

Either service values or minimum values of illuminance are recommended, depending on the country in which the code was originated, table 12.1.

The service illuminance is the mean illuminance throughout the life of the lighting system and averaged over the relevant area, which may be the whole area of the interior or the area occupied by the visual task and its immediate surround. This means that the initial illuminance must be higher than the recommended value to allow for the fact that the illuminance will inevitably drop below this value by the end of the cleaning and relamping period.

Minimum illuminance values represent minimum values on the task at any time. This means that the initial illuminance on the task must be considerably higher – the exact amount will depend on the degree of light depreciation due to lamp ageing and the accumulation of dust and dirt – and that regular maintenance has to be ensured.

The recommended illuminance, whether it be a service value or a minimum, is valid for the horizontal, oblique or vertical working plane or, where this is not known, for the horizontal plane 0.85 m above the floor.

In the British IES Code, most of the illuminance values are specified in terms of the 'standard service illuminance'. This is the service illuminance recommended for standard conditions. A 'flow chart' is included in the code (figure 12.1) which shows how the standard illuminance recommended

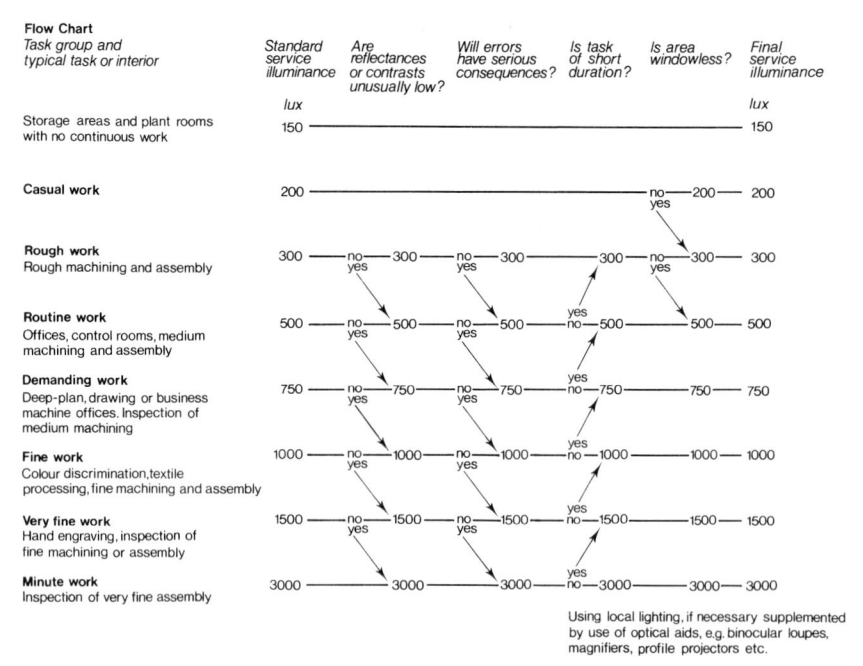

Flow Chart Task group and typical task or interior	Standard service illuminance	Are reflectances or contrasts unusually low?	Will errors have serious consequences?	Is task of short duration?	Is area windowless?	Final service illuminance
	lux					lux
Storage areas and plant rooms with no continuous work	150					150
Casual work	200				no—200 yes ↘	200
Rough work Rough machining and assembly	300	no—300 yes ↘	no—300 yes ↘	300	no—300 yes ↗	300
Routine work Offices, control rooms, medium machining and assembly	500	no—500 yes ↘	no—500 yes ↘	yes no—500 ↗	500	500
Demanding work Deep-plan, drawing or business machine offices. Inspection of medium machining	750	no—750 yes ↘	no—750 yes ↘	yes no—750 ↗	750	750
Fine work Colour discrimination, textile processing, fine machining and assembly	1000	no—1000 yes ↘	no—1000 yes ↘	yes no—1000 ↗	1000	1000
Very fine work Hand engraving, inspection of fine machining or assembly	1500	no—1500 yes ↘	no—1500 yes ↘	yes no—1500 ↗	1500	1500
Minute work Inspection of very fine assembly	3000	3000	3000	yes no—3000 ↗	3000	3000

Using local lighting, if necessary supplemented by use of optical aids, e.g. binocular loupes, magnifiers, profile projectors etc.

Figure 12.1 Flow Chart of the British IES Code showing the steps by which the standard service illuminance should be increased when one or more special conditions apply. The resulting final service illuminance should then be used as the design value.

for a particular activity should be increased to compensate to some extent for unusual features in the task; the resulting final service illuminance derived from the flow chart is then used as the design value.

The illuminance values in the German code are also derived from the standard service illuminance, figure 12.2. For example, the minimum *initial* value at any working position is required to be not less than 0.8 times the service illuminance. This value will drop to not less than 0.5 times the service value during the life of the system, as is shown by the lower curve in figure 12.2.

This method has the advantages of a logical approach and simplicity at the same time if, with respect to visual performance and comfort, 50 per cent of the standard service illuminance is specified for the minimum illuminance level at any working position at any time.

There are also differences in the way in which light loss (maintenance) factors and lamp lumen values are applied in lighting design. Great Britain uses 'lighting design lumens' (average lumen output after 2000 hours) for lighting calculations, instead of the 100-hour value as generally agreed. These differences in approach lead to the need to design for different initial illuminances, as shown in table 12.2.

Table 12.1 Illuminance values recommended in various countries

Recommended illuminance value	Country	
Service value	Australia Austria Brazil France Germany Great Britain	Italy Japan The Netherlands Norway Switzerland
Minimum value	Belgium Canada Denmark India	South Africa Sweden USA USSR

Table 12.2 Examples of national illuminance recommendations

Country	Recommended illuminance value	Recommended maintenance factor in clean conditions	Lamp lumen value to be applied	Initial illuminance to be designed in % of recommended value
Germany and the Netherlands	Service value	0.8	100 h	125
Great Britain	Service value	0.8	2000 h	140
Belgium	Minimum value	0.8	100 h	150

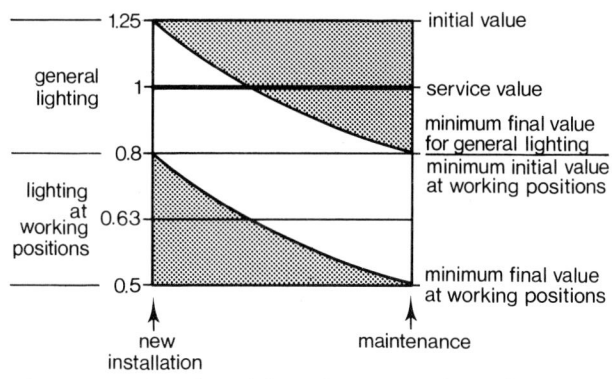

Figure 12.2 The various illuminance values derived from the service value in the German code of lighting.

Most of the national codes contain a schedule giving recommended illuminances (see previous chapter) for a large number of interiors and activities. Within Europe, the levels recommended in the different schedules for similar types of application are roughly comparable. Illuminance levels as recommended within Europe for a selection of areas and activities are given in table 12.3.

Table 12.3 Some illuminance levels, as recommended within Europe, for a selection of areas and activities

Area or Activity	Service illuminance (lx)	Area or Activity	Service illuminance (lx)
Bakeries:			
General working areas	300	Forming, blowing	300
Decorating, inspection	500	Decorating	500
		Etching	750
Breweries	300		
		Leather Factories:	
Canning and Preserving Factories	500	Pressing, glazing	750
		Cutting, sewing	1 000
Chemical Works:		Grading, matching	1 500
Interior plant areas	200		
Grinding, mixing	300	*Machine Shops:*	
Calendering, injection	500	Rough bench and machine work,	
Control rooms	500	welding	300
Laboratories	750	Medium bench and machine work	500
Colour matching	1 000	Fine bench and machine work	750
		Very fine work	1 000
Chocolate Factories:		Very fine precision work	2 000
General working areas	300		
Decorating, inspection	500	*Paper Mills:*	
		Paper and board making	300
Dairies:			
Bottling milk	300	*Potteries:*	
		Firing	200
Electrical Industries:		Moulding, pressing	300
Coil winding	500	Enamelling, decorating	750
Assembly work: Fine	1 500		
Very fine	2 000	*Printing Works:*	
Adjustment, inspection	1 000	Printing machines, book binding	500
		Hand composing	750
Foundries:		Retouching, etching	1 000
Rough moulding, pouring	300		
Fine moulding, core making,		*Textile Mills:*	
inspection	500	Carding, spreading	300
		Reeling, spinning	500
Glass Works:		Weaving plain cloth	750
Mixing rooms	200		

Area or Activity	Service illuminance (lx)	Area or Activity	Service illuminance (lx)
Weaving fine worsteds	1 000	*Theatres and Concert Halls:*	
Inspection	1 500	Auditoria	100
		Foyers	200
Warehouses:			
Storage rooms	150	*Churches:*	
Packing and dispatch	300	Nave	100
		Choir	150
Woodworking Shops:			
Rough sawing and cutting	200	**Homes and Hotels**	
Rough bench work	300		
Medium bench work	500	*Homes:*	
Finishing, final inspection	750	Bedrooms:	
		General	50
Offices and Schools		Bed-head	200
		Bathrooms:	
Offices:		General	100
Conference rooms	300	Shaving, make-up	500
General offices:		Living-rooms:	
Normal	500	General	100
Deep-plan	750	Reading, sewing	500
Drawing boards	1 000	Stairs	100
		Kitchens:	
Schools:		General	300
Classrooms, lecture theatres	300	Working areas	500
Laboratories, libraries, reading		Workroom	300
rooms, art rooms	500	Nursery	150
Shops, Stores and Exhibition Areas		*Hotels:*	
		Entrance halls	300
Shops:		Dining rooms	200
Conventional shops	300	Kitchens	500
Self-service shops	500	Bedrooms, bathrooms:	
Supermarkets	750	General	100
		Local	300
Show Rooms	500		
		Miscellaneous	
Museums and Art Galleries:			
General:		*Indoors:*	
Light-sensitive exhibits	150	Circulation areas, corridors and	
Exhibits insensitive to light	300	stairs in industry	150
Public Buildings		*Outdoors:*	
		Entrances, exits	30
Cinemas:		Industrial covered ways, gantries	50
Auditoria	50	Docks, quays	100
Foyers	150	Service station forecourts	200

In areas that must give the impression of being well-lit and in which the appearance of people is important – circulation areas and the like – the value of the vertical illuminance on objects and walls is more meaningful than the horizontal illuminance since it has been found to be more indicative of lighting quality. Illuminance recommendations for these areas are, for this reason, given in the British IES Code in terms of scalar illuminance – also known as mean spherical illuminance. (See Chapter 2, Sec. 2.6.) Thus, the amount of light is indicated independently of the direction of incidence. The Russian code, however, uses the mean cylindrical illuminance for these areas because, in their view, it is more closely related to the vertical illuminance on objects and walls than is scalar illuminance.

12.2 Luminance Distribution in the Visual Field

There are at present no detailed recommendations in national codes relating to the luminance of the major surfaces in the visual field – walls, ceilings, etc. There are, however, methods whereby such luminances may be deduced indirectly.

There are two approaches open. Either the colour and reflectance of the surface in question can be fixed and the luminance arrived at by noting the surface illuminance recommended for a given task illuminance – as is done for walls in the French code – or the illuminance on the task can be taken as the starting point and the luminance calculated by noting the corresponding relative illuminances and effective reflectances for the various room surfaces as read from the recommendations. This is the approach adopted in the British Code, IES (1977), which recommends that the ceiling cavity reflectance (defined as the equivalent reflectance of the room volume

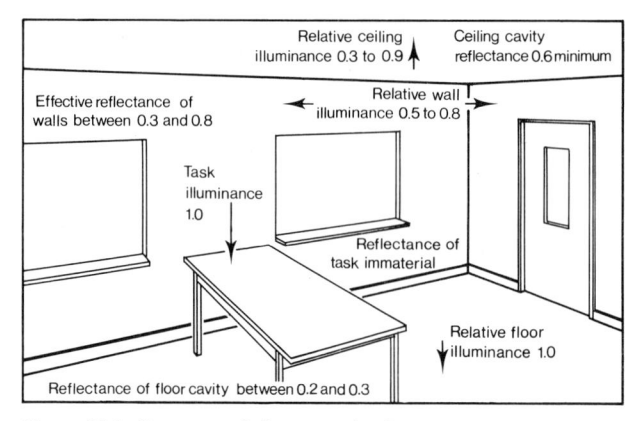

Figure 12.3 Recommended ranges of reflectance and relative illuminance for room surfaces as given in the British IES Code.

above the plane of the luminaires) in working interiors should be as high as practicable and generally at least 0.6. The effective reflectance recommended in this code for walls is 0.3 to 0.8, depending on room size – the smaller the room the higher the reflectance. The equivalent reflectance recommended for the floor cavity (viz. the room volume below the working plane) is 0.2 to 0.3. The recommendations are illustrated in figure 12.3.

12.3 Glare Control

There are two systems currently in use within Western Europe for measuring and specifying glare in working interiors. These are the British IES Glare Index System (IES, 1967), which has also been adopted by Belgium and Scandinavia, and the modified Luminance Curve System (which has been described in Chapter 3) which is being adopted by an ever increasing number of European countries including Austria, France, Germany, Italy, Switzerland and the Netherlands.

Where luminous ceilings are concerned, most countries have adopted a luminance limit of 500 cd/m^2 for any luminaire viewed at angles greater than 45° to the downward vertical.

12.4 Directional Effects in Lighting

12.4.1 Shadows

Quantitative specifications for the avoidance of excessive shadow effects are given in the Dutch and French codes, which both advise an upper limit of 4:1 for the ratio of the horizontal to the vertical illuminance at a point.

12.4.2 Modelling

A British proposal for the evaluation of modelling (given in an appendix to the code, IES, 1973) is that the flow of light be treated as a vector quantity whose magnitude and direction can be specified. The ratio of the magnitude of the illuminance vector to the scalar illuminance can be related to the subjective impression of the modelling qualities of the lighting. The relationship of vector/scalar ratio to assessment of directional qualities of the lighting is described in a table, which also includes photographs of the human face under different lighting conditions.

12.4.3 Contrast Rendering/Veiling Reflections

Only general recommendations are given in the codes mentioned above for obtaining good contrast rendering and the avoidance of veiling reflections;

for example, by carefully arranging the luminaires to lie outside the 'offending zone', by the use of luminaires of large flashed area and low luminance, by arranging for more light to fall on the task from the sides, and by the avoidance of glossy surfaces in the task area.

12.5 Colour

The lamps commonly used for interior lighting are classified with respect to their colour appearance as 'cool', 'intermediate' and 'warm'.

Colour rendering requirements are given in terms of the general colour rendering index, R_a (see Sec. 4.3.2). The British code, in addition, lists fourteen different lamp types in an extended table which describes their colour rendering effects on red, orange, yellow, green, and blue surface colours.

Recommendations concerning the minimum colour rendering index for specific applications are incorporated in the lighting codes of the different countries as shown in tables 12.4 to 12.6.

Table 12.4 Recommended minimum colour rendering index (French code)

Required quality	Minimum colour rendering index	Typical applications
Optimum appreciation of primary colours Excellent colour rendering	$R_a > 90$	Control, selection, examination... laboratories, textile industries, printing Selection of farm produce
Good colour rendering and comfortable illumination Acceptable colour rendering	$R_a > 80$ $R_a > 70$	Offices, department stores, schools, certain industries
Moderate colour rendering (colour rendering of secondary importance)	$60 < R_a < 70$	Light industry: mechanical workshops
No colour rendering requirement	$R_a < 60$	Heavy industry: foundries Store areas

Table 12.5 Recommended ranges of colour rendering index (German code)

Range of colour rendering index (R_a)	Typical applications
85–100	Textile and graphic industries, shops, offices, schools, homes, restaurants
70–84	Workshops, offices, schools, shops, corridors, staircases, outdoor lighting
40–69	Workshops and storerooms, outdoor lighting
<40	Floodlighting, outdoor lighting

Table 12.6 Recommended minimum colour rendering index and colour temperature (Dutch code)

Required quality	Minimum colour-rendering index (R_a)	Recommended colour temperature (K)	Examples of rooms
As high as possible	90	6500–7400	Colour-judging rooms in the textile, tobacco, paint and printing industries
		approx. 4000	Rooms used for medical examinations and treatment, museums, printing industries
Good	80	approx. 4000	Offices, department stores and shops; storerooms and workshops where sorting by colour is important
		approx. 3000	Places where people meet, conference rooms, ships, hotels
Medium	60	–	Corridors, staircases, storerooms, and workshops where colour rendering is of minor importance
None	–	–	Foundries, steel rolling mills i.e. heavy industries

Chapter 13

Calculations and Measurements

13.1 Calculations

Lighting calculations fall into two main groups: those performed by the equipment manufacturer in converting hardware measurement data into a form suitable for presentation to the lighting engineer, and those performed by the lighting engineer himself during the actual lighting design phase.

Little need be said here concerning the first group of calculations, other than that today increasing use is being made of the computer in this field. This is only to be expected, for the computer is able to process a large amount of data at less cost, far faster and with much less chance of error than was ever possible using manual calculation techniques alone. The sort of technical design data supplied in this way are summarised in this chapter by taking a look at a typical luminaire data sheet.

There is no reason, in theory at least, why the computer should not be called upon to go a step further and perform the task of designing a complete lighting installation. Properly programmed, it could be used to calculate such things as the average illuminance and the illuminance distribution on planes of interest – and hence uniformity of illuminance – it could even forecast luminance values and provide data on the degree of discomfort glare to be expected. Universally applicable computer programmes are in fact known to have been written by specialist organisations. In practice, however, a considerable amount of time must be spent in feeding the computer with the necessary design data, and for routine design work it will invariably prove quicker and quite sufficient to make use instead of simple, manual design techniques. The main types of calculation met with in such an approach to lighting design, namely those concerned with the determination of illuminance, luminance and running costs, are outlined in this chapter.

13.1.1 Technical Design Data

Much of the information on which lighting calculations are based is supplied by the equipment manufacturer in the form of technical data sheets. A typical data sheet for a luminaire will contain the sort of information given

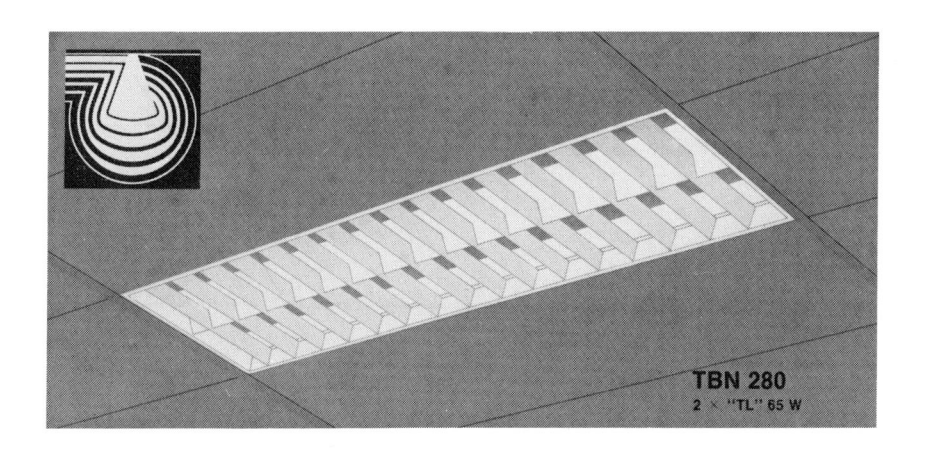

PHOTOMETRIC DATA

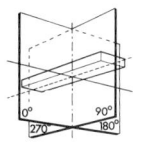

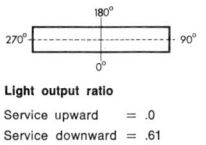

TBN 280
2 × "TL" 65 W

Light output ratio

Service upward	=	.0
Service downward	=	.61
Total	=	.61
Optical total	=	.70
Luminous area: L	=	1508 mm
W	=	287 mm

Zonal luminous flux diagram

61%

Luminous intensity diagram

— 0°–180°
---- 90°–270°

cd/1000 lm

γ	PER 1000 LM				
	INTENSITY		LUMINANCE		ZONAL FLUX
	0–180	90–270	0–180	90–270	0–γ
0	276	276	638	638	0
5	275	273	639	633	7
10	274	264	643	619	26
15	272	252	651	603	58
20	268	236	659	580	100
25	259	218	660	556	151
30	246	198	656	530	210
35	226	178	637	502	272
40	198	155	597	468	335
45	165	131	539	428	395
50	128	107	461	385	449
55	95	82	382	331	494
60	68	59	315	274	529
65	48	44	262	241	556
70	35	33	235	222	576
75	23	23	209	204	591
80	15	14	201	185	601
85	7	6	183	154	607

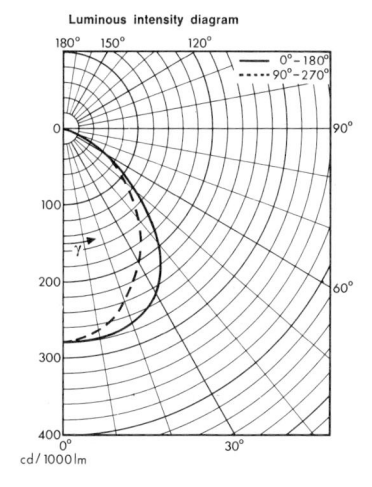

Figure 13.1 Extracts from a manufacturer's data sheet, giving the various items of information referred to in the text.

227

UTILIZATION FACTOR TABLE FOR THE CALCULATION OF AVERAGE ILLUMINANCES AT WORKING PLANE, CEILING AND WALLS

	K	REFLECTANCES OF CEILING, WALLS, WORKING PLANE																						DR	BZ
		.70 .90 .50	.70 .30 .10	.70 .10 .10	.50 .50 .10	.50 .30 .10	.50 .10 .10	.30 .30 .10	.30 .10 .10	.70 .50 .30	.70 .30 .30	.70 .10 .30	.50 .50 .30	.50 .30 .30	.50 .10 .30	.30 .30 .30	.30 .10 .30	0 0 0								
WORKING PLANE	0.60	.31	.27	.24	.31	.27	.24	.27	.24	.33	.28	.24	.32	.27	.24	.27	.24	.23	.38	3					
	0.80	.38	.34	.31	.37	.33	.31	.33	.30	.40	.35	.31	.39	.34	.31	.34	.31	.29	.48	3					
	1.00	.42	.38	.35	.41	.37	.35	.37	.35	.45	.40	.36	.43	.39	.36	.38	.35	.33	.55	3					
	1.25	.46	.42	.39	.45	.42	.39	.41	.39	.49	.45	.41	.47	.43	.40	.42	.40	.38	.62	3					
	1.50	.49	.45	.43	.47	.45	.42	.44	.42	.53	.48	.45	.51	.47	.44	.45	.43	.41	.67	3					
	2.00	.52	.49	.47	.51	.49	.47	.48	.46	.58	.54	.50	.55	.52	.49	.50	.47	.45	.73	3					
	2.50	.55	.52	.50	.53	.51	.49	.51	.49	.61	.57	.54	.58	.55	.52	.53	.50	.47	.78	3					
	3.00	.56	.54	.52	.55	.53	.52	.52	.51	.63	.60	.57	.60	.57	.55	.55	.53	.49	.81	3					
	4.00	.58	.57	.55	.57	.56	.54	.55	.53	.66	.63	.61	.63	.60	.58	.57	.56	.52	.85	3					
	5.00	.60	.58	.57	.58	.57	.56	.56	.55	.68	.66	.64	.64	.62	.60	.59	.58	.54	.88	3					
CEILING	0.60	.08	.04	.02	.07	.04	.02	.04	.02	.10	.06	.03	.10	.06	.03	.06	.03								
	0.80	.08	.04	.02	.08	.04	.02	.04	.02	.12	.07	.04	.11	.07	.04	.07	.04								
	1.00	.08	.05	.02	.08	.05	.02	.05	.02	.13	.09	.06	.13	.09	.06	.08	.05	SPACING							
	1.25	.08	.05	.03	.08	.05	.03	.05	.03	.14	.10	.07	.14	.10	.07	.10	.07	———— = 1.00							
	1.50	.08	.05	.03	.07	.05	.03	.05	.03	.15	.11	.08	.15	.11	.08	.11	.08	HEIGHT							
	2.00	.08	.05	.04	.07	.05	.04	.05	.04	.17	.13	.10	.16	.13	.10	.12	.10								
	2.50	.07	.06	.04	.07	.06	.04	.05	.04	.18	.15	.12	.17	.14	.12	.13	.11								
	3.00	.07	.06	.04	.07	.06	.04	.06	.04	.18	.16	.13	.17	.15	.13	.14	.12	SUSPENSION							
	4.00	.07	.06	.05	.07	.06	.05	.06	.05	.19	.17	.15	.18	.16	.14	.15	.14	———— = 0							
	5.00	.07	.06	.05	.07	.06	.05	.06	.05	.20	.18	.16	.19	.17	.16	.16	.15	HEIGHT							
WALLS	0.60	.18	.15	.13	.18	.15	.13	.15	.13	.21	.17	.14	.20	.17	.14	.16	.14								
	0.80	.20	.17	.14	.19	.16	.14	.16	.14	.23	.19	.17	.23	.19	.16	.18	.16								
	1.00	.21	.18	.16	.20	.18	.16	.17	.16	.26	.22	.19	.24	.21	.18	.20	.18								
	1.25	.22	.19	.17	.21	.19	.17	.18	.17	.27	.24	.21	.26	.23	.20	.22	.20								
	1.50	.22	.20	.18	.22	.19	.18	.19	.18	.29	.25	.23	.27	.24	.22	.23	.21								
	2.00	.23	.21	.19	.22	.21	.19	.20	.19	.31	.28	.25	.29	.26	.24	.25	.23								
	2.50	.24	.22	.21	.23	.21	.20	.21	.20	.32	.29	.27	.30	.28	.26	.26	.24								
	3.00	.24	.22	.21	.23	.22	.20	.21	.20	.33	.31	.28	.31	.29	.27	.27	.26								
	4.00	.24	.23	.22	.24	.22	.21	.22	.21	.35	.32	.30	.32	.30	.29	.28	.27								
	5.00	.25	.24	.22	.24	.23	.22	.22	.22	.35	.34	.32	.33	.31	.30	.29	.28	LVO 04875							

Initial average illuminance = utilization factor x flux of lamps installed per square metre ceiling area.

quality class	service value of illuminance (lux)			
I	≥ 750	≤ 500		
II		≥ 750	≤ 500	
III			≥ 750	≤ 500
	a	b	c	d	e

Data for the determination of glare limitation according to the C.I.E. Publication No. 29.

0 - 180		
	33/84	34
γ	CD/M2	CD/M2
85	1866	1215
75	2131	1387
65	2677	1743
55	3895	2536

90 - 270		
	33/84	34
γ	CD/M2	CD/M2
85	1568	1021
75	2076	1352
65	2454	1597
55	3378	2199

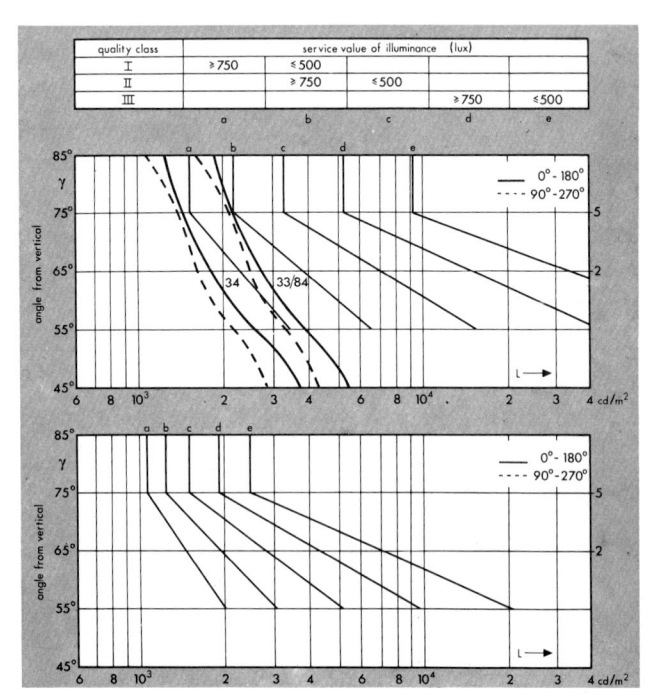

RETURN AIR DATA

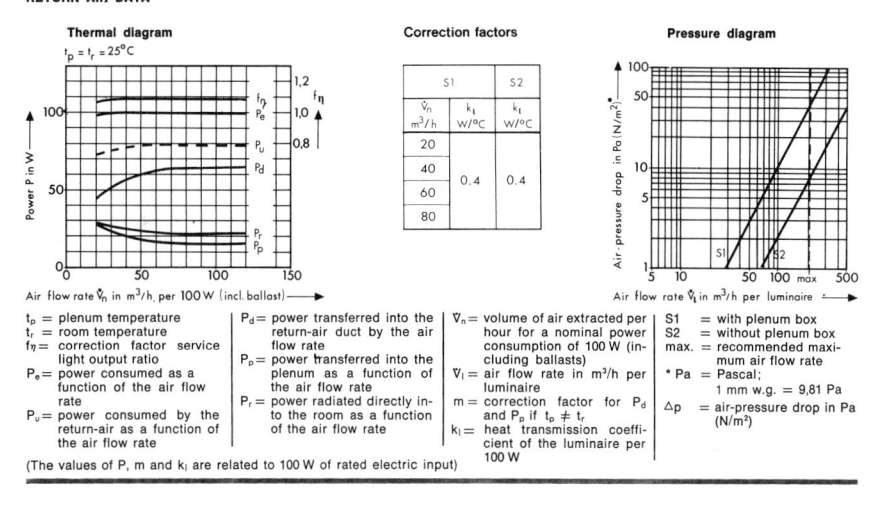

Thermal diagram
$t_p = t_r = 25°C$

Correction factors

S1		S2	
$\dot{V}_n$ m³/h	k_l W/°C		k_l W/°C
20			
40	0.4		0.4
60			
80			

Pressure diagram

Air flow rate $\dot{V}_n$ in m³/h per 100 W (incl. ballast)

Air flow rate $\dot{V}_l$ in m³/h per luminaire

t_p = plenum temperature
t_r = room temperature
f_η = correction factor service light output ratio
P_e = power consumed as a function of the air flow rate
P_u = power consumed by the return-air as a function of the air flow rate

P_d = power transferred into the return-air duct by the air flow rate
P_p = power transferred into the plenum as a function of the air flow rate
P_r = power radiated directly into the room as a function of the air flow rate

$\dot{V}_n$ = volume of air extracted per hour for a nominal power consumption of 100 W (including ballasts)
$\dot{V}_l$ = air flow rate in m³/h per luminaire
m = correction factor for P_d and P_p if $t_p \neq t_r$
k_l = heat transmission coefficient of the luminaire per 100 W

S1 = with plenum box
S2 = without plenum box
max. = recommended maximum air flow rate
* Pa = Pascal;
  1 mm w.g. = 9,81 Pa
Δp = air-pressure drop in Pa (N/m²)

(The values of P, m and k_l are related to 100 W of rated electric input)

SOUND DATA

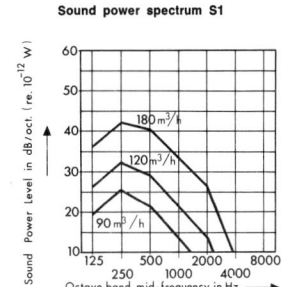

Sound power spectrum S1

Sound power diagram

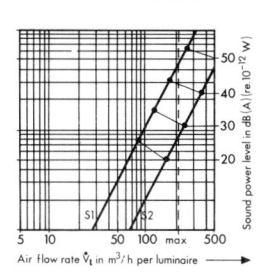

in figure 13.1 (pages 227–229). This information can, so far as lighting calculations are concerned, be listed as follows:

Photometric data

Zonal flux. Information concerning the luminous flux distribution of a luminaire is given both in diagrammatic and tabular form.

The zonal luminous flux diagram shows at a glance what percentage of the luminaire's total installed luminous flux is emitted within any given cone, the cone being defined by its half apex angle.

The tabulated zonal flux values enable the user to determine the exact value of the luminous flux emitted by the luminaire for a given half-apex value. The flux is specified in lumens per 1000 lumens installed.

Light output ratio. This is the ratio of the flux emitted by the luminaire to the sum of the individual fluxes emitted by the lamps operating outside the luminaire under standard conditions

$$OR = \frac{F}{n \times PHI}$$

where OR = light output ratio
 F = flux emitted by the luminaire
 n = number of lamps per luminaire
 PHI = nominal flux of one lamp (PHI is computer language for Φ).

The light output ratio is divided into the upward light output ratio and the downward light output ratio. The nomenclature used on the data sheet is
Light output ratio (upward + downward) = Total
Light output ratio upward = Service upward
Light output ratio downward = Service downward

Optical light output ratio. This is the ratio of the flux emitted by the luminaire to the sum of the individual fluxes emitted by the lamps operating inside the luminaire.

Note: If the optical light output ratio is considerably greater than the service light output ratio this indicates that the lamps are operating within the luminaire under unfavourable conditions. Ventilation of the luminaire, in many cases, will improve these conditions and help towards achieving the ideal situation where the optical light output ratio and the service light output ratio are equal.
The service light output ratio, mentioned above, is normally given for the luminaire operating without ventilation.

Luminous intensity. The luminous intensity distribution of a luminaire is shown in the form of a polar diagram in which intensity, in cd per 1000 lm of nominal lamp flux, is plotted as a function of γ for two planes mutually at right angles: in a vertical plane through the longitudinal axis of the luminaire (the 90°–270° plane) and in a plane at right angles to this axis (the 0°–180° plane).

The polar diagram, or luminous intensity diagram, can be used:
a) to provide a rough idea of the light distribution of the luminaire;
b) for the calculation of illuminance values at a point (although the data given in the 'luminous intensity table' – see below – is more suitable for this purpose); or

c) for the calculation of the luminance distribution of the luminaire (same comment as for b).

Note: In the case of obvious asymmetry the number of planes may be extended, while for completely symmetrical light distribution the number of planes will be reduced to one.

The luminous intensity distribution of a luminaire is also specified by means of a luminous intensity table. The luminous intensity table is for use when it is necessary to know the exact luminous intensity of the luminaire in a particular direction. This table gives the luminous intensity values, per 1000 lm of nominal lamp flux, as measured in the laboratory, at every 5°, in two planes, one passing through the longitudinal axis of the luminaire (90°–270°) and one at right angles to this axis (0°–180°). These are the same planes as those in the luminous intensity diagram.

Luminaire luminance. Given in the data sheet is a table in which are listed luminaire luminance values in cd/m² per 1000 lm of lamp flux for angles of view γ (measured from the downward vertical through the luminaire's centre) from 0° to 85°. These values are given for the two planes of interest, viz. that parallel to the lamp axis (the 90°–270° plane) and that at right angles to this axis (the 0°–180° plane).

Note: Where the luminance distribution of a luminaire is not specified by the manufacturer, this will have to be calculated (see Sec. 13.1.3).

Utilization factor. The utilization factor, UF, for a reference plane is the ratio between the flux received on the reference plane, FT, and the sum of the nominal fluxes, SPHI, from all the lamps in the installation

$$UF = \frac{FT}{SPHI} = \frac{FT}{n \times N \times PHI} \quad \text{in which } N \text{ is the number of luminaires.}$$

The average illuminance on the working plane, walls and ceiling (E4, E3 and E1 respectively) are given by:

E4 = UF4 × PHID
E3 = UF3 × PHID
E1 = UF1 × PHID

in which UF4, UF3 and UF1 are the utilization factors for these planes and PHID is the installed lamp flux density.

$$PHID = \frac{n \times N \times PHI}{A} = \frac{SPHI}{A}$$

where A = area of the plane considered.

Note: The utilization factors are calculated for (a) a regular and rectangular arrangement of luminaires with a spacing-to-height ratio as specified and a distance from the perimeter luminaires to the nearest wall equal to half the spacing and (b) a suspension-to-height ratio (see definition below) as specified.

Room index. This is an index of the geometry of the room. The greater the room index the greater the utilization factor. The room index is given by the formula

$$k = \frac{a \times b}{h3 \times (a + b)}$$

where a and b are the lengths of the sides of the room and $h3$ is the mounting height, which is the distance between the plane of the luminaires and the working plane.

Note: The working plane is the imaginary (normally) horizontal plane considered to be at the height of the work above the floor (normally 0,75 m sitting or 0,85 m standing) and covering the entire floor area.

The utilization factor values are arranged in the tables according to the relevant room index (from $k = 0.6$ to $k = 5.0$).

Room reflectances. The ratio of the luminous flux reflected by a room surface to the flux incident upon that surface is called the reflectance of that surface.
The utilization factor tables include combinations of different values of reflectance for the ceiling R1, walls R3 and working plane R4: (ceiling $R1 = 0.70; 0.50$ and 0.30; walls $R3 = 0.50; 0.30$ and 0.10; working plane $R4 = 0,30$ and $0,10$), as recommended by the CIE.

Direct ratio. The direct ratio (DR) is the ratio of the luminous flux directly incident on the working plane to the downward flux of the installation.

BZ classification. For the benefit of those countries where the BZ method (British Zonal method) of luminaire classification is used, the BZ classification is given in the last column of the utilization factor tables. This classification can be used for the calculation of the approximate average illuminance on the working plane and the IES Glare Index (for further details see IES Technical Report No. 2 – IES, 1971 and IES Technical Report No. 10 – IES, 1967).

Spacing-to-height ratio. The spacing-to-height ratio is the ratio of the distance between the centre of the luminaires and the distance between the plane of the luminaires and the working plane.

Suspension-to-height ratio. The suspension-to-height ratio is the ratio of the distance between the ceiling and the plane of the luminaires and the distance between the plane of the luminaires and the working plane.

Luminance diagram and glare limitation curves. The CIE Guide on Interior Lighting (CIE Publication No. 29) gives rules for the control of direct discomfort glare. (See also Sec. 11.3.2) Depending on the 'Quality Class' chosen, the luminance of luminaires should not exceed values tabulated for emission angles $\gamma = 85°, 75°, 65°$ and $55°$, a distinction being made between different levels of illuminance. The luminance limits are represented in a diagram by means of luminance curves that pass through the tabulated values. The plotted luminance curve of the luminaire immediately reveals for which quality class and for which range of illuminance levels the luminaire complies with the CIE glare limiting rules. When the curve is on the left-hand side of one of the standard curves indicated by a, b, c, d or e, it means that the luminaire can be used for the conditions defined by that curve and by all curves to the right of it. These conditions are described in the block immediately above the diagram. A table of the luminance values for two types of lamp is given, enabling a direct comparison to be made with the CIE tables.

Return air data (for air-handling luminaires only)

Correction factor for light output ratio. Given in the thermal diagram is a curve, f_η, that indicates the increase in service light output ratio as a function of air flow rate per 100 watt of nominal installed lighting load (including ballast).

Thermal characteristics. The curves P in the thermal diagram specify how the electrical energy consumed by the luminaire (lamps and ballast) is converted into heat, the rate of production of heat being given as a function of air flow rate for a nominal load of 100 watt.

For the luminaire installed in a plenum-exhaust system (i.e. no plenum box attached) the total rate of production of heat, curve P_e, has two components: P_u, the heat carried by the return air into the plenum, and P_r, the heat radiated directly into the room. Thus

$$P_e = P_u + P_r$$

Where the luminaire is provided with a plenum box the curve P_e will have three components: P_d, the heat carried by the return air into the return-air duct; P_p, the heat radiated from the luminaire into the plenum; and P_r as above. Thus, in this case

$$P_e = P_d + P_p + P_r$$

Correction factor for heat flow through ceiling. The thermal diagram is standardised for $t_p = t_r = 25°C$. If these temperatures are not equal, there will be a heat flow through the false ceiling. In order to be able to calculate this heat flow the user needs to know the heat transmission coefficient of the false ceiling, k_{fc}, per 100 watt of installed electrical load. This coefficient is given by

$$k_{fc} = \frac{k_c (A - A_1) + k_1 A_1}{A}$$

in which k_c = heat transmission coefficient of the false ceiling material
k_1 = heat transmission coefficient of the luminaire, per 100 watt
A = area of the ceiling, per 100 watt
A_1 = area of the luminaire, per 100 watt

The value of k_1 for a luminaire with or without a plenum box can be obtained from the correction factor table (columns S1 and S2 respectively) for a number of air flow rates.

Air pressure difference. To exhaust a volume of air through a luminaire an air pressure difference across the luminaire is needed. The pressure difference (given either in millimetres water gauge, mm. w. g., or in pascals, Pa, – 1 mm. w.g. = 9.81 Pa) needed to create a given air flow rate can be read from the pressure diagram. The maximum permitted air flow rate per luminaire, expressed in m^3/h, is indicated in the diagram by a dotted line.

13.1.2 Illuminance Calculations

In many working interiors an average illuminance level has to be created on the working plane by a regular pattern of ceiling-mounted luminaires. In order to determine either the necessary number of lamps and luminaires for a specified lighting level or the average illuminance obtained from a particular lighting design, the so-called Lumen Method of calculation is employed.

Limitations of the straightforward lumen method are that a) it considers only the average illuminance specified for the working plane, and b) it can only be used for standard luminaire arrangements, that is to say arrangements defined by the luminaire manufacturer in his utilisation factor tables. Should it be necessary to design an installation that will yield certain specified illuminances on the ceiling and walls as well as on the working plane, or should it be necessary for some reason to depart from a standard luminaire arrangement, then the more sophisticated design approach offered by the so-called Applied Method of the CIE referred to below can be used. Finally, for some purposes it may be necessary to calculate the illuminance provided at a point in an interior, or over a small defined area, by a single luminaire. (A spotlit picture on a wall and the lighting of an office desk by a single overhead luminaire are examples.) Here the Point Method of calculation is used.

The Lumen Method

The object of the lumen method of design is to determine a lighting layout that will provide a specified service illuminance on the horizontal working plane from an installation of luminaires mounted overhead in a substantially regular pattern.

The lumen method is based on the formula

$$n = \frac{E \times A}{PHI \times UF \times MF}$$

where n = the number of lamps required
A = the area of the working plane
E = the specified illuminance
PHI = the luminous flux of the lamp type used
UF = utilisation factor for the working plane
MF = maintenance factor for the installation

The formula used to calculate the total luminous flux, SPHI, that must be installed to give the specified illuminance, E4, on the working plane is

$$SPHI = \frac{E4 \times A}{UF4 \times f_\eta \times MF}$$

where UF4 is the utilisation factor for the working plane (as defined under 'Utilisation factors') and f_η is the correction factor for the light output ratio (applicable only in the case of air-handling luminaires) – the light output ratio itself is incorporated in the utilisation factor (UF = light output ratio × utilance).

The utilisation factor is found as follows

a) Determine the room index, k, according to the formula

$$k = \frac{a \times b}{h3 \times (a + b)}$$

b) Determine the reflectances of the ceiling, walls and working plane, For this, the following scale can be used

white and very light colours	0.7
light colours	0.5
medium colours	0.3
dark colours	0.1

The average reflectance for the working plane, which is often made up to a large extent by furniture and floor, is normally taken to be 0.1. Where light coloured office desks or similar work surfaces occupy a substantial part of the working plane an average reflectance of up to 0.3 would be more appropriate.

The designer is frequently faced with the situation that the reflectances of room surfaces are not known at the time when the lighting design is made. In such cases it is recommended to use for offices the triplet 0.7/0.5/0.3 for the reflectances of ceiling, walls and working plane respectively, and for other premises the triplet 0.7/0.5/0.1.

c) Select the utilisation factor table appropriate to the type of luminaire and lamp under consideration and read the value of UF4 from the table at the corresponding calculated value of the room index and the particular combination of room reflectances.

The correction factor for the light output ratio is found (if applicable) by determining the air flow rate, per 100 watt of electrical load, and then reading the value of f_η from the thermal diagram.

The value chosen for the maintenance factor will depend largely upon the degree of pollution expected in the interior concerned. (See Chapter 10 Lighting Maintenance.)

Having calculated total flux SPHI to be installed, the next step is to determine the number of lamps and luminaires needed to give this flux

$$n = \frac{\text{SPHI}}{\text{PHI}}$$

where n = total number of lamps
and PHI = nominal luminous flux per lamp

Knowing n, the number of luminaires of a chosen lamp-carrying capacity can be simply derived.

In practice, it may be necessary to employ a greater or lesser number of luminaires than that calculated in order to arrive at an acceptable lighting layout. The effect that this change in number may have on the average illuminance is, of course, likely to be negligible in the case of a large interior employing many luminaires, but it is usual in the case of small rooms to calculate the illuminance given by the actual number of luminaires finally decided upon to see that this is within the illuminance limits specified. The formula used for the illuminance E4 on the working plane is

$$E4 = \frac{\text{UF4} \times n \times \text{PHI} \times f_\eta \times \text{MF}}{A}$$

and similarly for the walls (E3) and ceiling (E1).

The two worked examples which follow illustrate the calculation technique described above.

Example 1:
To calculate the number of luminaires needed to provide an office with an average illuminance of 800 lx on the working plane.
The dimensions of the room are:
length $a = 30$ m
width $b = 7.5$ m
height $h = 3.15$ m
height of the working plane $= 0.75$ m
Reflectances of ceiling, walls and working plane are 0.70; 0.50 and 0.10 respectively.
Type of luminaire: TBN 280 (2 × 'TL' 65 W lamps).

Calculation
Room index:
$$k = \frac{a \times b}{h3 \times (a + b)} = \frac{30 \times 7.5}{(3.15 - 0.75)(30 + 7.5)} = 2.5$$

Utilization factor:
For a room index of 2.5 and reflectances of 0.70; 0.50 and 0.10 the UF for the luminaire TBN 280 is found to be 0.55. Total luminous flux to be installed is therefore

$$SPHI = \frac{E4 \times a \times b}{UF4 \times f_\eta \times MF} = \frac{800 \times 30 \times 7.5}{0.55 \times f_\eta \times MF} = \frac{327 \times 10^3}{f_\eta \times MF}$$

Luminaires without air exhaust:
Correction factor, $f_\eta = 1.0$
Maintenance factor, $MF = 0.80$

Luminaire with air exhaust:
Air flow rate per luminaire, 100 m³/h
Air flow rate per 100 W,
$$\dot{V}_n = \frac{100 \times 100}{153} = 65.4 \text{ m}^3/\text{h}$$
Correction factor, $f_\eta = 1.12$
Maintenance factor, $MF = 0.85$

$SPHI = \dfrac{327 \times 10^3}{0.8} = 409 \times 10^3$ lm $SPHI = \dfrac{327 \times 10^3}{1.12 \times 0.85} = 343 \times 10^3$ lm

The number of fluorescent lamps type 'TL' 65 W/84/5100 lm required, will thus be:

$\dfrac{409 \times 10^3}{5.1 \times 10^3} = 80$ lamps $\dfrac{343 \times 10^3}{5.1 \times 10^3} = 67$ lamps

For which the number of luminaires type TBN 280 (2 × 'TL' 65 W) required will be:

$$\frac{80}{2} = 40 \text{ luminaires} \qquad \frac{67}{2} = 33 \text{ luminaires}$$

The luminaires will be arranged in three rows along the length of the office. In the case of luminaires not having an air-exhaust facility, this will mean taking 13 luminaires per row, i.e. 39 luminaires instead of the calculated 40. In the case of air-exhaust luminaires, three rows of 11 will give the required number of 33 in total.

The illuminance E4 in each case will then be

$$E4 = \frac{UF4 \times n \times PHI \times f_n \times MF}{A}$$

Without air exhaust:

$$E4 = \frac{0.55 \times (2 \times 3 \times 13) \times 5100 \times 0.8}{30 \times 7.5}$$

$$E4 = 778 \text{ lx}$$

With air exhaust:

$$E4 = \frac{0.55 \times (2 \times 3 \times 11) \times 5100 \times 1.12 \times 0.85}{30 \times 7.5}$$

$$E4 = 783 \text{ lx}$$

Example 2:

To calculate the horizontal illuminance on the working plane in an office measuring 20 m × 10 m illuminated by means of 65 W 'TL' fluorescent lamps in twin-lamp luminaires type TBN 280.

The luminaires are mounted at a height of 3 m above the floor in eight rows of four, spaced 2.5 m apart. Reflectances of ceiling, walls and working plane are 0.50; 0.30 and 0.10 respectively.

MF = 0.85
height of the working plane = 0.85 m
PHI = 5100 lm
$\dot{V}$ = 3000 m³/h

Calculation
Room index:

$$k = \frac{a \times b}{h3 \times (a + b)} = \frac{20 \times 10}{(3 - 0.85)(20 + 10)} = 3.1$$

Utilization factor:
Found from the table for the given reflectances and room index: UF4 = 0.53

Installed nominal lamp flux density:

$$\text{PHID} = \frac{8 \text{ rows} \times 4 \text{ luminaires} \times 2 \text{ lamps} \times 5100 \text{ lm}}{20 \text{ m} \times 10 \text{ m}} = 1632 \text{ lm/m}^2$$

Air flow rate per luminaire:

$$\dot{V}_e = \frac{\text{total volume exhausted}}{\text{number of luminaires}}$$

$$\dot{V}_e = \frac{3000}{8 \times 4} = 93.75 \text{ m}^3/\text{h}$$

Air flow rate per 100 W:

$$\dot{V}_n = \frac{\text{air volume per luminaire} \times 100}{\text{nominal power of the luminaire (incl. ball.)}}$$

$$\dot{V}_n = \frac{93.75 \times 100}{153} = 61.3 \text{ m}^3/\text{h}$$

Correction factor for light output ratio (found from the thermal diagram for this air flow rate): $f_\eta = 1.11$

Calculation of illuminances:

$$\begin{aligned}
E4 \text{ (UF4} = 0.53) &= \text{UF4} \times \text{PHID} \times f_\eta \times \text{MF} \\
&= 0.53 \times 1632 \times 1.11 \times 0.85 \\
&= 816 \text{ lx}
\end{aligned}$$

$$\begin{aligned}
E3 \text{ (UF3} = 0.22) &= 0.22 \times 1632 \times 1.11 \times 0.85 \\
&= 339 \text{ lx}
\end{aligned}$$

$$\begin{aligned}
E1 \text{ (UF1} = 0.06) &= 0.06 \times 1632 \times 1.11 \times 0.85 \\
&= 92 \text{ lx}
\end{aligned}$$

The CIE Applied Method

As was pointed out earlier, the lumen method as described above cannot be used where the design brief specifies the illuminances to be obtained on the ceiling and walls in addition to that required on the working plane, or where the luminaire arrangement is anything but standard. It was partly for design work such as this that the CIE Applied Method was evolved. This is again a lumen method of lighting design, but one based on the use of extensive precalculated tables of photometric data covering all the many aspects of luminaire performance.

Without going into detail here (a full description of the Applied Method, along with all the necessary tables and numerous worked examples is to be found in CIE Report No 40 – see reference CIE, 1978) the essence of the Applied Method is that the luminaires (as described by their light distributions) and luminaire arrangements needed to give the required illuminances on the room surfaces are selected using the tables provided, applying correction factors where necessary to allow for any departures from standard luminaire arrangements. This is the so-called design phase.

In general, there will be more than one design solution; but the more limiting the design requirements, the more limited also will be the number of solutions possible. For instance, if the arrangement of the luminaires is specified, then the number of possible solutions will be reduced considerably.

The final choice of installation is made once the illuminance values given by each tentative design have been checked using a technique very similar to that used in the lumen method described above.

The Point Method

The direct illuminance obtained at a point P on a horizontal or vertical plane (figure 13.2) from a single luminaire can be calculated using the fomulae

$$E_h = I_\alpha \cos^3 \alpha / h^2$$

for the horizontal illuminance at P, and

$$E_v = I_\alpha \cos^2 \alpha \sin \alpha / h^2$$

for the vertical illuminance at P.

The luminous intensity I_α of the luminaire at angle α is obtained from the photometric data for the luminaire.

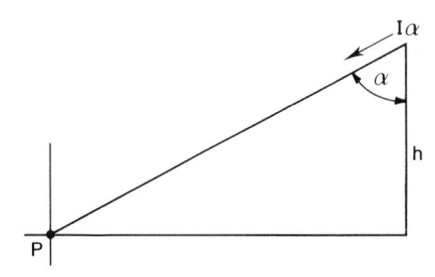

Figure 13.2 Calculation of direct component of illuminance at a point.

13.1.3 Luminance Calculations

Surface luminance

The luminance, L, of a diffusely reflecting wall, ceiling or working surface can be determined by first calculating the average illuminance, E, on the surface concerned using the lumen method, and then applying the formula

$$L = \frac{E\rho}{\pi} \quad \text{where } \rho \text{ is the reflectance of the surface considered.}$$

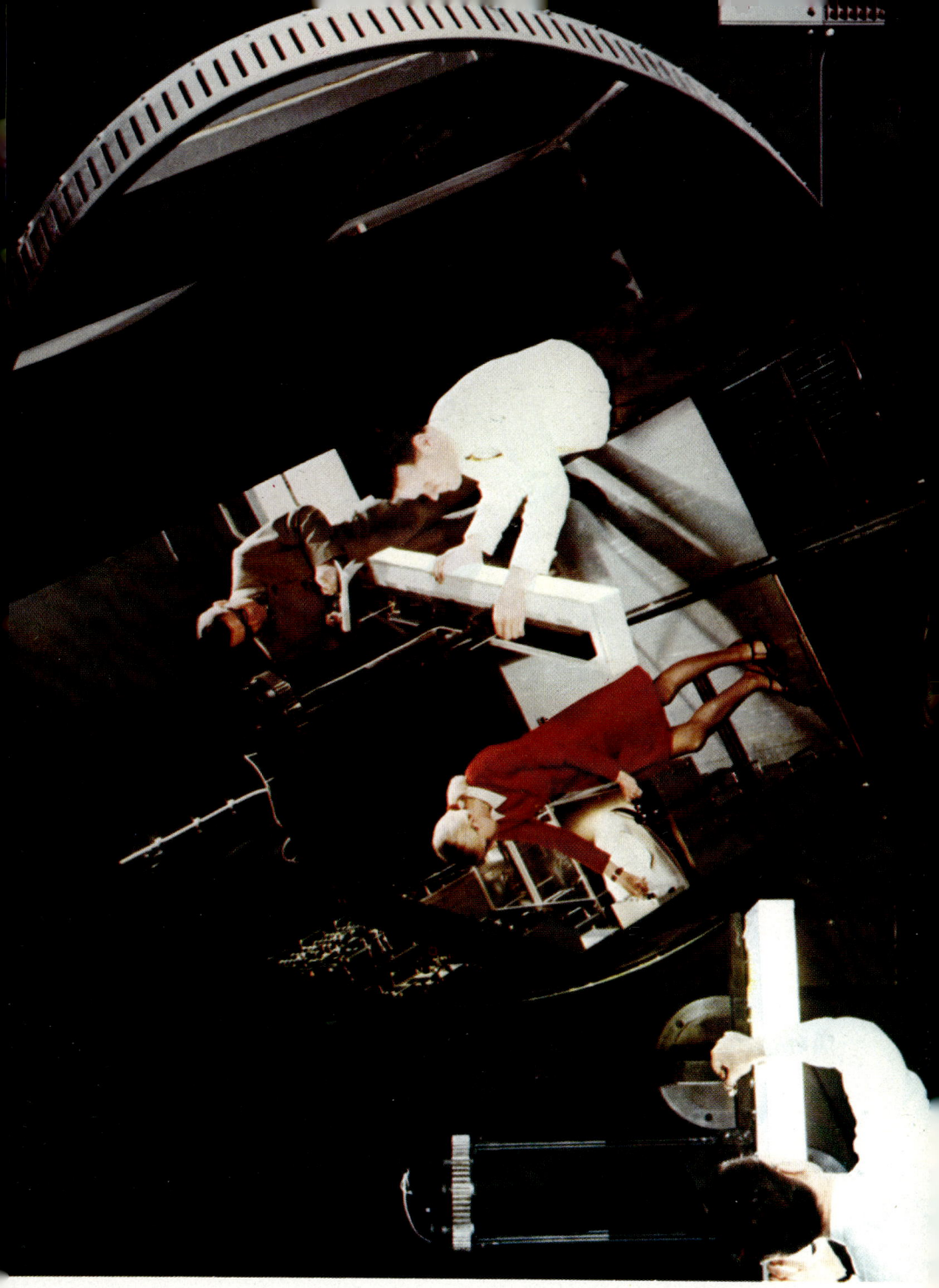

A goniophotometer set up. The optical path of the instrument is lengthened using the large mirror which rotates about the luminaire, seen in the lower left of the photo. Reflected in the mirror can be seen the control console and the paper disc on which the luminous intensity distribution of the luminaire is automatically plotted.

7 Two devices used in the assessment of surface reflectance, the colour fan and the perforated colour chart. (The latter, seen against a grey background to produce the match seen in the bottom left-hand corner, appears in the book Handbuch für Beleuchtung published by W. Girardet, Essen, Germany.)

Luminaire luminance

The luminance of a luminaire when viewed from an angle γ to the normal to its surface is given by

$$L_\gamma = \frac{I_\gamma}{A_\gamma}$$

where I_γ = the luminous intensity of the luminaire at angle γ
A_γ = the apparent area of the luminaire's luminous surface at angle γ
From figure 13.3 the apparent area is

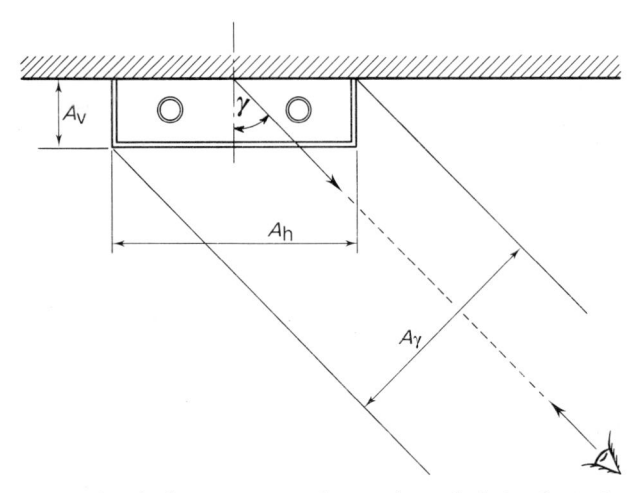

$$A_\gamma = A_h \cos \gamma + A_v \sin \gamma$$

Figure 13.3 The apparent area $A\gamma$ of a luminaire at angle γ used in calculating luminaire luminance.

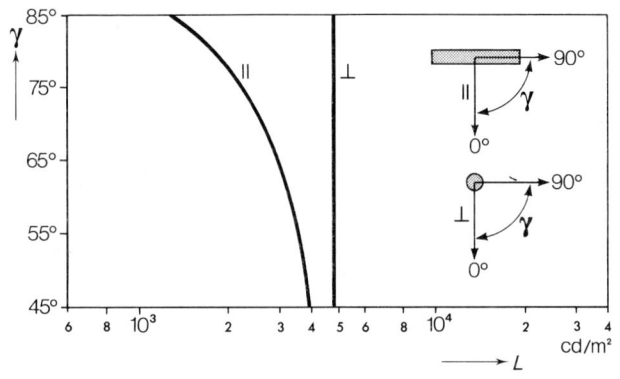

Figure 13.4 Luminance distribution ∥ lengthwise and ⊥ crosswise of a bare 40 watt tubular fluorescent lamp of 2000 lm.

In the case of a simple batten luminaire, the lamp is fully exposed to view. The average luminance of a bare fluorescent lamp viewed in a plane passing through the lamp axis decreases as the angle of view γ approaches $90°$ (figure 13.4) and follows approximately the equation (Fischer, 1972)

$$L_{av} = L \cos^{0.5} \gamma$$

At right angles to the lamp axis the luminance is independent of the viewing angle. The average luminance (in cd/m^2) can in this case be determined either:

(a) from the lamp flux Φ (in lm) and the projected luminous area A_o (in m^2) of the lamp using the equation

$$L_{av} = \frac{\Phi}{9.25 \, A_o}$$

(b) from the luminous intensity I_o (in cd) and the projected area A_o (in m^2) using the equation

$$L_{av} = \frac{I_o}{A_o}$$

(c) from the maximum luminance L_{max} measured at the centre of the lamp using the equation

$$L_{av} = 0.8 \, L_{max}$$

13.1.4 Cost Calculation

Listed below are some of the factors – many of them interdependent – having a direct influence on the costs of an interior lighting installation:

Lighting quality	level and uniformity, degree of glare control, colour rendering
Lamps	wattage, light output, lifetime, price
Luminaires	type, number of lamps per luminaire, light distribution, price
Control gear	ballast losses, compensation, price
Installation costs	cabling, switches, mounting system, labour
Maintenance costs	luminaire accessibility, maintenance system

Traditionally, costs are separated into initial and running costs, the former covering the equipment and its installation, the latter energy costs and maintenance (including cleaning and replacement costs). Together, these costs give the annual cost in use of an installation. This can be calculated using the formula

$$K = n_t \left[\frac{P.p/100 + I.q/100 + R}{n_l} + t_B \left(\frac{L + W}{t_L} + a.N \right) \right]$$

where:
- P = Price of a luminaire
- p = Capital for P as percentage (interest and depreciation)
- I = Costs for installation material and mounting per luminaire
- q = Capital for I as percentage (interest and depreciation)
- R = Cleaning costs per luminaire and year
- L = Price of a lamp
- n_t = Total number of lamps
- n_1 = Number of lamps per luminaire
- W = Cost of replacing a lamp
- N = Consumption of a lamp, including ballast, in kW
- a = Cost of electrical energy per kWh
- t_L = Useful life of the lamp in hours (approx. 8000 hours for fluorescent lamps)
- t_B = Yearly period of use in hours

It need scarcely be added, that when using this formula to compare the costs of different alternative lighting installations a meaningful result will only be obtained if the installations are first comparable in terms of lighting quality.

13.2 Measurements

Photometry is a basic, indispensable part of lighting engineering, ranging from the very exact measurements carried out in the laboratory by standards institutes when calibrating reference sources, to routine measurements in research and quality control of light sources and to field measurements, which must sometimes be very exact but are very often only needed to give a global impression of existing lighting levels.

As far as project design is concerned, the only laboratory measurements of real interest are those made to determine the luminous intensity distribution of luminaires.

Most field measurements are concerned with the determination or checking of illuminances. Luminances may also be of interest, but more often than not they are calculated from other photometric data rather than measured. Designers, in order to be able to make proper use of utilisation factor tables, may also want to determine the reflectances of room surfaces.

When making field measurements one should always first establish the degree of accuracy required for the case in question; knowing this, one can then decide whether or not all the precautions described in this chapter should be followed. It should be noted, that the accuracy achieved in field measurements is not normally better than $\pm\ 10\%$.

13.2.1 Laboratory Measurements

The basic laboratory measurements made in the photometric test of a luminaire are those necessary to determine its luminous intensity output in specified planes and angles. The resulting candlepower distribution is used to determine the luminaire efficiency, light output ratios, zonal flux distribution and luminance distribution referred to in the previous section.

The luminous intensity distribution of a luminaire (or bare lamp) can be measured with either a direct reading photometer or with a photometer that produces a graphical readout. The photometer most used in laboratories is of the automatically recording type in which a system of mirrors rotating about the light source reflects the light in the direction of the photocell, the light source remaining stationary in its normal burning position (see colour plate 6). Equipment used in association with these photometers – or goniophotometers as they are more properly called – traces the luminous intensity distribution curves in the various planes of interest.

13.2.2 Field Measurements

Field measurements made on a completed lighting installation can be used to check for compliance with the tendered specifications or with recommended practice, or they can be compared with the results of previous measurement surveys to see whether or not there is a need for maintenance, modification or replacement. Comparison surveys can also be used to advantage when seeking to design an installation that will be expedient from the viewpoints of both lighting quality and economy.

Field measurements are, of course, only valid for the conditions existing at the time of the survey. It is important, therefore, to record a detailed description of the surveyed area and to make a note of all the factors that might affect the results, such as lamp type and age, luminaire and ballast type, supply voltage, interior surface reflectances, state of maintenance (including date when last cleaned) and type of instrument used in the survey.

Illuminance measurements

For accurate measurements, photometers of the photocell type should be used that have been cosine and colour corrected. The former correction is to allow for the effects of light falling on the cell at oblique angles. Colour correction is necessary in order to match the spectral sensitivity of the cell – which left uncorrected may differ from the spectral sensitivety of the human eye and extend beyond the visible region of the spectrum – to that of the human eye, as defined by the spectral response of the CIE Standard Observer.

The calibration of the photocell should be checked at least once a year. The mechanical zero of the indicating instrument should be checked immediately prior to use and before switching on.

Care should be taken not to cast a shadow over the photocell whilst taking a reading.

Measurements of the illuminance obtained with an electric lighting installation should be made after dark, or with daylight excluded from the interior.

An installation containing discharge lamps should be switched on at least twenty minutes before measurements are taken. This is to allow the lamps to stabilise. Where fluorescent lamps are mounted inside totally enclosed luminaires stabilisation may take longer.

In installations with new discharge lamps, at least 100 hours of operation should have elapsed before measurements are taken.

The procedure adopted for the measurement of average horizontal illuminance will depend on whether the interior concerned is unfurnished or furnished.

In an unfurnished or a non-working interior the area over which measurements are to be taken should first be divided up into a number of squares. The illuminance at the centre of each square at a height of 0.85 metres above the floor is then measured and the readings averaged. A portable stand to support the photocell at the correct height is useful for maintaining positional accuracy during the measurement procedure.

The accuracy of the value of average illuminance arrived at will be largely determined by the number of measurement points taken, that is by the number of squares used. The minimum number of measurement points needed for a given degree of measurement accuracy can be related to the room index of the interior concerned (see table 13.1). It should be realised, however, that errors are possible if the grid for the measurement points coincides with that marking the positions of the luminaires. In such a case, the number of measurement points should be increased.

For working interiors in which the various work places (e.g. desks, benches) exist or their position is known at the time of measurement, the illuminance at each of these specific points should be measured and then averaged.

Where, in a working interior, the general lighting is supplemented by local lighting at the various work places, the spot illuminance at each of these places should be measured. Each measurement should be performed with the worker concerned in his normal working position and with the cell of the photometer located at the most critical zone of the visual task being performed, whatever the angle of the cell to the horizontal.

In a working interior containing tall machinery, racks, etc., a knowledge of the average illuminance would often be of little use. What should be measured in such cases is the spot illuminance prevailing in those zones or at those places where the work actually takes place.

For measuring cylindrical or scalar illuminance or the illumination vector, special devices are required. Approximations of these values can be gained by measuring the illuminance in the relevant directions and taking the mean of the readings.

Table 13.1 Relationship between room index and number of measurement points for given degrees of accuracy

Room index (k)	Minimum number of measurement points	
	$\pm 5\%$	$\pm 10\%$
$k < 1$	8	4
$1 \leqslant k < 2$	18	9
$2 \leqslant k < 3$	32	16
$3 < k$	50	25

Luminance measurements

The surfaces of primary interest in a luminance survey are the visual task and its immediate surround, walls and ceilings, windows and luminaires. These luminances may be derived by calculation from the measured illuminance and reflectance (see Sec. 13.1.3). The luminance of a light source may be calculated from a knowledge of its luminous intensity and apparent area (see again Sec. 13.1.3). Luminances may also be measured with a suitable luminance meter.

Luminance surveys, unlike illuminance surveys, should always be made under working conditions: during daytime including daylight, and after dark with electric lighting only. The luminances, which should be measured from the relevant workers' positions, can be recorded by marking the values obtained on a photograph or perspective drawing of the interior concerned.

Reflectance

Although special devices for measuring reflectances of surface colours are available, reflectances are mostly estimated by comparing the surface colours with those of calibrated colour samples which are available in the form of colour fans or colour charts perforated to simplify the comparison. (See colour plate 7.) Very rough estimations of reflectances can also be made knowing that the reflectances of the darkest surfaces occuring in interiors are approximately 0.1 and the brightest ones approximately 0.8.

Part 4

APPLICATION FIELDS

Chapter 14

Industrial Lighting

Industrial lighting covers an extremely wide range of different working interiors and work tasks: from small workshops to huge factory halls, and from the fine precision work often carried out in the former to the heavy industrial tasks associated with the latter. The design of a work place may make the task of lighting it easy; on the other hand, there may be obstructions formed by awkwardly shaped machines and the like to contend with. Again, the work task itself may be easy to light, or it may impose certain requirements on the lighting: such as, for example, freedom from producing reflections or, conversely, the deliberate creation of these to bring out surface detail or reveal imperfections in surface finish.

Careful attention paid to these and other aspects of lighting, which includes the need to study the cost effectiveness of the various lighting systems available, can increase productivity, reduce accidents and cut costs.

14.1 Lighting Levels

In the various codes of practice devoted to interior lighting, those chapters dealing with the lighting of industrial tasks and interiors are by far the most extensive. Most include a table giving illuminance recommendations for a wide variety of interiors and activities. Those tasks not covered by these tables must be dealt with by experiment or by comparison with a task of a similar nature, the recommended illuminance for which is known.

The illuminance values recommended in these codes are intended to be economically reasonable while ensuring good seeing conditions. Generally, higher values than those recommended would be preferred by most workers. These higher values may be justifiable on certain grounds: for example, where there is a special need (perhaps in the interests of reducing accidents and expensive human errors) to ensure an above normal accuracy of perception, where the speed of the work is unusually high or where unusually low reflectances or contrasts are present in the task.

Table 12.3 gives a survey of lighting levels recommended in Western Europe for different interiors and activities.

14.2 Lighting Systems

There are three systems of lighting used in industrial interiors: general lighting, localised lighting and local lighting. Only general lighting and localised lighting may be used independently; local lighting is a back-up system which may be used to supplement the main lighting as and where required.

14.2.1 General Lighting

General lighting is designed to produce a more or less uniform illuminance on the working plane throughout the area involved, uniformity generally being considered adequate if the ratio of the minimum to the average values at any given work position is not less than 0.8. General lighting with uniformity of this degree will ensure complete freedom in the placement of machinery and work benches. It is achieved by employing a more or less regular array of overhead luminaires. Of particular importance is the ratio between mounting height and spacing (the distance between the centres of adjacent luminaires). It follows, that the spacing for luminaires having a wide light distribution can be greater than for luminaires in which the distribution is concentrated. The maximum spacing/mounting height ratio for a specific type of luminaire is specified by the luminaire manufacturer.

The choice between tubular fluorescent and high pressure or metal halide lamps for the general lighting will be influenced primarily by the mounting height available. This can, of course, vary considerably from one type of industrial interior to another, but for the purposes of lighting design it is generally sufficient to consider these as falling into two groups: those areas where the mounting height is less than about six metres above floor level, and those where it is in excess of this figure. For the sake of convenience, the interiors comprising each of these groups will be referred to below as low-bay and high-bay interiors respectively.

Low-bay general lighting. The main problem encountered in low-bay lighting is that of designing an installation that is both economical and relatively free from glare. The tubular fluorescent lamp, with its high efficacy, large surface area and low luminance, is therefore used to the virtual exclusion of all other light sources.

In the majority of installations, the fluorescent tubes are housed in reflector luminaires. Those giving some light output in the upward direction serve to increase the ceiling luminance thereby reducing the luminance difference between ceiling and luminaire. This results in improved seeing comfort, and the air flow through the top openings in the luminaires reduces dirt accumulation so the level of illuminance can be more easily maintained.

With reflector luminaires the design of the reflector itself is generally such as to ensure that the fluorescent tube or tubes will be adequately screened at normal angles of view (see colour plate 8). Where glossy surfaces unavoidably present in the working area are likely to give rise to reflected glare or veiling reflections, it is advisable to employ reflector luminaires equipped with some form of additional screening, e.g., louvres or diffusing screens (see colour plate 9).

Special attention should be paid to the orientation of bright-sided luminaires. Where the work is such as to give a main direction of view these are generally placed in continuous or near-continuous rows running parallel to this direction, fluorescent tubes viewed end-on being less glaring than when viewed from the side.

High-bay general lighting. With increase in mounting height, the recommended illuminance level can be obtained using a lesser number of more powerful lamps spaced farther apart. This leads to major economies in both installation and maintenance.

The lamps used are of three types: high-pressure mercury, high-pressure sodium and metal halide.

Conventional high-bay luminaires are of the direct, reflector type having a more or less concentrated light distribution. The reflector, as well as providing the desired degree of light concentration, serves to shield the lamp within from direct view. This shielding, together with the fact that the luminaires are normally well above the normal line of sight, means that glare is easily avoided. Luminaires of this type are employed to advantage in those interiors where greater light penetration is needed in order to illuminate areas between tall, closely-spaced items of machinery, piles of packing cases, etc.

Wider beams are used in those areas where the presence of rather high machinery, control panels and the like makes it necessary to provide adequate illumination on vertical surfaces (see colour plate 10).

14.2.2 Localised Lighting

In those interiors where the arrangement of the work positions is permanent, the use of localised lighting in preference to general lighting can sometimes lead to advantages in terms of increased worker comfort and reduced maintenance and energy costs. The luminaires should be concentrated relatively low above the work areas so as to provide the higher illuminances at these points whilst providing at the same time an adequate level of lighting in the gangways where orientation is required.

14.2.3 Local Lighting

The requirements for certain types of task with regard to lighting level and lighting quality can be so stringent that it is neither technically nor economcally feasible to satisfy these requirements by employing a system of general lighting alone. Examples of such tasks are the marking out of materials and the final inspection of products in areas given over mainly to assembly. For work such as this, local lighting is to be preferred. This is lighting that is designed to illuminate the area occupied by the visual task, and its immediate surround. Such lighting may be needed for critical visual tasks performed in places where the general lighting is really only adequate for work of a less demanding nature. Local lighting is also employed to increase the illuminance at work positions that, due to the presence of obstructions, are not sufficiently well lighted by the general lighting.

From the point of view of maintaining the desired brightness balance in the area of a visual task and in the visual field beyond, it is advisable to look upon local lighting as a useful supplement to general lighting but never as a substitute for it.

Because of the comparatively short distance between the locally placed lamps and the work surface there is a danger, where incandescent lamps are used, that heat from these lamps can result in worker discomfort or adversely affect the materials being used, or both. Such like effects can often be obviated by careful positioning of the light sources or by employing instead lamps of the tubular fluorescent variety.

Local lighting luminaires mounted close to a work task might restrict the general view of the worker concerned and make supervision of that task difficult. Trouble of this sort can be avoided by opting for a compromise between local lighting and general lighting in which the luminaires are mounted just above head height, viz. normally at least two metres above floor level.

It should be borne in mind that where local-lighting luminaires are mounted on machinery they may be subjected to mechanical shock and vibration; this can result in a shortening of the normal lamp life, especially where normal incandescent lamps are concerned. For this reason, such luminaires should be given a suitably resilient mounting. Where incandescent lamps are employed these should be of the reinforced-construction type, the filament and support of which are specially designed to make these lamps suitable for use in applications of this kind. It is often easy, however, to avoid such mounting places altogether, making use instead of a convenient, isolated structure of a rigid nature.

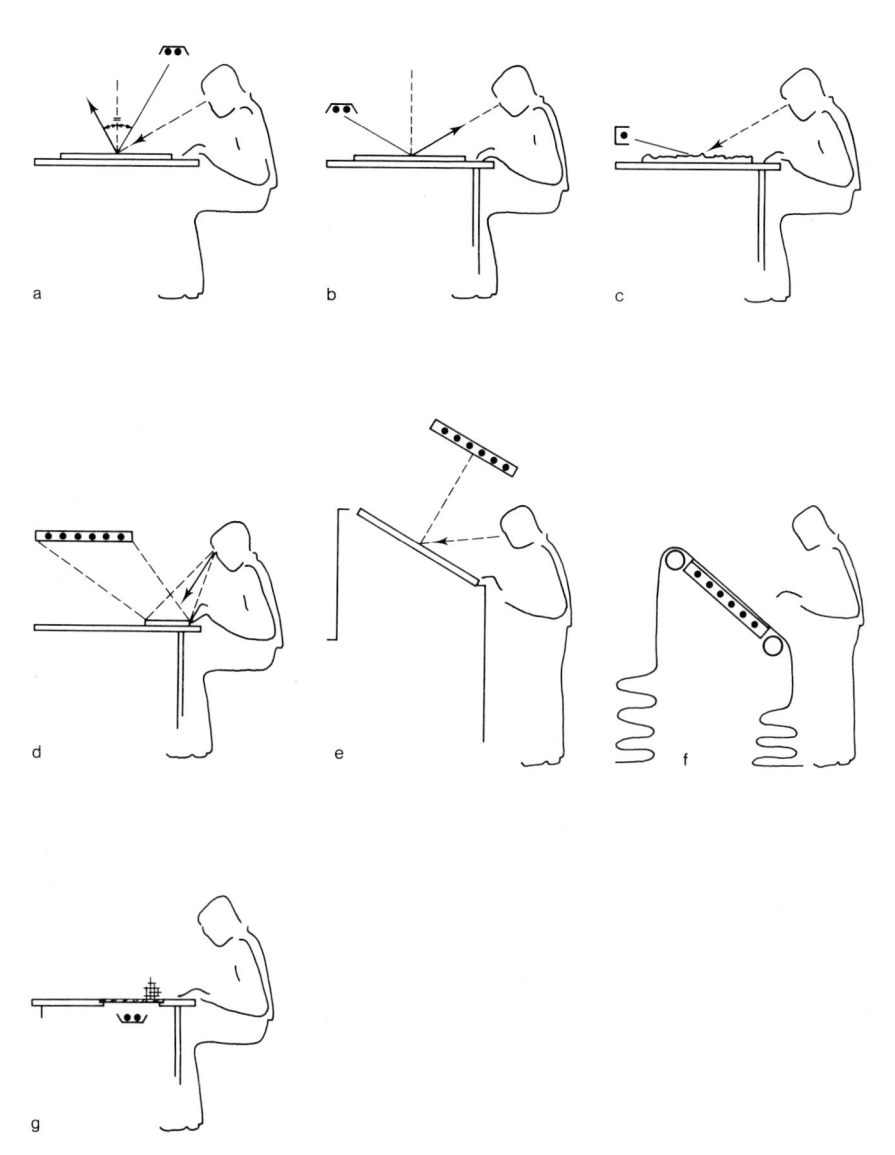

Figure 14.1 Some examples of how the proper choice and placement of a supplementary luminaire can help to improve task visibility. (a) Veiling reflections on a specular surface are eliminated by ensuring that light reflected from the surface does not *coincide with the angle of view. (b) The observation of specular detail against a diffuse background, on the other hand, is aided if reflected light* does *coincide with the angle of view. (c) Low-angle lighting can be used to emphasise surface irregularities. (d) Reflected light from a source having a large surface area facilitates the detection of blemishes in a polished surface. (e) Diffuse lighting from an extended source placed parallel to the work surface facilitates the identification of specualr objects (e.g., as in typesetting). (f) Irregularities in transparent materials can be clearly revealed using transmitted light from a diffuse source. (g) Throwing an object into silhouette by viewing it against a diffusely lighted background is an effective way of checking its contour.*

14.3 Special Lighting Effects and Techniques

Many of the visual tasks occuring in industry call for more than usual care in the choice and positioning of the local lighting (figure 14.1).

Consider, for example, tasks involving the discrimination of fine surface detail. The purpose of the lighting is, of course, to emphasise the detail by creating a contrast between it and the background. Where both the detail and the surface are specular, this can best be done by ensuring that light striking the work-piece is reflected away from the worker. This means employing local lighting, with the luminaires mounted towards the front of the work-bench (figure 14.1a and figure 14.2). Should the detail itself be specular and the surface diffuse, then the luminaire should be positioned farther away from the worker so as to direct the reflected light toward his eyes (figure 14.1b and figure 14.3).

The detection of gross irregularities in surface finish is facilitated using low-angle lighting which throws the irregularities into relief by virtue of the shadows produced. Such lighting should be positioned so as to direct the reflected light toward the observer but below his line of sight (figure 14.1c). A similar technique is often employed where it is desired to examine fine

Figure 14.2 A well-screened luminaire mounted towards the front of the work bench and aimed away from the worker in the direction of the workpiece is used here to provide the very exacting lighting needed for watch assembly.

Low-bay general lighting in which fluorescent tubes have been mounted in open-trough reflectors to give good screening for normal angles of view.

9 Low-bay general lighting in which direct glare has been reduced by providing the luminaires with screening louvres and arranging for them to run end-on to the main direction of view.
10 High-bay lighting employing wide-beam reflectors.

Low-brightness, twin-lamp fluorescent luminaires of the mirror reflector type produce just the right degree modelling in this open-plan office.

12 *A typical primary school classroom with multi-directional viewing in which glare has been combated by employing low-luminance fluorescent lamp luminaires partly screened from view by the ceiling structure. The good colour rendering given by the lamps both enhances the classroom décor and, even more important, ensures that colours will be correctly identified by the pupils.*

Figure 14.3 Light is here directed towards the worker by means of a plastics 'light bender' (working on the principle of total internal reflection), the source itself being hidden from view.

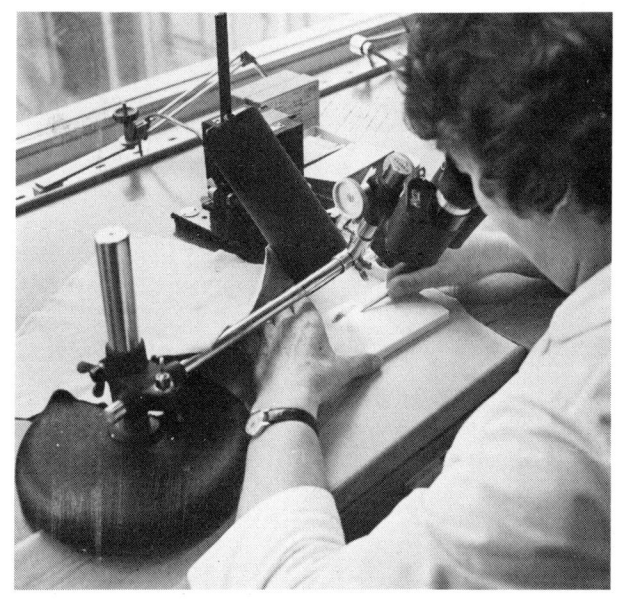

Figure 14.4 Local lighting used in conjunction with a magnifying device. In this case the source itself forms an integral part of the viewing set-up and so can be placed very close to the detail being examined.

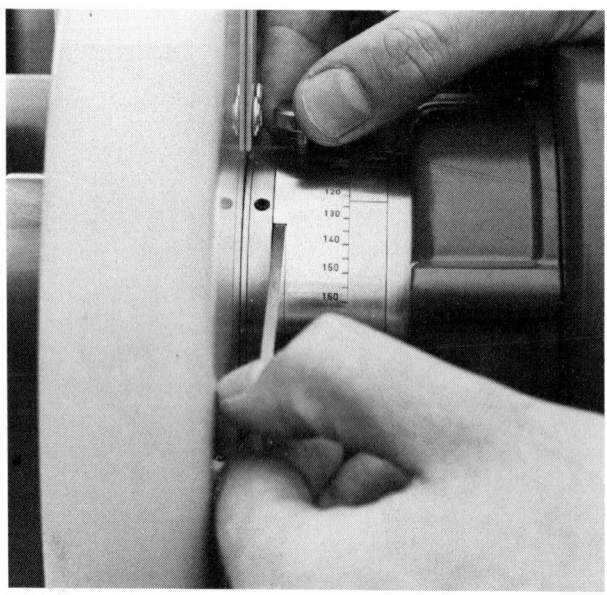

a

b

Figure 14.5 The engraved numbers and lines on this scale seen under fluorescent strip lighting (photo a) are less clearly visible than when seen under the light from a large, diffuse source (photo b).

detail with the aid of a magnifying device, but here it is better to place the local lighting as close as possible to the detail concerned (figure 14.4).

To reveal blemishes or diffuse detail (e.g. engraving) in a polished surface a source of large surface area should be reflected toward the eye of the observer (figure 14.1d and figure 14.5).

The same large area source, similarly placed, is also employed where the need is to provide comfortable viewing of small specular objects seen against an extended background (figure 14.1e).

The inspection of semi-transparent or translucent materials is a further example of where an extended, diffuse source can be used to advantage. In this case, the source is situated immediately behind the object being examined, the details of which are revealed by virtue of the light transmitted through it (figure 14.1f). A similar technique can be used where deformities in fully transparent objects must be detected. The source, which in this case is positioned some distance from the object being viewed, may be covered by an opaque grid-like pattern which will appear kinked when seen through an object containing flaws (figure 14.6). The inspection of contours may also be done in this way. Alternatively, the object being examined may be viewed against a diffusely lighted background to throw the contour into silhouette (figure 14.1g).

Figure 14.6 A glass vessel is seen here being inspected using the technique described in the text. The distortions to the illuminated grid caused by irregularities in the glass are clearly visible.

The accurate assessment or matching of colour calls for the use of specially developed sources designed to comply with certain standards of colour rendering. It is important that the task be isolated from the effects of other, extraneous sources, which may not be suitable for colour matching purposes. This can best be done by using some form of inspection booth in which sources of the requisite type are mounted above an opalescent screen to give a diffused, downward light. The inner surfaces of the booth should have a neutral matt finish, and the illuminance should be at least 1000 lx.

Common to all of the above situations is the need for the lighting, especially the general lighting, to help create a pleasant working environment. Glare of all forms must of course be avoided, but in addition careful attention should be paid to the establishment of a satisfactory luminance balance between the various surfaces in the visual field of the worker – e.g., task, background – as discussed in Chapter 2.

Chapter 15

Offices and Schools

The office worker and school pupil have in common the fact that a very large part of their working day is spent either reading or writing. It follows, of course, that the primary function of the lighting must be that of making these tasks easier to perform. But no lighting installation can compensate fully for deficiencies in the task itself, such as low reflectance or specular materials, low contrasts and ill-defined characters. These deficiencies can often be avoided by paying careful attention to the work routine: for example, by using light-coloured, good quality paper; ink instead of pencil; and by cleaning typewriters and replacing typewriter ribbons more frequently.

The lighting levels recommended within Western Europe for office and school lighting are detailed in tables 15.1 and 15.2 respectively.

Table 15.1 Recommended illuminances for office lighting

Location	Illuminance (lx)
General offices, normal	500– 750
deep-plan	750–1 000
Private offices	500– 750
Conference rooms	300– 500
Drawing offices, general	500– 750
drawing boards	750–1 000

Table 15.2 Recommended illuminances for school lighting

Location	Illuminance (lx)
Classrooms, general	300–500
chalkboard	300–500 (vertical)
Lecture rooms, normal	300–500
when dimmed	150 and lower
Arts and crafts rooms, workshops, laboratories	500–750
Assembly halls	300–500

15.1 Office Lighting

The interiors included here under the heading office lighting are: general offices, private offices, conference rooms and drawing offices.

15.1.1 General Offices

Most general offices are moderate to large in area and their layout, in common with that of many other types of working area, is seldom fixed; office furniture is re-arranged from time to time, and partition walls may be added, shifted or removed.
There are, theoretically at least, a number of ways of ensuring that all work positions will receive an adequate level of illumination, no matter what the office layout.

General lighting

The approach adopted for the vast majority of general offices is to employ ceiling-mounted luminaires in a regular, fixed pattern designed to provide a satisfactory level and uniformity of illuminance on the working plane. So long as the arrangement is made acceptable with regard to glare, for all angles of view, it need not be modified with changes in office layout.
Where it is possible that a large office will be subdivided in the future using floor to ceiling partitions, the lighting arrangement should be planned with this possibility in mind. No luminaire should be badly positioned with respect to these partitions, and this normally means that the layout of the luminaires will be a function of the window spacing, with no luminaires located between windows where partitions are most likely to be placed. Should subdivision subsequently take place, any adjustment to the lighting level in the smaller areas created can be made by replacing the luminaires concerned with units containing a greater or lesser number of lamps, as appropriate.
A pleasant lighting arrangement that both facilitates wiring and makes provision for future subdivision of the office area, is that in which fluorescent luminaires are mounted in near-continuous straight lines running end-on to the main direction of view.
The brightness contrasts between luminaires and ceiling should not be disturbing. Where the luminaires are of the recessed type, the luminance of the ceiling will be determined by the amount of light reaching it indirectly, that is to say from the working surfaces but mainly from the floor. The reflectance of the latter should therefore be high, but not so high as to create problems with regard to its cleaning.

There is also a need to avoid unpleasant brightness contrasts at the boundaries of the visual scene. This is especially true in the case of a wall pierced by rather small windows; the comparatively large wall surfaces between such windows, if not adequately illuminated or of sufficiently high reflectance, could be too dark by contrast with the window area itself during the hours of daylight.

The modelling effect of fluorescent lighting is inherently rather limited and additional, carefully placed directional downlighting will be needed if the outstanding features of an office, e.g. wall coverings, plants, etc., are to be shown to the best advantage. Where some form of suspended ceiling is employed, these downlights can be conveniently recessed into it above the objects to be lighted.

Figure 15.1 Suspended (or integrated) ceiling system in the course of construction. The photo is of a plenum exhaust system (see Sec. 8.2). It shows elongated supply air diffusers connected via flexible piping to the main air supply duct and the luminaires (of the slotted-top variety) through which the return air passes on its way to the plenum.

The benefits to be gained from integrating the general lighting with the ventilation or air conditioning and ceiling acoustics using a suspended ceiling system (figure 15.1) are discussed in Chapter 5. To be fully effective the plans for integration must be formulated at a very early stage of building design.

Flexible lighting installations

Energy savings can be obtained by employing a flexible approach to the design and use of the lighting within a building. The installation should of course be designed to give the recommended illuminances in the various working areas, with correspondingly lower illuminances in non-working, storage and circulation areas and the like. There are, however, a number of ways of going about this, and each approach has its own advantages and disadvantages.

There are four approaches open:

1. Lighting control by switching or dimming
2. Repositioning luminaires as the occasion demands
3. Localised lighting
4. Combination of relatively low level general lighting and local lighting given by luminaires attached to the work stations

Lighting control by switching or dimming. Control by switching, which allows any unneccessary lighting to be turned off, increases installation costs but reduces energy consumption and lowers running costs.

It should at least be possible to switch off the row of luminaires closest to the windows, since this lighting is often not required during the hours of daylight.

The ability to switch each individual luminaire on or off as required goes a step further towards cutting running costs.

Lighting control by dimming is also sometimes put forward as a possible solution to the problem of how to economise in the use of lighting energy, the idea being that as the amount of daylight increases so the contribution made by the artifical lighting may be reduced.

Automatic switching systems controlled from a stored memory programme are already being considered.

Repositioning Luminaires. A flexible lighting system in which the number and position of the luminaires can be altered offers the advantage that the number of luminaires needed can be kept to a minimum, and this will yield obvious savings in running costs. But these savings must be balanced against the more costly wiring involved and the extra cost of repositioning and rewiring the luminaires where the need arises, including the indirect cost of work lost due to any disturbance caused during the repositioning process.

Another possibility is to mount the luminaires on a grid made up from ceiling-mounted lighting track.

Localised lighting. Localised lighting, in which the luminaires are concentrated at and around the various work stations, can be used to some advantage in certain smaller offices. By placing the desks in the well-lighted window zones and using the remainder of the office space for circulation and filing purposes, savings on annual energy consumption of up to 25 per cent can be achieved as compared with a uniformly lighted office.

Combined local and general lighting. Still more energy (up to 50 per cent of total) can be saved by employing a combination of local lighting and low level general lighting. The latter should give at least 200 lx for task illuminances of 500 lx, and approximately 300 lx for task illuminances of 750 lx, the difference in each case being made up by the local lighting.

The saving in running costs is achieved since fewer general lighting luminaires will be needed and the local lighting at unoccupied work positions can be switched off. Such lighting must, however, be carefully planned if the irregular, and possibly unpleasant, luminance pattern created by its use is to be avoided.

The local lighting should, of course, allow a task to be performed in comfort for all possible positions of the worker – for those engaged in reading, where it is common practice to adopt a reclining attitude some distance away from the normal, well-lighted work position, some additional, suitably positioned local lighting unit may be called for.

15.1.2 Private Offices

The lighting of a private office (figure 15.2) may be decided more from the viewpoint of the artistic effect or atmosphere that it is desired to create than may that of a general office. The general lighting should, of course, be designed to adequately cover the desk and its immediate surround – a secretary seated near the desk will need sufficient light to facilitate note-taking – but the luminances in the remainder of the room can often best be provided by supplementary lighting, and this leaves the lighting engineer or interior designer full scope for the application of a decorative lighting treatment.

The more sumptuous the furnishings and decor, the more elaborate is the lighting needed to do the office justice. Window drapery, for example, is favourably lighted by concealed strip lighting. Use here of a valence of the open-top variety will allow up-light from the concealed strip lighting to reflect off the ceiling, thus providing a useful supplement to the general lighting of the office interior. Other decorative elements in the office such as plants, murals and paintings, can be 'picked out' using ceiling-mounted narrow beam spots or downlights. Wide-beam, or more ideally fan-beam spots can be used to 'wash' a wall or walls with light, perhaps to reveal texture and provide a pleasing variation in depth of colour.

Uniformity of the lighting within a private office is not called for and may

Figure 15.2 A private office lit by a combination of tubular fluorescent lighting and ceiling-mounted spots. The fluorescent tubes are housed in luminaires of the mirror reflector type to give a certain degree of modelling on the desk. The spots, as well as providing strong modelling on selected objects (note that on the figure of the monkey), create a pleasing tonal gradation on an otherwise uninteresting wall.

in fact go counter to the decor, which is often such as to provide one or more points of focal emphasis.

15.1.3 Conference Rooms

Many of the principles of lighting a private office apply also to conference rooms. Again, the main work surface, in this case the conference table, should be adequately covered by the general lighting, bearing in mind that if the table is polished (as is often the case) the luminaires will have to be carefully sited to avoid producing troublesome reflections in its surface at virtually all angles of view.

This general lighting, and any supplementary lighting – for example, that which may be employed to enhance the room decor or provide illumination on a display stand or blackboard – is often provided with a switching or dimming control to facilitate the showing of slides or films, or for other reasons.

Particular care should be taken to avoid creating a situation in which persons seated with their backs to a window are seen in silhouette by those seated opposite. Either the frontal lighting at these seating positions must be sufficient to maintain a brightness balance, or the offending window must be provided with a suitable blind or curtain.

15.1.4 Drawing Offices

Drafting involves very accurate discrimination of fine detail and therefore calls for high-quality, high-level lighting. Glare in general, and veiling reflections in particular must be avoided, as must the creation of hard shadows from hands and drafting instruments. An illuminance on the boards in the order of between 750 lx and 1000 lx is generally recommended.

Figure 15.3 Drawing office lighting of the type described in the text in which the emphasis is on the reduction of glare and veiling reflections and the elimination of harsh shadows.

The problem of providing suitable lighting is much simplified if it can be arranged that all occupants of the office face one way; direct glare can then be minimised by employing ceiling mounted fluorescent luminaires running in rows end-on to everybody. A well-tried arrangement, which can be adopted where the office layout is fixed, is that in which the rows are located to either side of the drafting machines (figure 15.3). With this arrangement, the absence of any luminaire directly above a given work position serves to keep glare and veiling reflections to a minimum and the light coming from both sides of a worker effectively eliminates hard shadows.

Shadows and all forms of glare can also be minimised by using large-area luminaires. Luminaires of this type will therefore help to maintain lighting quality, especially where due to possible alterations to the office layout the arrangement of the luminaires cannot be optimised.

15.2 School Lighting

The primary areas of interest in school lighting are the classrooms, the lecture rooms, the arts and crafts rooms or workshops and the assembly hall.

15.2.1 Classrooms

The tendency in school design has always been to provide separate classrooms each with a generous amount of daylighting, the light coming from large areas of glazing in one or more window walls. In an increasing number of new schools, however, the classrooms are comparatively large deep-plan areas in which individual teaching areas are defined by means of semi-permanent partition walls or articles of furniture, those areas remote from the windows receiving little or no daylight. This latest approach to classroom

Figure 15.4 A conventionally lit classroom. Note especially the well-screened ceiling-mounted luminaire above the chalkboard.

design has resulted in a change in the type of artificial lighting needed to create a satisfactory visual environment.

In a conventional classroom the window wall will (ideally) be to the left of the students when they are seated normally so as to face the chalkboard. Good, glare-free lighting can then be provided by employing low-brightness or well-screened ceiling luminaires arranged in rows running parallel to the window wall (figure 15.4) with the rows spaced sufficiently far apart to allow the rows of desks to be positioned between rows. This last precaution serves especially to reduce reflected glare from the work surface.

The chalkboard should be provided with its own lighting system in which both direct glare and veiling reflections in the board are eliminated. The simplest arrangement is to have one or more fluorescent luminaires mounted on the ceiling and screened from the pupils so as to light the board at an angle of not less than sixty degrees from the normal to any point of its surface. Where necessary, window blinds can be employed to prevent reflected glare from windows occurring in the chalkboard and to eliminate sun on desks. These same blinds, perhaps in combination with a dimming device for the artificial lighting, will in any case be needed if it is planned to use the classroom for slide or film shows.

Depending on the size of the classroom, it may be necessary to arrange that the luminaires remote from the window wall can be switched on independently of the remainder of the installation so as to compensate for fading daylight.

The larger, deep-plan type of classroom has many features in common with the open-plan general office, the lighting for which was discussed earlier. Again, the fact that certain areas will, inevitably, be remote from a natural source of fresh air, means that it will probably be necessary to install a ventilating or air conditioning system. The ceiling-mounted elements of such a system can be profitably combined with the lighting luminaires and with acoustical ceiling tiles to form one, fully integrated system. The arrangement of the ceiling-mounted luminaires should of course be chosen to suit the smallest sub-divided area within the classroom concerned.

15.2.2 Lecture Rooms

The view of the chalkboard from high up at the back of a lecture room is generally such as to bring the ceiling-mounted luminaires very close to the direct line of sight. Glare in such a situation can be avoided by concealing these luminaires behind downward projections from the ceiling (figure 15.5), or else by employing luminaires having an asymmetrical light distribution. The chalkboard itself, with its own local lighting, is best kept separate from the projection screen; the board can then be lit while projection is in progress (figure 15.6).

The frontal lighting at the lecturer's position must be sufficient to prevent the lecturer or the equipment used by him from being thrown into silhouette by the bright background of the lighted chalkboard.

The general lighting in a lecture room should be dimmer controlled to facilitate the showing of slides and films. The control panel, which in

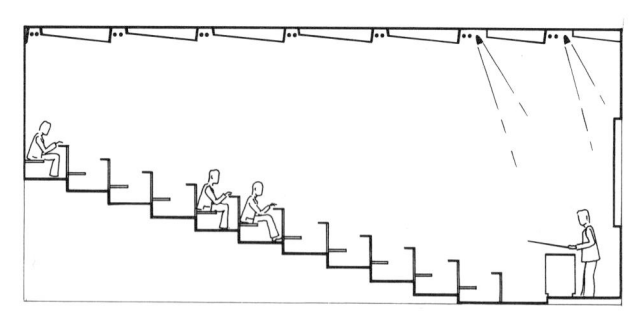

Figure 15.5 Glare-free lecture room lighting obtained by concealing the luminaires between downward projections in the acoustic ceiling. Frontal lighting at the lecturer's position and chalkboard lighting comes from ceiling-mounted spots.

Figure 15.6 The projection screen in this lecture room has been sited to the side of the chalkboard, so allowing the latter to be lighted for use if needed while projection is in progress.

addition to the dimmer control might include switches for various groups of lights and even an automatic projection system, is best located adjacent to the lecturer's rostrum.

It is important, because of the possible need to vacate the room during a period of darkness, that special attention be paid to the provision of emergency lighting and exit lighting. Steps and stairs should be equipped with local orientation lighting.

15.2.3 Arts and Crafts Rooms, Workshops

Rooms set aside for arts and crafts should preferably have light of 'daylight' colours. Art rooms in particular should be provided with additional lighting from spots to give the necessary degree of modelling as and where required. A pleasantly-lit room with light on a generous scale should be aimed at.

School workshops are often modelled along the same lines as their counterparts in industry and so should be treated accordingly.

15.2.4 Assembly Halls

The assembly hall is usually the focal point of the school building and, as such, should be lighted attractively. Apart from ensuring that the required lighting level is attained, and provided that the basic principles of lighting are adhered to, there should be as little restriction as possible placed on the design of the installation.

If the hall is used for games, concerts or as a theatre, provision must of course then be made for lighting such activities in an appropriate manner.

Chapter 16

Shops and Stores

There are many ways in which shop lighting can help the shopkeeper to sell his goods. In a great many cases a selection from the goods on offer is presented in the form of a window display. The power of this display to attract the attention of passers by will be greatly increased if special care is given to the lighting. The interior of a large shop or store needs a general lighting installation for orientation purposes, and this is generally augmented by emphasis lighting on special displays and points of interest to attract customers to selected parts of the floor.

This and subsequent chapters deal with interiors in which a clear distinction can be drawn between the public and the private areas of the interior concerned – a shop, for example, may have in addition to the area entered by the public, a private area or areas set aside for administration or storage. In each case, the discussion has been confined to the lighting of the public area concerned.

16.1 Basic Principles of Shop Lighting

16.1.1 Lighting Levels

The illuminance levels recommended for shoplighting are very much dependent on the type and size of shop considered and its situation. Even the country and area of that country in which the shop is situated, and the climatic conditions, play their part in determining the lighting requirements. It is extremely difficult, therefore, to give detailed lighting recommendations with regard to lighting level; suffice it to say that an illuminance of 500 lx to 1000 lx should be aimed at for the general lighting of a shop situated in a large shopping centre, and 300 lx to 500 lx for a shop situated elsewhere.

16.1.2 Window Displays

The power of a window display to attract the attention of passers by often lies in the dramatic effect created by the lighting (see colour plate 13). In the majority of cases, however, the primary function of the lighting is to

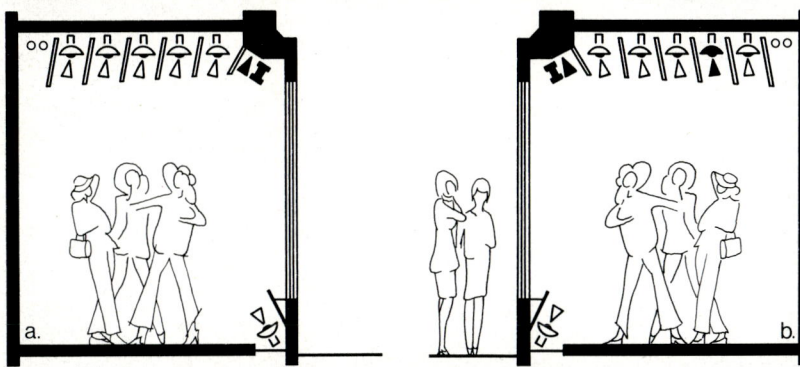

13 *A display window incorporating a number of fixed luminaires any combination of which can be selected to achieve the desired lighting effect. For example (a) a dramatic lighting effect given by pressed glass and halogen lamps mounted at the top front of the window, and (b) High-key top lighting achieved by adding the light from bowl reflector lamps and pressed glass lamps mounted directly above the figures.*

14 The discomforting reflections seen in the glass of this window could possibly have been reduced by increasing the lighting level on the goods displayed.
15 Spotlights mounted on power track, as in this boutique, provide a flexible and attractive solution to the problem of lighting ever-changing display layouts.

bring out some special feature or quality of the goods on display. Clothing, for example, should be lighted using spots in addition to the general lighting to bring out the texture and finish of the materials. For jewellers' windows and the like, where the aim is to enhance the natural sparkle of the pieces on display, the light from conventional incandescent lamps and spots can be used to great effect.

Many show windows require a great deal of flexibility in the lighting installation. The use of spotlights on power tracks is one solution. An even more sophisticated approach is to use a dynamic lighting system. Such a system, which contains an electronic programming unit controlling a number of dimming devices connected to groups of lamps, is capable of providing a virtually unlimited variety of striking lighting effects.

In the case of display windows opening onto the street the luminance of surfaces inside the display area should be sufficiently high to lessen the possiblity of daylight producing discomforting reflections in the glass (see colour plate 14). Again, the actual illuminance level recommended will depend on the situation of the shop concerned: a level of 1000 lx to 2000 lx for shops in large shopping centres, with 500 lx to 1000 lx for those away from the centre is typical, but even these levels can at times prove ineffectual in combating these reflections. In some cases the problem can be partially solved by angling the window glass or by curving it in some way such that light striking it, particularly that from the sky, is reflected towards the pavement.

16.1.3 General Lighting

General lighting coming from a regular array of fairly large fluorescent luminaires having a good colour rendering index is acceptable over the extensive areas of a typical sales floor in a large store, provided there is plenty of visual variety in other ways. Recessed modular luminaires containing, say, four 1.2 or 1.5 metre fluorescent tubes would be typical in a modern building with suspended ceilings, with incandescent downlights added at random intervals to give sparkle. Display areas given over to luxury goods are often lighted solely with incandescent lamps, and these are often recessed in the case of a suspended ceiling. Some typical mounting patterns for luminaires of the recessed type are illustrated in figure 16.1.

Where conventional (i.e. non-suspended) ceilings of low to moderate height are concerned, effective general lighting can be obtained using surface-mounted fluorescent luminaires. For high, exposed ceilings, pendant mounted luminaires are more appropriate. These may be open-topped to provide generous upward light to create a fairly uniform 'sky' above, or they can be of the direct type producing purely downward lighting to provide a higher

Figure 16.1 Some typical mounting patterns for the recessed, ceiling mounted luminaires used in shop lighting: (a), (b) and (c) Tubular fluorescent lamps, (d) Incandescent downlights, (e) A mixture of tubular fluorescent lamps and incandescent downlights.

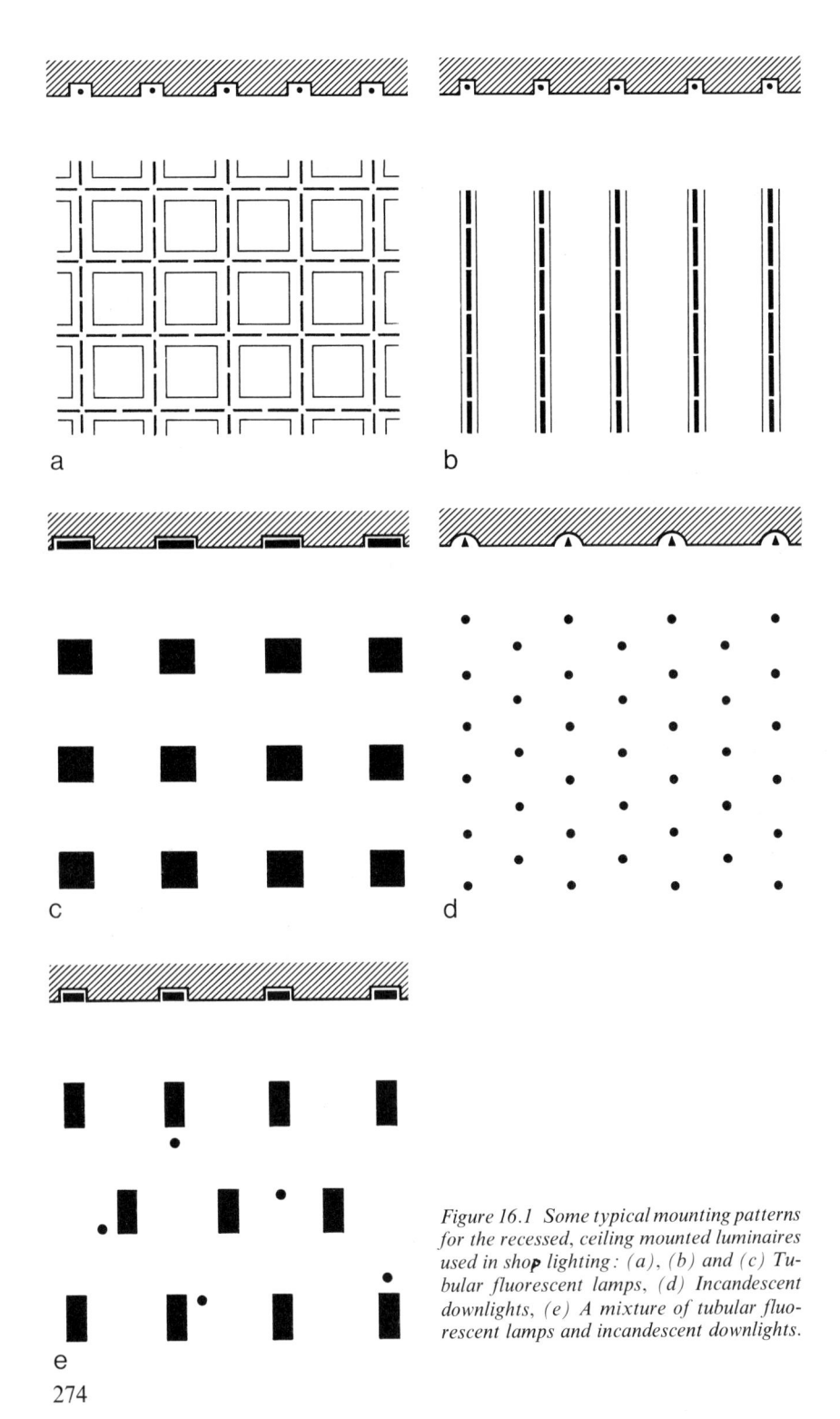

illuminance at the display level. The choice may be influenced by the type of ceiling, but in many cases it is simply a question of taste on the part of the interior designer.

High-pressure mercury lamps and metal halide lamps have certain points in their favour as sources suitable for the general lighting of large, high-ceilinged interiors. They are more compact and of higher intensity than fluorescent lamps, and this means that they require a much smaller portion of the ceiling surface to give the same level of illuminance. An important consequence of this is that maintenance of the installation is facilitated, as is its integration with the other services commonly housed in the ceiling.

However, it must be borne in mind that the high luminance of these light sources may give rise to a certain amount of glare unless the luminaires are carefully screened or else equipped with optical devices, hence their restriction to use in high-ceiling areas. Another point, is that the concentration of high-powered luminaires in or near the ceiling can lead to high temperatures, both at the luminaires and in their immediate surround, unless special precautions are taken.

16.1.4 Local Lighting

Local lighting may be added to give emphasis and modelling to special displays or it may merely serve to light goods that would otherwise be poorly lit by the general lighting alone.

The possibilities for building local lighting into showcases, cabinets, counters, clothes racks and the many other types of display unit are almost without limit. Linear sources are particularly suitable, and although the incandescent variety is perhaps easier to install and does not require bulky control gear, the advantage often lies with the smaller diameter fluorescent lamps. The fluorescent lamp has a longer life (leading to lower replacement costs), its luminous efficacy is higher (resulting in lower heat dissipation) and, unlike the incandescent tube, its colour appearance and colour rendering can be chosen to suit the needs of the application. The operating temperature of the fluorescent tube is also much lower than that of the incandescent lamp, and this means that it can be safely positioned closer to heat-sensitive materials.

However, the ultimate criterion governing the choice of lamp type must be how the merchandise will appear to the prospective purchaser. Certain types of jewellery, glass, china and silver, for example, will have a much livelier appearance under the light from a clear incandescent lamp than under that from a diffuse fluorescent source. Finally, it should be noted that lighting incorporated in display units is almost always more effective when the lamps are completely concealed.

Luminaires appearing to have a purely decorative function can in fact perform a useful task in providing local emphasis. Decorative cylindrical pendants mounted over a glass-topped counter showcase and given the extra 'punch' of 'Super Lux' lamps can prove invaluable in this respect. Care should be taken, however, to avoid specular reflection by mounting the light sources well to the front of the showcase so that the light can only be reflected away from the customer (figure 16.2).

Figure 16.2 Local emphasis provided by pendants. Note that the pendants are positioned above the front edge of the counter so as to avoid producing reflected glare in the eyes of customers.

16.2 Special Considerations

Shops can be divided into three main categories: small, specialist shops; self-service shops and supermarkets; and department stores. What may constitute a suitable lighting installation for one type of shop interior could prove entirely unsuitable in another. The following points should be borne in mind.

16.2.1 Small Shops

In small shops good counter lighting is particularly important. The general lighting in a small shop is more often than not provided by the spill light coming from incandescent or tubular fluorescent lamps mounted in fixed positions above the counters and the general display areas. Special articles on display can be picked out using flexible spotlighting, and this can serve also to create the desired decorative effect in the interior as well as an atmosphere appropriate to the special character of the shop (see colour plate 15).

16.2.2 Self-service Shops and Supermarkets

Self-service shops and supermarkets also generally have fixed lighting arrangements, but unlike the small specialist shop illuminance levels are high and uniform. The sources generally used are fluorescent lamps or the high-intensity discharge lamps.
Local lighting is used only for emphasising special offers and the like. Spotlights mounted on power track are frequently used for this purpose.

16.2.3 Department Stores

In department stores regular alterations to the display layout take place. The general lighting, which is often fixed, is similar to that employed in large open-plan offices, but a certain degree of flexibility can be achieved by means of spotlights that can be quickly and easily repositioned to suit any arrangement of the merchandise.

Chapter 17

Museums and Art Galleries

The visual conditions in the public areas of a museum or art gallery should be both pleasing and free from distraction so that the attention is concentrated on the exhibits. To permit of easy viewing, these should be well illuminated by supplying light of suitable quantity, diffusion and direction in such a way that glare is avoided. When planning such an installation, notice should be taken of the fact that some of the more sensitive materials on display may be damaged in one way or another by the presence of light, whether it be daylight or artificial.

17.1 Lighting Requirements

The lighting installation for a museum or art gallery should be capable of producing all the lighting effects appropriate to the character of the objects being exhibited, and the style of presentation should fully underline the original intentions – where these are known – of the individual artists or exhibitors.

Many exhibits require that their shape or texture be revealed using the modelling effect of directional lighting. Such lighting can be built into special showcases (see colour plate 16) or it can come from spots mounted some distance away on power track (figure 17.1). In both cases, the lighting is given a high degree of flexibility to allow for possible changes in the layout of the exhibition.

Special exhibits can be emphasised using localised lighting, but this must not be overdone, and some general lighting is almost always desirable (see colour plate 17).

When lighting paintings using localised lighting great care must be taken to avoid producing reflections in the varnish or protective glass of the exhibit. Such reflections can be minimised by arranging for the luminaires to have an asymmetrical light distribution, with the main component of the light striking the paintings at an angle of at least 60° to the normal to the wall (figure 17.2). An elegant solution where small paintings, etchings and drawings are concerned is to enclose the exhibits in a showcase containing its own built-in lighting. By sloping the front glass and arranging for the

Figure 17.1 Free-standing show-cases with the light coming from 150 watt spotlights mounted some distance away. Flexibility has here been achieved by mounting the spots on power track.

brightness of the surroundings to be low in comparison with that inside the showcase, reflections in the glass of the latter can be virtually eliminated (figure 17.3).

For exhibits not sensitive to light an illuminance of 300 lx to 500 lx is recommended; providing, that is, that the radiant heat emitted by the light sources is not such as to present problems.

It has been recommended (Thomson, 1961 and IES, 1970) that the illuminance in museums be limited to not more than 150 lx for the exhibits on display that are moderately sensitive to light (e.g. paintings done in oil or tempera and exhibits containing leather, bone, ivory or wood) and to not

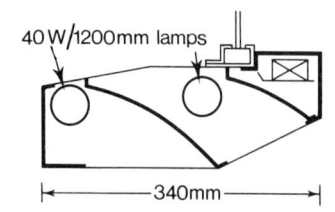

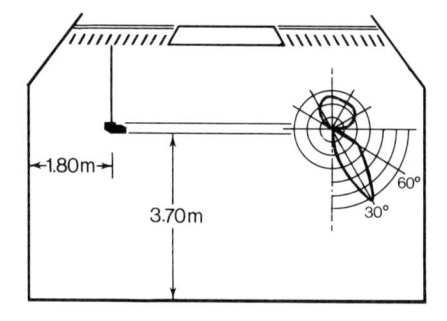

Figure 17.2 Boymans-Van Beuningen Museum, Rotterdam. The photo shows a general view of a gallery with natural lighting from a louvred ceiling. Artificial lighting is by mirror-reflector luminaires equipped with tubular fluorescent lamps. The lighting at the four corners is from 100 watt tungsten filament lamps. None of the lamps are visible from normal viewing positions. The drawings show a cross-section of the luminaires and of the gallery, with in the latter the light distribution curve of the luminaire.

more than 50 lx for specially sensitive objects (e.g. textiles, watercolours, gouaches, sketches and manuscripts).

The lower the lighting levels employed, the greater is the need to ensure good adaptation; only than will the display be prevented from assuming a gloomy appearance. This means, for example, that no part of any general view should be greatly brighter than the prevailing key, although the exhibits themselves should, within the illuminance range permitted, be brighter than their surroundings.

Figure 17.3 Show-cases with front lighting by tubular fluorescent lamps mounted at the top to give an illuminance on the back wall of 60–120 lx. The front glasses are set at an angle of 10° to overcome problems of veiling reflections for normal viewing positions.

One technique that has been successfully employed to this end is that of lighting the exhibits themselves, relying solely on spill light to provide the necessary orientation lighting. Each display is in fact 'tuned' for overall balance, using dimmers where necessary to create the desired effect. Where additional lighting is deemed necessary, this can be provided by ceiling-mounted fluorescent strip lighting. Diffusion is helped by employing fairly high reflectances for floors and walls.

The lighting should be such as to enable the visitor upon entering and moving through the building to adapt sufficiently to the differing lighting levels of the various exhibition areas. Areas of highly-lit exhibits should not immediately precede areas which, perhaps for reasons of conservation, are relatively dimly lit, as the latter will then appear gloomy.

17.2 Conservation

The extent of possible damage caused by light, for a given material, depends on three factors: the illuminance on the material, the duration of its exposure to light, and the spectral composition of that light. (For the purpose of this chapter the term 'light' is taken to include the invisible radiation regions of the spectrum adjacent to the visible region, and in particular the ultraviolet region.)

Damage to light-sensitive materials can be slowed down by (a) limiting the illuminance to the values already mentioned, (b) reducing the time of exposure and (c) reducing as far as possible the short-wave components of the light – especially the u.v.

The combined effect of level of radiation and time of exposure to it is expressed in the law of reciprocity. This states that the effect is proportional to the product of irradiance level and time of exposure. Thus, reduction of both illuminance and time of exposure are important in limiting any possibly harmful effects of light on very-light-sensitive materials.

Exposure time is limited, in practice, by switching off the artificial lighting and excluding daylight when it is not needed – principally outside of museum visiting hours – but it is of course possible to take conservation a step further and cover those exhibits that are very sensitive to light right up to the moment of view.

17.3 Choice of Lamps

With regard to the spectral composition of light, it has been known for some time that damage to light-sensitive materials increases as the wavelength of the incident radiation decreases through the visible region of the spectrum towards the blue end and on into the ultraviolet region. In the interests of conservation, therefore, the sources employed in museum lighting are invariably those in which relatively little u.v. is emitted.

Daylight is rich in u.v., even after penetrating window glass. The tendency in recent years has therefore been to make only limited use of daylight where conservation measures are in force.

Of the artificial light sources, the ordinary tungsten filament lamp, which is much used in museum lighting to bring form and sparkle to a display, emits so little u.v. that precautions with regard to its suppression are unnecessary. These lamps do, however, have a relatively high output of infrared radiation and should therefore be kept well away from heat-sensitive exhibits.

The ubiquitous tubular fluorescent lamp is much favoured in museum lighting chiefly on account of its low brightness and high efficacy. Of particular importance with regard to conservation, however, is the fact that the u.v. emitted by most fluorescent lamps is very low. It is in fact lowest in the case of the colours 27 and 37 lamps.

Taking the colour 27 fluorescent tube just mentioned as reference, it is possible to place the various light sources used in museum lighting in order according to their so-called relative damage factors, the illuminance being constant throughout. This has been done in table 17.1.

Table 17.1 The relative damage factor and other technical data of various light sources

Light source*	Relative damage factor	Colour temperature (K)	Luminous flux per 40 W lamp (lm)	Colour rendering index (R_a)
Fluorescent tube /27	1	2700	1750	94
Incandescent lamp	1½	2800	500	100
Fluorescent tube /37	2	4000	1820	96
Fluorescent tube /32	2	2950	1950	85
Fluorescent tube /83	2½	3000	3200	86
Fluorescent tube /84	2½	4000	3200	86
Fluorescent tube /33	3	4200	3100	66
Fluorescent tube /34	3½	3900	2120	86
Daylight from overcast sky filtered through window glass	9	–	–	–

* For fluorescent tubes the Philips colour code number is given (See Sec. 7.3.2)

Chapter 18

Hotels

It has been said that 'lighting creates the hotel image'. It is certainly true that the lighting in the public areas of a hotel is very much part of its decor and that even the most expensive decor will look garish if the lighting is not in keeping with it. But in addition to the decorative lighting, which is designed to supplement and support the style and character of the hotel, there is an equally important need for various types of amenity lighting. A hotelier's first consideration is for the comfort and safety of his guests, and it is now becoming increasingly realised that amenity lighting is just as important to all concerned as the rest of the creature comforts offered.

18.1 The Hotel Approaches and Entrance

The lighting needs of these areas will, of course, vary depending upon whether the hotel is situated in the middle of an already brightly lit city or hidden away in the depths of the countryside. But whatever its location, the traveller must be able to find and easily identify the hotel.

If the hotel is in its own grounds, all driveways, access roads, car parks, gardens and terraces need to be adequately lit and the routes signposted to ensure that the approaches are not confusing. For car parks and their approaches a minimum horizontal illuminance at ground level of 10 lx is recommended.

Where the main entrance has an overhanging canopy, an attractive lighting design beneath the canopy that complements the lighting used for the hotel name and other signs can be made (figure 18.1). A minimum illuminance under the canopy of 100 lx is recommended.

18.2 The Foyer, Reception Area and Lounge

It is essential that the lighting in the reception area be so planned that the reception desk itself and any hotel shops (figure 18.2) become the focal points for all persons entering the hotel. This is achieved by making the lighting level in these areas somewhat higher than that recommended for the general lighting – say 500 lx rather than 200 lx (table 18.1).

Figure 18.1 This hotel entrance stands out from its surroundings mainly by virtue of the lighting. Note especially the well-lighted steps.

Figure 18.2 The brightness of this hotel shop relative to its surroundings helps to make it the focal point and thus easily located by guests.

The lighting in entrance halls and foyers must be equipped with switching and regulating facilities to allow for the differing day and night-time requirements.

It is desirable that the hotel lounge should afford a certain degree of privacy, a feeling of intimacy even, to the hotel guests and their friends. The lighting can help in this respect by creating within the area concerned a number of separate focal points or areas of interest, each with its own particular character and atmosphere. The large decorative table lamp is much used to

Table 18.1 Recommended illuminances for hotel lighting

Location	Illuminance (lx)
Entrance halls	
general	150–200
reception, cashier, shop	300–500
Public rooms	
bars, coffee bars	150–200
dining rooms, restaurants	
general	100–150
cash desks	300
lounges, writing rooms, cloakrooms	150–200
Bedrooms	
general	50–100
bedhead	150–300
Bathrooms	100–200

Figure 18.3 A hotel lounge with large table lamps used to establish focal points.

this end (figure 18.3). Its upward component of light serves to lighten the ceiling between the recessed incandescent or fluorescent luminaires commonly used for inconspicuously providing the general illumination. The downward light from the table lamp provides the local addition to the general lighting needed to bring the total illumination up to a reasonable level on the book or newspaper in the hands of a guest sitting in an easy chair or settee.

Lounges that are intended to be used for several different types of function should, of course, be provided with a suitably flexible system of lighting.

18.3 Restaurants and Bars

The general level of illuminance in a restaurant should be comparatively high during the day (figure 18.4), but may be lower at night to help create an intimate atmosphere.

Figure 18.4 A hotel restaurant in which extensive use has been made of low-brightness downlights to create emphasis on the tables.

Fluorescent luminaires at the perimeter of the dining area can contribute unobtrusively to the general level of illuminance. They should, however, be supplemented by local lighting at the tables. Dimming and partial switching of the lighting is often desired.

The atmosphere aimed at will depend of course on the type of restaurant. Where strictly functional lighting is desired, a rather uniform lighting level of several hundred lux may be required. Where the aim, on the other hand, is to create an intimate atmosphere the general lighting should be kept rather low (e.g. 100 lx) with local increases at the tables, cash desk, waiter stations and serving points.

Bar lighting (figure 18.5) is an area in which hidden spotlights, recessed downlights, and other forms of concealed lighting, suitably regulated, all come into their own.

Figure 18.5 Low-key bar lighting

18.4 Corridors and Stairs

Hotels usually have rather long corridors on the bedroom floors situated well inside the building and thus away from sources of natural daylight. Fluorescent lamps are recommended for use here as they show substantial savings in running costs. The illuminance during the day should be at approximately 150 lx, whereas during the evening and night a level of as low as 20 lx will suffice – experience has shown that a low night-time level in corridors serves to quieten revellers returning to their rooms.

Arrangements for all-night pilot lighting and emergency lighting will also be necessary on both corridors and stairs, especially those leading to fire exits.

18.5 Bedrooms

There is a tendency to design hotel rooms in the form of bed-sitting rooms, complete with toilet facilities (figure 18.6). The lighting of the rooms may

16 *A free-standing show-case with tubular fluorescent lamps mounted inside the top and screened by a special wedge-shaped mirror louvre to give the light a more directional character and to reduce the luminaire luminance in the direction of the observers' eyes.*

17 *The Roman-Germanic Museum, Cologne. The individual exhibits in this hall are accentuated using 150 watt PAR 38 spotlights mounted in the ceiling. Additional ceiling-mounted 150 watt downlights provide a general illuminance of 150–200 lux.*

18 View of the reception and lobby areas of the Airport Hotel, Calcutta. The lighting of the former comes principally from the incandescent bowl reflector lamps recess mounted in the decorative modular ceiling. This contrasts pleasantly with the subdued lighting in the lobby area beyond, where ceiling downlights have been used in combination with large decorative table lamps.

be combined with the decor, which is usually custom built. It should consist of general lighting (for example, curtain coves lighting with fluorescent lamps and, depending on the size of the room, additional recessed indirect lighting) together with bed-head lighting and, where a desk is provided, local lighting for this also.

The bed-head lighting should provide sufficient light for reading, without disturbing any other occupants of the room. Bed-side table lamps are not recommended for this purpose. They take up valuable space, and in any case are easily damaged. Bed-head wall lights, if used, should be mounted high enough to clear the head of a person sitting up in bed.

For the dressing-table or wall mirror, the best solution is to mount a fluo-

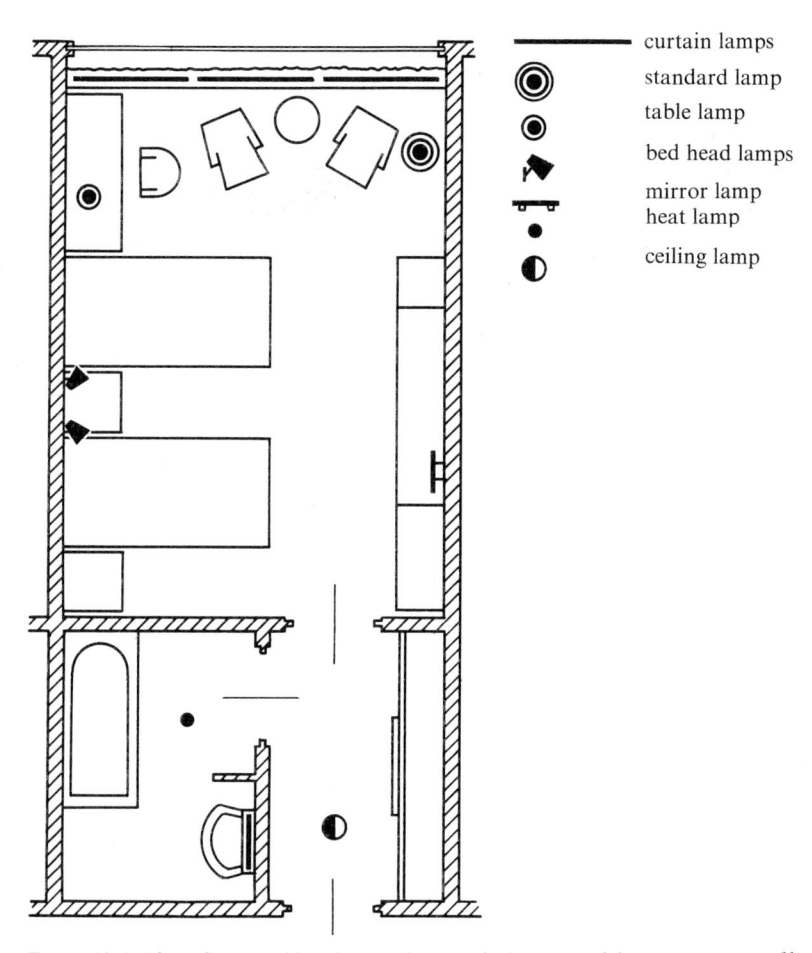

Figure 18.6 Plan of a typical hotel room showing the location of the various types of lighting used.

rescent lamp concealed by an opal diffuser either above or on either side of the mirror (figure 18.7).

In the bathroom, general lighting is usually combined with fluorescent mirror lighting – the lighting set to light the face and not the mirror – one or two 40 W or 65 W fluorescent tubes being used for this purpose.

Figure 18.7 A hotel room with hidden indirect lighting and mirror lighting of the type described in the text.

Chapter 19

Hospitals

The problems most frequently encountered in hospital lighting are not primarily technical. There are many cases where it is simply a question of settling a conflict of interests between the lighting needs of the patient and the medical staff.
It has been realised for a long time that a patient is likely to benefit more from a given course of treatment if he is in a relaxed frame of mind during his stay in the hospital. Every effort must therefore be made to create wherever possible in areas frequented by the patient a sympathetic and restful environment, one with domestic rather than constitutional associations. At the same time, however, the work of the medical staff has to be carried out efficiently and safely; warm, low-intensity lighting may be ideal for bringing a feeling of comfort to a patient's surroundings, but is clearly not suitable for the purposes of carrying out a detailed clinical examination.

19.1 General Lighting Requirements

A factor of great psychological importance, especially to the sick, is colour; a light source that works with the hospital decor to help create a pleasant, friendly atmosphere in terms of colour will inevitably contribute towards the recovery of many types of patient.
Colour is also of great importance, but in quite another way, to the medical staff. The primary concern here is that the sources used give the truest possible colour rendering of the human skin, the colour and change in colour of the skin being important indications of a patient's condition.
Tubular fluorescent lamps of the warm-white colour giving good colour rendering are considered eminently suitable for use in hospitals in colder climates to bring a feeling of warmth to surroundings in which trueness of colour rendering is not of paramount importance. Similarly, for hospitals in the tropics, the cooler 'daylight' types of lamps should be used.
Rooms where examination regularly takes place call for lamps giving the truest possible colour rendering and a colour temperature of around 4000 K. In those rooms where the use of radiation-sensitive electronic equipment is anticipated, the lighting should be interference-free.

Emergency lighting should be installed in all internal traffic areas and exits, and in all other areas where life and safety would be endangered by the absence of lighting.

19.2 Specific Lighting Techniques

19.2.1 Ward Lighting

General lighting
In the first place, wards should have a general lighting which, as the patients themselves are often obliged to view their surroundings from recumbent or semi-recumbent positions, should be totally free from glare. Indirect lighting is therefore often preferred for this purpose.

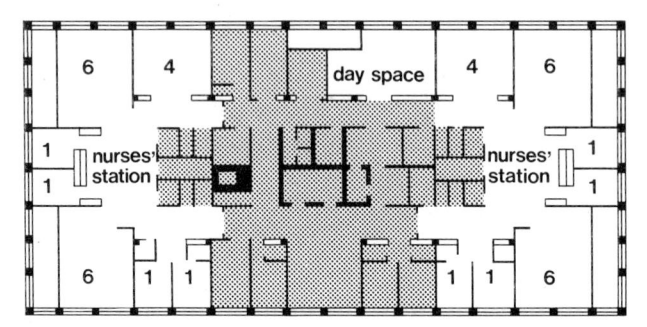

Figure 19.1 Plan of 'race-track' type ward (number of beds indicated) on a typical floor of a hospital block. Parts of the inner zone (hatched), which comprises service and ancillary rooms, are entirely reliant on artificial lighting, and this must be such as to facilitate visual adaptation for staff moving about the floor.

The illuminance recommended for the general lighting in the patient area is 100 lx. In wards of the 'race track' type (figure 19.1), the nurses' stations are located in the inner zone of the building and are therefore often lit entirely by artificial light. The patients, on the other hand, are accommodated in the outer zone of the building, an area which will more than likely be well provided with daylight. It is important, therefore, in wards such as these, that the general lighting be carefully planned so as to facilitate the visual adaptation of the nursing staff when passing from the one zone to the other.

Local lighting

Local lighting at the bed-head, covering the full width of the bed, must be available for the use of patients wishing to read, etc. Such lighting, which should provide a local illuminance of between 100 lx and 300 lx to supplement the general lighting (figure 19.2), must not disturb patients in adjacent beds or in any beds opposite. The luminance of the luminaire providing the bed-head lighting and the luminance of the wall above the bed, as seen by either patients or medical staff, should not be greater than about 350 cd/cm². Heat radiated by the source should of course be kept as low as possible. There should be a light switch located within easy reach of the patient.

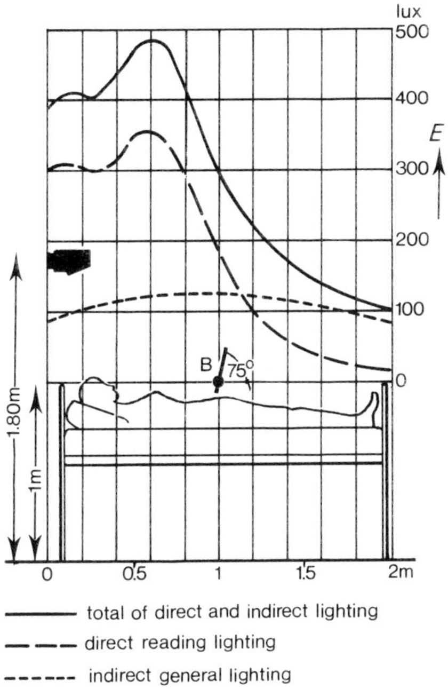

Figure 19.2 Local lighting at the bed-head. The measurements were made in a one-bed room, height 2.8 m, with normal room-surface reflectances, using an integrated ward lighting unit of the type illustrated in figure 19.3. The illuminance levels (vertical scale) were measured at a height of 1 m along the longitudinal axis of the bed. Point B shows the usual position of a book, the illuminance on the plane of which is 320 lx.

——— total of direct and indirect lighting
— — — direct reading lighting
------ indirect general lighting

Examination lighting

If examination or treatment of the patient is not carried out in a room set aside for this purpose, suitable supplementary luminaires may be used in the ward. The lamps, which should be so screened that only the bed area is illuminated, should give a minimum illuminance of 1000 lx. The light source should, as already mentioned above, have the requisite colour rendering properties.

Night lighting

Night lighting should be sufficient to provide the minimum amount of light necessary for nurses and patients to find their way about during the hours of darkness, when the general lighting has been turned off. This corresponds to an illuminance of 0.5 lx at floor level. The lamp providing this illumination should be adequately screened so as not to disturb sleeping patients.

Night observation lighting

Night lighting intended for the observation of patients should cause the minimum disturbance to other patients in the wards. For this reason, an illuminance of between 5 lx and 20 lx, restricted to the bed-heads and provided by well-screened sources, is recommended. The light switch, located at the bed, should not be within reach of the patient.

Integrated ward lighting

The most striking development of recent years in the fitting out of both open and private wards has been the tendency to integrate the various types of lighting described above with the medical services and communications systems. A typical integrated ward-lighting system is illustrated in figure 19.3.

From the point of view of building economics, the great advantage of the package approach offered by such a system is that all piping and wiring is

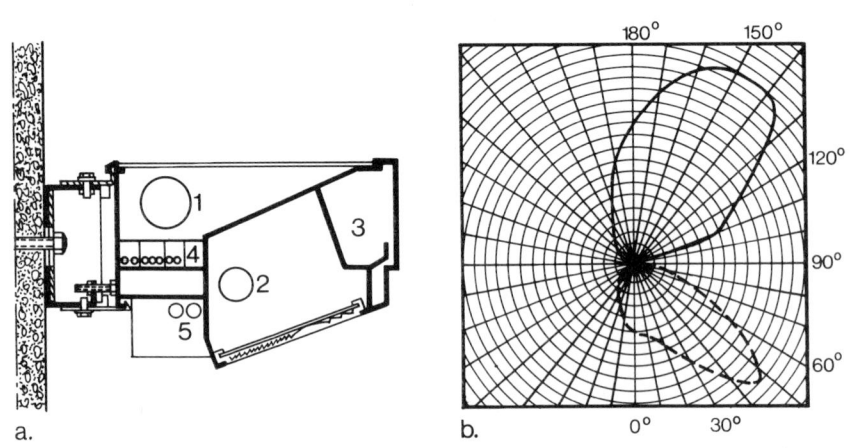

Figure 19.3 Integrated ward lighting. (a) Cross-section of a special-purpose unit showing 1. Indirect general lighting compartment (65 watt fluorescent lamp colour 34) 2. Direct lighting compartment (30 watt fluorescent lamp colour 34 for reading or 6 watt incandescent lamp for examination purposes) 3. Channel for communications cables 4. Channel for mains wiring 5. Channel for medical pipes (b) Light distribution of the luminaire – direct (dotted line) and indirect (solid line). The Photos show the unit in operation. The patient's night light (seen vertically above the vase of flowers) burns at all times and casts a pool of light on the floor at the bedside.

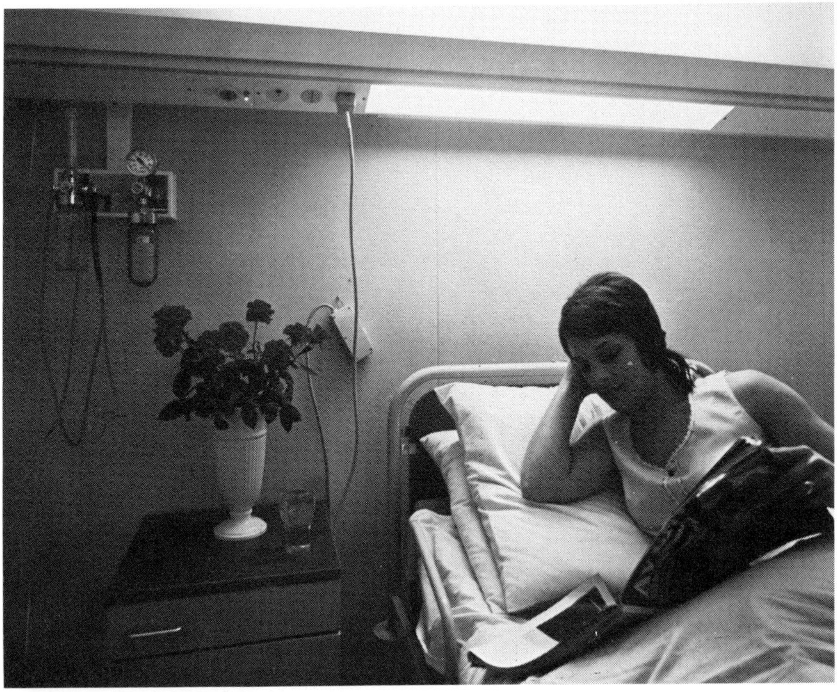

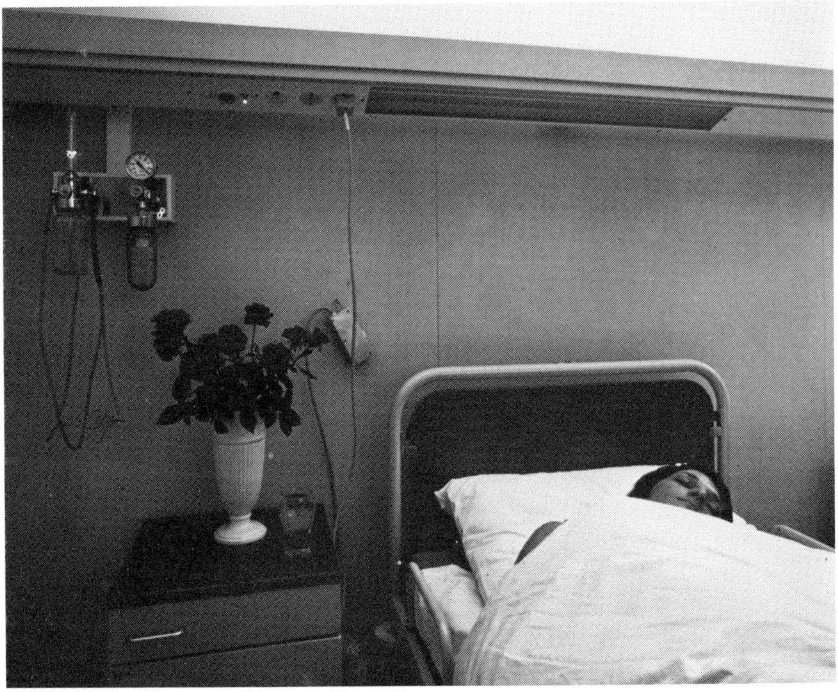

incorporated in the unit, which is wall mounted and so does not have to be actually built into the wall. Special examination lighting, however, is often not included; instead, there is generally provision for connection of a separate examination lamp, permanent or otherwise. Disturbance to the patient can be minimised by arranging for the examination lighting to be dimmer controlled.

19.2.2 Corridors

The lighting in corridors should be related to the lighting in adjacent rooms so that there is no marked difference in illuminance when passing from the one to the other. This often means that provision must be made for reducing the illuminance in the corridor at night. In those cases where the corridor does not receive sufficient natural light during the day, the artificial lighting in the corridor should facilitate visual adaptation by providing a rather high luminance on the wall opposite the doors of rooms that are illuminated by daylight (figure 19.4).

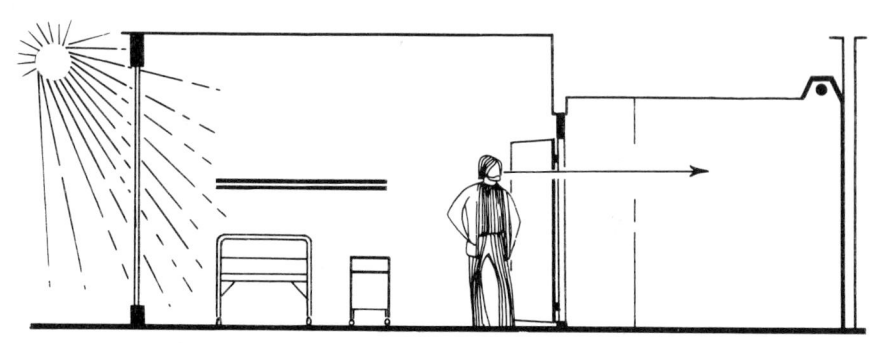

Figure 19.4 Corridor lighting placed to facilitate visual adaptation.

The disturbance to patients being wheeled along the corridors on trolleys, caused by glimsing the luminaires as they pass overhead, can be minimised by ensuring that these are mounted off-centre. (See again figure 19.4.)
The day-time illuminance in corridors should be between 200 lx and 300 lx. This can be reduced at night to between 3 lx and 5 lx for corridors opening onto bed-bays and to between 5 lx and 10 lx for all other corridors.

19.2.3 Examination Rooms

The lighting in examination rooms should be planned to accommodate a wide variety of visual tasks. This is normally achieved using a combined system of general and local lighting, with the former giving an illuminance of between 500 lx and 1000 lx. The two systems should be matched as closely as possible for colour temperature.

19.2.4 Theatre Suites

The lighting of the operating theatre (figure 19.5) calls for a delicate balance between the very special lighting used to light the centrally placed operating table and that providing the illumination in the remainder of the theatre.

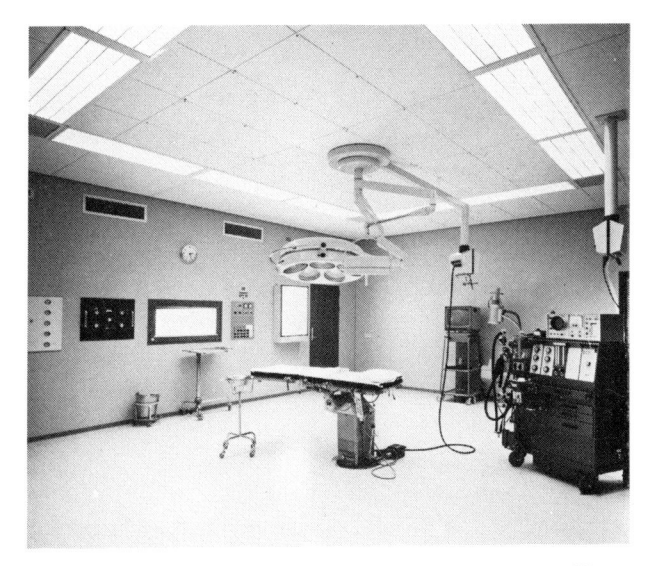

Figure 19.5 The general lighting in this operating theatre is provided by 10 recessed luminaires with mirror optics, each housing four 65 watt fluorescent reflector lamps, colour white de luxe. It is possible to switch one, two, three or four lamps per luminaire, so providing illuminances ranging from 250 lx to 1000 lx.

The operating luminaire (a description of which is beyond the scope of this book) is designed to give shadow-free lighting of very high illuminance on the table variable in intensity between certain prescribed limits. The illuminance provided by the general lighting should be in the order of 1000 lx in order to always keep luminance differences within the theatre to an acceptable maximum.

The colour of the general illumination in an operating theatre should also be compatible with the illumination from the operating light, that is to say the colour temperature of the two sources should match as closely as possible.

The preferred source for the general theatre lighting is the tubular fluorescent lamp having a colour temperature of around 4000 K and good to optimum colour rendering. Luminaires should be of the multi-lamp recessed type, equipped with mirror reflectors to give maximum light output and low source luminance.

The illuminance level given by the general lighting in the other rooms comprising the theatre suite, viz. surgeons' and nurses' changing rooms, scrub room, sterilising room and recovery room, should be at least fifty per cent of that given by the general lighting in the theatre itself in order to facilitate visual adaptation when passing from one to the other. Colour rendering should be the same throughout the suite.

19.2.5 Intensive Care Rooms

The illumination here must be suitable for a wide variety of visual tasks. Furthermore, the lighting system should include provision for changing the illuminance level quickly in order to satisfy emergency requirements.

The illuminance given by the general lighting should be variable from 300 lx down to almost zero. The preference is for fluorescent tubes identical to those used in the operating theatre.

Supplementary luminaires are needed to provide the localised lighting used for examination and treatment purposes, but these must not encroach on the bed surrounds. Portable surgical luminaires (operating lights) should also be available.

Curtains are needed to screen off the area in which medical staff are active from the rest of the room, so minimising the disturbance to other patients.

19.2.6 X-ray Rooms

For the positioning of patients and for the purposes of room cleaning, a dimmer-controlled general lighting installation that gives an illuminance of 100 lx will suffice. Other tasks, e.g. the giving of injections, will require localised lighting.

An institutional atmosphere can be avoided by adding some decorative lighting: for example, a wall luminaire giving a low, comfortable level of lighting.

Chapter 20

Sports Buildings

An indoor sports lighting installation should provide good visual conditions for both the players, so as to promote the speed and accuracy of their performance, and the spectators, so that the play can be followed with the minimum of effort. Where television or film coverage is anticipated, the lighting should be such that the demands placed upon it by these recording media are satisfied. Finally, the lighting should integrate with and, if possible, enhance the architectural style of the hall or stadium concerned.

20.1 Lighting for Players and Spectators

20.1.1 General Requirements

Illuminance levels

For many sports, viewing is omnidirectional and both the horizontal and the vertical illuminances are important. (This is particularly true of sports that are to be televised or filmed in colour, see Sec. 20.2 below.) For practical reasons, however, many recommendations for sports lighting refer only to the horizontal illuminance required. The vertical illuminance at a level of 1.5 m above the ground on a vertical plane facing the centre of the playing

Table 20.1 Recommended minimum illuminances and uniformities for sports lighting

	Horizontal illuminance E (lux)		Uniformity (E_{min}/E_{av})	
	Training	Matches	Training	Matches
Halls	200	500	1:2	1:1.5
Swimming-pools	200	500	1:1.5	1:1.5
Skating-rinks	200	500	1:2	1:1.5
Tennis courts	200	500	1:2	1:1.5
Ten-pin bowling alleys	200	200	1:2	1:2
Shooting ranges	100	100	1:3	1:3
Horse-jumping arenas	150	300	1:2	1:2

area should then always be more than half the recommended horizontal illuminance.

For most sports, a horizontal illuminance of approximately 500 lx is adequate for the players. Higher illuminances are necessary at those matches where spectators are present than for those games that are solely for training purposes.

Recommended illuminance levels for a selection of indoor sports areas are given in table 20.1.

Should lighting of more than 50 W/m^2 of floor surface have to be installed in order to achieve the recommended illuminance, then the effect of this on the indoor climate must be taken into consideration.

Reflections from walls, floor and ceiling

Large differences in the luminosity of floor, walls and ceiling should be avoided. For this reason no glossy materials or paints should be used for the finish of these surfaces.

The luminance pattern of the walls and ceiling, which often serve as a background to the perception of a ball (for example), should be kept subdued. It is recommended, therefore, that a ceiling or wall with a line pattern full of contrasts be avoided, although in the latter case this should not be absolutely monotonous. In order to be able to realise acceptable luminance ratios the following reflectances are to be preferred: walls, 0.3 to 0.6; ceilings, above 0.6. For badminton, tennis and volleyball especially, walls with unsaturated, cool colour should be given preference over grey walls.

Dark shiny floors should be avoided. The reflectance of the floor should be at least 0.25.

Daylight

A hall may be used for other purposes in addition to sport, for which the entry into the hall of daylight – or even direct sunlight – may be of no consequence. When sport is in progress, however, direct sunlight should not be allowed to reach the playing area. Care should also be taken to ensure that sky luminances seen through windows do not distract or annoy either the players or the spectators.

Modelling

The effectiveness of modelling is determined by the direction or directions from which the lighting comes and the number and type of light sources used.

Modelling can range from 'harsh' to 'flat'. Harsh modelling, with its characteristic deep shadows, will result if single, high-intensity sources (for example, narrow-beam floodlights) are so positioned as to light the scene from predominantly one direction. Flat, or shadowless, modelling results if the scene is lighted uniformly from all directions (the sort of lighting produced, for example, by a luminous ceiling). Either of these extremes is, of course, undesirable although, in the latter case, the addition of a few spotlights to improve the modelling is feasible.

In practice, acceptable modelling is generally achieved by employing one or other of two basic lighting arrangements: line or spot. The line arrangement, in which medium intensity sources are mounted in continuous or near-continuous lines above and along either side of the area concerned, is generally considered to give slightly better modelling than the spot arrangement in which a lesser number of grouped, higher-intensity sources are employed.

Glare

In the majority of sports the players must frequently look upwards; the complete avoidance of glare is then made rather difficult. Glare can be reduced to an acceptable level, however, by ensuring that the lamps are well screened and that they provide a certain amount of up light to lighten the roof or ceiling above.

Light sources of high luminous intensity should be carefully grouped and positioned so as to keep the number of individual sources visible in a given direction of view to a minimum.

In many sports – such as mini-football, tennis and volleyball – there is a main direction of play and therefore a main direction of view along the length of the playing area. Side lighting is preferred for sports falling into this category, the light sources being arranged in rows running along either side of the playing area. This arrangement reduces the risk of glare, provides good modelling and also supplies the necessary vertical component of the lighting.

20.1.2 Requirements for Specific Sports
Badminton, volleyball and tennis

For sports such as these – sports in which the players are constantly required to look upwards – the brightness contrasts on the ceiling above the playing area should be kept to a minimum.

With badminton and tennis, players often prefer the illuminance level at the net to be higher than that on the rest of the court; the emphasis here must be on providing a glare-free area directly above the net. Side lighting is preferred for all three sports.

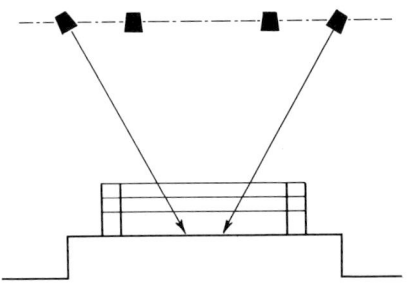

Figure 20.1 Recommended lighting arrangement for boxing rings.

Boxing

Boxing is a sport that requires very high local illuminances. A common lighting arrangement (figure 20.1) uses high-intensity floodlights mounted some six metres above the canvas.

Swimming

The lighting in a swimming pool should satisfy two basic requirements. In the first place, it should be glare-free and provide an adequate and uniform level of illuminance on the water surface. Secondly, and particularly important from the viewpoint of safety, the light should penetrate the water without giving rise to reflections in its surface; submerged swimmers will then be made clearly visible to onlookers on the poolside.

In order to satisfy the second of these requirements the ratio of the luminance of the luminaires (in all directions that can lead to reflections in the water surface) to the average illuminance on the water surface should be as low as possible. Also, it is well known that the reflection of light from a water surface decreases with decrease in the angle of light incidence (measured from the vertical). The application of this principle by employing luminaires for HID lamps having a concentrated, or narrow-beam, output directed vertically downwards can help in providing a practical solution to preventing troublesome reflections. Finally, the contribution made by underwater lighting to increased visibility should not be overlooked. Such lighting is inherently incapable of producing surface reflections, and can even serve to lessen the disturbing effect of such reflections should they already exist.

General lighting. The three main systems of general lighting worthy of consideration are:
1. Fluorescent lamps mounted to form a luminous ceiling (see colour plate 19). Such a ceiling can lead to reflections in the water surface by virtue of the diffuse character of the light distribution from the ceiling itself. The disturbance caused by these reflections will, however, be minimal because the luminance/illuminance ratio mentioned above will be relatively low. Lamp replacement is best carried out from above the ceiling.
2. A variant of (1) wherein the luminous ceiling is limited to a number of rows of fluorescent lamps mounted in luminaires with either diffuse or downward-directed light distributions.

   For a restful lighting effect the luminaires should be mounted in the form of continuous broad bands. The number of bands should be kept to the minimum necessary to preserve lighting uniformity.

   The limited ceiling height in indoor swimming pools means that, in the interests of uniformity, the luminaires usually have to be mounted over the surface of the water as well as above the pool surrounds. This solution is economically attractive and has found a wide field of application.
3. Indirect lighting in which large, wall-mounted floodlights fitted with tungsten halogen lamps or a combination of metal halide and high-pressure sodium lamps are aimed at the ceiling (see colour plate 20).

   With this system it is impossible for the light sources to be reflected in the surface of the water. The ceiling, if diffusely reflecting, can itself be reflected in the water surface, but the disturbance produced will be minimal on account of the relatively low ceiling luminance involved.

Maintenance is easy because the luminaires are both limited in number and conveniently placed. The height and reflectance of the ceiling, however, must be suitable for indirect lighting.

This system is best used in combination with lighting for the pool surrounds that uses well-screened tubular fluorescent lamps.

Combinations of systems are also possible. For example, a combination of systems (2) and (3) above (figure 20.2), in which direct lighting using tubular fluorescent lamps is mounted above the pool surround with indirect, wall-mounted luminaires to provide adequate illuminance in the central area of the pool. The lamps used in this system should be well-screened, give good colour rendering and create a lively appearance.

Underwater lighting. The part played by underwater lighting in helping to make swimmers underwater visible to onlookers on the poolside has been mentioned above. This aspect of pool safety is of course particularly important in public swimming baths. But underwater lighting can also be used

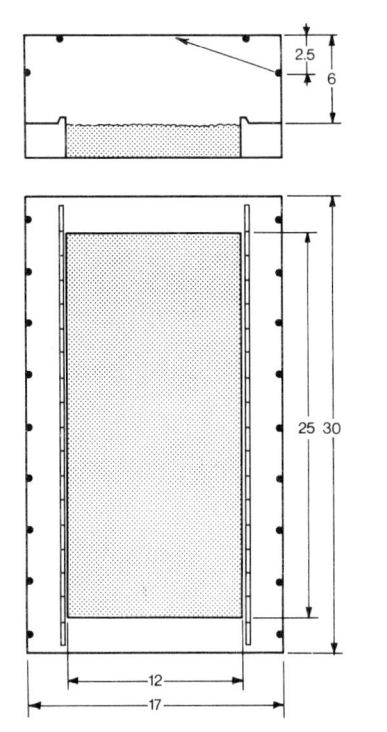

Figure 20.2 Combination of direct and indirect swimming-pool lighting (distances in metres).

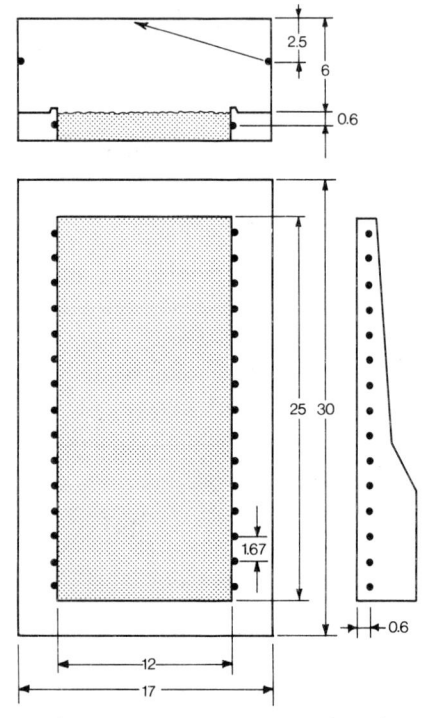

Figure 20.3 Underwater lighting, shown here in combination with an indirect general lighting system (distances in metres).

19 Swimming-pool lighting provided by a luminous ceiling.
20 Swimming-pool lighting of the indirect type.

21 An ice-rink lit predominantly from overhead to give a good luminance uniformity on the ice.
22 To obtain an acceptable lighting uniformity where, as here, only limited mounting height is available, the luminaires can be mounted overhead in a regular arrangement rather than along the side walls as would normally be the case. Note the increased luminaire spacing above the stands and the fact that the luminaires run end-on to the main direction of play.

to good effect in improving the aesthetic appearance of a pool, and this makes such lighting equally attractive to the private pool owner.

Usually, either incandescent, metal halide, or high-pressure sodium lamps are used for underwater lighting. The light sources are normally placed along the longitudinal sides of the pool so that the luminaires aim their beams in the cross-wise direction. In this way the beams have only to penetrate the shortest distance through the water.

In order to take advantage of the phenomenon of total reflection that can be produced at the water surface, the luminaires should be mounted between 0.5 m and 1.0 m below this level (figure 20.3). For deep pools and diving areas, two rows of luminaires should be employed, one above the other, at depths of 0.5 m to 1.0 m and 3.0 m.

A distinction is made between the dry and wet niches built into the walls of the pool to house the underwater light sources. A dry niche is equipped with a watertight porthole behind which the luminaire is placed, whereas a wet niche is open to the water and the luminaire itself is equipped with the necessary water proofing. Dry niches offer certain advantages over wet ones, namely that the luminaires used are cheaper and can be more easily adjusted. Maintenance, with access possible from a service corridor or pit outside the pool basin, is also facilitated.

Really effective underwater lighting calls for an installation giving a high luminous flux per unit area of water surface. Figures based on present-day practice are 150 W/m^2 to 225 W/m^2 for incandescent lamps and 100 W/m^2 for discharge lamps. For small pools, a figure of 100 W/m^2 using incandescent lamps may be taken as a compromise. In order that this installed flux is not wasted, the walls of the pool basin should be given a high-reflectance surface finish.

Ten-pin bowling

The light sources used to illuminate a bowling alley – and which also often form an architectural element of the ceiling – should be well screened from the bowler. Often the ceiling is of 'saw-tooth' construction and tubular fluorescent lamps can be mounted on the side hidden from view and at right angles to the alleys.

The average horizontal illuminance in the bowling centre should be about 200 lx, with additional, local lighting above the pins.

Ice-hockey

For the lighting of ice-hockey, and ice-skating in general, the luminaires can either be mounted immediately above the ice-rink or adjacent to it, although it is generally easier to satisfy the requirements relating to lighting level, uniformity and glare with the former arrangement than with the latter. The area in the immediate vicinity of the goals should receive extra light, but not so much that the requirements with respect to illuminance uniformity are left unsatisfied. This extra lighting should come from the sides of the goals rather than from behind them, so as to avoid producing reflected glare from the ice.

20.2 Lighting Requirements for TV or Film Coverage in Colour

Lighting that satisfies the quality requirements of players and spectators and produces a horizontal illuminance on the playing area in excess of 300 lx will generally prove adequate for the operation of black/white television and film cameras. Colour recording, however, imposes far more stringent requirements with regard to the level and quality of the lighting.

20.2.1 Illuminance Levels

Three factors combine to determine the illuminance level needed for the good reproduction of a scene in colour: the sensitivity of the film or television camera in use, the exposure time, and the effective aperture of the camera lens.

Film cameras

Film sensitivity. The sensitivity of colour film may be taken as being about 160 ASA. This sensitivity will, however, be effectively reduced if, because of a discrepancy in colour temperature between film and illuminant, the colour temperature of the latter has to be altered by using a colour-correcting filter on the camera – the reduction in sensitivity brought about by the use of such a filter can be as much as 50 per cent.

Exposure time. For a cine camera the exposure time is determined by the film speed used (viz. the speed of the film through the camera; in order to avoid confusion, the term 'film sensitivity' is preferred to 'film speed' when referring to the speed of the emulsion of cine film).
At the standard film speed of 24 frames per second, the exposure time is approximately 1/50 s. For slow motion effects, however, a film speed of twice this is quite usual (i.e. 48 frames per second), giving an exposure time of 1/100 s or less.

Effective aperture. Because of the need to ensure adequate depth of field, the effective aperture of the camera lens will be limited to about $f/2$.

To sum up. As far as filming in colour is concerned, the illuminance level must be such as to allow the correct exposure to be obtained when limited to a film sensitivity of about 160 ASA, an exposure time of 1/100 s or less and an effective aperture of no greater than $f/2$.

TV cameras

Camera sensitivity. Colour TV cameras suitable for televising sports events have a sensitivity equivalent to about 125 ASA – or 250 ASA if a reduction in picture quality is acceptable.

Exposure time. On account of the fact that a fixed scanning frequency (25 complete pictures per second) is employed, the TV camera has a fixed exposure time. Slow-motion effects are obtained by magnetic storing and multi-reading of shots taken under normal conditions – thus no additional light is needed.

Effective aperture. This is again dictated by the need to ensure an adequate depth of field. An f-number of between $f/2$ and $f/5.6$ is common.
From an analysis of the sort of technical information outlined above it is possible to arrive at the vertical illuminance needed to obtain a satisfactory exposure under given conditions for both film cameras (table 20.2) and TV cameras (table 20.3).

Table 20.2 Required illuminance (vertical) in lux for colour films of 160 ASA sensitivity

Exposure time	Lens aperture			
	$f/(2)$	$f/2.8$	$f/4$	$f/5.6$
1/ 50 s	(300)	600	1 200	2 400
1/100 s	(600)	1 200	2 400	4 800

Table 20.3 Required illuminance (vertical) in lux for colour TV based on 2 mlm at a signal-to-noise-ratio of about 40 dB.
$f/4$ can be regarded as a normal aperture corresponding to an illuminance of 1 500 lx

Lens aperture			
$f/(2)$	$f/2.8$	$f/4$	$f/5.6$
(375)	750	1 500	3 000

Note: The figures specified between brackets can only be used in exceptional cases where some loss of picture quality can be tolerated

The vertical illuminance recommended for a given situation is that needed in the direction of the camera or cameras. In all other directions away from the main angle of view the illuminance can be less than the value recommended, but should never be less than 50 per cent of this value. The illuminance uniformity in the vertical plane as measured at a height of 1.5 m above the playing area should be 1:3 or better.

Where the camera angle is such as to include an area outside the field of play, occupied by spectators, a horizontal illuminance on this area of 25 per cent of the average horizontal illuminance on the playing area will be needed to give adequate picture quality.

20.2.2 Colour Temperature and Colour Rendering

Colour film calls for the use of lamps having a correlated colour temperature of between 3000 K and 7000 K, the preferred value being dependent upon whether the artificial lighting is used to supplement daylight or replace it entirely. Where the former is the case the colour temperature of the artificial lighting should, in the interests of preserving colour quality, be near to 5000 K so as to match that of the daylight. Light of a lower colour temperature is, however, perfectly acceptable so long as daylight is excluded from the scene entirely.

The point on the colour triangle defining the colour of the light should lie near to the locus of the black body radiator; the need to use filters on the camera, other than those normally employed to match film to light source, is thereby lessened.

The colour television camera is not so critical with regard to colour temperature, so long as this is consistent throughout the scene being televised, and provided there is sufficient energy radiated in the visible region of the spectrum.

Tests and experience have shown that for film and television alike, as well as for players and spectators, the lamps used should have a general colour rendering index in excess of 70.

20.2.3 Suitable Light Sources

Table 20.4 lists those light sources suitable for lighting sports events that are to be filmed or televised in colour.

Table 20.4 Light sources suitable for colour TV broadcasting in sports halls and grounds

Light source	Luminous efficacy up to (lm/W)	Colour temperature (K) about
Projector lamps	25	3 000
Tungsten-Halogen lamps	30	3 200
Fluorescent lamps	50*	3 000 to 6 000
Metal halide lamps	70*	3 000 to 6 000

* Including ballast

Bibliography

Allphin, W., *Sight Line to Desk Tasks in Schools and Offices*. Illuminating Engineering vol. 58 p. 244 (1963).

Arndt, W., Bodmann, H. W. and Muck, E., *Blendung durch einzelne Lichtquellen im Sehfeld* (Glare from single light sources in the field of vision). Lichttechnik, vol. 11 p. 22 (1959a).

Arndt, W., Bodmann, H. W. and Muck, E., *Untersuchung über die psychologische Blendung durch mehrere Lichtquellen* (Investigation on discomfort glare caused by several light sources). Compte Rendu CIE p. 59 5 (1959b).

Aston, S. M. and Bellchambers, H. E., *Illumination, Colour Rendering and Visual Clarity*. Lighting Research and Technology 1 pp. 259–261 (1969).

Balder, J. J. and Fortuin, G. J., *The Influence of Time of Observation on the Visibility of Stationary Objects*. Compte Rendu, CIE Zurich, 1955 N-F/3 (1955).

Balder, J. J., *Erwünschte Leuchtdichten in Büroräumen* (Preferred Luminance in Offices). Lichttechnik, vol. 9 p. 455 (1957).

Barthès, E. and Richard, J., *Étude expérimentale du confort visuel à travers l'équilibre des luminances* (An experimental study of visual comfort as determined by the balance of brightness). Lux, vol. 54 p. 298 (1969).

Bedocs, L. and Simons, R. H., *The accuracy of the IES Glare Index System*. Lighting Research and Technology, vol. 4 p. 80 (1972).

Bellchambers, H. E. and Godby, A. C., *Illumination, Colour Rendering and Visual Clarity*. Lighting Research and Technology. vol. 4 pp. 104–106 (1972).

Bellchambers, H. Collins, J. and Crisp, V., *Relationship between two systems of glare limitation*. Lighting Research and Technology, vol. 7 no. 2 p. 106 (1975).

Blackwell, H. R. et al., *Development and Use of a Quantitative Method for Specification of Interior Illumination Levels on the Basis of Performance Data*. Illuminating Engineering, vol. LIV p. 317 (1959).

Blackwell, O. M. and Blackwell, H. R., *Visual Performance Data for 156 Normal Observers of Various Ages*. J. Illum. Eng. Soc. 1, 3–13 (1971).

Bodmann, H. W., *Illumination Levels and Visual Performance*. International Lighting Review, vol. 13 p. 41 (1962).

Bodmann, H. W. and Voit, E. A., *Versuche zur Beschreibung der Hellempfindung* (Experiments to describe brightness perception). Lichttechnik, vol. 14 p. 394 (1962).

Bodmann, H. W., Söllner, G. and Voit, E., *Bewertung der Beleuchtungsniveaus bei verschiedenen Lichtarten* (Evaluation of Lighting Levels with Various Kinds of Light), Compte Rendu CIE Wien, S. 502–509 (1963).

Bodmann, H. W. Söllner, G. and Senger, E., *A Simple Glare Evaluation System*. Illuminating Engineering, vol. 61 p. 347 (1966).

Bodmann, H. W., *Quality of Interior Lighting Based on Luminance*. Transaction of the IES, vol. 32 no. 1 p. 22 (1967).

Bodmann, H. W., *Light and the total energy input to a building*. Light and Lighting, September 1970 (1970).

Bodmann, H. W., *Visibility Assessment in Lighting Engineering*. J. Illum. Eng. Soc. 2, 437–443 (1973).

Boer, J. B. de, *Strassenleuchtdichte und Blendungsfreiheit* (Road luminance and Freedom from Glare). Lichttechnik, vol. 10 p. 359 (1958).

Boer, J. B. de, *Glanz in der Beleuchtungstechnik* (Glare in Lighting), Lichttechnik, vol. 28 pp. 227 and 263 (1976).

Boer, J. B. de, *Performance and Comfort in the presence of Veiling Reflections*, Lighting Research and Technology (1977).

Bouma, P. J., *Two methods of characterizing the colour rendering properties of a light source*. CIE Proceedings, Scheveningen, vol. II p. 57 (1939).

Bouma, P. J., *Physical aspects of colour*. Philips Technical Library, Mac Millan, London (1971).

Boyce, P. R., *The Influence of Illumination Level on Prolonged Work Performance*. Lighting Research and Technology, vol. 2 p. 74 (1970).

Boyce, P. R., *Age, Illuminance, Visual Performance and Preference*. Lighting Research and Technology, vol. 5 p. 125 (1973).

Boyce, P. R., *Investigations of the Subjective Balance Between Illuminance and Lamp Colour Properties*. Lighting Research and Technology 9, pp. 11–24 (1977).

CIE, *A Unified Framework of Methods for Evaluating Visual Performance Aspects of Lighting*. Publication CIE No. 19/2 (TC-3.1) Draft of June 1977 (preliminary sixth Draft) (1973).

CIE, *Guide on Interior Lighting*. Publication CIE No. 29 (TC-4.1) (1975).

CIE, *Calculations for Interior Lighting – Applied Method*. Publication CIE No. 40 TC-1.5 (1978).

Collins, J. B. and Plant, C. G. H., *Preferred Luminance Distributions in Windowless Spaces*. Lighting Research and Technology, vol. 3 p. 219 (1971).

Cuttle, C. Burt, W. and Valentine, B., *Beyond the Working Plane*. CIE, Washington P-67. 12 (1967).

Epaneshnikov, M. M., Obrosova, N. A., Sidorova, T. N. and Undasynov, G. N., *New Characteristics of Lighting Conditions for Premises of Public Buildings and Methods for their Calculation*. CIE XVII Session, Barcelone P-71.30 (1971).

Fischer, D., *The European approach to the integration of lighting and air-conditioning.* Lighting Research and Technology, vol. 2 p. 150 (1970a).

Fischer, D., *Optimale Beleuchtungsniveaus in Arbeitsräumen* (Optimum Lighting Levels in Working Interiors). Lichttechnik, vol. 22 p. 61 and 103 (1970b).

Fischer, D., *Lichttechnische Konditionierung von Arbeitsräumen* (Lighting Conditioning of Working Interiors). Lux. no. 57 p. 206 (1970c).

Fischer, D., *Betrachtungen und Messungen über die Leuchtdichteverteilung von Leuchtstofflampen* (Considerations and Measurements on the Luminance Distribution of Fluorescent Lamps). Optik, vol. 31 p. 477 (1970d).

Fischer, D., *The European Glare Limiting Method.* Lighting Research and Technology, vol. 4 no. 2 (1972).

Fischer, D., *A Luminance Concept for Working Interiors.* Journal of the IES, vol. 2 p. 92 (1973a).

Fischer, D., *Comparison of some European Interior Lighting Recommendations.* Lighting Research and Technology, vol. 5 p. 186 (1973b).

Fischer, D. and Hendriks, R., *Qualitativer und quantitativer Vergleich der Blendungsbewertungssysteme verschiedener Länder* (Qualitative and Quantitative Comparison of the Glare Evaluation Systems in Various Countries). Lichttechnik, vol. 25 p. 186 (1973).

Fortuin, G. J., *Visual Power and Visibility.* Philips Research Report 6, p. 251–287 (1951).

Hardy, A. C., *Proceedings of the Conference on Electric Space Heating and Air Conditioning.* Gothenburg, June 1972 (1972).

Helson, H. and Lansford, T., *The role of Spectral Energy of Source and Background Colour in the Pleasantness of Object Colours.* Appl. Opt. vol. 9 p. 1513 (1970).

Henderson, R. L., McNelis, J. F. and Williams, H G.. *A Survey and Analysis of Important Visual Tasks in Offices.* Journal of the Illuminating Engineering Society, vol. 4 p. 150 (1975).

Hentschel, H. J., Kringer, W., Pfeffer, K. A., Roedler, F., Schreiber, L., Söllner, G. and Steck, B., *Kalorimetrische Messungen an Luftgekühlten Leuchten* (Calorimetric Measurements with Ventilated Luminaires). Lichttechnik, vol. 24 p. 509 (1972).

Hopkinson, R. G., *Evaluation of Glare.* Illuminating Engineering, vol. 52 p. 316 (1957).

Hopkinson, R. G. and Longmore, J., *The Permanent Supplementary Lighting of Interiors.* Trans Illum. Eng. Soc. (London), vol. 24 p. 121 (1959).

Hopkinson, R. G. and Collins, W. M., *An Experimental Study of the Glare from a Luminous Ceiling.* Trans. Illum. Eng. Soc. (London), vol. 28 No. 4 p. 142–148 (1963).

IEC, *Electrical Installations of Buildings.* Publication No. 64 (1973).

IES, *Outline of a Standard Procedure for Computing Visual Comfort Ratings for Interior Lighting.* Committee on Recommendations of Quality and Quantity of Illumination of the IES, Report No. 2, Illuminating Engineering, vol. LVIII p. 643 (1966).

IES, *Depreciation and Maintenance of Interior Lighting.* Technical Report No. 9 (1967).

IES, *Evaluation of Discomfort Glare – the IES Glare Index System for Artificial Lighting Installations.* IES Technical Report No. 10 (1967).

IES, *A Method of Evaluating the Visual Effectiveness of Lighting Systems.* RQQ report No. 4A, Illum. Eng. Vol. 65, p. 505 (1970).

IES, *Lighting of Art Galleries and Museums.* Technical Report No. 14 of the British Illum. Eng. Soc. p. 6 (1970).

IES, *An Alternate Simplified Method for Determining the Acceptability of a Luminaire, from the VCP Standpoint, for Use in Large Rooms.* RQQ Report No. 3, Journal of the IES vol. 1 p. 256 (1972).

IES, *The Predetermination of Contrast Rendition Factors for the Calculation of Equivalent Sphere Illumination.* (LM–39) RQQ Report No. 5, Journal of IES/January, vol. 2 p. 149 (1973).

IES, *Code for Interior Lighting.* p. 16 (1977).

Jay, P. A., *Inter-relationship of the design criteria for lighting installations.* Trans. Illum. Eng. Soc. (London), vol. 33 p. 47 (1968).

Judd, D. B. MacAdam, D. L. and Wyszecki, G., *Spectral Distributions of Typical Daylight as a Function of Correlated Colour Temperature.* J. Opt. Soc. Am. vol. 54 p. 1031 (1964).

Kruithof, A. A., *Röhrenlampen mit Leuchtstoffen für allgemeine Beleuchtungszwecke* (Tubular fluorescent lamps for general lighting). Philips Technical Review, No. 6 p. 65 (1941).

Noguchi, T., Ejima, Y., Nagai, H. and Nakano, T., *Influence of light direction on appearance of solid object.* Journal of Light & Visual Environment, vol. 1 No. 1 pp. 64–69 (1977).

Ouweltjes, J. L., *The specification of colour rendering properties of fluorescent lamps.* Die Farbe vol. 9 p. 207 (1960).

Range, D., *Bevorzugte Beleuchtungsniveaus im Freien* (Preferred Lighting Levels in The Open Air). Lichttechnik, vol. 23 p. 356 (1971).

Saunders, J. E., *The role of the level and diversity of horizontal illumination in an appraisal of a simple office task.* Lighting Research and Technology, vol. 2 p. 150 (1969).

Schröder, G. and Steck, B., *Die empfindungsgemässe Bewertung der gesamtbestrahlungsstärke von Beleuchtungsanlagen mit Leuchtstofflampen* (Sensory evaluation of the total radiation of lighting installations with fluorescent lamps). Lichttechnik, vol. 25 p. 17 (1973).

Schröder, D. and Steck, B., *Zur Beurteilung der Lichtfarbe in der Innenbeleuchtung* (On the evaluation of colour appearance in interior lighting). Paper presented to the Lighting Congress, Salzburg 1974 (1974).

Söllner, G., *Ein einfaches System zur Blendungsbewertung* (A Simple Glare Evaluation System). Lichttechnik, vol. 17 p. 59a (1965).

Söllner, G., *Bemerkungen zu einigen Verfahren der Blendungsbewertung* (Comments on some Glare Evaluation Systems). Lichttechnik, vol. 20 p. 111A (1968a).

Söllner, G., *Kombinierte Beleuchtung und Klimatisierung zur Konditionierung von Arbeits-*

räumen (Combined lighting and air conditioning for conditioning of working interiors). Heizung-Lüftung-Haustechnik 19 p. 339 (1968b).

Söllner, G., *Blendung durch leuchtende Decken* (Glare from luminous Ceilings). Lichttechnik, no. 11 (1972).

Stiles, W. S., *The effect of glare on the brightness difference threshold.* Proc. Roy. Soc., London, B, vol. 104, p. 322 (1929).

Studiengemeinschaft Licht, *Untersuchungen über Leistung und Ermüdung des Menschen bei verschiedenen Lichtbedingungen* (Investigations into performance and fatigue of workers under different lighting conditions). Lichttechnik, vol. 8 p. 297 (1956).

Thomson, C. G., *A New Look at Colour Rendering, Level of Illumination and Protection from Ultraviolet Radiation in Museum Lighting.* 'Conservation' – The Journal of the International Institue for Conservation of Historic and Artistic Works, vol. 6 No. 2 and 3 p. 49–70 (1961).

Touw, L. M. C., *Preferred Brightness Ratio of Task and its Immediate Surround.* Proc. CIE Stockholm (1951).

Tregenza, P. R., Romaya, S. M., Dawe, S. P., Heap, L. J. and Tuck, B., *Consistency and Variation in Preferences for Office Lighting.* Lighting Research and Technology, vol. 6 no. 4 p. 205 (1974).

Uitterhoeve, W. L. and Kebschull, W., *Sehleistung und Sehkomfort im Büro* (Visual Performance and Visual Comfort in Offices). Second European Light Congress, Brussels, September 1973 (1973).

Vermeulen, D. and de Boer, J. B., *The Admissible Brightness of Lighting Fixtures.* (Paper read at the CIE Congress, Paris, 1948.) Applied Scientific Research, vol. B2 1950 p. 85 (1948).

Weston, H. C., *The Relation Between Illumination and Visual Performance.* Medical Research Council, H.M.S.O. Code No. 46-2-87-53 (1953).

Wyatt, T. J., *Building economics and energy conservation.* International Lighting Review, vol. XXIV No. 3, 85–92 (1973).

Glossary

The terms and definitions given below are in alphabetical order using the most common form of the term.

A more comprehensive list of such terms and definitions will be found in CIE publication No. 17, the International Lighting Vocabulary, the third edition of which was published in 1970 and with which the terms used in this glossary are in close agreement.

Accommodation: focal adjustment of the eye, generally spontaneous, made for the purpose of looking at an object situated at a given distance.

Adaptation: 1. The process by which the properties of the visual system are modified according to the luminances or the colour stimuli presented to it.
2. The final state of the process.

Black body: see **Planckian radiator**.

Black body locus: see **Planckian locus**.

Blended-light lamp: lamp contaning in the same bulb a mercury vapour lamp element and an incandescent lamp filament connected in series. The bulb may be diffusing or coated with a fluorescent material.

Brightness (or luminosity): attribute of visual sensation according to which an area appears to emit more or less light.

Note: Brightness according to the definition is also an attribute of colour.
In British recommendations the term 'brightness' is now reserved to describe brightness of colour; luminosity should be used in all other instances.

CIE standard photometric observer: receptor of radiation whose relative spectral sensitivity curve conforms to the $V(\lambda)$ curve or to the $V'(\lambda)$ curve.

Colour: see **Perceived colour**, and **Object colour**.

Colour rendering: general expression for the effect of an illuminant on the colour appearance of objects in conscious or subconscious comparison with their colour appearance under a reference illuminant.

Colour rendering index (R_a): of a light source. Measure of the degree to which the psychophysical colours of objects illuminated by the source conform to those of the same objects illuminated by a reference illuminant for specified conditions.

Colour temperature: temperature of the black body that emits radiation of the same chromaticity as the radiation considered. Unit: Kelvin, K.

Colour triangle: see **Chromaticity diagram.**

Contrast: subjective assessment of the difference in appearance of two parts of a field of view seen simultaneously or successively.

Correlated colour temperature: the colour temperature corresponding to the point on the Planckian locus which is nearest to the point representing the chromaticity of the illuminant considered on an agreed uniform-chromaticity-scale diagram.
Unit: Kelvin, K.

Cosine law of incidence: the law which states that illuminance at a point on a plane is proportional to the cosine of the angle of incidence (the angle between the direction of the incident light and the perpendicular to the plane).

$$E = \frac{I}{d^2} \cos \alpha$$

Depreciation factor (deprecated): the reciprocal of the maintenance factor.

Diffuse transmission: transmission in which on the macroscopic scale, diffusion occurs independently of the laws of refraction.

Diffuse transmission: transmission in which, on the macroscopic scale, diffusion occurs independently of the laws of refraction.

Diffused lighting: lighting in which the light on the working plane or on an object is not incident predominantly from any particular direction.

Diffuser: device used to alter the spatial distribution of a radiant or luminous flux and depending essentially on the phenomenon of diffusion.

Dimmer: device enabling the luminous flux from lamps in a lighting installation to be varied in order to adjust the level of the illuminance.

Direct flux: of an installation, is the luminous flux that reaches the reference plane directly from the luminaires of the installation.

Direct ratio: of an installation, is the ratio of the direct flux to the downward flux of the installation.

Disability glare: glare that impairs the vision of objects without necessarily causing discomfort.

Discharge lamp: lamp in which the light is produced, either directly or by means of phosphors, by an electric discharge through a gas, a metal vapour, or mixture of several gases and vapours.

Discomfort glare: glare that causes discomfort without necessarily impairing the vision of objects.

Drip-proof luminaire: luminaire so constructed that, when mounted in its designed position, it will withstand drops of water falling in a substantially vertical direction.

Dustproof luminaire: luminaire so constructed that dust of specified nature and fineness cannot enter it in an amount sufficient to impair its satisfactory operation in a dust-laden atmosphere.

Dust-tight luminaire: luminaire so constructed that dust of a specified nature and fineness cannot enter it when it is used in a dust-laden atmosphere.

Emergency lighting: lighting intended to allow the occupants to find the exits from a building with ease and certainty in the case of failure of the normal lighting system.

Explosion proof luminaire (USA): Enclosed lighting fitting which satisfies the appropriate regulations for use in situations where there is risk of explosion.

Flameproof lighting fitting (UK): see **Explosion proof luminaire.**

Flameproof luminaire: see **Increased safety luminaire.**

Floodlight: projector designed for floodlighting, usually capable of being pointed in any direction and of weatherproof construction.

Fluorescence: photoluminescence that persists for an extremely short time after excitation.

Fluorescent lamp: discharge lamp in which most of the light is emitted by a layer of fluorescent material excited by the ultraviolet radiation from the discharge.

Note: This term is most commonly applied to low-pressure tubular fluorescent lamps. – for example: 'TL', 'TL'F, 'TL'E lamps.

Fluorescent mercury lamp: a high pressure mercury lamp in which the light is produced partly by the mercury vapour and partly by a layer of fluorescent material on the inner surface of the outer bulb excited by the ultraviolet radiation of the discharge – for example: HPL-N, HPLR-N lamps.

Full radiator: see **Planckian radiator.**

Gaseous discharge lamp: discharge lamp in which the discharge takes place in a gas – for example: xenon, neon, helium, nitrogen, carbon dioxide.

Note: The term 'neon tube' is sometimes wrongly used to denote any such tubular discharge lamp.

General lighting: lighting designed to illuminate an area without provision for special local requirements.

Glare: condition of vision in which there is discomfort or a reduction in the ability to see significant objects, or both, due to an unsuitable distribution or range of luminance or to extreme contrasts in space or time.

Halide lamp: discharge lamp in which the light is produced by the radiation from a mixture of a metallic vapour (for example, mercury) and the products of the dissociation of halides (for example, halides of thallium, indium or sodium) – for example: HPI/T lamps.

Halogen lamp: gas-filled lamp containing a tungsten filament and a small proportion of halogens.

High-pressure mercury (vapour) lamp: mercury vapour lamp, with or without a coating of phosphor, in which during operation the partial pressure of the vapour is of the order of 10^5 N/m^2 – for example: HPR and HGK lamps.

High-pressure sodium (vapour) lamp: sodium vapour lamp in which the partial pressure of the vapour during operation is of the order of 10^4 N/m² – for example: SON, SON/T lamps.

Hue: attribute of visual sensation which has given rise to colour names such as blue, green, yellow, red, purple, etc., but excluding colours in the white, grey, black range.

Illuminance, (E_v, E): at a point on a surface. Quotient of the luminous flux incident on an element of the surface containing the point and the area of that element.
Unit: lux, lx.

Illuminance meter: an instrument for the measurement of illuminance.

Illumination: the application of visible radiation to an object.

Incandescence: emission of visible radiation by thermal excitation.

Incandescent (electric) lamp: lamp in which light is produced by means of a body heated to incandescence by the passage of an electric current.

Note: According to whether the luminous element is a filament of carbon, tungsten or other metal, the lamp is called a 'carbon filament lamp' a 'tungsten filament lamp' or a 'metal filament lamp'. Tungsten and other metal filament lamps may be 'straight filament lamps', 'single-coil lamps' or 'coiled-coil lamps'.

Increased safety luminaire: enclosed luminaire that satisfies the appropriate regulations for use in situations where there is risk of explosion.

Indirect flux: of an installation, is the luminous flux reaching the reference plane after reflection against other surfaces.

Indirect lighting: lighting by means of luminaires with a light distribution such that not more than 10% of the emitted luminous flux reaches the working plane directly, assuming that this plane is unbounded.

Infrared radiation: radiation for which the wavelengths of the monochromatic components are greater than those for visible radiation and less than about 1 mm.

Inter-reflection (or interflection): general effect of the reflections of radiation between several reflecting surfaces.

Inverse Square Law: the law which states that the illuminance at a point on a plane perpendicular to the line joining the point and a source is inversely proportional to the square of the distance between the source and the plane.

$$E = \frac{I}{d^2}$$

Isocandela curve (diagram): curve traced on an imaginary sphere with the source at its centre and joining all adjacent points corresponding to those directions in which the luminous intensity is the same, or a plane projection of this curve.

Isoluminance curve (diagram): locus of points on a surface at which the luminance is the same, for given positions of the observer and of the source or sources in relation to the surface.

Isolux curve (diagram): locus of points on a surface where the illuminance has the same value.

Jet-proof luminaire: luminaire constructed to withstand a direct jet of water from any direction.

Lamellae louvre: a louvre of which the main shielding elements are in the form of straight strips of opaque or translucent material.

Lamp: source made in order to produce light.

Lens panel: a refracting panel consisting of one or more, usually cylindrical, fresnel lenses.

Light: any radiation capable of causing a visual sensation directly i.e. **Visible radiation.**

Light distribution curve: see **Luminous intensity distribution curve.**

Light controller: that part of a luminaire designed to control the spatial distribution of the luminous flux of the lamp(s).

Note: In practice a light controller will also act as a screen.

Light output ratio: of a luminaire, is the ratio of the light output of the luminaire, measured under specified practical conditions, to the sum of the individual light outputs of the lamps operating outside the luminaire under specified conditions.

Note 1: For luminaires using incandescent lamps, the optical output ratio and the light output ratio are the same in practice.

Note 2: For luminaires using discharge lamps the light output ratio may be less than or greater than the optical output ratio depending upon:
(1) The internal temperature of the luminaire
(2) The setting of the lamp ballast in the luminaire.
The term 'light output ratio (working)' is used when including the effects of both the above conditions; the term 'light output ratio (luminaire)' is used when including only the effect of the internal temperature of a luminaire.

Lighting: application of visible radiation to an object.

Lightness: attribute of visual sensation in accordance with which a body seems to transmit or reflect diffusely a greater or smaller fraction of the incident light.

Localized lighting: lighting designed to increase the illuminance at certain specified positions, for instance those at which work is carried on.

Note: The term 'local lighting' is often applied to lighting designed to illuminate a particularly small area, e.g. a desk top.

Louvre: screen made of translucent or opaque components and geometricelly disposed to prevent lamps from being directly visible over a given angle.

Low-pressure mercury (vapour) lamp: mercury vapour lamp, with or without a coating of phosphor, in which during operation the partial pressure of the vapour does not exceed 100 N/m^2 – for example: a 'TL' or a TUV lamp.

Low-pressure sodium lamp: sodium vapour lamp in which the partial pressure of the vapour during operation does not exceed 5 N/m^2 – for example: a SOX lamp.

Luminaire: apparatus that distributes, filters or transforms the lighting given by a lamp or lamps and which includes all the items necessary for fixing and protecting these lamps and for connecting them to the supply circuit.

Note: In road lighting the term 'lantern' is also used.

Luminance, (L): (in a given direction, at a point on the surface of a source or a receptor or at a point on the path of a beam). Quotient of the luminous flux leaving, arriving at, or passing through an element of surface at this point and propagated in directions defined by an elementary cone containing the given direction, and the product of the solid angle of the cone and the area of the orthogonal projection of the element of surface on a plane perpendicular to the given direction.
Unit: candela per square metre, cd/m².

Luminaire contrast, (C_L): between two parts of a visual field, is the relative luminance difference of those parts in accordance with the formula:

$$C_L = \frac{L_2 - L_1}{L_1}$$

where the size of the two parts differs greatly and where
L_1 = luminance of the smallest part,
L_2 = luminance of the greatest part,

or $$C_L = \frac{(L_2 - L_1)}{(L_2 + L_1)}$$

where the size of the two parts is of the same order and where
L_1 = luminance of one part
L_2 = luminance of the other part,

or $$\frac{L_2}{L_1}$$

Luminance distribution curve: curve representing the luminance of a luminaire in a vertical plane as a function of the angle from the nadir.

Luminance meter: an instrument for the measurement of luminance.

Luminescence: phenomenon of the emission by matter of electromagnetic radiation which for certain wavelengths or restricted regions of the spectrum is in excess of that due to the thermal radiation from the material at the same temperature. The radiation is characteristic of the particular material.

Note: In lighting this term is generally restricted to the emission of radiation in the visible or near visible spectrum.

Luminosity: see **Brightness**

Luminous efficacy (of a source): quotient of the luminous flux emitted and the power consumed.
Unit: lumen per watt, lm/W

Luminous flux, $(\Phi_v), (\Phi)$: the quantity derived from radiant flux by evaluating the radiation according to its action upon a selective receptor, the spectral sensitivity of which is defined by the standard spectral luminous efficiencies
Unit: lumen, lm

Luminous intensity, (I_v, I): of a source in a given direction. Quotient of the luminous flux leaving the source, propagated in an element of solid angle containing the given direction, and the element of solid angle.
Unit: candela, cd

Note: The luminous intensity of luminaires is normally given either in a **Luminous intensity diagram** or in an **Isocandela diagram**.

Luminous intensity diagram (table): luminous intensity shown in the form of a polar diagram or table, in terms of candelas per 1000 lumens of lamp flux.
The diagram (table) for non-symmetrical light distributions gives the light distribution of a luminaire in at least two planes:
1. In a vertical plane through the longitudinal axis of the luminaire,
2. In a plane at right angles to that axis.

Note: The luminous intensity diagram (table) can be used:
a. To provide a rough idea of the light distribution of the luminaire,
b. For the calculation of illuminance values at a point,
c. For the calculation of the luminance distribution of the luminaire.

(Luminous) intensity distribution curve: of a light source is the curve, generally polar, which represents the luminous intensity in a plane passing through the source, or in a cone with its apex at the source, as a function of the angle measured from some given direction.

Note 1: When the source has a symmetrical luminous intensity distribution a meridian plane is generally chosen.

Note 2: In the case of a vertical plane, angles are measured from the downward vertical.

Lux meter : see **Illuminance meter**

Maintenance factor: ratio of the average illuminance on the working plane after a specified period of use of a lighting installation to the average illuminance obtained under the same conditions for a new installation.

Note: The use of the term **Depreciation factor** as the reciprocal of maintenance factor is deprecated.

Metal halide lamp: see **Halide lamp**

Metal vapour lamp: discharge lamps such as the 'mercury (vapour) lamp' and the 'sodium (vapour) lamp' in which the light is mainly produced in a metallic vapour.

Mirror reflector: see **Specular reflector**

Mixed transmission: partly regular and partly diffuse transmission.

Monochromatic radiation: radiation characterized by a single frequency or wavelength. By extension, radiation of a very small range of frequencies or wavelengths which can be described by stating a single frequency or wavelength.

Mounting height: the distance between the reference plane and the plane of the luminaires.

Object (perceived) colour: colour perceived to belong to an object either self-luminous or non-self-luminous.

Optical output ratio: of a luminaire, is the ratio of the light output measured under specified practical conditions, to the sum of the individual light outputs of the lamps when inside the luminaire.

Pendant luminaire: luminaire provided with a cord, chain, tube, etc. which enables it to be suspended from a ceiling or other support.

Perceived colour: aspect of visual perception by which an observer may distinguish between two fields of view of the same size, shape and structure such as may be caused by differences in the spectral composition of the radiation concerned in the observation.

Phosphorescence: photoluminescence that persists for an appreciable time after excitation.

Photometry: measurement of quantities referring to radiation evaluated according to the visual effect which it produces, as based on certain conventions.

Planckian locus: the line in a chromaticity diagram representing full (or Planckian) radiators of different temperatures.

Planckian radiator: thermal radiator that absorbs completely all incident radiation, whatever the wavelength, the direction of incidence or the polarization.
This radiator has, for any wavelength, the maximum spectral concentration of radiant exitence at a given temperature.

Preheat lamp: hot cathode lamp designed to start with preheating of the electrodes – for example: 'TL'M, 'TL'RS lamp.

Radiant efficiency, (η_e): of a source of radiation, ratio of the radiant flux (power) emitted to the power consumed.

Radiant energy, (Q_e, Q): energy emitted, transferred, or received in the form of radiation. Unit: joule, J.

Radiant flux: see **Radiant power.**

Radiant power, (Φ_e, Φ): power emitted, transferred, or received in the form of radiation. Unit: watt, W.

Radiation:
1. Emission or transfer of energy in the form of electromagnetic waves or particles.
2. These electromagnetic waves or particles.

Rainproof luminaire: luminaire so constructed as to withstand the penetration of rain, and for use out of doors.

Recessed luminaire: luminaire mounted above the ceiling or behind a wall or other surface so that any visible projection is insignificant.

Reference surface: surface on which illuminance is measured or specified.

Reflectance (formerly **Reflection factor**): ratio of the reflected radiant or luminous flux to the incident flux.

Reflection: return of radiation by a surface without change of frequency of the monochromatic components of which the radiation is composed.

Reflector lamp: Incandescent or discharge lamp in which part of the bulb, generally of suitable shape, is coated with a reflecting material so as to control light.

Note: Among the types of lamps in this class is the *pressed glass lamp*, the bulb of which consists of two glass parts fused together, namely a metallized reflecting bowl and a patterned cover forming an optical system.

Refracting louvre: a louvre in which the screening depends essentially on the phenomenon of refraction.

Note: A refracting louvre simultaneously serves as a light controller.

Refraction: change in the direction of propagation of radiation determined by change in the velocity of propagation in passing through an optically non-homogeneous medium, or in passing from one medium to another.

Refractor: device in which the phenomenon of refraction is used to alter the spatial distribution of the luminous flux from a source.

Room index: code number, representative of the geometry of a room, used in calculation of the utilization factor or the utilance.

Note 1: Unless otherwise indicated, the room index is given by the formula
$$\frac{l.b}{h(l+b)}$$
Where: l is the length of the room, b is the width and h is the distance of the luminaires above the working plane.

Note 2: The 'ceiling cavity index' is calculated from the same formula except that h is the distance from ceiling to luminaires.

Saturation: attribute of visual sensation which permits a judgement to be made of the proportion of pure chromatic colour in the total sensation.

Screen: that part of a luminaire designed to prevent the lamps from being directly visible over a given range of angles.

Note: In practice a screen will also act as a light controller.

Solid angle (Ω): the angle subtended at the centre of a sphere by an area on its surface numerically equal to the square of the radius.
Unit: steradian, sr.

Spacing: the distance between the centres of two successive luminaires in an installation.

Spectral distribution:
a. Of a photometric quantity: luminous flux, luminous intensity, etc. The spectral concentration of the photometric quantity as a function of wavelength.
b. Of a radiometric quantity: radiant flux (power), radiant intensity, etc.
    The spectral concentration of the radiometric quantity as a function of wavelength.

Note: Commonly the relative spectral distribution is used, i.e. the spectral concentration of the photometric or radiometric quantity measured in terms of an arbitrary value of this quantity.

Spectral energy distribution: of a radiation. Description of the spectral character of a radiation by the relative spectral distribution of some radiometric quantity (radiant flux [power], radiant intensity, etc.).

Spectral light distribution: of a radiation. Description of the spectral character of a radiation by the relative spectral distribution of some photometric quantity (luminous flux, luminous intensity, etc.).

Specular reflection: reflection without diffusion in accordance with the laws of optical reflection; as in a mirror.

Specular reflector: that part of a luminaire designed to reflect the luminous flux of the lamps in required directions by means of specular reflection.

Stand-by lighting: lighting that enables work to continue in the case of failure of the normal lighting system.

Starter: device for starting a discharge lamp (in particular a fluorescent lamp) that provides for the necessary preheating of the electrodes and/or causes a voltage surge in combination with the series ballast.

Starting device: electrical apparatus that provides the conditions required for starting a discharge.

Switch-start fluorescent lamp: fluorescent lamp suitable for operation with a circuit requiring a starter for the preheating of the electrodes for example: 'TL' standard type.

Thermal radiation: process of emission in which the radiant energy originates in the thermal agitation of the particles of matter (atoms, molecules, ions).

Transmission: passage of radiation through a medium without change of frequency of the monochromatic components of which he radiation is composed.

Transmittance (formerly **Transmission factor**): ratio of the transmitted radiant or luminous flux to the incident flux.

Ultraviolet radiation: radiation for which the wavelengths of the monochromatic components are smaller than those for visible radiation and more than about 1 nm.

Uniform-chromaticity-scale (UCS) diagram: chromaticity diagram in which the coordinate scales are chosen with the intention of making equal intervals represent approximately equal steps of discrimination for colours of the same luminance at all parts of the diagram.

Uniformity ratio of illuminance: on a given plane, is a measure of the variation of illuminance over the plane expressed as either:
(1) The ratio of the minimum to the maximum illuminance.
(2) The ratio of the minimum to the average illuminance.

Note: In some countries, the reciprocal of these ratios is used, characterized by values greater than unity.

Upper [lower] (hemispherical) (luminous) flux (fraction): of a source, is the luminous flux emitted above [below] a horizontal plane passing through the source.

Note: It is essential that the plane be specified in every case.

Upward [downward] light output ratio (luminaire efficiency): the product of the upward [downward] flux fraction and the light output ratio.

Utilance, (U): ratio of the utilized flux to the luminous flux leaving the luminaires.

Utilization factor: ratio of the utilized flux to the luminous flux emitted by the lamps.

Note: The term 'coefficient of utilization' is deprecated.

Utilized flux: luminous flux received on the reference surface under consideration.

Note: Unless otherwise indicated, the reference surface is the working plane.

Vapour-tight luminaire: luminaire so constructed that a specified vapour or gas cannot enter its enclosure.

Visible radiation: any radiation capable of causing a visual sensation directly.

Visual acuity; sharpness of vision:
1. Qualitatively: Capacity for seeing distinctly objects very close together.
2. Quantitatively: Reciprocal of the value (generally in minutes of arc) of the angular separation of two neighbouring objects (points or lines) which the eye can just see as separate.

Visual field: of the eye or eyes, is the angular extent of the space in which an object can be perceived when the eye(s) regard(s) an object directly ahead. The field may be monocular or binocular.

Visual system: the group of structures comprising the eye, the optic nerve and certain parts of the brain, which transforms the light stimulus into a complex of nerve excitations, whose subjective correlate is visual perception.

Watertight luminaire: luminaire constructed to withstand the penetration of water when immersed to a specified depth, but not intended for permanent use under water.

Note: The term 'submersible luminaire' applies to a luminaire constructed to withstand indefinitely submersion in water to a specified depth.

Wavelength, (λ): distance in the direction of propagation of a periodic wave between two successive points at which the phase is the same (at the same time).
Unit: metre, m.

Working plane: reference suface defined as the plane at which work is usually done.

Note: In interior lighting, and unless otherwise indicated, it is assumed to be a horizontal plane 0,85 m above the floor and limited by the walls of the room.

Zonal luminous flux diagram: the graphical representation of the luminous flux distribution of a luminaire or a lamp in which the luminous flux emitted within a cone is plotted against the half-apex angle of that cone.

Appendix A

Fundamental Photometric and Radiometric Quantities

The symbols for photometric quantities are the same as those for the corresponding radiometric quantities. When it is necessary to differentiate between them the subscripts v and e respectively should be used, e.g. Q_v and Q_e where v = visible radiation and e = radiant energy.

Any of the quantities listed in the following tables may be restricted to a narrow wavelength band by adding the word 'spectral' and indicating the wavelength. The corresponding symbols may be changed by adding a subscript λ, e.g. Q_λ, for a spectral concentration or a λ in parentheses, e.g. $K(\lambda)$, for a function of wavelength.

Standard Units, Symbols and Defining Equations for Photometric Quantities

Quantity	Symbol	Defining Equation	Unit	Symbolic Abbreviation
Luminous energy (quantity of light)	Q	$Q = \int \Phi \, dt$	lumen-hour lumen-second	lm.h lm.s
Luminous flux	Φ	$\Phi = dQ/dt$	lumen	lm
Luminous exitance	M	$M = d\Phi/dA$	lumen per square metre	lm/m²
Illuminance	E	$E = d\Phi/dA$	lux	lx
Luminous intensity (candlepower)	I	$I = d\Phi/d\Omega$ (Ω = solid angle through which flux from point source is radiated)	candela	cd
Luminance	L	$L = dI/dA \cos\Theta$ (Θ = angle between line of sight and normal to surface considered)	candela per square metre	cd/m²
Luminous efficacy	K	$K = \Phi_v/\Phi_e$	lumen per watt	lm/W
Luminous efficiency	V	$V = K/K_{max}$ (K_{max} = maximum value of $K(\lambda)$ function)	(percentage)	
Scalar illuminance	E_{sc}	$E_{sc} = \int E/4\pi \, d\Omega$	lux	lx
Light exposure	H	$H = dQ/dA$	lux-second	lx.s

Standard Units, Symbols and Defining Equations for Radiometric Quantities

Quantity	Symbol	Defining Equation	Unit	Symbolic Abbreviation
Radiant energy	Q		joule kilowatt-hour	J kWh
Radiant flux	Φ	$\Phi = dQ/dt$	watt joule per second	W J/s
Radiant exitance	M	$M = d\Phi/dA$	watt per square metre	W/m²
Irradiance	E	$E = d\Phi/dA$	watt per square metre	W/m²
Radiant intensity	I	$I = d\Phi/d\Omega$ (Ω = solid angle through which flux from point source is radiated)	watt per steradian	W/sr
Radiance	L	$L = dI/dA \cos\Theta$ (Θ = angle between line of sight and normal to surface considered)	watt per steradian and square metre	W/sr.m²
Absorptance	α	$\alpha = d\Phi_a/d\Phi_o$*	(numerical ratio)	
Reflectance	ρ	$\rho = d\Phi_r/d\Phi_o$*	(numerical ratio)	
Transmittance	τ	$\tau = d\Phi_t/d\Phi_o$*	(numerical ratio)	
Radiant exposure	H	$H = dQ/dA$	joule per square metre watt-second per square metre	J/m² Ws/m²

* Φ_a = absorbed flux, Φ_r = reflected flux, Φ_t = transmitted flux, Φ_o = incident flux.

Appendix B

Conversion Factors

Luminance Units

To convert	Candelas per sq. metre (cd/m^2)	Stilb (cd/m^2)	Footlambert (fl)
To		Multiply by	
Candelas per sq. metre (cd/m^2)	1.0	10 000	3.43
Stilb (cd/m^2)	0.0001	1.0	0.00034
Footlambert (fl)	0.2919	2919	1.0

Illuminance Units

To convert	Lux	Footcandle
To	Multiply by	
Lux	1	10.76
Footcandle	0.0929	1

List of colour plates

Plate	Page
1–3	96–97
4–5	112–113
6–7	240–241
8–12	256–257
13–15	272–273
16–18	288–289
19–22	304–305

Index

A

absorption 127
accommodation 315
acoustical control 130
acoustic ceiling panels 178
acoustics 127
actual contrast ratio 52
adaptation 33, 315
adaption luminance 43
admissibility table 211
age and visual performance 39
age and visual satisfaction 39
air conditioning 114
air diffusers 174
air-handling luminaires 123
air supply 116
– – diffusers 177
American VCP method 82
art galleries 278
Australian code system 82

B

badminton 301
ballasts 160
bibliography 310
black body 315
– – locus 315
– – radiator 95
black limit 43, 46
blended light lamp 158, 315
blown-bulb reflector lamps 150
boxing 302
bright limit 43, 46
brightness 315, 320
– discrimination 43
British IES glare index system 81
building shape 133
BZ classification 232

C

calculations 226
calorimeter 125
ceiling cavity reflectance 222
ceiling luminance 60, 204
ceiling systems 121
chroma 91
chromatic adaptation 109
chromaticity 104
– coordinates 93
– diagram 90, 94, 316
CIE applied method 239
CIE standard photometric observer 315
CIE system 91
circulation areas 37
cleaning lamps and luminaires 195
cleaning room surfaces 196
clear-glass 156
colour 315
– appearance 89, 95, 213
– designations 152
– grading 110
– matching 110
– points 94
– rendering 89, 100, 152, 213, 315
– – groups 214
– – index 102, 315
– reproduction 111
– schemes 111
– shading 111
– shift 103
– space 92
– specification 90
– temperature 95, 97, 315
– triangle 90, 316
conservation 282
contrast 12, 316
– reducing visibility meter 25
– rendering 223
– rendition factor 48

control gear 160
conversion factors 330
correlated colour temperature 97, 316
cosine law of incidence 316
cost calculation 242
cut-off angle 167

D
data sheets 226
daylight 61, 101, 136
degree of dust protection 169
degree of moisture protection 168
degree of visibility 50
depreciation factor 316, 321
diffused lighting 316
diffuser 316
diffuse transmission 316
dimmer 316
dimming 179
direct flux 316
direct glare 73
direct ratio 232, 316
disability glare 316
discharge lamp 316
discomfort glare 73, 86, 316
drip-proof luminaire 316
dustproof luminaire 316
dust-tight luminaire 317

E
efficacy 146, 152
electrical protection 173
electricity supply 181
emergency lighting 186, 317
– – luminaires 170
energy conservation 133
equivalent contrast 25
equivalent glare indices 85, 86
equivalent sphere illuminance 49
European glare limiting method 78
European quality class 84
evaluation of direct glare 207
explosion proof luminaire 317

F
facial luminance 35
false ceiling 174
fatigue 22
field luminance 13
field measurements 244

flameproof lighting fitting 317
flexibility 121, 185
floodlight 317
flow chart 218
fluorescence 317
fluorescent lamps 150, 317
–, instant start 164
–, starterless 163
–, switch-start 163
fluorescent mercury lamp 317
full radiator 317

G
gaseous discharge lamp 317
Gaussian distribution 30
general colour rendering index 102, 105, 106
general lighting 252, 317
– – service lamps 147
glare 73, 205, 317
– control 205
– evaluation systems 74
– – comparison 83
– formula 73
– limit 46
– mark 74
glossary 315
group replacement 194

H
halide lamp 317, 321
halogen lamp 317
heat load 115
heat transfer 122
high-bay general lighting 253
high-bay luminaires 170
high-pressure discharge lamps 154
high-pressure mercury lamps 154, 317
high-pressure sodium lamps 159, 317
hospitals 291
hotels 284
hue 90, 318
hypothetical colours 93

I
ice-hockey 305
ignitors 163
illuminance 11, 318
– calculations 234
– – CIE Applied Method 239

– – Lumen Method 235
– – Point Method 240
– levels 220
– measurements 244
– meter 318, 321
– vector 64
illumination 318
incandescence 318
incandescent lamps 144, 318
increased safety luminaire 317, 318
index of modelling 64
indirect flux 318
indirect lighting 318
industrial lighting 251
infrared radiation 318
instant start fluorescent lamp 164
integrated ceilings 174
integration 120
inter-reflection (or interflexion) 318
inverse square law 318
isocandela curve (diagram) 318, 320
isoluminance curve (diagram) 318
isolux curve (diagram) 318

J

jet-proof luminaire 319

L

laboratory measurements 244
lamellae louvre 319
lamp 143, 195, 319
– ageing 192
– cleaning 195
– cooling 120
– failure 192
– life 146
– replacement 192
Landolt ring 13
lens panel 319
light 319
– controller 319
– distribution curve 319
– loss factor 196
– output ratio 230, 319
– regulators 179
lighting 319
– circuits 183
– codes 216
– criteria 201

– heat 138
– level 201, 217
– maintenance 192
– requirements for TV 306
lightness 319
localised lighting 253, 319
local lighting 254
louvre 167, 319
low-bay general lighting 252
low-pressure mercury (vapour) lamp 319
low-pressure sodium lamp 319
lumen method 235
luminaire 165, 319
– air handling 123
– classification 172
– cleaning 195
– contrast 320
– light output ratio 171
– luminance 206, 231, 241
luminance 11, 42, 320
– calculations 240
– curve method 74, 79, 207
– diagram 233
– distribution 222, 320
– limits 43, 208
– measurements 246
– meter 320
luminescence 320
luminosity 320
luminous ceilings 86
luminous efficacy 320
luminous flux 320
luminous intensity 230, 320
– – diagram 320, 321
– – distribution 319, 321
lux meter 321

M

maintained emergency lighting 189
maintenance 192
– factor 196, 321
– operations 192
mean cylindrical illuminance 37
mean spherical illuminance 37
measurements 243
metal halide lamp 158, 321
metal vapour lamp 321
metamerism 109
minimum illuminance 217
mirror reflector 321

mixed transmission 321
modelling 64, 215, 223
– index 64
monochromatic radiation 321
mounting height 321
Munsell book of color 91
Munsell system 90
museums 278

N

noise rating curves 130
non-maintained emergency lighting 187

O

object colour 315, 321
object contrast 12
object size 12
offending zone 54
office lighting 262
optical light output ratio 230
optical output ratio 321

P

pendant luminaire 321
perceived colour 315, 321
permanent artificial lighting 61
phosphorescence 322
photometric data 229
photometric quantities 328
photometry 322
Planckian locus 95, 315, 322
Planckian radiator 102, 315, 317, 322
Planck's law 95
plenum 121
point method 240
power tracks 178
preferred illuminances 30
preferred luminances 204
preheat lamp 322
pressed-glass reflector lamps 149
primary colours 91
prismatic diffuser 168

R

radiant efficiency 322
radiant energy 322
radiant flux 322
radiant power 322
radiation 322
radiometric quantities 329

rainproof luminaire 322
rapid start 163
recessed luminaire 322
recommended illuminances 203
reconstituted daylight 96, 101
reference illuminance 18
reference luminance 18
reference sources 101, 102
reference surface 322
reflectance 246, 322
reflected glare 47, 55, 210
reflection 322
reflector lamps 149, 322
refracting louvre 322
refraction 323
refractor 323
relative contrast sensitivity 18
relative visual performance 20
relative wall illuminance 60
restaurants 287
RGB colorimetric system 91
RGB colour triangle 92
room index 232, 323

S

safety regulations 190
saturation 91, 323
scalar illuminance 38, 64
school lighting 268
screen 323
SELV wiring 186
semi-maintained emergency lighting 188
service illuminance 217
shadows 223
shielding angle 167
shop lighting 272
size 12
sky luminance 62
solar radiation 115
solid angle 323
sound absorption 127
sound insulation 127
sound power diagram 126
sound power level 128
sound power spectrum 126
sound pressure level 128
source colour 97
spacing 323
spacing-to-height ratio 232
special colour rendering index 105

335

special lighting 256
spectral band method 102
spectral distribution 323
spectral energy distribution 323
spectral light distribution 323
spectral tristimulus values 93
specular reflection 323
specular reflector 321, 323
speed of perception 13
sphere illumination 49
sports lighting 299
standard chromaticity diagram 94
standard colorimetric system 91
standard service illuminance 217
stand-by lighting 324
stand-by power 188
starter 163, 324
starterless fluorescent lamps 163
starting device 324
structure-factor 51
sub-switchboard 183
supra-threshold conditions 19
surface luminance 240
suspended ceiling 175
suspension-to-height ratio 233
swimming 302
switch-start fluorescent lamp 324

T
task luminance 47
task visibility 255
tennis 301
ten-pin bowling 305
test colours 103
thermal characteristics 233
thermal load 115
thermal radiation 324
thyristor ignitor 164
threshold contrast 18
threshold visibility 12
transformer sub-station 181
transmission 324
transmittance 324
tristimulus values 93
tungsten halogen lamps 147

U
UCS diagram 95
ultraviolet radiation 324
uniform chromaticity scale 90, 95, 324
uniformity ratio of illuminance 324
upper [lower] (hemispherical) (luminous) flux (fraction) 324
upward [downward] light output ratio (luminaire efficiency) 324
utilance 324
utilization factor 231, 324
utilized flux 324

V
vapour-tight luminaire 324
vector/scalar ratio 64
veiling glare 51
veiling reflections 47, 210, 223
ventilation 114
visibility level 25
visibility reference function 18
visibility reference task 18
visible radiation 319, 324
visual acuity 13, 325
visual clarity 107
visual environment 32
visual field 325
visual performance 19
visual satisfaction 27
visual system 325
volleyball 301

W
wall luminance 56, 205
watertight luminaire 325
wavelength 325
Weber-Fechner rule 46
weighted decibel 129
window size 134
working areas 27
working plane 325

Z
zonal flux 229
zonal luminous flux diagram 325